# The Luminous Image

Dirick Vellert. *The Triumph of Faith*. 1517. (see cat. no. 68)

# The Luminous Image

## Painted Glass Roundels in the Lowlands, 1480–1560

by TIMOTHY B. HUSBAND

with an introductory essay by
ILJA M. VELDMAN

and contributions by
Ellen Konowitz and Zsuzsanna van Ruyven-Zeman

THE METROPOLITAN MUSEUM OF ART, NEW YORK

This volume is published in conjunction with the exhibition
"The Luminous Image: Painted Glass Roundels in the Lowlands, 1480–1560,"
held at The Metropolitan Museum of Art, New York, May 23–August 20, 1995

The exhibition is made possible in part by the National Endowment for the Arts.

Published by The Metropolitan Museum of Art, New York

Library of Congress Cataloging-in-Publication Data

Husband, Timothy, 1945–

    The luminous image: painted glass roundels in the lowlands, 1480–1560 /

by Timothy B. Husband; with an introductory essay by Ilja M. Veldman; and

contributions by Ellen Konowitz and Zsuzsanna van Ruyven-Zeman.

      p.  cm.

    Catalog of an exhibition held at The Metropolitan Museum of Art,

May 23–August 20, 1995.

    Includes bibliographical references and index.

    ISBN 0-87099-748-3 (paper)

    1. Glass painting and staining, Renaissance—Netherlands—Exhibitions.

2. Glass painting and staining—Netherlands—Exhibitions.   I. Konowitz,

Ellen.   II. Ruyven-Zeman, Zsuzsanna van.   III. Metropolitan Museum of

Art (New York, N.Y.)   IV. Title.

NK5353.H87   1995

748.599492'09'0310747471—dc20                    95-11656

                                      CIP

John P. O'Neill, *Editor in Chief*
Ellen Shultz, *Editor*
Malcolm Grear Designers, Inc., *Designer*
Jay Reingold and Chris Zichello, *Production*
Jayne Kushna, *Bibliographer*

COVER: The Pseudo-Ortkens group. *Susanna and the Elders*. About 1520–40
(see cat. no. 65)

# Contents

# Foreword

Were one to reflect on the painterly arts in the Burgundian-Habsburg Lowlands in the late fifteenth century and the first half of the sixteenth, masterpieces by such artists as Hugo van der Goes, Jan Gossaert, Barent van Orley, Lucas van Leyden, and Maarten van Heemskerck would likely come to mind. However, the small-scale silver-stained glass paintings that graced the windows of the imposing town houses and the guildhalls, hospices, town halls, and other civic buildings in the thriving mercantile centers of Bruges, Ghent, Brussels, Antwerp, Rotterdam, Leiden, and Amsterdam are not likely to figure among them. In fact, few but a handful of specialists are even familiar with this exceptional art form. Yet, these and other outstanding artists of the period, including Dirick Vellert, Jan Swart van Groningen, Lambert van Noort, and Dirck Crabeth, all produced designs for silver-stained roundels.

"The Luminous Image: Painted Glass Roundels in the Lowlands, 1480–1560," the first exhibition devoted to this material, surveys small-scale glass painting at the height of its production. Because many roundels were intended for private and secular contexts, their rich imagery addresses a broad range of issues and candidly reflects the attitudes and preoccupations of the clients who commissioned them. Thus, we encounter such divergent subjects as the story of Sorgheloos (cat. nos. 30–37), a cautionary morality tale on a theme of financial irresponsibility, and Dirck Crabeth's *Christ as the Redeemer of Mankind* (cat. nos. 127 and 128), a polemical, if not heretical, reading of mankind's best route to salvation. The styles are diverse, whether Late Gothic or Mannerist, but there is a coherence to the works as a whole, given the prevalence of strong artistic traditions and conventions. The techniques employed are often astonishing in their accomplishment and breathtaking in their impact. One can only marvel at the subtle shifts of light and shadow and the fine gradations of tonalities in Dirick Vellert's signed and dated *Triumphs* (cat. nos. 67 and 68), as well as in the *Triumph of David* (cat. no. 56), after—perhaps even by—Lucas van Leyden, on loan for the first time through the generosity of the Biblioteca Ambrosiana in Milan. The exhibition does not, however, consist solely of painted glass roundels, but includes many of the designs and related drawings; these provide a singular opportunity both to admire masterpieces of draftsmanship and to study the artistic process. The chiaroscuro effects of the *Beheading of John the Baptist*, the only signed drawing by Jan Gossaert (cat. no. 58), may have been intended merely to delight the eye of an aristocratic patron, while the two versions of the *Presentation in the Temple* (cat. nos. 74 and 75) reveal Dirick Vellert altering a tracing of his preliminary design, thereby refining his composition for one in a series of roundels devoted to the Life of the Virgin.

Timothy B. Husband, curator of this exhibition, deserves the highest praise for his initiative and scholarship—qualities that have assured this project's high level of seriousness and originality. Our debt of gratitude to the many institutions and the several private collectors who have unstintingly lent these fragile but singularly beautiful works of art cannot be adequately expressed. We wish to give special thanks to the Rijksmuseum in Amsterdam, which has been uncommonly generous in lending an extraordinarily large number of objects, each filling a crucial role in our exhibition; we would, therefore, like to offer our profound appreciation to Professor Henk van Os, the director, and to his colleagues.

PHILIPPE DE MONTEBELLO
*Director*
The Metropolitan Museum of Art

# Acknowledgments

"The Luminous Image: Painted Glass Roundels in the Lowlands, 1480–1560" has been five years in the making, developing out of an interest in the collection of silver-stained roundels at The Cloisters and an effort of many years to expand, upgrade, and reinstall these holdings. As I progressed, the logical conclusion to my study of the material was an exhibition that would introduce this engaging but little-known art form to a broader public, presenting examples of the highest quality selected to demonstrate the range of stylistic, iconographical, and technical achievement while illuminating the cultural context in which painted glass roundels flourished. The realization of this project, however, would not have been possible without the contributions of many individuals and institutions.

From the outset, Yvette Vanden Bemden, Corpus Vitrearum, Belgique, has continually offered encouragement and assistance, whether facilitating the Belgian loans or extending her kind hospitality in Brussels. Jan Piet Filedt Kok has, with unflagging resolution, long extended his support to the exhibition and has generously given of his scholarly insights. The Rijksmuseum has been especially generous in lending both roundels and drawings, in addition to prints; the exhibition would have been greatly diminished, therefore, without the exceptional support and commitment of that institution's general director, Henk van Os. I am deeply indebted to Ilja M. Veldman for her learned essay, which provides a valuable overview of the iconographical influences on roundel production, and, likewise, to Ellen Konowitz and Zsuzsanna van Ruyven-Zeman for their scholarly contributions on Dirick Vellert and Lambert van Noort, respectively, as well as to Linda Evers, whose studies pertaining to the Pseudo-Ortkens problem in large part have been incorporated into the catalogue. Alessandro Rovetta of the Università Cattolica, Milan, and Pamela M. Jones of the University of Massachusetts, Boston, graciously shared their expertise. Professor Herman Pleij of the Vrije Universiteit, Amsterdam, very kindly directed me in the arcane territory of sixteenth-century literature and popular culture. Madeline H. Caviness of Tufts University, Medford, in her role as international president of the Corpus Vitrearum, has done much to engender good will and interest in the exhibition.

While colleagues at all the lending institutions were exceedingly helpful, I am particularly indebted to Daniel Alcouffe, Musée du Louvre; Peter Barnet, The Detroit Institute of Arts; Mària van Berge-Gerbaud, Collection Frits Lugt, Institut Néerlandais, Paris; Holm Bevers, Kupferstichkabinett, Berlin; Monique Blanc and Chantal Bouchon, Musée des Arts Décoratifs, Paris; Émmanuelle Brugerolles, École Nationale Supérieure des Beaux-Arts, Paris; Mungo Campbell, National Gallery of Scotland; Stephen Fliegel, The Cleveland Museum of Art; Antony V. Griffiths, British Museum; Marijn Schapelhouman and Peter Schatborn, Rijksprentenkabinet, Amsterdam; Francis Van Noten, Musées Royaux d'Art et d'Histoire, Brussels; André Van den Kerkhove, Bijlokemuseum, Ghent; Christiaan Vogelaar, Stedelijk Museum de Lakenhal, Leiden; Oliver Watson and Michael Archer, Victoria and Albert Museum; Hilary Wayment, King's College, Cambridge; and Timothy Wilson, Ashmolean Museum, Oxford.

For the first time, the Pinacoteca of the Biblioteca Ambrosiana, Milan, has agreed to lend the *Triumph of David*; this would not have been possible without the cooperation and good offices of Monsignor Gianfranco Ravasi, Marco Navoni, and Angelo Colombo. Additionally, we are very grateful to Paolo Vitti; Antonella Camerana; Bona Borromeo; and Caterina Pirina, Corpus Vitrearum, Italia.

Many colleagues at The Metropolitan Museum of Art have lent invaluable assistance, but special thanks are owed to Maryan W. Ainsworth and to Catherine Bindman. To Mary B. Shepard I am much indebted for her enthusiastic support, in general, and for her organization of the educational aspects of the exhibition, in particular. Nina S. Maruca handled the responsibilities of registrar with admirable efficiency. Mary C. Higgins is responsible for the impressive conservation and restoration work done on the Metropolitan Museum's roundels, as well as on those from Detroit, Pittsburgh, and Toledo; Michele D. Marincola was a great support in this effort of over a year's duration. Cathryn Steeves did much preliminary research and bibliographic work for the catalogue while shouldering administrative duties; in this latter role she was ably succeeded by Timothy S. Riley, who streamlined the operation with his computer skills. For the last year, however, Anna Gendel has served as exhibition assistant with admirable tenacity; without her determined efforts, conducted with infectious good cheer and utter dependability, the realization of the catalogue and the exhibition would have been a far more trying affair. Danielle Tilkin, with her usual efficiency, was extremely helpful in assisting with the French loans. The design of the exhibition installation is the inspired work of Stephen Saitas; the challenge of designing the lighting was effectively surmounted by Zack Zanolli, and the graphics were produced by Barbara Weiss. The catalogue was edited with elegant clarity and unfailing precision, often under difficult constraints of time and space, by Ellen Shultz. The design is the lucid work of Malcolm Grear Designers, Inc. Jay Reingold, with the assistance of Chris Zichello, skillfully shepherded the catalogue through production. For his support throughout I am grateful to John P. O'Neill. Barbara Bridgers and the Photograph Studio at the Metropolitan Museum, along with Eli Valeton and Florence Albers at the Rijksmuseum, were especially helpful in assembling large amounts of photographic material. William Cole generously provided photographs from his archives.

For her commitment to this exhibition from its inception I wish to express my appreciation to Mahrukh Tarapor. Linda Sylling ably managed an array of logistical problems. To William D. Wixom, for his unwavering support and wise counsel, I am ever grateful. Without the firm commitment of our director, Philippe de Montebello, to whom I am much indebted, the exhibition would not have taken place. Sibyll Kummer-Rothenhäusler, who is responsible for sparking my interest in this material, has been an enthusiastic and learned advocate of this project from the beginning.

Finally, I would like to express my deep gratitude to Jane Hayward and Ruth Blumka, both of whom, in very different ways, lent their encouragement, advice, and support; their loss is felt throughout the museum world, and I am much saddened that neither can see the realization of a project they both so ardently championed.

The exhibition is made possible in part by the National Endowment for the Arts. We are also grateful for the support of The Netherlands-American Amity Trust, Inc., and Rabobank Nederland.

TIMOTHY B. HUSBAND

# Lenders to the Exhibition

| | |
|---|---|
| AMSTERDAM | Rijksmuseum, *cat. nos. 3, 5, 41, 42, 46, 47, 68, 76, 79, 80, 84–90, 95, 97, 105, 106, 128* |
| | Rijksmuseum, Rijksprentenkabinet, *cat. nos. 30, 34, 39, 48, 54, 81, 91, 93, 102, 126, 127* |
| | Collectie Stichting P. en N. de Boer, *cat. no. 35* |
| ATLANTA | Curtis O. Baer Collection, *cat. no. 6* |
| BERLIN | Staatliche Museen zu Berlin, Preußischer Kulturbesitz, Kupferstichkabinett, *cat. nos. 2, 8, 15, 19, 38, 69, 71* |
| BOSTON | Museum of Fine Arts, *cat. nos. 1, 107* |
| BRUSSELS | Musées Royaux d'Art et d'Histoire, *cat. nos. 13, 14, 67* |
| CAMBRIDGE | Fitzwilliam Museum, *cat. nos. 82, 100* |
| | King's College Chapel, *cat. nos. 12, 115, 116* |
| CLEVELAND | The Cleveland Museum of Art, *cat. no. 60* |
| DARMSTADT | Hessisches Landesmuseum, Darmstadt, *cat. nos. 36, 55, 73* |
| DETROIT | The Detroit Institute of Arts, *cat. no. 40* |
| EDINBURGH | National Gallery of Scotland, *cat. no. 59* |
| GHENT | Bijlokemuseum, *cat. nos. 44, 45, 109, 110* |
| LEIDEN | Prentenkabinet der Rijksuniversiteit, *cat. nos. 121, 122* |
| | Stedelijk Museum de Lakenhal, *cat. nos. 31, 124, 125* |
| LEUVEN | Katholieke Universiteit, Kunstpatrimonium, *cat. no. 114* |
| | Stedelijk Museum Vander Kelen-Mertens, *cat. no. 98* |
| LONDON | British Museum, *cat. nos. 43, 49, 57, 70, 74, 75, 77, 78, 94, 96* |
| | Victoria and Albert Museum, *cat. nos. 7, 20, 28, 37, 64, 99, 103, 104* |
| MILAN | Pinacoteca della Biblioteca Ambrosiana, *cat. no. 56* |
| MUNICH | Staatliche Graphische Sammlung München, *cat. no. 113* |
| THE NETHERLANDS | Private collection, *cat. no. 123* |
| NEW YORK | The Metropolitan Museum of Art, *cat. nos. 10, 22* |
| | The Metropolitan Museum of Art, The Cloisters Collection, *cat. nos. 17, 18, 21, 23, 26, 27, 29, 33, 61, 65, 92, 101* |
| OXFORD | Ashmolean Museum, *cat. nos. 11, 24, 66* |
| PARIS | Collection Frits Lugt, Institut Néerlandais, *cat. nos. 62, 63, 112* |
| | École Nationale Supérieure des Beaux-Arts, *cat. nos. 58, 83, 111* |
| | Musée des Arts Décoratifs, *cat. nos. 117–120* |
| | Musée du Louvre, Département des Arts Graphiques, *cat. nos. 16, 25* |
| | Musée du Louvre, Département des Objets d'Art, *cat. nos. 50, 52, 53* |
| PITTSBURGH | University Art Gallery, *cat. no. 9* |
| ROTTERDAM | Museum Boymans-van Beuningen, *cat. nos. 4, 51, 108* |
| TOLEDO | The Toledo Museum of Art, *cat. no. 32* |
| VIENNA | Graphische Sammlung Albertina, *cat. no. 72* |

# Introduction

TIMOTHY B. HUSBAND

## Painted and Silver-Stained Roundels

In 1506–7, the abbess of Rijnsburg, a convent near Leiden, commissioned designs for painted glass roundels from "Cornelis the painter" (perhaps Cornelis Engebrechtsz., a teacher of Lucas van Leyden); the same archival documents further inform us that the designs were executed by Ewout Vos and two assistants and that these roundels were to be installed in the "Blue Room" located in the abbess's private suite.[1]

Although not described in the documents, the painted glass or silver-stained roundels ordered by the abbess were, no doubt, of the very sort that is the subject of this volume. Each was a single piece of colorless glass (as opposed to the colored pot-metal glass employed in cathedrals), usually round but often rectangular (the term "roundel" is thus innately contradictory), rendered in a vitreous paint, and fired. It was then enhanced with silver sulfide or silver oxide, which, when likewise fired, fused with the glass, imparting translucent tones ranging from pale yellow to deep amber or copper, depending upon the amount of silver in the suspension. Painting on roundels was, in general, reductive: The outlines of forms were indicated with dark trace lines, but the contours and modeling and the gradations of light and dark were achieved by working away the mattes in subtle, increasingly thinner gradations, allowing more and more light through until the mattes were completely removed, leaving only colorless glass. The mattes could be worked while either wet or dry with a variety of stippling brushes and badger brushes, each producing its own effect. The point of a stick or a fine metal stylus was used to cut through the matte to indicate highlights or to accent hair or ornament. The subsequent firing of the roundel fused these vitreous mattes and trace paints with the glass. Roundels were glazed, painted side toward the interior, into diamond-paned or leaded quarry windows, at a point close to eye level to best appreciate their stylistic and technical refinements. The images were brought to radiant life by natural light from without (see plate 1).

The abbess of Rijnsburg installed her roundels not in the abbey nor even in her private chapel—which had been completed in 1483–84—but in one of a suite of rooms that constituted her private living quarters. Roundels likewise graced the fenestration of civic or official structures, guilds, hospitals, mercantile buildings, courts, and town halls, as well as chapels and possibly even glazed cloisters. Victims of vicissitude, all appear to have been extirpated from their original settings; only in one instance—the Dirck Crabeth panels from the house at Pieterskerkgracht 9, in Leiden (see cat. nos. 117–125)—can the original context of surviving glass be documented. While it is impossible to identify a roundel with a particular building, the nature of the setting is often suggested by the iconography. Subjects concerned with sound administration of justice—Susanna and the Elders (see cat. nos. 62–64) or the Judgment of Cambyses (see cat. no. 80), for example—were thoroughly appropriate in a governmental or judicial setting, while unorthodox interpretations of theological matters (see cat. nos. 126–128) were more prudently displayed in the privacy of one's home.

Painted and silver-stained roundels initially relied on a broad but relatively conventional choice of subject matter: Iconic images, such as patron saints; devotional imagery including the Crucifixion, the Man of Sorrows, the Pietà, or the Trinity; a variety of secular themes, such as genre scenes or those with *Vanitas* or *Memento mori* imagery, and allegories; and, above all, narrative series based on both Old and New Testament texts. By the opening decades of the sixteenth century, the repertoire expanded considerably; the new and wide-ranging sources of roundel iconography during the period in which this exceptional art form flourished is a subject that Ilja M. Veldman addresses with admirable lucidity in the essay that follows these introductory remarks.

While numerous roundels are extant, these cannot represent more than the merest fraction of the original production, and, moreover, not one has survived in its original context. Although the production must have reached proto-industrial proportions by the second decade of the sixteenth century, lamentably little is known about the glass painters or the working methods of the shops that produced these luminous images. The scant details provided by the archival references to the Rijnsburg roundels reinforce, in a near void of documentary evidence, the inferences drawn from a study of the glass and related drawings that, by fortuitous historical accident, remain intact.

Virtually every major artist of the period in the Lowlands, as well as in Germany, created designs for roundels; the designers, however, were generally not—as in the case of Rijnsburg Abbey—glass painters. Dirick Vellert (see cat. nos. 67–80) and, later, Dirck Crabeth (see cat. nos. 117–128) were notable exceptions, as each was remarkably accomplished at both arts; whether Lucas van Leyden was likewise so gifted remains, in the face of inconclusive evidence, uncertain (see cat. no. 56). When the designer and glass painter were not one and the same, as was the usual case, numerous workshop copies of the designs were required (see the section on drawings below); attributions, as a consequence, are offered with considerable apprehension. An anonymous design with distinct stylistic affinities to a particular artist, workshop, or regional style may be localized, with reasonable probability, in corresponding proximity to the source of its inspiration. The designs of the van der Goes group (see cat. nos. 1, 2, 4, 6, 8, and 10), for example, were assuredly produced—if not in Ghent where Hugo himself worked, then in the South Lowlands and probably in Flanders or Brabant. A design, however, could be copied readily or otherwise widely disseminated, becoming available to glass painters wherever their workshops might be established. Thus, an Antwerp design could be executed in Leiden—a fact that only telltale stylistic or technical details would betray. The converse premise—that the executed roundel was produced in a locale in close propinquity to the origin of its design—is, therefore, in all probability less accurate. As a result, even when a roundel is based on an extant design of known authorship, the glass painting is here generally given a broad attribution: often no more than North or South Lowlands, and, in many cases, merely the Lowlands.

It is possible, but not yet proven, that particular glass-painting workshops or centers favored particular techniques, so that the careful study of the brush- and stylus work, the physical properties of the paint, and the treatment of mattes, assessed in conjunction with stylistic considerations, eventually may aid in localizing roundels. As the styles and techniques of the glass painters in a given workshop were probably fairly homogeneous—the reputation of a workshop rested in part upon a recognizable style of consistent quality—it seems likely, for example, that the *Betrayal* and the *Crowning with Thorns* (cat. nos. 41 and 42), while based on the same series of designs, must have been painted in different workshops, for the techniques are at considerable variance: The former relies on the reductive method of working away the mattes to create a rich texture

of densities and tonalities, while the latter, in a more painterly style, builds up the mattes to define the forms with the almost exclusive use of the point of a brush.

The demand for painted glass roundels was evidently sufficient to spawn an artistic industry that flourished from the last quarter of the fifteenth century through the first half of the sixteenth. The clientele consisted predominantly of well-to-do urban denizens and the professional and mercantile classes—the civic, political, and economic hierarchy of the burgeoning cities of Flanders, Zeeland, Brabant, and Holland. A similar enthusiasm for roundels in aristocratic circles, while wholly probable, is unestablished: Jan Gossaert, the only major artist of the period who spent most of his career at court, produced highly finished designs, but there is no evidence that these were ever executed in glass (see cat. nos. 58–61). The van Orley workshop in Brussels produced tapestry designs for Mary of Hungary, who, as regent of the Lowlands, ruled from her court in that city until 1555; there is no compelling reason to assume that the court would disdain the prodigious production of roundel designs that also emanated from the van Orley workshop (see cat. nos. 62, 63, and 66).

## Silver Stain

Medieval recipes for silver stain called for a compound of silver and antimony sulfide in a liquid suspension, which, given the small amount of silver required, was diluted with six to ten parts of a medium that comprised red or yellow ocher, pipe clay, or brick dust; it was then applied with an ordinary brush, a spatula, or a brush made of soft, fine badger fur. The firing of the silver-sulfide solution left a chalky residue on the painted glass that had to be buffed to reveal the tones of the silver stain. In large part for this reason, the silver stain was always applied to the back of the glass, while the mattes or flat, vitreous paints—usually shades of reddish brown to dark umber in the Lowlands but almost uniformly black in Germany—were always applied to the front surface. To achieve a range of hues, glass painters could apply solutions of different concentrations, firing after each application; because the color of the silver stain depended on the chemical composition of both the compound and the glass, as well as on the duration of firing, the balance and control encountered in the finest roundels could be achieved by only the most talented and experienced of glass painters. As the glass used in large-scale leaded panels is colored by the additives mixed into the batch of molten mass, silver-stained roundels are the only form of glass that truly can be called stained.

The date of the earliest use of silver stain in Northern Europe long has been a matter of scholarly debate. Jean Lafond's claim that the first appearance of the technique was in Normandy has never been convincingly refuted; he cites the glass in the church at Mesnil-Villeman (Manche) of 1313 as the earliest dated example, and notes the extensive use of silver stain in the opening decades of the fourteenth century in the glazing programs of Saint-Ouen in Rouen, and of churches in Jumièges and Évreux.[2] Meredith Lillich, however, has hypothesized that a translation of the *Lapidario*, an Arabic manuscript acquired in 1243 by Alfonso X of Spain, which contained a recipe for silver stain, was brought to Paris about 1300, and found its way into the hands of Marie de Brabant in Mantes, which

FIG. 1 The Burgundian-Habsburg Lowlands in 1555

Gossaert produced these sheets solely for the visual delight of his aristocratic clientele. The other types of drawings all appear to be more directly related to roundel production. In this volume the term "design" signifies an original composition executed by the artist, sometimes a relatively finished sheet but usually a sketch or a rapidly penned drawing, that expresses the artist's conception. A design can also be a tracing or a copy of a composition that has then been reworked, altered, or otherwise refined, often in a darker ink (see cat. nos. 75, 77, and 78, for excellent examples of this type). A drawing that codifies the original sketch or a reworked design into a more studied linear drawing, with no further traces of reworking, clarifying the artist's intentions for the glass painter, is here called a "working design." Some artists produced working designs in the form of highly finished drawings, with little or no alterations; in a number of cases, notably that of Vellert, the modeling and shading are fully indicated with washes (see cat. nos. 69, 70, 71, and 72), while in others hatchings were preferred. Some form of this "working design" seems to have been turned over to the glass-painting workshop for execution. Other than the rare signed examples, such as those by Dirick Vellert, Jan Gossaert, and Lambert van Noort, few of these drawings can be considered autograph. While some, on the basis of style and technique, convincingly can be attributed to particular artists, most must be viewed as workshop replicas or copies, not infrequently of a somewhat later date. Although there were workshops that persisted in the fifteenth-century practice of cobbling together compositions from diverse, accumulated models, increasingly in the sixteenth century workshops relied on commissioned original—and expensive, one imagines—designs. This may have been dictated by the growing demand of an ever more sophisticated and wealthy clientele for works of the highest quality, but it may also reflect a tradition rooted in the fifteenth century whereby the greatest artists willingly lent their talents to all manner of creation. Dürer, for example, perceived no diminution of his stature by designing wallpaper, lighting fixtures, and the like. Given the expense and the inherent artistic value of the "working design," it behooved the glass-painting workshop into whose custody it passed to preserve it, which appears to have been accomplished through making a copy by tracing. These drawings, any number of which, no doubt, could have been made according to demand, are here called "workbench drawings"; they have a somewhat studied and mechanical appearance, lacking the fluid line and telltale alterations of the master. It was probably a drawing of this type that was either pinned up in front of the glass painter for freehand copying or placed under the glass for tracing.

accounts for the early emergence of silver stain in Normandy.[3] Whatever the reasons for its renascent popularity in the later fifteenth century, the golden hue and the translucence of silver stain afforded a warm coloration to an image without impeding the transmission of light through it—a matter of some concern in the interior of an urban town house, the fenestration of which necessarily was limited.

## The Drawings

A study of the drawings related to silver-stained roundels quickly reveals that a variety of different types exists, and, because of the almost total lack of documentation pertaining to artistic methods, their precise function, insofar as it can be determined, is adducible only by comparative examination. The most refined of these drawings are highly finished works by the hand of the master in pen or point of the brush with wash and white highlights on prepared paper, often in stunning tones of ocher, gray, blue, or green (see cat. nos. 58, 59, and 102, and plates 11 and 14). These splendid drawings, erroneously thought to have been the final step in the process of developing a roundel design, can now be shown to be the first step.[4] It is also possible that these sheets were not, in any practical sense, designs at all. As nearly all the known roundel drawings associated with Jan Gossaert, for example, are of this finished type, and none seems to have been executed as roundels, it may well be that

## The Burgundian-Habsburg Lowlands up to 1560

The Burgundian-Habsburg Lowlands[5] correspond roughly to modern Luxembourg, Belgium, and the Netherlands—a patchwork territory that had been assembled by the Valois dukes of Burgundy through marriage, treaty, purchase, coercion, and conquest (see fig. 1).[6] A brief historical overview of the period bracketed by the works in this volume may be helpful. In 1475, Charles the Bold (r. 1467–77) conquered the duchy of Lorraine, which essentially connected the French Burgundian territories; these increasingly were referred to as the "landen van derwaerts overe" (lands over there), and the Burgundian Lowlands were called the "landen van herwaerts overe" (lands over here). After the death of Charles the Bold in the battle of Nancy in 1477, the Lorraine and the duchy of Burgundy were absorbed by the French crown, reducing Burgundian hegemony to the territories of the Lowlands. Charles's daughter Mary of Burgundy (r. 1477–82) married the Holy Roman Emperor Maximilian I, bringing the Habsburgs into the succession. Philip the Handsome (r. 1482–1506), the son of Mary of Burgundy and Maximilian I, married Joan the Mad, daughter of Ferdinand and Isabella of Aragon and Castile, and was succeeded by Charles of Ghent (r. 1506–56), who, in turn, succeeded to the Spanish realms in 1516 and became Holy Roman Emperor, as Charles V, in 1519. Charles added successive territories to the Lowlands, including the Tournaisis, Friesland, Overijssel, Utrecht, Drenthe, Groningen, and, finally, Guelders-Zutphen in 1543, thus unifying the Seventeen Provinces.[7] By 1529, Charles V had forced the French to renounce any claims over the Lowlands; with the Augsburg Interim of 1547 he removed all authority of the Holy Roman Empire; and in the Pragmatic Sanction of 1549, he declared the Lowlands forever an indivisible territory. After the death of Philip the Handsome in 1506, his sister, Charles V's aunt, Margaret of Austria, acted as governess of the Lowlands until her death in 1530; from 1531 until 1555, Mary of Hungary, a younger sister of Charles V, served as regent of the Lowlands. In the following year Charles V abdicated; his son Philip II became ruler of all the territories of Spain and the Lowlands, although he entrusted the rule of the Lowlands, from 1559 to 1567, to his illegitimate half sister Margaret of Austria, Duchess of Parma.

About 1480, the population of the Lowlands was about 2.7 million, over a third of whom lived in the principal cities in Flanders, Brabant, and Holland; by 1560, the population had risen to over three million, with nearly two million people living in these three prospering counties as well as in Zeeland. Thirteen of the fifteen largest cities were in these counties, and some of them, such as Antwerp, Gouda, Amsterdam, Rotterdam, and Leiden, doubled their populations in this period. The population of Antwerp, for example, about thirty thousand at the end of the fifteenth century, rose to nearly ninety thousand by the 1560s; in Northern Europe, only London and Paris had larger populations at this time.

The economic fortunes of many of these provinces and their cities frequently were reflected in their swelling populations. Cities with ready access to the seas—Bruges, in the fifteenth century, then Antwerp, and ultimately Amsterdam in the sixteenth—enjoyed flourishing international trade, particularly in the textile industries. By 1550, exports from the Lowlands were three times those of England. Economic booms from about 1495 to 1525 and again from about 1540 to 1565 resulted in great wealth for the burgeoning mercantile classes, no insignificant amount of which was directed toward the arts and brought prosperity to artists in commercial and governmental centers. By the late 1550s, however, manufacturing, agriculture, shipping, and other key industries began to slide into a depression. Beset by trade conflicts, severe grain shortages in 1565, and soaring unemployment and widespread poverty, the Lowlands sank into economic crisis. Against this background, the duke of Alva and his army arrived, threatening draconian religious and political repression. In 1566, iconoclastic rampages broke out, adding to the upheaval. In 1567, and during the several years following, thousands of artists and craftsmen emigrated to France, England, Germany, and the peripheral regions of the Lowlands. Thus, the climate that had been so favorable to artistic production deteriorated ruinously.

## The Luminous Image

In Joos van Cleve's painting of *The Annunciation* (plate 1), following fifteenth-century Lowlands tradition, the setting is a domestic interior of the period. The comfortable room, no doubt, was quite typical of those found in affluent dwellings in the thriving urban centers of the Lowlands in the early sixteenth century. Yet, here, the bedroom serves not as the place of repose for a mercantile prince, but as a stage for the announcement of the coming Incarnation of Christ. The panel at once records a paramount event in the Life of the Virgin, made all the more immediate by the contemporary setting, while inviting the viewer to contemplate the full meaning of the subject it presents. The devotional aspect of the image is underscored by other pietistic objects in the room, such as the elaborate triptych placed as an altarpiece on the draped cabinet and the simple, hand-colored single-leaf wood-block print tacked to the wall. Both objects, through their imagery, aid the viewer in comprehending the significance of the principal scene: Moses holding the tablets of the law, as seen in the print, signifies the transition from the era before law (*ante legem*) to the era under law (*sub lege*), while the Incarnation represents the transition from the era *sub lege* to the era under grace (*sub gratia*). The meeting of Abraham and Melchizedek, depicted in the triptych, was understood as a prefiguration of the Last Supper, and, by extension, of the redemption of mankind through Christ's sacrifice on the cross—the proof of the Incarnation, which is here being announced.

Although the two roundels set into the transoms of the window are in close proximity to the print and the triptych, seemingly they were not meant to play a similar thematic role, as their subjects cannot be identified (each seems to represent two standing figures, perhaps saints). Roundels with iconic subject matter—whether a saint, the Virgin and Child, the Crucifixion, the Pietà, the Man of Sorrows, or the Trinity—certainly availed as devotional images, a function well served both by the intimacy with which they were intended to be viewed and by the arresting radiance with which they were illuminated. However, their apparent ubiquity in affluent households, guildhalls, and civic buildings cannot be explained entirely by their pietistic purpose, particularly as roundels generally were produced in narrative series rather than as singular scenes, and these series, instead of inspiring devotionalism, evidently were intended to convey some more prosaic form of edifying allegory, ethical instruction, or cautionary tale. Thus, Tobit is not merely the protagonist of an Old Testament saga, but an exemplum of patience and steadfast faith in a time of religious questioning (see cat. nos. 13 and 14); Susanna and the Elders is not a tale of virtue besmirched and then fortuitously restored, but a paradigm of justice both subverted and well served (see cat. nos. 63, 64, 65, and 104); and Sorgheloos is not simply a secularized version of the parable of the Prodigal Son, but a starchy allegory inveighing against spendthriftiness (see cat. nos. 30–37). Indeed, a propensity for moralizing appears to be a fundamental characteristic of art in the Lowlands throughout this period. While artists from the Lowlands flocked to Italy to study classical sculpture and Renaissance painting, the artistic vocabulary that they learned was employed, by and large, to tell a very different story. In Jan Gossaert's *Venus and Amor* (fig. 13, p. 23), for example, any overtone of unselfconscious sexuality has been abandoned in favor of an admonishment against carnal gratification, as the inscription on the original frame suggests. The same predisposition seems to have prevailed in the literary realm as well: Humanist pursuits were aimed not so much at reviving knowledge of classical languages and literature as at providing a new and improved means of revitalizing Christian faith.[8] It is not that the denizens of the North and South Lowlands—which remained a fairly coherent political and cultural entity up until about 1579—were any more concupiscent or morally bankrupt; more spendthrifty, or more miserly, for that matter; or more faithless, adulterous, profligate, or corrupt than any other Northern Europeans (or perhaps they were, but no matter). Yet, the urge to give a moralizing, admonitory gloss to all manner of subject— "a finger raised in warning," as Ilja M. Veldman puts it, in her eloquent casting of this argument[9]—would seem inherent in their artistic expression.

The predominant overtone of painted and silver-stained roundels from the Lowlands is likewise that of "the finger raised in warning"—an idiosyncrasy that differentiates them from examples produced elsewhere in Northern Europe. Thus, inspiring the viewer to vigilance in the face of all forms of human frailty and alerting him to the many pitfalls to be avoided would seem to have been the ascendant intention of these roundels. From another point of view, however, the flourishing roundel production in the Lowlands, until the calamitous reversal of circumstances in the 1560s, was at an artistic zenith. The most prominent artists of the day produced designs of exceptional quality to satisfy their increasingly demanding clientele. The resulting glass paintings were exceptional works of art, executed with dazzling technique and animated by subtle gradations of tonality and light, vibrant and translucent golden hues, and rich painterly textures. The admitted salutary effect notwithstanding, these luminous images also must have been highly valued for the sheer visual delight they accorded.

1. The Rijnsburg Abbey documents are housed in the Algemeen Rijks-Archief in The Hague; see Jeremy M. Bangs, "Rijnsburg Abbey: Additional Documentation on Furniture, Artists, Musicians, and Buildings, 1500–1570," *Bulletin van de Koninklijke Nederlandse Oudheidkundige Bond* 74, 1975, p. 186.

2. See "Un vitrail de Mesnil-Villeman (1313) et les origines du jaune d'argent," *Bulletin de la Société nationale des antiquaires de France*, 1954, pp. 93–95, which updates Lafond's earlier and more extensive study. "Essai historique sur le jaune d'argent," in *Pratique de la peinture sur verre à l'usage des curieux, suivie d'un essai historique . . .* , Rouen, 1943, pp. 39–116.

3. "European Stained Glass around 1300: The Introduction of Silver Stain," in *Europäische Kunst um 1300*, Vienna, 1986, p. 46.

4. See Ellen Konowitz, "Drawings as intermediary stages: some working methods of Dirk Vellert and Albrecht Dürer re-examined," *Simiolus* 20, 1990–91, pp. 143–52.

5. The Lowlands (from *païs bas* or *pays bas*) rather than the Netherlands (or Netherlandish) is the preferred terminology throughout this volume, as it avoids any confusion with the modern country the Netherlands.

6. For a concise and authoritative discussion of the political and economic history of the Lowlands see Hugo de Schepper, "The Burgundian-Habsburg Netherlands," in *Handbook of European History 1400–1600, Late Middle Ages, Renaissance and Reformation 1, Structures and Assertions*, ed. by Thomas A. Brady, Jr., Heiko A. Oberman, and James D. Tracy, Leiden and New York, 1994, pp. 499–533. For a detailed study of the Habsburg rule see James D. Tracy, *Holland under Habsburg Rule 1506–1566. The Formation of a Body Politic*, Berkeley, 1990.

7. The Seventeen Provinces were Brabant, Limburg, Luxembourg, Gelderland, Flanders, Artois, Hainault, Holland, Zeeland, Namur, Zutphen, East Friesland, West Friesland, Mechelen, Utrecht, Overijssel, and Groningen. The prince-bishopric of Liège was never politically incorporated into the Lowlands.

8. See Jozef IJsewijn, "The Coming of Humanism to the Low Countries," *Itinerarium Italicum: The Profile of the Italian Renaissance in the Mirror of its European Transformations* (Studies in Medieval and Reformation Thought, 14), ed. by Heiko A. Oberman with Thomas A. Brady, Jr., Leiden, 1975, pp. 193–301.

9. "Elements of continuity: a finger raised in warning," *Simiolus* 20, 1990–91, pp. 124–41, esp. pp. 134–35.

# Characteristics of Iconography in the Lowlands during the Period of Humanism and the Reformation: 1480 to 1560

ILJA M. VELDMAN
Vrije Universiteit, Amsterdam

Perhaps nowhere more than in the Lowlands—one of the most densely populated areas in Europe in the sixteenth century—did the iconography of works of art mirror the interests of the public for which they were intended. The art of this period was primarily created for the upper middle classes eager to acquire illuminated manuscripts and books, small panel paintings, drawings, prints, small-scale stained glass, and other such objects suited to domestic or civic surrounds as well as to the tastes and pocketbooks of a growing market force. The wide-ranging imagery was in direct response to the concerns, preoccupations, and ideals of an educated public comprised not only of the nobility and the clergy but also of the burgeoning classes of wealthy merchants, Humanists, educators, artists, and skilled craftsmen. In addition to the aesthetic pleasure afforded the buyers of works of art, the content and meaning of this art were of fundamental importance as reflections of the culture of the time.

The years from 1480 to 1560 are generally considered to have been a period of great social, religious, and intellectual change in the Lowlands, influenced largely by the Reformation and by the conflict with traditional Catholicism that occurred. Expanding this point of view, H. A. Enno van Gelder proposed that—beyond the concerns of traditional Catholic dogma and of new reformist trends—devotional and cultural life from 1450 to 1560 was marked by an even more embracing reform movement, which far exceeded the boundaries of the ecclesiastical Reformation. This encompassing change, which he termed the "Broad Reformation," was rooted in Humanism and Renaissance ideals, and deeply affected the outlook of the upper classes of society. Characteristic of these new attitudes were an ethical philosophy of life, a broadened view of religious issues, and a reformulation of the means by which man hoped to attain heavenly salvation.[1]

This "Broad Reformation" is irrefutably reflected in the visual arts. Under the influence of Humanism and the Reformation, the accent clearly shifted in the choice, treatment, and function of subject matter during the course of the sixteenth century. However, despite all of the innovations, the iconographic repertoire in the 1500s remained primarily religious in nature and relied at least in part on the heritage of the Late Middle Ages. Of course, more secular themes increasingly made their appearance in the visual arts, but even then they generally contained a moral lesson consistent with Christian principles.

The discussion of developments in iconography in the Lowlands will be divided into four thematically organized sections. The order is not meant to suggest a chronology for, in practice, a variety of subjects prevailed simultaneously, and the categories themselves overlapped. The analysis here, furthermore, is not confined to silver-stained roundels and panels, but applies equally well to illuminated manuscripts, books, prints, drawings, and small panel paintings designed for the same audience. Indeed, the majority of artists discussed worked in more than one of the above-mentioned mediums.[2]

## Devotional Themes

### The Influence of the devotio moderna on the Iconographic Repertoire

Devotional imagery in this period had its roots in earlier fifteenth-century miniature painting in the Lowlands. Its flowering was due in large part to the religious movement known as the *devotio moderna*, whose spiritual father was Geert Groote (d. 1384). The influence of the *devotio moderna* prevailed until the Reformation and the

FIG. 1. Master of the Suffrages. *The Descent of the Holy Spirit.* Miniature from a Book of Hours. About 1480–90. The Hague, Koninklijke Bibliotheek (Ms. 130 E 5, f. 86 *v*)

Counter-Reformation, affecting the activities of the pious lay communities known as the Brothers and the Sisters of the Common Life, and the association of monasteries under the rule of the Canons Regular of Saint Augustine, known as the Windesheim Congregation.[3] Their new piety was rooted in a desire to counteract the abuses and corruption of the Church, and they sought a renewed spirituality inspired by a personal reading of the Gospels. The primary inspiration to their devotion was Christ's Passion—the proof of Christ's love for mankind and the climax of the drama that held the hope of man's redemption.

In order to give this new spirituality broad support, as many books as possible were produced in the vernacular. The Delft Bible (1477), based on the Windesheim revision of the Vulgate, was the first printed book in the Lowlands. Geert Groote himself compiled a new version of the Book of Hours: an abridgment of the Holy Office (the official prayers of the Church) suitable for laymen. This Book of Hours in the vernacular was thus accessible to a large public, and enjoyed even greater currency after the invention of printing in the Lowlands.

The *devotio moderna* not only advanced the production and use of bibles, Books of Hours, and other pious literature among laymen and clergy, but also encouraged the illustration of these texts to further stimulate the reader's piety. The Life of Christ and, to a lesser degree, representations of the Virgin were the most common subjects. Books of Hours were lavishly decorated.[4] They contained, for example, illustrations of the Annunciation (in the Hours of the Virgin), the Birth and Infancy of Christ, events in his public life, the Passion (in

the Hours of the Holy Cross), and the Transfiguration and Descent of the Holy Spirit (in the Hours of the Holy Spirit; see fig. 1).[5]

Most of the subjects illustrated in Books of Hours recur in glass paintings, drawings, and prints produced in the Lowlands. The Passion was among the most prevalent themes in all mediums (see cat. nos. 38, 39, 40, 41, and 42). Many of the major events in the Life of the Virgin and in the Life and Passion of Christ were celebrated with Church festivals and feast days, confirming their importance for society and, by extension, for the visual arts.[6] In addition, medieval legends not found in biblical texts were widely illustrated in Books of Hours and other prayer books; the Mass of Saint Gregory, for example (see cat. no. 103), was extensively represented because of Gregory the Great's vital role in formulating the liturgy. Likewise, the Occupations of the Months (see cat. nos. 28 and 29), on the surface a secular subject, was the traditional choice for illustrating the liturgical calendar usually found at the beginning of a Book of Hours.

### The Emergence of New Themes from the New Testament

Although the New Testament—with the exception of the Apocalypse—was only minimally illustrated in early printed bibles, a variety of other printed books based on or inspired by the Gospels increasingly was produced from the end of the fifteenth century on, with extensive woodcut illustrations. These included homilies (familiar explications, sermons, moralizations, or paraphrases of the Gospels), *plenaria* (popular vernacular translations of the Epistles or Gospels for all the Sundays and feast days of the year, along with expositions or instructions), evangelistaries (liturgical books with passages from the Gospels and Epistles that were read at Mass), passionals (various devotional books based on the sufferings of Christ or of the saints), and Ammonian sections or harmonies of the Gospels (a chronological story of the Life of Christ, based on all four Gospels, or concordances of parallel passages from the last three books of the Gospels arranged alongside the text of Matthew).

While these last books were used in conjunction with the celebration of the Mass and of various feast days, others were strictly intended for private devotion or meditation. Included in this group are such texts as *Tboeck vanden leven ons heeren Ihesu Christi* (published by Gerard Leeuw in Antwerp, 1487)[7]—a Netherlandish version of the *Meditationes vitae Christi* by the Carthusian Ludolphus of Saxony, a fourteenth-century devotional treatise in the form of a compilation of partially apocryphal stories from the Life of Christ. The seventy-four woodcuts depict subjects seldom illustrated before, such as Christ's parables and acts of healing (see fig. 2), subjects that also appeared in painted glass panels (see cat. nos. 46 and 47, fig. 5).

In the sixteenth century, the influence of Humanism and reformism enkindled the study of the text of the Bible, resulting not only in more scholarly recensions on the one hand, but also in more accessible editions for the less erudite on the other. Mattheus Crom published *Dat leven ons Heeren Christi Jesu* (Antwerp, 1537) by the Carthusian Willem van Branteghem, a Gospel harmony embellished with more than two hundred woodcuts by the Ghent painter Lieven de Witte,[8] and with an ode by the Humanist Georg Cassander that not only names the artist—unusual in itself—but also praises his illustrations. Events from the Four Gospels are carefully illustrated in accordance with the biblical texts: not just narrative accounts of Christ's life, or even of the parables, but also his more abstract teach-

FIG. 2. *The Healing of Two Possessed People*. Woodcut from *Tboeck vanden leven ons heeren Ihesu Christi* (1487). Amsterdam, Vrije Universiteit

FIG. 3. Lieven de Witte. *The Parable of the Laborers in the Vineyard*. Woodcut from *Dat leven ons Heeren Christi Jesu* (1537) by Willem van Branteghem. The Hague, Koninklijke Bibliotheek

ings, which had never been interpreted visually before (see fig. 3). As a result, the entire text of the Gospels was made "legible" through the illustrations, with the biblical text—condensed in this case—serving an almost subsidiary role. (The woodcuts by Lieven de Witte were later copied in numerous other bibles in the Lowlands.)[9]

In engravings and single-leaf woodcuts as well the accent shifted from scenes of the Infancy of Christ, the Passion, and the Resurrection to representations of Christ's life on earth and of the parables and those of his other teachings with a moral thrust. Increasingly, artists began to produce prints in series. The stories were visualized from beginning to end in multiple scenes with an emphasis on the narrative aspect, so that the content was made infinitely more comprehensible. Dirck Volckertsz. Coornhert's series of thirty etchings for *The Fall and Salvation of Mankind through the Life and Passion of Christ* (1548), after designs by Maarten van Heemskerck, devotes considerable space to Christ's acts of healing.[10] The biblical parables, which, in the Middle Ages, were interpreted in a mystical fashion, now came to serve as moral lessons to be applied to daily life, and also to help one attain eternal salvation. Prints by Coornhert after Heemskerck, such as *The Unmerciful Servant* (1549 and 1554, respectively), *The Good Samaritan* (1549), and *The Rich Man on His Deathbed* (1551; see fig. 4), were intended to promote mercy and charity in the viewer.[11] Identical themes also were embraced in *rederijker* (rhetoricians') plays and in Latin-school dramas, which were aimed at the same public that acquired these prints as well as glass paintings. Coornhert was also the author of the *Comedie vande Rijckeman* of about 1550, inspired by the parable of Lazarus and the Rich Man,[12] and Macropedius, in his Latin-school drama *Lazarus mendicus* (1541), told of the life of luxury and the tragic end of the wealthy Laemargus as an admonitory example.[13]

The parable of the Prodigal Son received much attention both in art and in literature (*De Historie van den verloren Sone* was published in Antwerp in 1540).[14] Illustrations of the wayward existence of the Prodigal Son were strongly influenced by popular literature, and tales of vagabonds who had lost all of their possessions to

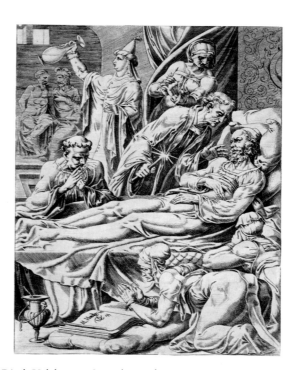

FIG. 4. Dirck Volckertsz. Coornhert, after Maarten van Heemskerck. *The Rich Man on His Deathbed*: from a series of the Parable of Lazarus and the Rich Man. Etching and engraving. 1551. Amsterdam, Rijksmuseum, Rijksprentenkabinet

FIG. 5. Hieronymus Bosch. *The Seven Deadly Sins and the "Four Last Things."* Tempera and oil on panel. About 1490–1500. Madrid, Museo del Prado

women, alcohol, and gambling developed into an extremely popular genre.[15] Dissolute tavern scenes featuring personifications of Poverty and of the Common Lass (*Gemene deerne*) frequently were the subjects of prints, drawings, and glass paintings.[16] In Cornelis Anthonisz.'s series of woodcuts from 1541 (see cat. nos. 30 and 34), the central character, Sorgheloos (Carefree), disports himself with such companions as Gemack (Ease) and Weelde (Luxury), who eventually and irretrievably reduce him to beggary.[17] The forgiving nature of the parable is thus abandoned in favor of stringent moralizing.

Didactic and moralizing tendencies are encountered in other themes as well. Prints, drawings, and glass paintings illustrating the Acts of Mercy, for example (see cat. nos. 46–50), represent contemporary citizens performing their tasks among their neighbors. In a series of prints from 1552 by Coornhert, after Heemskerck, illustrations of these Acts of Mercy are preceded by an image of the Last Judgment.[18] Likewise, the theme of Souls in Hell (see cat. no. 26), also illustrated in Books of Hours and other prayer books, should be examined in relation to the Last Judgment and the doctrine of the "Four Last Things" (death, the Last Judgment, Heaven, and hell),[19] which became known through a devotional treatise by Dionysius the Carthusian, *Novissima quattuor*, designed to prepare one for salvation. In addition to Latin versions, there were also vernacular editions of the treatise, such as *Die vier uterste* (Gouda, Gerard Leeuw, 1482), which were illustrated with woodcuts.[20] The so-called "table-top" by Hieronymus Bosch (see fig. 5) represents the "Four Last Things" in combination with the Seven Deadly Sins, which man must avoid at all costs should he want to ascend to Heaven after death.[21] Related to the theme of the "Four Last Things" is the *Ars moriendi* (*The Art of Dying*), a collection of late medieval illustrated texts originally compiled for priests who had to assist the dying,

but later on used by the laity. Even when a deathbed scene was not described in the actual biblical story it often was illustrated in art: A case in point is the biblical account of the parable of Lazarus and the Rich Man, which does not allude to the scene of the rich man on his deathbed, as depicted by Coornhert (see fig. 4).

## The Flourishing of Themes from the Old Testament

### The Typological Tradition

In the Late Middle Ages, many events in Old Testament stories traditionally were considered as prefigurations of events in the New Testament and therefore were widely illustrated. Together with their New Testament parallels, these typologies were collected in the *Biblia pauperum* and the *Speculum humanae salvationis*, from the fourteenth century on; they were available first in handwritten and later in printed versions.[22] For example, the Sacrifice of Isaac was depicted in connection with the Crucifixion; the Meeting of Abraham and Melchizedek and the Fall of Manna were paired with the Last Supper; David and Goliath, with the Temptation of Christ; Joseph being thrown into the well, with the Burial of Christ; Joseph's brothers showing his bloody coat to Jacob, with the Lamentation; and the selling of Joseph to the Ishmaelites was thought to prefigure Judas receiving the thirty pieces of silver.

Such typological arrangements endured in the Lowlands well into the sixteenth century. The third edition of Jacob Cornelisz.'s circular Passion woodcut series of 1511–14, for instance, published in Amsterdam about 1520 by Doen Pietersz., incorporated woodcuts of

Old Testament parallels to New Testament events (see cat. nos. 38–42).[23] About 1530, Doen Pietersz. issued an even more extensive *Biblia pauperum*, combining woodcuts from Jacob Cornelisz.'s Small Passion (1523) with woodcuts of Old Testament scenes by the same artist and Lucas van Leyden (fig. 6).[24] Even when they were not accompanied by New Testament counterparts, Old Testament representations in the first half of the sixteenth century automatically would have evoked associations with the Life of Christ in the minds of their beholders, as, for example, Gideon and the Miracle of the Fleece (cat. no. 70, fig. 1), which, traditionally, prefigured the Annunciation.

### Expansion of the Old Testament Repertoire

The oldest handwritten bibles in the Lowlands were not bibles per se, but combined selections from the Old Testament, a Gospel harmony, and sometimes commentaries, along with a scattering of popular secular history, such as the life of Alexander the Great. Most of these "history bibles" originated in Utrecht between 1430 and 1445, and included an abundance of images to elucidate the biblical passages.[25] These richly illustrated manuscripts were designed for a few exclusive users, but from the late fifteenth century on, printed bibles with woodcuts were issued for a far larger public. Enormously influential in this regard was the Cologne Bible of about 1478, published by Heinrich Quentell;[26] with more than one hundred woodcuts illustrating the books of the Old Testament, this bible served as a model for artists well into the sixteenth century, for it contained many scenes that did not belong to the traditional typological repertoire. The Story of Joseph, for example, was told in ten woodcuts, and that of Moses in thirty.[27] Following the model of the Cologne Bible and of the illustrated German editions of Luther's Bible, more and more Dutch-language bibles were produced in which the Old Testament contained abundant illustrations—as, for instance, the Liesveldt Bible (Antwerp, 1526) and the Vorsterman Bible (Antwerp,

FIG. 7. Lucas van Leyden. *The Repudiation of Hagar.* Engraving. 1516. Amsterdam, Rijksmuseum, Rijksprentenkabinet

1528), the latter featuring woodcuts after designs by Jan Swart van Groningen.[28]

Old Testament events enjoyed enduring popularity because the main characters and the infinite trials and tribulations they suffered before their stories came to happy conclusions could readily be identified with, and the central dramas raised issues that seemed relevant in the readers' own times. In the case of the Story of Joseph, events

FIG. 8. Jan Swart van Groningen. *The Healing of Tobit.*
Pen and brown ink on paper. About 1535. Leipzig, Museum
der bildenden Künste

FIG. 9. Philips Galle, after Maarten van Heemskerck. *Samson Smiting
the Philistines with the Jawbone of an Ass*: from a series of the Story of
Samson. Engraving. About 1560. Rotterdam, Museum Boymans-van
Beuningen

are fraught with sibling rivalry and dramatic reversals of fortune, comprising a complex saga that ultimately is resolved with the restoration of honor and family unity. Its appeal is evidenced by the continuing ubiquity of its representations: It was the subject of a series of six tondi by the Master of the Joseph Sequence dating to about 1500, each painting combining multiple scenes to fully convey the narrative (see cat. nos. 8 and 9, figs. 2 and 7, and cat. no. 10, figs. 1 and 2);[29] and the theme was treated by Lucas van Leyden in a series of five engravings in 1512 (see cat. no. 56, fig. 3), and by Heemskerck in a series of eight prints etched by Coornhert in 1549–50 (see cat. no. 108).[30]

The life of the patriarch Abraham, who was forced to abandon his country; to repudiate Hagar, the mother of his firstborn; and to offer in sacrifice his only other son, Isaac, enjoyed similar favor. Lucas van Leyden depicted *Abraham and the Three Angels*, *The Repudiation of Hagar* (1516; fig. 7), and *The Sacrifice of Isaac*; the subject of Abraham was extensively represented by Dirick Vellert (cat. nos. 77–79); and Heemskerck devoted a series of prints to the Story of Abraham and one to that of Isaac in 1549.[31]

The Story of Tobit, the virtuous old man whose blindness was healed by his son, Tobias, was an exemplum of patient endurance *par excellence* and, likewise, inspired extensive representations: The Hugo van der Goes group produced designs for a series of roundels with that theme at the end of the fifteenth century (cat. nos. 12–14); Jan Swart also made a series of drawings of the story that possibly were intended for glass panels (fig. 8);[32] about 1548 Heemskerck produced a series of woodcuts, and in 1555 a series of ten engravings of the subject;[33] and, about 1555, Lambert van Noort executed a design for a painted glass panel depicting *The Healing of Tobit* (cat. no. 113).

Among painters in the Lowlands, it was primarily Lucas van Leyden, and Maarten van Heemskerck a generation later, who extensively illustrated Old Testament events in prints. In addition to those of his works discussed above, Lucas produced a series of prints related to the Story of Adam and Eve, as well as *David Playing the Harp for Saul*, *David and Abigail*, *David and Goliath*, *Esther and Ahasuerus* (1518), *The Triumph of Mordecai* (1518), and *Susanna and the Elders*.[34] The subjects of Heemskerck's Old Testament series are Judith (about 1548), Jacob (1549), Judah and Tamar (about 1549), Lot (about 1551), Susanna (1551), Solomon (1554), Abigail (1555), David (about 1556), Noah (1559), Tamar and Amnon (1559), and Samson (about 1560; see fig. 9).[35]

## Old Testament Stories as Moral Examples

As noted earlier, under the influence of Humanism and the Reformation the moral and didactic content of biblical stories increasingly was emphasized. Jacob van Liesveldt, in the preface to his Dutch translation of the Bible, published in 1536, described the function of stories from the Old Testament as guides to good and evil. The core of his argument, based on Martin Luther's September Testament, was that Old Testament events were to be considered as a "fixed code of laws" from which man could learn what he should and should not do.

Luther's premise was fully exploited, for example, by the association of each of the Ten Commandments (Exodus 20: 1–17) with an Old Testament story of transgression. This practice had already been adopted in late medieval manuscripts, such as the *Concordantiae caritatis*, and in incunabula of the *Zielentroost*, a collection of exempla in the Decalogue.[36] During the German Reformation, as well, it was customary to illustrate the catechism (Christian lessons for laymen) with prints in which violations of each of the Ten Commandments were exemplified by scenes from the Old Testament.[37] For instance, the Mocking of Noah repudiates the commandment "Honor thy father and mother"; Cain Killing Abel, "Thou shalt not kill"; David and Bathsheba, "Thou shalt not commit adultery"; Susanna before the judge, "Thou shalt not bear false witness against thy neighbor"; and Joseph and the wife of Potiphar, "Thou shalt not covet thy neighbor's wife."[38]

The visual narrative was contrived to make the moral underpinnings of the Old Testament stories as explicit as possible. In the case of the perennially popular tale of the beautiful and virtuous Susanna (see cat. nos. 63–65), the moral issues are revealed in the principal events of the story: Susanna withstanding attempts at seduction and blackmail by the two elders was seen as a warning against both adultery and false accusation, while the revelation of the elders' perjury through Daniel's cross-examination (see fig. 10)[39] and their subsequent lapidation represented both good judgment and a vindication of marital fidelity and chastity. As with the subject of Joseph and the wife of Potiphar, early portrayals of *Susanna and the Elders* are rather chaste; both scenes, however, ironically would acquire a distinctly erotic character during the course of the sixteenth century.

Less well-known stories also yielded moral lessons. In 1558 Hans Liefrinck devoted a series of eight prints to the Story of Nebuchadnezzar, after designs by Lambert van Noort.[40] The dream of King Nebuchadnezzar and its realization (Daniel 4: 1–34), for example, may be interpreted as a warning against the sin of pride: The king is admonished by God for his vanity and is punished for it, but when Nebuchadnezzar repents he is restored to his former power (see cat. nos. 115 and 116).

Numerous Old Testament females, both heroines and deceivers, came to be viewed as quintessential exempla; Susanna, Judith, and Esther, for instance, are generally regarded as positive models, but others such as Eve, Jezebel, and Delilah, as a result of their deceitful behavior, are cited as admonitory figures.[41] Lucas van Leyden made two series of woodcuts that depict the deceptions wrought by women in the Bible and in other literary works.[42] In one of these series, the images were printed within ornamental frames inscribed with biblical passages, including quotes from Ecclesiastes warning against the pernicious influence of women (see, for example, cat. nos. 51, 52, 53, and 55). It was usually of little consequence whether these women were heroic or troublemakers; the artists' intentions were to elucidate and then warn against the seductive power of women in general. Such was the case with Coornhert's series of etchings from 1551, after works by Maarten van Heemskerck, which features not only Eve, Lot's daughters, Jael, Delilah, and the wives of Solomon (fig. 11), but also the brave and virtuous Judith, who slew Holofernes and thus delivered her city of Bethulia from siege.[43]

That such representations conveyed current understanding is confirmed by contemporary literature, such as *Dat bedroch der vrouwen. Tot een onderwijs ende exempel van allen mannen ionck ende out, om dat si sullen weten, hoe bruesch, hoe valsch, hoe bedriechlijk dat die vrouwen zijn* (*The Deceit of Women. Being a Lesson and Example for All Men Young and Old, As They Should*

FIG. 10. Lucas van Leyden. *Susanna in Judgment* (destroyed). Tempera and oil on panel. About 1509–12. Formerly Bremen, Kunsthalle

FIG. 11. Dirck Volckertsz. Coornhert, after Maarten van Heemskerck. *The Idolatry of Solomon*: from a series of the Power of Women. Etching and engraving. 1551. Amsterdam, Rijksmuseum, Rijksprentenkabinet

*Know How Weak, How False, How Deceptive Women Are*), published in Utrecht about 1532. This volume was richly illustrated with woodcuts;[44] in addition to contemporary examples and those from antiquity, the deceptions of Eve, Lot's daughters, Jael, Jezebel, Delilah, the wives of Solomon, and Herodias were cited as cautionary exempla. *Der sotten schip* (Antwerp, 1548), a Netherlandish version of Sebastian Brant's *Das Narrenschiff* (1494), also names famous victims of women: Adam, Lot, Samson, David, Solomon, Joseph, Aristotle, and Hercules.[45] Moreover, in such etiquette books as *Boec van den loveliken leven ende staet der echten* (*In Praise of Marriage*), by Dionysius the Carthusian (Gouda, 1479), men were warned never to heed the advice of women lest they find themselves in the greatest of difficulties.[46]

## Humanism

### Characteristics of Netherlandish Humanism

Humanism in the Lowlands originated in the cloisters and the circles of the *devotio moderna*, rather than in cities, at courts, or at universities, as was the case in Italy. Humanism was not considered a goal in itself, but a means of improving theological studies and Christian living. Education was, in this respect, a necessity. Because most writers were clergymen or teachers, neo-Latin literature in the Lowlands had a strongly moralizing and Christian character. As a result, Netherlandish Humanism is often referred to as Christian or biblical Humanism.[47]

The most famous Humanist in the Lowlands was Erasmus of Rotterdam. In his *Enchiridion militis christiani* (1503; translated into Dutch in 1524), Erasmus describes the struggle between mind and body and stresses the importance of knowledge and insight as weapons in the fight against the cardinal sins.[48] The book became an enormously popular moral text, including passages from the Bible and writings by classical authors. In other works as well, Erasmus argued for a Christian theology capable of being understood by all, which could be applied in daily life. In addition to the Gospels and the Epistles of the apostles, he viewed the study of classical languages and literature as an important instructive tool for the attainment of a high moral standard.[49]

The Humanists studied the literature of classical antiquity and attempted to relate its lessons to their own culture and way of thinking. The philosophies of Cicero and Seneca and of the Early Christian writer Boethius were particularly embraced because of their moral content. Not coincidentally, the first book that Dirck Volckertsz. Coornhert translated into Dutch and published in 1561 was Cicero's *De officiis*; his translation of Seneca's *De beneficiis* appeared the following year. Boethius's famous *De consolatione philosophiae* had already been published in a Dutch-language version in 1485 in Ghent and in 1558 in Deventer, the latter possibly by Coornhert; Coornhert issued a revised edition in 1584, translated directly from the Latin.[50]

### The Role of the Latin-School Drama and the Rederijker *Plays*

Moral interpretation was likewise disseminated through Latin-school dramas written by Humanists who were usually affiliated with Latin

FIG. 12. Cornelis Anthonisz. *The Prodigal Son Welcomed into the Church*: from a series of the Allegory of the Prodigal Son. Woodcut. About 1540. Amsterdam, Rijksmuseum, Rijksprentenkabinet

schools.[51] Aside from the utility of these school dramas in furthering a pupil's knowledge of Latin, their didactic possibilities were amply exploited. One of the oldest of the school dramas is *Grisellis* (1511) by Eligius Houcharius (Gillis Hoockaert), a theatrical version of the last novella of Boccaccio's *Decameron*, which was translated into Latin by Petrarch in 1373 and was known in several Lowlands versions, such as the *Historie van Griseldis* (Antwerp, 1519);[52] the story was also a subject for glass painting (see cat. no. 111).

Like the *rederijker* plays, many of the school dramas dealt with biblical themes; Cornelius Crocus's *Joseph* (Antwerp, 1536), which had been reprinted eleven times by 1549,[53] concerned the attempts of Potiphar's wife to seduce Joseph. In 1544 Macropedius wrote about Joseph's experiences in Egypt. The story of the Jewish heroine Esther, who saved her people from destruction, was the subject of a play by Petrus Philicinus in 1545, and of one by Frans Goethals in 1549. In addition, several school dramas portrayed the courageous and chaste Susanna, among them Johannes Placentius's *Suzanna* of 1534.[54]

Adaptations of the Story of the Prodigal Son were also popular among Latin playwrights. Macropedius's *Asotus*, written in 1507 and published in 1537, describes a rake who disports among the whores in his father's house and subsequently sails with them to Mileteus, while his father awaits his return at the harbor.[55] Gulielmus Gnapheus (Willem Claesz. de Volder)—who, incidentally, was arrested several times for being a follower of Lutheranism and took exile in Germany in 1529—wrote the play *Acolastus* (Antwerp, 1529) shortly before his emigration; the forty-seventh edition appeared in 1585. In this work, as well, the profligate life of the young man takes center stage.[56] Barbara Haeger has convincingly demonstrated the similarities between *Acolastus* and Cornelis Anthonisz.'s woodcut series of the Allegory of the Prodigal Son (about 1540; see fig. 12).[57]

As the Humanists revived interest in classical culture by producing dramas based on works by some of the foremost authors—notably Terence—the *rederijkers* also, on occasion, based their Dutch-language plays on classical models, but infused them with a Christian moral;[58] examples include *Mars en Venus* (1551); *Eneas en Dido*; *Charon* (1551), which contains a commentary on man's sinful pursuit of sensuality and gold; *Narcissus ende Echo*; and *Pyramus en Thisbe*,[59] in which Pyramus appears to represent Christ and Thisbe the bride in the Song of Songs.

### Humanistic Subjects in the Visual Arts

In addition to monasteries, the court of Philip of Burgundy—who became Bishop of Utrecht in 1517—was also an important Humanist center. Philip surrounded himself with scholars and artists, one of whom, Jan Gossaert, decorated Philip's castle at Wijk bij Duurstede in the "antique" style.[60] Philip took Gossaert with him to Rome (1508–9), where the artist made drawings after antique sculptures. Later on, he painted various mythological pictures for his patron, including *Venus and Amor* in 1521 (see fig. 13). The paintings were provided with frames bearing moralizing Latin inscriptions written by Philip's court Humanist, Gerrit Geldenhauer. The Latin inscription on *Venus and Amor* refers to the adultery of Mars and Venus, as described in Homer's *Odyssey* and in Ovid's *Metamorphoses*, and may be translated: "Shameless son, you who are wont to provoke gods and men, even your mother is not sacred to you. Have done with that, lest you perish."[61]

As a result of artists' travels in Italy and the influence of prints and editions of classical literature imported from there, diverse themes from ancient history, mythology, and Italian Humanism were soon introduced into the art of the Lowlands. The *Trionfi* of Petrarch, in particular, enjoyed great popularity.[62] Despite the fact that Petrarch borrowed from classical authors and incorporated numerous mythological motifs in his writings, his point of departure was Christian: Petrarch's text—demonstrating the transience of worldly matters such as love, fame, and time—in turn, was the inspiration for a popular cycle of images that made use of certain conventions not found in the sonnets themselves. Each of the victorious personifications is depicted in a triumphal chariot pulled by an animal in keeping with the subject's symbolism, although Petrarch describes a chariot only in the first triumph: that of Cupid is drawn by four white horses. By convention, however, the chariot of Chastity is led by unicorns, that of Death by bullocks, that of Fame by elephants (see cat. nos. 81 and 82), that of Time by deer (see cat. no. 67), and that of Divinity by the Four Evangelists or their symbols (see cat. nos. 83 and 84).

Ancient history was also a very popular subject in art. Livy's *Ab urbe condita* was printed in Antwerp in 1519;[63] the Story of Lucretia, whose suicide was the subject of many prints and panel paintings in the Lowlands, was a popular episode from Livy, and was understood

FIG. 13. Jan Gossaert. *Venus and Amor*. Tempera and oil on panel. 1521. Brussels, Musée d'Art Ancien

as an example of marital fidelity and chastity. Also based on Livy are Barent van Orley's designs of 1524 for tapestries depicting the founding of Rome by Romulus and Remus,[64] which can be considered something of a royal allegory, relating in an exemplary fashion the accession to the throne and the kingship of a young ruler. The Judgment of Cambyses, an episode from Herodotus's *Histories* and, as an exemplum, widely disseminated through the *Gesta Romanorum*, was often represented as an admonition to corrupt judges (see cat. no. 80), as were such subjects as Susanna before the Judges and the Judgment of Solomon.[65]

During the Renaissance, mythological stories attained a contemporary moralizing significance and were summarized in the compilations of sixteenth-century Italian mythographers.[66] The Judgment of Paris, known in the Lowlands by the fifteenth century,[67] was enacted in *tableaux vivants* at royal pageants, among them the Entry of Philip the Good into Ghent in 1457, that of Charles the Bold into Lille in 1468, and that of Philip the Handsome into Antwerp in 1494.[68] The story may be seen as a royal allegory—a lesson for a king's son to choose wisely, not for sensuality (Venus), but for power (Juno) or wisdom (Minerva).[69] The myth must have been regarded as equally applicable to lesser men, for it inspired roundels (see cat. nos. 59 and 60), drawings, and small panel paintings, like the one by a follower of the Master of the Female Half-Lengths (see fig. 14).[70] From the 1540s on, in paintings by such artists as Maarten van Heemskerck

FIG. 14. Follower of the Master of the Female Half-Lengths (Monogrammist L.D.H. ?). *The Judgment of Paris*. Tempera and oil on panel. 1532. Amsterdam, Rijksmuseum

FIG. 15. Lucas van Leyden. *Pyramus and Thisbe*. Engraving. 1514. New York, The Metropolitan Museum of Art, Harris Brisbane Dick Fund, 1934

and Frans Floris—as a result of their travels to Italy—depictions of mythological subjects took on an increasingly more classical aspect.[71]

The most important source for mythological subjects was Ovid's *Metamorphoses*; it became known in the Lowlands via a French edition published by Colard Mansion in Bruges in 1484: *Cy commence Ovide . . . son livre intitulé Métamorphose*, which, in turn, was based on the *Ovidius moralizatus* by Bersuire and the *Ovide moralisé* from the first half of the fourteenth century.[72] *Cy commence Ovide . . .* was a compilation of tales from Ovid rendered as Christian allegories for the edification of the reader. The edition by Mansion was illustrated with lively woodcuts, albeit devoid of classical elements.[73] Early painted and graphic representations of mythological subjects, whether the Pseudo-Ortkens scene from the second *Eclogue* of Virgil (cat. no. 66) or Lucas van Leyden's engraving of *Pyramus and Thisbe* of 1514 (fig. 15), similarly have little that is "classical" about them.[74]

## The Reformation

### The Reformation in the Lowlands

As opposed to Germany, where Lutheranism played an important role in political developments, in the Lowlands the Reformation manifested itself only inconspicuously in the visual arts. The central government's fervent repression of all attempts at reform reinforced the sectarian nature of Protestantism. Initially, many hoped for a thoughtful, gradual reform of the Catholic Church, rather than its wholesale abandonment.[75]

Reformist doctrine in the Lowlands originally was based on that of Martin Luther, which was disseminated in Ghent and Antwerp from about 1525 on. In addition to the influence of an Erasmian Christian Humanism, there was also a strong spiritual current from Switzerland and southern Germany. The early Reformation was thus a melting pot of various beliefs and diverse doctrines, which were often difficult to distinguish from one another. At first, only the

Anabaptists were well organized and promoted a well-defined credo, but they were severely suppressed after their attempt to seize power in Amsterdam in 1535.[76]

The various denominations were not clearly defined until about 1566—the year of the violent outbreak of iconoclasm and the beginning of a strong political polarization—but many of the doctrinal differences with traditional Catholicism are distinct. For Protestants, salvation was to be achieved through faith and grace, not through the sacraments or the performance of good deeds. The leitmotif was "justification through faith alone" (*sola fide*), as described in Saint Paul's Epistle to the Romans. Of the original Seven Sacraments of the Catholic Church, the Protestants recognized only Baptism and Communion. For Calvinism, moreover, predestination—the conviction that one already was destined for Heaven or hell before birth—was a central tenet.

At the start, Protestantism appealed primarily to the middle class. It is, therefore, not surprising that it found many sympathizers in *rederijker* milieus. The "morality plays" (*spelen van sinne*)—those *rederijker* dramas with a moral content and in which most characters were personifications of vices and virtues—frequently exhibit reformist sentiments.[77]

From 1539, especially in Flanders, reformist currents were strictly suppressed. In 1546 a list of forbidden books was drawn up and attempts were made to reform the Catholic Church from within, but despite the persecution, about 1560 the larger Flemish cities had organized Protestant congregations, and political and religious dissidents began to join forces.

### Reformist Elements in the Visual Arts

Satirical prints depicting the pope and the clergy—common in Germany during the period of struggle between Lutherans and Catholics—hardly existed in the Lowlands before 1566. Other specifically reformist representations were also rare.[78] It must be said that it is not easy to distinguish among reformist and Catholic imagery, as the Bible was the source for all denominations and the old visual traditions persisted. Progressive Catholic artists, such as Maarten van Heemskerck, incorporated reformist elements in their work or gave expression to an Erasmian-Humanistic vision of faith.[79] Furthermore, art-historical opinion often conflicts in efforts to identify the motivating religious sympathies of specific reformist images.

As mentioned earlier, subject matter in the visual arts underwent certain changes under the influence of Humanism and the Reformation, beginning in the second quarter of the sixteenth century. Devotional images of the Virgin and of the saints became less common and representations of Christ's suffering and death and of the Resurrection gave way to depictions of Christ's teachings and of the miracles he performed, as well as of Old Testament events with moral content. A new genre was introduced in the form of Christian allegories concerning the contrast between good and evil and the way in which man could attain heavenly salvation. The power of faith in Christ, who redeemed man from transgression and death, was the obvious key to these allegories. Illustrations of explicitly Protestant subjects, however, remained limited to unsigned drawings, stained-glass paintings, and prints, which were probably private commissions and not intended for the art market. Their iconography in many instances can be traced back to that of earlier German reformist imagery.

For the Protestants, the Word, the text of the Bible, was the guiding principle. Ever-increasing numbers of representations took the form of literal depictions of a biblical passage, or else were provided with accompanying biblical verses. Artists often derived inspiration from the apostolic Epistles. Saint Paul's exposition of justification through faith became a tenet of the Lutherans, earning him the sobri-

quet "apostle of the Reformation"; the resulting diminished popularity of this saint among Catholics in the sixteenth century is, therefore, hardly surprising. Thus, a work such as Dirck Crabeth's *Preaching of Paul* of 1543 (cat. no. 119) would appear to voice Protestant sympathies. The same may be said for a glass panel of about 1560 stylistically related to the work of Jan Swart, *Followers*

FIG. 16. *Followers of Christ Each Bearing His Cross.* Woodcut of "Thy will be done, on earth as it is in heaven," from *Een wtlegginghe des Pater noster* (about 1544–50) by Erasmus of Rotterdam. Amsterdam, Universiteitsbibliotheek

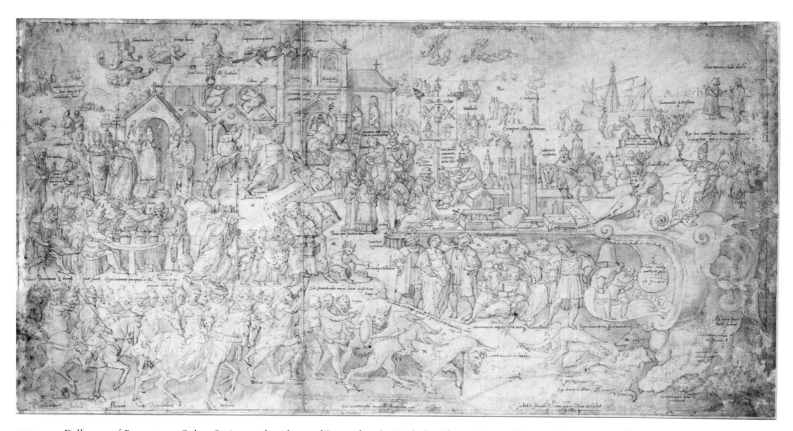

FIG. 17. Follower of Barent van Orley. *Satire on the Abuse of Power by the Catholic Clergy.* Pen and brown ink on paper. About 1530–40. Amsterdam, Rijksmuseum, Rijksprentenkabinet

FIG. 18. Master A.P., after the Workshop of Barent van Orley. *The Struggle of Faith against Unbelief*. Woodcut. 1536. Staatliche Museen zu Berlin, Preußischer Kulturbesitz, Kupferstichkabinett

FIG. 19. Master A.P., after the Workshop of Barent van Orley. *The Struggle between Patience and Wrath*. Woodcut. 1536. Staatliche Museen zu Berlin, Preußischer Kulturbesitz, Kupferstichkabinett

of *Christ Each Bearing His Cross* (cat. no. 106). Its iconography is derived from German reformist prints in which the subject functioned as an illustration of the third plea of the Lord's Prayer: "Thy will be done, on earth as it is in heaven";[80] the same theme appears in contemporary illustrations in Dutch books devoted to an elucidation of the Lord's Prayer (fig. 16). Even though the subject reflects the spirit of the Reformation, the exhortation it embodies, in fact, would have applied equally to all denominations.

In contrast to book publishers, who were considered especially suspect by the Inquisition,[81] only a few artists were persecuted. The image was apparently considered less threatening than the word. Moreover, in proceedings against artists their conduct was more of an issue than their work. In 1527 Barent van Orley had to appear before the Inquisition with his family members and friends because he was present when a Lutheran sermon was delivered in his house.[82] Orley was convicted, but due to the intercession of Margaret of Austria—he was her court painter—he was punished lightly. As a result of this case, the presence of heterodox subject matter or "Protestant elements," such as are encountered in the drawing *Satire on the Abuse of Power by the Catholic Clergy* (see fig. 17),[83] has been used to support attributions to Orley. The iconography of this drawing, however, does not so much promote a particular reformed faith as it indicts the traditional practices of the Catholic clergy.

According to Karel Boon, Orley or a workshop assistant designed two woodcuts executed by the Master A.P.: *The Struggle of Faith against Unbelief* and *The Struggle between Patience and Wrath* (figs. 18 and 19), which were published by Willem Liefrinck in Antwerp in 1536.[84] Faith is seen leading a battle with her sword "Verbum Dei"; Patience stands on the "rock of Christ" and protects herself with the "shield of faith" and the "anvil of tolerance." The labels (by the unknown "Lucas Volder") proclaim that true faith is not an institution of the Church manifested, for example, in the doing of good works, but rather represents the belief of every individual in Christ.

The designer of the woodcuts in the above-mentioned *Dat leven ons Heeren*, Lieven de Witte, was fined in Ghent in 1528 because he conversed with people suspected of heresy.[85] The book by Cornelis van der Heyden, *Corte instruccye ende onderwijs* (1545), for which de Witte also designed the woodcuts, was banned immediately after it was issued, and the Ghent publisher Joos Lambrechts was sentenced to prison.[86] The main objection must have been to the text, but it is worth noting that de Witte, in addition, had included a tetragram in many of his illustrations—a symbol that in Germany was used exclusively in reformist circles.

Despite the persecutions, several images were produced with an unambiguously reformist character. The unsigned drawing *Christ as the Light of the World* of about 1530 (fig. 20)[87] might be the work of Lucas Cornelisz. Cock, the son of the Leiden painter Cornelis Engebrechtsz., who emigrated to England after 1542. The sheet was inspired by a woodcut by Hans Holbein the Younger, which may have been intended to illustrate a pamphlet written by the reformer Guillaume Farel in 1527. In both the drawing and the woodcut Christ shows the true believers the giant candelabrum that is the symbol of his light—an image inspired by various biblical passages: "No man lighteth a candle, and putteth it in a hidden place, nor under a bushel; but upon a candlestick, that they that come in, may see the light" (Luke 11:33); *"The people that sat in darkness, hath*

FIG. 20. Attributed to Lucas Cornelisz. Cock. *Christ as the Light of the World*. Pen and brown ink on paper. About 1530. Paris, Collection Frits Lugt, Institut Néerlandais

*seen a great light"* (Matthew 4:16); and, especially, "I am the light of the world: he that followeth me, walketh not in darkness" (John 8:12). This last passage was interpreted by the Protestants as the new light of the Gospel shining in the darkness that had been precipitated by Catholicism. At the right in the drawing and in the woodcut, clergymen, led by the pope, turn away from the light and tumble into a pit; in Holbein's woodcut, Plato and Aristotle are also seen in their company. In contrast, the group of believers, who turn toward the light, consists of simple burghers and farmers—an allusion to the distinction between the "true church" (an intangible, spiritual congregation of believers) and the "church of Satan, the anti-Christ or the pope."

Although there is no evidence to indicate a Protestant background for Cornelis Anthonisz., his woodcut series of the Allegory of the Prodigal Son contains several anti-Catholic and Lutheran elements.[88] In the third print, the personification of Superstition dressed as a pilgrim directs the Prodigal Son to the "Temple of Satan," in which the personification of Illness is seated, wearing a papal tiara (fig. 21). In the sixth print, the Prodigal Son is united with the personification of Peace in a church interior; the image of the crucified Christ on the altar and the representation of Baptism and Communion—as noted, the only two sacraments accepted by the

FIG. 21. Cornelis Anthonisz. *The Prodigal Son Is Driven from the Inn and Is Directed by Superstition to the Temple of Satan*: from a series of the Allegory of the Prodigal Son. Woodcut. About 1540. Amsterdam, Rijksmuseum, Rijksprentenkabinet

FIG. 22. Jan Swart van Groningen. *The Broad Path*. Pen and brush, with brown ink, on paper. About 1530–35. Staatliche Museen zu Berlin, Preußischer Kulturbesitz, Kupferstichkabinett

Protestants—make it clear that the Prodigal Son was saved by the sacrifice and mercy of Christ.

Jan Swart, whose woodcuts illustrated the Vorsterman Bible, was even more clearly influenced by Protestantism. Paired drawings of *The Broad Path* and *The Narrow Path* of about 1530–35 (figs. 22 and 23), perhaps working designs for glass panels,[89] illuminate a biblical passage from Matthew (7: 13–14): "Enter ye in at the narrow gate: for wide is the gate, and broad is the way that leadeth to destruction, and many there are who go in thereat. How narrow is the gate, and strait is the way that leadeth to life: and few there are that find it!" The drawings leave no doubt that representatives of the established worldly and ecclesiastical order take the broad path to ruin, and that only the community of the ordinary, anonymous faithful knows how to find the difficult path to Heaven. On the broad path (fig. 22), a long procession, preceded by a flute player and drummer, descends into hell. At the head of the group are a pope and a cardinal, followed by other clergymen, a king, and burghers. Death and the devil hover above their heads. In the other drawing (fig. 23), the righteous (significantly fewer in number), led by the tetragram, undertake their journey after being baptized by an angel, climbing a steep and narrow path that leads to Heaven; snakes, hell-

ish monsters, and thorns impede their passage. This scene also portrays average, hardworking people, such as a peasant with a flail and a farmer with a harrow. Swart probably was influenced by German reformist woodcuts; the man with the flail resembles the figure of Karsthans, the incarnation of the simple, pious layman who follows the reformed doctrine.[90]

In his drawing *The Allegory of Salvation*, Jan Swart depicted a woman (Faith ?) and a burgher drinking from a goblet filled with the blood of Christ, before the image of Christ on the cross rising from a baptismal font. This is a reference to the reception of the Eucharist by laymen—one of the most important Protestant reforms. Swart expressed anticlerical sentiments in his drawing of the *Five Wise and the Five Foolish Virgins* by representing the foolish virgins as nuns with rosaries; in *The Unworthy Wedding Guest* he depicted a monk as the improperly attired guest.[91]

Finally, mention should be made of Dirck Crabeth, primarily known for the stained-glass windows of 1555–71 in the church of Saint John in Gouda. Despite the fact that he worked for many years for the Catholic Church Council in Gouda, the imagery in his designs for stained-glass panels displays a decidedly unorthodox religious approach; this is evident in his drawing of *Christ as the*

FIG. 23. Jan Swart van Groningen. *The Narrow Path.* Pen and brush, with brown ink, on paper. About 1530–35. Staatliche Museen zu Berlin, Preußischer Kulturbesitz, Kupferstichkabinett

FIG. 24. Dirck Pietersz. Crabeth. *A Tormented Man Asks for Mercy.* Pen and brown ink on paper. About 1550–55. Utrecht, Rijksmuseum Het Catharijneconvent

*Redeemer of Mankind* (see cat. no. 127),[92] a composition that is derived from an etching of 1547 by the Protestant Augustin Hirschvogel. The verse on the back of Crabeth's drawing also has a Protestant slant: As told in the Bible, by faith man learns that the only path to Heaven is through Christ.

This drawing is part of a group by Dirck Crabeth and his workshop whose theme is man's path to salvation. The underlying message is that man frequently stumbles on his way and mistakenly seeks salvation through good works but is ultimately saved by the grace of God. This is evident in *A Tormented Man Asks for Mercy* (fig. 24), as well as in the many other drawings in this complex series (see cat. nos. 127 and 128).[93] Daniel Horst suggests that Crabeth's iconography was either derived from Frans Huys's series of reformist etchings Man's Way to Salvation of about 1560 or was based on an earlier common model.[94] Karin van Schaik-Scheers recently discovered that the drawings display strong similarities to an older cycle of German reformist woodcuts on the Origin of Sin and the Justification of Man before God, by the Master N.G., a follower of Lucas Cranach.[95] The cycle shows, for example, how man, as the slave of sin, is tortured by conscience and despair despite his good deeds. When he is threatened by death man receives grace in the form of the Holy Spirit, so that he recognizes his sins. He abandons the performance of good deeds and chooses Christ's teachings above Blind Reason. Patience brings man to the Gospel and Christ redeems him from sin through the Crucifixion.

Artists of the Lowlands who produced reformist images concentrated primarily on one point of vital importance: portraying the new vision of the path to heavenly salvation. They even may have been prepared to risk their own lives for this conviction. With the growing political independence and the concomitant freedom of opinion in the North Lowlands, this situation changed radically, heralding the final political and artistic break between the North and South Lowlands. After a brief intervening period of stagnation brought about by war and a deteriorating economy, the arts would once again flower, abandoning traditional avenues and assuming new forms of expression.

Translated by
Timothy B. Husband
Jennifer M. Kilian
Marjorie E. Wieseman

1. See H. A. Enno van Gelder, *The Two Reformations in the 16th Century. A Study of the Religious Aspects and Consequences of the Renaissance and Humanism*, The Hague, 1961.

2. Glass painters belonged to the Guild of Saint Luke and generally seem to have been trained as painters. Lucas van Leyden, for example, was described by van Mander as an "excellent painter, engraver, and glass painter." See R. Vos, "The Life of Lucas van Leyden by Karel van Mander," *Nederlands Kunsthistorisch Jaarboek* 29, 1978 (1979), pp. 462–63.

3. See A. Hyma, *The Brethren of the Common Life*, Grand Rapids, 1950; R. R. Post, *The Modern Devotion: Confrontation with Reformation and Humanism*, Leiden, 1968; C. C. de Bruin, E. Persoons, and A. G. Weiler, *Geert Grote en de Moderne Devotie*, Zutphen, 1984.

4. See *The Golden Age of Dutch Manuscript Painting* (exhib. cat.), Utrecht, Rijksmuseum Het Catharijneconvent, and New York, The Pierpont Morgan Library, eds. H. L. M. Defoer, A. S. Korteweg, and W. C. M. Wüstefeld, intro. by J. H. Marrow, Stuttgart and Zurich, 1989; J. H. Marrow, *A Descriptive and Analytical Catalogue of Dutch Illustrated Manuscripts of the 15th and 16th Centuries*, 2 vols., Doornspijk, forthcoming.

5. For an iconographical index of illustrations in books in the Koninklijke Bibliotheek, The Hague, see J. P. J. Brandhorst and K. H. Broekhuijsen-Kruijer, *De verluchte handschriften en incunabelen van de Koninklijke Bibliotheek*, The Hague, 1985.

6. For popular Netherlandish saint's day festivals from the thirteenth through the sixteenth centuries see E. I. Strubbe and L. Voet, *De chronologie van de middeleeuwen en moderne tijden in de Nederlanden*, Antwerp and Amsterdam, 1960; reprinted, Brussels, 1991, pp. 155–97.

7. See W. M. Conway, *The Woodcutters of the Netherlands in the Fifteenth Century*, Cambridge, England, 1884; reprinted, Hildesheim and Nieuwkoop, 1970, p. 229, no. 6.

8. See I. M. Veldman and K. van Schaik, *Verbeelde boodschap. De illustraties van Lieven de Witte bij "Dat leven ons Heeren"* (1537), Haarlem and Brussels, 1989.

9. See B. Rosier, "De Nederlandse bijbelillustratie in de zestiende eeuw," Ph.D diss., 2 vols., Amsterdam, Vrije Universiteit, 1992.

10. See I. M. Veldman, comp., and G. Luijten, ed., *The New Hollstein. Dutch & Flemish Etchings, Engravings and Woodcuts 1450–1700, Maarten van Heemskerck*, part 1, Roosendaal and Amsterdam, 1993, nos. 273–302.

11. See I. M. Veldman, ed., "Dirck Volckertsz. Coornhert," *The Illustrated Bartsch*, vol. 55 [New York], 1991, pp. 127–35, 147–50; I. M. Veldman, comp., and G. Luijten, ed., *The New Hollstein. Dutch & Flemish Etchings, Engravings and Woodcuts 1450–1700, Maarten van Heemskerck*, part 2, Roosendaal and Amsterdam, 1994, nos. 338–342, 350–353, and 368–371.

12. See P. van der Meulen, ed., *Het Roerspel en de Comedies van Coornhert*, Leiden, 1955, pp. 15–79.

13. See J. A. Worp, *Geschiedenis van het drama en van het tooneel in Nederland*, vol. 1, Rotterdam, 1904, pp. 213–14.

14. See W. Nijhoff and M. E. Kronenberg, *Nederlandsche Bibliographie van 1500 tot 1540*, vol. 1, The Hague, 1923, no. 1909.

15. See K. Renger, *Lockere Gesellschaft. Zur Ikonographie des Verlorenen Sohnes und von Wirtshausszenen in der niederländischen Malerei*, Berlin, 1970, pp. 17–36; H. Pleij, *Het gilde van de Blauwe Schuit. Literatuur, volksfeest en burgermoraal in de late middeleeuwen*, Amsterdam, 1983.

16. See Renger, op. cit., pp. 37–42, figs. 13–24.

17. Ibid., pp. 42–70, figs. 25–38. See also C. M. Armstrong, *The Moralizing Prints of Cornelis Anthonisz*, Princeton, 1990, pp. 19–34, figs. 37 a–f.

18. See Veldman, "Dirck Volckertsz. Coornhert," op. cit., pp. 151–57; Veldman, *New Hollstein, Maarten van Heemskerck*, part 2, op. cit., nos. 330–336.

19. See L. Malke, "Zur Ikonographie der 'Vier Letzten Dinge' vom ausgehenden Mittelalter bis zum Rokoko," *Zeitschrift des Deutschen Vereins für Kunstwissenschaft* 30 (1976), pp. 44–66.

20. See Conway, op. cit., p. 220, no. 4. For somewhat later Netherlandish editions see Nijhoff and Kronenberg, op. cit., nos. 2089–2090, vol. 2, 1940, nos. 4000–4001.

21. See C. de Tolnay, *Hieronymus Bosch*, New York, 1966, ill. p. 65.

22. See H. T. Musper, *Die Urausgaben der holländischen Apokalypse und Biblia Pauperum*, Munich, 1961; A. Henry, *Biblia pauperum. A Facsimile and Edition*, Ithaca, 1987; E. Breitenbach, *Speculum humanae salvationis. Eine typengeschichtliche Untersuchung*, Strasbourg, 1930.

23. See J. P. Filedt Kok, "Een *Biblia pauperum* met houtsneden van Jacob Cornelisz. en Lucas van Leyden gereconstrueerd," *Bulletin van het Rijksmuseum* 36 (1988), pp. 83–116, fig. 10.

24. Ibid., pp. 96–114, figs. 3, 17–28.

25. See S. Hindman, *Text and Image in Fifteenth-Century Illustrated Dutch Bibles*, Leiden, 1977; *The Golden Age of Dutch Manuscript Painting*, op. cit., pp. 129–45. For example, the *Historiebijbel* in the Koninklijke Bibliotheek, The Hague, contains 509 miniatures from Genesis through the Apocalypse; see *The Golden Age of Dutch Manuscript Painting*, op. cit., pp. 131–35, no. 38 (K.B. Ms. 78 D 38 1 and 2).

26. An edition of the same year in *Niederrheinisch* made the text available to the Dutch-speaking population.

27. See A. Schramm, *Der Bilderschmuck der Frühdrucke*, vol. VIII, *Die Kölner Drucker*, Leipzig, 1924, p. 9, figs. 369–378, 379–408.

28. See N. Beets, *De houtsneden in Vorsterman's bijbel van 1528*, Amsterdam, 1915.

29. See A. E. Popham, "Notes on Flemish Domestic Glass Painting-I," *Apollo* 7 (1928), pp. 175–79; K. Arndt, "Ein Bildfragment aus den Niederlanden," *Niederdeutsche Beiträge zur Kunstgeschichte* 27 (1988), pp. 85–88.

30. See E. S. Jacobowitz and S. Loeb Stepanek, *The Prints of Lucas van Leyden & His Contemporaries* (exhib. cat.), Washington, D.C., National Gallery of Art, 1983, pp. 89–101, nos. 31–32; Veldman, *New Hollstein, Maarten van Heemskerck*, part 1, op. cit., nos. 43–50.

31. See Jacobowitz and Stepanek, op. cit., nos. 6, 42, 69; Veldman, *New Hollstein, Maarten van Heemskerck*, part 1, op. cit., nos. 8–13, 17–22.

32. See L. von Baldass, "Notizen über holländische Zeichner des XVI. Jahrhunderts. III. Jan Swart van Groningen," *Mitteilungen der Gesellschaft für vervielfältigende Kunst*. Beilage der "Graphischen Kunst" 41 (1918), pp. 11–21, nos. 32–39. For a comparison with another drawing by Swart of Tobias see K. G. Boon, *The Netherlandish and German Drawings of the XVth and XVIth Centuries of the Frits Lugt Collection*, 3 vols., Paris, 1992, pp. 362–63, no. 204.

33. See Veldman, *New Hollstein, Maarten van Heemskerck*, part 1, op. cit., nos. 183–188, 189–198.

34. For works relating to Adam and Eve, and a survey of Lucas's entire graphic *oeuvre* see J. P. Filedt Kok, *Lucas van Leyden—grafiek* (exhib. cat.), Amsterdam, Rijksmuseum, Rijksprentenkabinet, 1978; Jacobowitz and Stepanek, op. cit., nos. 1–2, 13, 15, 40, 48.

35. See Veldman, *New Hollstein, Maarten van Heemskerck*, part 1, op. cit., nos. 1–7, 14–16, 23–30, 35–38, 85–90, 94–109, 110–122, 199–206, 215–218.

36. See C. Laun-Gocht, "Bildkatechese im Spätmittelalter: Allegorische und typologische Auslegungen des Dekalogs," Ph.D. diss., Munich, Universität, 1979, pp. 88–104.

37. See G. Schiller, *Ikonographie der christlichen Kunst*, vol. IV-1, *Die Kirche*, Gütersloh, 1976, pp. 121–34.

38. See Veldman, *New Hollstein, Maarten van Heemskerck*, part 1, op. cit., pp. 66–73, nos. 65–74. In a series of engravings of the Ten Commandments (1566) by Herman Muller, after Maarten van Heemskerck, each is illustrated with appropriate Old Testament scenes (largely following Lucas Cranach's iconography).

39. See E. Lawton Smith, *The Paintings of Lucas van Leyden: A New Appraisal, with Catalogue Raisonné*, Columbia, Missouri, and London, 1992, pp. 92–95.

40. See Z. van Ruyven-Zeman, "Lambert van Noort Inventor," Ph.D. diss., 2 vols., Amsterdam, Vrije Universiteit, 1990, pp. 99–100, 203–4, figs. 65–72.

41. See S. L. Smith, "'To Women's Wiles I Fell'": The Power of Women *Topos* and the Development of Medieval Secular Art," Ph.D. diss., University of Pennsylvania, 1978; *Tussen heks en heilige. Het vrouwbeeld op de drempel van de moderne tijd, 15de/16de eeuw* (exhib. cat.), Nijmegen, Museum "Commanderie van Sint-Jan," 1985, pp. 164–79.

42. See Jacobowitz and Stepanek, op. cit., pp. 102–23, 164–83, nos. 10, 46. Lucas also treated the Idolatry of Solomon (1514) and Samson and Delilah as independent subjects.

43. See Veldman, *New Hollstein, Maarten van Heemskerck*, part 1, op. cit., nos. 259–264. Philips Galle chose exactly the same scene to include in a print series of about 1565; see A. Dolders, "Philips Galle," *The Illustrated Bartsch*, vol. 56, New York, 1987, pp. 97–102.

44. See W. L. Braekman, ed., *Dat bedroch der vrouwen*, Bruges, n.d. [1983]. The Antwerp publisher Jan van Ghelen published an edition about 1560; see H. Pleij, "Een fragment van de oudste Nederlandse Novellenbundel te Cambridge," in H. Heestermans, *Dr. C. H. A. Kruyskamp. Opstellen door vrienden en vakgenoten*, The Hague, 1977, pp. 142–55.

45. See L. Geeraedts, ed., *Der sotten schip oft dat Narren schip*, Middelburg, 1981, chapter XIII, "Venus goddinne van sotter minne / Jaecht menighen mensche wt den sinne."

46. See M. F. A. G. Campbell, *Annales de la typographie Néerlandaise au XVe siècle*, The Hague, 1874, no. 592.

47. See J. IJsewijn, "The Coming of Humanism to the Low Countries," in H. A. Oberman and T. A. Brady, Jr., eds., *Itinerarium Italicum. The Profile of the Italian Renaissance in the Mirror of Its European Transformations. Dedicated to Paul Oskar Kristeller on the Occasion of His 70th Birthday*, Leiden, 1975, pp. 193–304.

48. R. Himelick, trans. and ed., *The Enchiridion of Erasmus*, Bloomington, 1963.

49. See C. Augustijn, *Erasmus en de Reformatie. Een onderzoek naar de houding die Erasmus ten opzichte van de Reformatie heeft aangenomen*, Amsterdam, 1962.

50. See A. Geerebaert, *Lijst van de gedrukte Nederlandsche vertalingen der oude Grieksche en Latijnsche schrijvers*, Ghent, 1924, p. 91, XCVII, nos. 1–3, p. 102, CIII, no. 1, p. 161, CXXXIII, no. 2; H. Bonger, *Leven en werk van D. V. Coornhert*, Amsterdam, 1978, pp. 358–89.

51. For a survey see Worp, op. cit., pp. 202–39; L. Bradmer, "The Latin Drama of the Renaissance (1340–1640)," *Studies in the Renaissance* 4, 1957, pp. 31–70.

52. See Nijhoff and Kronenberg, op. cit., vol. 3, The Hague, 1942, no. 0617.

53. See A. von Weilen, *Der ägyptische Joseph im Drama des XVI. Jahrhunderts. Ein Beitrag zur vergleichenden Litteraturgeschichte*, Vienna, 1887, pp. 25–26.

54. See R. Pilger, "Die Dramatisierungen der Susanna im 16. Jahrhundert," *Zeitschrift für deutsche Philologie* 11 (1880), pp. 129–217.

55. See Worp, op. cit., pp. 212–13; H. M. P. Puttiger, *Georgius Macropedius' Asotus. Een Neolatijns drama over de verloren zoon door Joris van Lanckvelt*, Nieuwkoop, 1988.

56. See J. Bolte, *Gvlielmvs Gnaphevs Acolastvs*, Berlin, 1891; J. F. M. Kat, *De verloren zoon als letterkundig motief*, Amsterdam, 1952, pp. 35–74; W. E. D. Atkinson, *Acolastus: A Latin Play of the Sixteenth Century by Gulielmus Gnapheus*, London and Ontario, 1964.

57. See B. Haeger, "Cornelis Anthonisz's Representation of the Parable of the Prodigal Son: A Protestant Interpretation of the Biblical Text," *Nederlands Kunsthistorisch Jaarboek* 37 (1986), pp. 133–50.

58. See Worp, op. cit., pp. 137–44.

59. See W. M. H. Hummelen, *Repertorium van het rederijkersdrama 1500–ca. 1620*, Assen, 1968, pp. 34–36; W. L. de Vreese, ed., *Een spel van sinne van Charon, de helsche schippere (1551)*, Antwerp, 1896; G. A. van Es, *Piramus en Thisbe. Twee rederijkersspelen uit de zestiende eeuw*, Zwolle, 1965.

60. See J. Sterk, *Philips van Bourgondië (1465–1524) bisschop van Utrecht als protagonist van de renaissance, zijn leven en maecenaat*, Zutphen, 1980.

61. See H. Pauwels, H. B. Hoetink, and S. Herzog, *Jan Gossaert genaamd Mabuse* (exhib. cat.), Rotterdam, Museum Boymans-van Beuningen, and Bruges, Groeningemuseum, 1965, pp. 121–22, no. 15, with the Latin text: "Nate effrons homines superos que lacessere suet[us] non matri parcis: parcito, ne pereas."

62. See Prince d'Essling and E. Münz, *Pétrarque, ses études d'art, son influence sur les artistes, ses portraits et ceux de Laure, l'illustration de ses écrits*, Paris, 1902.

63. See Nijhoff and Kronenberg, op. cit., vol. 2, no. 3412.

64. See H. Bevers, in *Niederländische Zeichnungen des 16. Jahrhunderts in der Staatlichen Graphischen Sammlung München* (exhib. cat.), Munich, 1989, pp. 63–65, nos. 50–53. For the tapestries see *Koninklijke pracht in goud en zijde. Vlaamse wandtapijten van de Spaanse kroon* (exhib. cat.), Mechelen and Amsterdam, 1993, pp. 64–91.

65. Bruges, Groeningemuseum. See H. J. van Miegroet, "Gerard David's *Justice of Cambyses*: *exemplum iustitiae* or political allegory?" *Simiolus* 18 (1988), pp. 116–33; H. van der Velden, "Cambyses for example: the origin and function of an 'exemplum iustitiae' in fifteenth-, sixteenth- and seventeenth-century Netherlandish art," and "Cambyses reconsidered: Gerard David's 'exemplum iustitiae' for the Bruges town hall," *Simiolus* 23, no. 1, forthcoming [1995].

66. See, for example, Giraldi's *De deis gentium* (1548), Conti's *Mythologiae sive explicationis fabularum* (1551), and Cartari's *Le imagini colla sposizione degli dei degli antichi* (1556).

67. The story was disseminated via Apollodorus's *Epitome*, Ovid's *Heroides*, Hyginus's *Fabulae*, Lucian's *Dialogues of the Gods*, and Apuleius's *The Golden Ass*.

68. See J. Huizinga, *The Waning of the Middle Ages*, London, 1927, pp. 280–90.

69. Compare the interpretation of the story by Karel van Mander, *Wtleggingh op den Metamorphosis Pub. Ovidij Nasonis*, in *Het Schilder-boeck*, Haarlem, 1604, fol. 94.

70. See M. J. Friedländer, *Early Netherlandish Painting*, vol. 12, Leiden and Brussels, 1975, fig. 107.

71. See I. M. Veldman, "The Judgment of Paris, a Newly Discovered Painting by Maarten van Heemskerck," *Mercury* 7 (1988), pp. 13–22.

72. See B. Guthmüller, *Ovidio Metamorphoseos vulgare. Formen und Funktionen der volkssprachlichen Wiedergabe klassischer Dichtung in der italienischen Renaissance*, Boppard am Rhein, 1981.

73. See M. D. Henkel, "Illustrierte Ausgaben von Ovids Metamorphosen im XV., XVI. und XVII. Jahrhundert," *Vorträge der Bibliothek Warburg 1926–1927*, Leipzig and Berlin, 1930, pp. 58–144 (especially pp. 61–65).

74. See Jacobowitz and Stepanek, op. cit., no. 44.

75. For a survey see A. Duke, *Reformation and Revolt in the Low Countries*, London and Ronceverte, West Virginia, 1990; on the Reformation in Flanders see J. Decavele, *De dageraad van de reformatie in Vlaanderen (1520–1565)*, 2 vols., Brussels, 1975.

76. See A. F. Mellink, *De wederdopers in de Noordelijke Nederlanden 1531–1544*, Groningen, 1954.

77. See L. M. van Dis, *Reformatorische Rederijkersspelen uit de eerste helft van de zestiende eeuw*, Haarlem, 1937; B. H. Erné and L. M. van Dis, *De Gentse Spelen van 1539*, 2 vols., The Hague, 1982.

78. For examples see C. Tümpel, "Die Reformation und die Kunst der Niederlande," in W. Hofmann, ed., *Luther und die Folgen für die Kunst* (exhib. cat.), Hamburger Kunsthalle, Munich, 1983, pp. 309–21; P. W. Parshall, "Kunst en reformatie in de Noordelijke Nederlanden—enkele gezichtspunten," and R. P. Zijp, "De iconografie van de reformatie in de Nederlanden, een begripsbepaling," *Bulletin van het Rijksmuseum* 35 (1987), pp. 164–75, 176–92.

79. See I. M. Veldman, "Maarten van Heemskercks visie op het geloof," *Bulletin van het Rijksmuseum* 35 (1987), pp. 193–210.

80. See Schiller, op. cit., figs. 365, 370.

81. See M. E. Kronenberg, *Verboden boeken en opstandige drukkers in de hervormingstijd*, Amsterdam, 1948.

82. See J. Duverger, "Lutherse predicatie te Brussel en het proces tegen een aantal kunstenaars (April–Juni 1527)," *Wetenschappelijke tijdingen* 36 (1977), cols. 221–228; J. Decavele, "Vroege reformatorische bedrijvigheid in de grote Nederlandse steden: Claes van Elst te Brussel, Antwerpen en Leiden (1524–1528)," *Nederlands Archief voor kerkgeschiedenis* 70 (1990), pp. 13–29.

83. See K. G. Boon, *Netherlandish Drawings of the Fifteenth and Sixteenth Centuries*, 2 vols., The Hague, 1978, no. 380; N. Beets, "Een godsdienstige allegorie door Barent van Orley," *Oud Holland* 49 (1932), pp. 129–37; K. G. Boon, "Divers aspects de l'iconographie de la pré-réforme aux Pays-Bas," *Gazette des Beaux-Arts*, 6th ser. 105 (1985), pp. 1–14; Boon, *Netherlandish and German Drawings*, op. cit., pp. xxvii–xxix.

84. See K. G. Boon, "Patientia dans les gravures de la Réforme aux Pays-Bas," *Revue de l'Art*, no. 56 (1982), pp. 10–12, figs. 5, 6.

85. See Veldman and van Schaik, op. cit., p. 47. The book itself was confiscated by reformists on several occasions about 1540 on the grounds that it was "an evil and suspect book"; see W. Bax, *Het protestantisme in het Bisdom Luik en vooral te Maastricht 1557–1612*, The Hague, 1937–41, vol. 1, 1937, p. 157 (no. 12), pp. 199–200.

86. See Decavele, *De dageraad van de reformatie in Vlaanderen*, op. cit., vol. 2, pp. 238–40.

87. See Boon, *Netherlandish and German Drawings*, op. cit., no. 13; Boon, "Patientia," op. cit., p. 8, fig. 1.

88. See Haeger, "Cornelis Anthonisz," op. cit., figs. 3, 6; B. Haeger, "The prodigal son in sixteenth and seventeenth-century Netherlandish art: depictions of the parable and the evolution of a Catholic image," *Simiolus* 16 (1986), pp. 128–38, figs. 1–2.

89. See Tümpel, op. cit., p. 310, figs. 2–3; *Kunst voor de beeldenstorm: Noordnederlandse kunst 1525–1580* (exhib. cat.), 2 vols., Amsterdam, Rijksmuseum, and The Hague, Staatsuitgeverij, 1986, no. 125.

90. See *Luther und die Folgen*, op. cit., nos. 55, 58, 61.

91. The first two drawings are in the Staatliche Museen zu Berlin, Preußischer Kulturbesitz, Kupferstichkabinett; the third is in the Bibliothèque Nationale, Paris. See Tümpel, op. cit., pp. 312–13, figs. 10–12.

92. See Amsterdam, *Kunst voor de beeldenstorm*, op. cit., nos. 240–241.

93. See K. G. Boon, "De glasschilder David Joris, een exponent van het Doperse geloof. Zijn kunst en zijn invloed op Dirck Crabeth," *Academia Analecta. Mededelingen van de Koninklijke Academie voor Wetenschappen, Letteren en Schone Kunsten van België* 49 (1988), pp. 117–37, figs. 22–24, 26–27.

94. See D. R. Horst, "Een zestiende-eeuwse reformatorische prentenreeks van Frans Huys over de Heilsweg van de Mens," *Bulletin van het Rijksmuseum* 38, 1 (1990), pp. 3–24, figs. 7, 16.

95. My thanks to Karin van Schaik-Scheers for the reference to R. W. Scribner, *For the sake of simple folk. Popular propaganda for the German Reformation*, Cambridge, England, and New York, 1981, pp. 208–11, fig. p. 196.

Plate 1

Joos van Cleve. *The Annunciation* (showing two silver-stained roundels glazed into the transoms
of the window). Tempera and oil on panel. About 1525. New York, The Metropolitan Museum
of Art, The Friedsam Collection, Bequest of Michael Friedsam, 1931 (*ex. cat.*)

Plate 2

The van der Goes group. *Abraham Blessing the Marriage of Isaac and Rebecca.* About 1480–90 (cat. no. 4)

Plate 3

The van der Goes group. *Abraham Blessing the Marriage of Isaac and Rebecca.* About 1480–1500 (cat. no. 5)

Plate 4

Master of the Joseph Sequence. *Joseph Interpreting the Dreams of the Butler and the Baker.*
About 1490–1500 (cat. no. 10)

Plate 5

The van der Goes group. *Tobias Drawing the Fish from the Water*.
Pen and brown ink on paper. About 1480–90.
Windsor Castle, Royal Library (*ex cat.*)

Plate 6

Simon Bening and Gheeraert Horenbout. *Tobias Drawing the Fish from the Water*. Manuscript illumination for Psalm 26, from the *Mayer van den Bergh Breviary*. About 1510–15. Antwerp, Museum Mayer van den Bergh (*ex cat.*)

Plate 7

*Christ Being Led Away from Herod Antipas.* About 1515–20 (cat. no. 21)

Plate 8

*Death with a Pope, a Prince, and a Peasant.* About 1510–20 (cat. no. 27)

Plate 9

*Sorgheloos and Lichte Fortune.* About 1520 (cat. no. 32)

Plate 10

Jacob Cornelisz. van Oostsanen. *The Last Supper.* About 1515–20 (cat. no. 40)

Plate 11

Pieter Cornelisz. Kunst. *Caring for the Dying*. About 1510–20 (cat. no. 47)

Plate 12

Lucas van Leyden. *Jael and Sisera*. After 1520 (cat. no. 51)

Lucas van Leyden. *The Triumph of David*. About 1510–30 (cat. no. 56)

Plate 14

Jan Gossaert. *The Beheading of John the Baptist.* About 1509–10 (cat. no. 58)

Plate 15

Dirick Vellert. *The Judgment of Cambyses*. 1542 (cat. no. 80)

Plate 16

Pieter Coecke van Aelst. *The Feast of Herod*. About 1540 (cat. no. 89)

Plate 17

Jan Swart van Groningen. *A Banquet before an Enthroned King*.
About 1540–45 (cat. no. 95)

Plate 18

Jan de Beer. *Christ at Emmaus*. About 1520 (cat. no. 102)

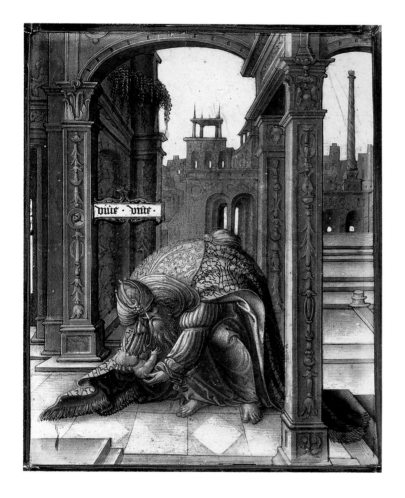

Plate 19

After the Master of the Miracles of the Apostles. *God Saving the Infant Jerusalem*. About 1525–30 (cat. no. 105)

Plate 20

Dirck Pietersz. Crabeth. *Christ as the Redeemer of Mankind*. About 1560–65 (cat. no. 128)

Plate 21

Dirck Pietersz. Crabeth. *Samuel Is Brought to the High Priest Eli.* 1543 (cat. no. 117)

# Catalogue

# 1

## The van der Goes Group:
## The Early Genesis and Tobit Series

A group of drawings and related roundels belonging to two or more Genesis cycles—and including histories of Abraham, Isaac, Jacob, and Joseph, as well as the story of Tobit—all appear to be dependent on the style of Hugo van der Goes (master from 1467 to 1482), although the precise nature of this relationship remains unclear. Both formal and stylistic correspondences with Hugo van der Goes's work suggest that, at the very least, a workshop or several workshops in Ghent or elsewhere in the South Lowlands had design or model books that borrowed from Hugo's compositions. A number of the roundel designs—cat. nos. 2, 6, 8, and 9, for example—quote specific passages in the Oxford *Meeting of Jacob and Rachel*, one of the very few drawings that is generally given to Hugo (fig. 1).[1] The well-known propensity for Lowlands artists of the fifteenth and early sixteenth centuries to copy in whole or part casts uncertainty on the propinquity of the roundel workshops to Hugo and compounds the difficulty of precisely establishing the relationships among the numerous drawings in this relatively homogeneous group. The related drawing of *Jacob with His Flock at the Fountain* (fig. 2),[2] in which the figure of Jacob clearly replicates that of the shepherd in the Oxford drawing, underscores the point. Popham's attribution of the surviving body of material—that is, the Abraham, Isaac, and Jacob series (cat. nos. 1–6), the Joseph series (cat. nos. 7–11), and the Story of Tobit series (cat. nos. 12–14)—to a single artist, the Master of the Story of Tobit,[3] overlooks the practice of synthesizing compositions from various models and then replicating the more popular of these compositions long after the career of a single artist.[4] Van Regteren Altena attributed the Abraham and Isaac series (cat. nos. 1–5) to Hugo Jacobsz., the father of Lucas van Leyden;[5] others continued to associate this group with a Leiden workshop in spite of the clear stylistic connections with the van der

FIG. 1 Hugo van der Goes. *The Meeting of Jacob and Rachel*. Pen and brush, with brown ink, brownish wash, and white body color, on gray prepared paper. 1470–80. Oxford, The Governing Body, Christ Church College

Goes group.[6] To this body of material Popham added other drawings, including a series of studies of female figures, several scenes from another Joseph series, and *The Death of Narcissus* (cat. no. 25);[7] these are not all by the same hand and possibly were not even produced by the same workshop. It does seem likely, however, that they all depend on models that ultimately can be traced back to Hugo van der Goes.[8] The sheer numbers of both roundels and drawings belonging to this group attest to the longevity of their vogue and provide the earliest unequivocal evidence of large-scale roundel production in the Lowlands.[9]

1. Christ Church College, 1335. Earlier authorities, such as Friedländer, Baldass, and Winkler (*Hugo van der Goes*, 1964, pp. 219–21, fig. 176), saw either later reworking in the background or considered it a sixteenth-century copy, although this has been refuted more recently. See Shaw, *Drawings at Christ Church Oxford*, 1976, p. 320, no. 1309, pl. 772. For the most recent scholarly exchange on this fine drawing see Sander, "*Jacob and Rachel*," 1989, pp. 39–52; this is rejoined by Schade, "*Jacob and Rachel*," 1991, pp. 187–93.

2. Detroit, *Flanders* (exhib. cat.), 1960, pp. 215–16, no. 59.

3. Popham, "Notes-I," 1928, pp. 176–79.

4. For the continued use of the compositions of the Joseph series see, for example, Jan Swart's adaptation of *Joseph Being Sold to the Ishmaelites* (cat. no. 96).

5. "Hugo Jacobsz," 1955, p. 116, n. 19, fig. 7.

6. Notably Amsterdam, *Middeleeuwse kunst* (exhib. cat.), 1958, p. 145, no. 188, pp. 173–74, nos. 240 and 241. Coebergh-Surie, "Leidse Glasruitje gemaakt in de periode 1480–1530," diss., Utrecht, n.d., no. 1, which, unfortunately, I have never seen, apparently attributed the drawings to the Master of the Story of Tobit and the roundels to Leiden; see Berserik, "Leiden, ca. 1480–1545," 1982, nos. 25 A and B, 26A and B, who somewhat tentatively associated the drawings and the roundels with the Master of the Story of Tobit.

7. See "Notes-I," 1928, pp. 177, 179.

8. Winkler, *Hugo van der Goes*, 1964, p. 284, accepts Popham's grouping but notes that these drawings seem "von oder nach demselben Zeichner zu sein." He remarks on

FIG. 2 After Hugo van der Goes. *Jacob with His Flock at the Fountain*. Pen and brown ink on paper. 1480–1500. Private collection

the apparent connection with van der Goes and suggests that the drawings are copies after the master, although some seem more akin to the Master of Moulins than to van der Goes.

9. For the numerous replicas, versions, and variants of the two scenes from the Story of Tobit (cat. nos. 12–14), for example, see Husband, *Silver-Stained Roundels*, 1991, pp. 141, 146.

FIG. 1 After the Hugo van der Goes group. *Abraham Repudiating Hagar and Ishmael.* Roundel. About 1490–1500. Brussels, Musée d'Art Ancien

## 1

### Abraham Repudiating Hagar and Ishmael

Close follower of Hugo van der Goes

South Lowlands, about 1480–90

Silverpoint on prepared paper, 7⅝ x 4⅞ in. (19.4 x 12.4 cm)

Boston, Museum of Fine Arts, Francis Bartlett Fund, 15.1244

Hagar was the Egyptian handmaid of Sarah, the wife of Abraham. Because Sarah was barren and despairing of an heir, she gave Hagar to Abraham—a union that produced Ishmael. Subsequently, in her old age, God made it possible for Sarah to give birth to a son, who was named Isaac. As the children grew older, Sarah increasingly viewed Ishmael as a threat to Isaac, and eventually prevailed upon Abraham, however reluctantly, to send Hagar and her son away. "So Abraham rose up in the morning, and taking bread and a bottle of water, put it upon her shoulder, and delivered the boy, and sent her away" (Genesis 21: 14).

The fragmentary Boston drawing records the moment in which Abraham gives Hagar a loaf of bread with one hand as he prepares to propel her on her way with the other. The curve at the lower right and the scale of the figures confirm that the drawing was intended as a design for a roundel. By deviating from the narrative and placing the water bottle in Hagar's hand rather than upon her shoulder the artist skillfully adjusts the composition to accommodate the circular format.

A damaged roundel in the Musée d'Art Ancien, Brussels, preserves the finished composition (fig. 1);[1] the correspondence of detail demonstrates that the workshop drawing and the present design were closely related. The background details in this sheet may be missing simply because they were the last elements of the design to be added, but the possibility that these details were left to assistants after the master had completed the principal figures—as often seems the practice in the painting of roundels—is intriguing.

The drawing is densely worked, with carefully constructed systems of shading; the darker areas are nearly filled with broad cross-hatching while the lighter passages are developed with fine, narrow parallel lines and the highlights are left as voids. The skillful handling of the pen brings an emotional intensity to the individual figures. Abraham seems at once determined to dispatch Hagar and regretful of having to do so. In Hagar's face one senses anxiety and a troubled concern for her son, down at whom she tenderly gazes. Both the emotive quality and the technique appear too close to the manner of van der Goes for this drawing to be considered a later copy.[2] In greater likelihood, it was a workshop design executed by an artist close to Hugo, on whose models or composition he relied.

1. Inv. no. 7549. See Berserik, "Leiden, ca. 1480–1545," 1982, nos. 25 A and B, 26 A and B, fig. 45.

2. Winkler, *Hugo van der Goes,* 1964, p. 270, considers the drawing to be "unverkennbar in Goes' Manier."

BIBLIOGRAPHY: Winkler, *Hugo van der Goes,* 1964, pp. 270–73, fig. 211.

## 2

### Rebecca Taking Leave of Her Parents

Follower of Hugo van der Goes

South Lowlands, about 1480–90

Pen and brown ink on paper: diameter, 8½ in. (21.6 cm)

Staatliche Museen zu Berlin, Preußischer Kulturbesitz, Kupferstichkabinett, KdZ 1981

## 3

### Rebecca Taking Leave of Her Parents

Lowlands, about 1480–1500

Roundel: diameter, 8½ in. (21.6 cm)

Amsterdam, Rijksmuseum, NM 12242

Abraham, seeking a wife of his own kindred for Isaac, sent his servant, Eliezer, to Mesopotamia. There, in fulfillment of God's word, he found Rebecca, daughter of Bathuel and sister of Laban. Eliezer presses his master's mission and, bowing to God's will and Rebecca's consent, the family of the intended bride of Isaac prepares for her to leave at once. "So they sent her away, and her nurse, and Abraham's servant, and his company" (Genesis 24: 59).

In the drawing, Eliezer gently pulls Rebecca's hand in an attempt to draw her away from the embrace of her parents, while her companions at the back of the group look on. In the right background Rebecca is seen atop a camel at the head of a caravan headed toward the home of Abraham and Isaac in Canaan.

2

3

The relationship of this drawing—trimmed vertically at both the left and right—to the Hugo van der Goes group is immediately evidenced by the figure of Eliezer, seen in three-quarter view from the rear; he appears to be modeled on the figure of the shepherd in the Oxford *Meeting of Jacob and Rachel* (fig. 1, p. 51)[1] and on its replication in the *Jacob with His Flock at the Fountain*, which is inscribed *hugues.* (fig. 2, p. 51).[2] Although reversed, the figure is shown in the same striking pose, standing with his weight on his right leg and his left leg bent at the knee, his face turned back over his left shoulder. The sense of arrested motion is echoed in the drapery patterns in which extended smooth planes are interrupted by passages of heavy, crumpled, angular tube folds, although less so here than in the Oxford drawing. An idiosyncratic detail—the gathering of tubular folds below the waists of the figures seen from the rear—is repeatedly encountered in the van der Goes group of roundel designs.

The drawing likewise exhibits many of the formal characteristics that typify the compositions of this body of drawings.[3] A central cluster of figures in the foreground dominates the composition while secondary scenes spiral off into the deep background, the figure scale ever diminishing. Spatial depth is indicated by raised outcroppings upon which figures stand or behind which they disappear. Topographical features also demarcate and isolate distinct narrative zones. The group in the foreground is usually given dramatic tension by the turning, rotating, or otherwise juxtaposing of individual figures. The torsion of the body of Abraham's servant creates a characteristic sense of

animation and activity—essential elements of an effective visual narrative. The frequent bleeding of the composition off one edge—here, the drapery of Bathuel at the left—further heightens the sense of narrative motion across the picture plane.

The modeling in the Berlin drawing is very economical. Tiny dots or short, fine parallel strokes define the lighter shaded areas, progressing to longer and broader parallel strokes; the spare use of dense cross-hatching or a solid field indicates the deepest passages. Faces, beyond the linear definition of features, are hardly worked at all—little dots and parallel lines are employed to shade chins, temples, or the areas under the eyes—and they lack the emotive depth of those in the Boston drawing. The gestures and articulation of the hands of the figures in the present sheet are also somewhat more wooden.[4] The drawing, nonetheless, appears to be an early copy, probably preserving the composition of the original working design.

The composition of the roundel corresponds to that of the Berlin drawing in all but the most insignificant details. Only in the contours of the land—of which just the barest indications are provided in the Berlin drawing—does the painter effectively develop the model in order to set off the group in the foreground from the ancillary scenes in the background. The painting is finely executed in reddish-brown and umber tones accented with several rich hues of silver stain from pale to deep golden yellow. The intermingling of hues on the sleeve of Bathuel and in the headdress of the female attendant immediately behind Rebecca creates the effect of shimmering textiles.

Similar mottled patterns are found throughout the landscape. Highlights in the drapery are achieved with networks of short, parallel strokes etched into the umber base with a very fine stylus, following the contours of the folds and the underlying forms. In the recessive areas, dark paint is applied with a fine-pointed brush, producing equivalent patterns of fine parallel lines to indicate the denser, shadowed passages. Back painting is used extensively to give a sense of depth. This particular technique of modeling is not found in later roundels. The dynamics of light and of tonal values endow this roundel with a particularly rich visual appeal. Reflecting, perhaps, the economy of the workshop, the very warped glass is marked with a large broken surface blister that was simply painted over.

1. See note 1, p. 51.

2. Private collection (formerly, de Hevesy, Paris). See Detroit, *Flanders* (exhib. cat.), 1960, pp. 215–16, no. 59. This drawing is also related to the *Annunciation to the Shepherds* in the Staatliche Kunstsammlungen, Dresden, 481. See also Winkler, *Hugo van der Goes*, 1964, p. 221; and Sander, "*Jacob and Rachel*," 1989, pp. 39–40, n. 6.

3. Châtelet (*Primitifs hollandais*, 1980, p. 240) has pointed out similarities between the present composition and that of the *David and Abigail* panel, a copy after van der Goes, now in Brussels (Musée d'Art Ancien, 755).

4. This is more evident in later copies of this group such as the example in the Kupferstichkabinett, Berlin, KdZ 774.

BIBLIOGRAPHY: (2) Bock et al., *Zeichnungen*, 1930, p. 4; Châtelet, *Primitifs hollandais*, 1980, p. 240,

4    5

FIG. 1 After the Hugo van der Goes group. *Abraham Blessing the Marriage of Isaac and Rebecca*. Roundel. About 1500–1510. London, British Museum

no. 152, fig. 240; Berserik, "Leiden, ca. 1480–1545," 1982, no. 25 A. (3) Beets, "Aanwinsten," 1911, p. 243, fig. 1; Popham, "Notes-I," 1928, p. 179; van Regteren Altena, "Hugo Jacobsz," 1955, p. 116, n. 19; Amsterdam, *Middeleeuwse kunst* (exhib. cat.), 1958, pp. 173–74, no. 240; Châtelet, *Primitifs hollandais*, 1980, p. 240, no. 152, fig. 241; Berserik, "Leiden, ca. 1480–1545," 1982, no. 25 B, fig. 41.

## 4    *see plate 2*

### Abraham Blessing the Marriage of Isaac and Rebecca

Follower of Hugo van der Goes

South Lowlands, about 1480–90

Pen and brown ink on paper, 8⅞ x 7¼ in. (22.5 x 18.3 cm)

Rotterdam, Museum Boymans-van Beuningen, N-192

## 5    *see plate 3*

### Abraham Blessing the Marriage of Isaac and Rebecca

Lowlands, about 1480–1500

Roundel: diameter, 8½ in. (21.6 cm)

Amsterdam, Rijksmuseum, NM 12243

This drawing appears to represent Isaac taking Rebecca as his wife while Abraham blesses their union by holding their hands, thus illustrating an event that is given little account in the biblical text. The scene could, in fact, be a visual elabora-

tion of either of the two references to the marriage: "[Isaac] Who brought her into the tent of Sara his mother, and took her to wife . . ." (Genesis 24: 67) and "[Isaac] Who when he was forty years old, took to wife Rebecca the daughter of Bathuel . . ." (Genesis 25: 20). Although late-fifteenth-century roundels series generally derive their compositions from a literal reading of the texts they illustrate, such narrative embellishments are not uncommon.

The present drawing—which has suffered losses at the right and along the upper-right edge—is finer and more finished than the one in Berlin. The modeling is rendered through innumerable short, variegated parallel lines, giving the Rotterdam drawing a feathery appearance more akin to that of the Boston and not the Berlin example. The physiognomies, rather than a sense of motion, animate the composition and evoke a calm serenity appropriate to the occasion. The polished execution of this sheet suggests that it was a finished design or an accomplished workshop copy.

The composition of the central group in the executed roundel corresponds in detail, but at least one major aspect in the background has been altered: The figure of Rebecca, seen astride the horse in the far background of the drawing, was moved to the middle group in the roundel, and a man on a camel occupies the more distant position on the road. As the background in the drawing is otherwise lost, it cannot be determined whether or not details in the roundel, such as the gate and the wattle fence to the right of the principal group, were indicated in the original design.

In the main, however, revisions or alterations of ancillary details were often undertaken by the glass painters. In a somewhat weaker roundel version of this composition, now in the British Museum (fig. 1),[1] the central group, excepting the costume of the attendant to the far left, remains unaltered, but the background is totally reconfigured with the addition of a church, a distant thatched-roofed house, and recontoured landscape. The identical technique and style of painting indicates that the present roundel and the companion piece above (cat. no. 3) were produced in the same workshop and by the same hand.

There is a large surface chip at the top of the roundel.

1. Inv. no. MLA 1852.3-27.3.

BIBLIOGRAPHY: (4) Rotterdam, *Noord-nederland-sche Primitieven* (exhib. cat.), 1936, p. 60, no. 8, fig. 10; Amsterdam, *Bijbelsche Kunst* (exhib. cat.), 1939, no. 15 A, ill. 28; van Regteren Altena, "Hugo Jacobsz," 1955, p. 116, fig. 7; Amsterdam, *Middeleeuwse kunst* (exhib. cat.), 1958, p. 145, no. 188, fig. 101; Berserik, "Leiden, ca. 1480–1545," 1982, no. 26 A; Husband, *Silver-Stained Roundels*, 1991, p. 16, fig. 4. (5) Beets, "Aanwinsten," 1911, p. 243, fig. 2; Popham, "Notes-I," 1928, p. 179; van Regteren Altena, "Hugo Jacobsz," 1955, p. 116, n. 19, fig. 7; Amsterdam, *Middeleeuwse kunst* (exhib. cat.), 1958, p. 174, no. 241, fig. 113; Berserik, "Leiden, ca. 1480–1545," 1982, no. 26 B; Husband, *Silver-Stained Roundels*, 1991, p. 16, fig. 5.

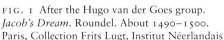

## 6

### Jacob's Dream

Follower of Hugo van der Goes

South Lowlands, about 1480–90

Pen and black ink on brown paper, 8³⁄₁₆ x 7¼ in. (20.8 x 18.4 cm)

Atlanta, Curtis O. Baer Collection

Isaac instructed his blessed son, Jacob, to go to Mesopotamia and marry a daughter of Laban, the brother of Rebecca and Jacob's uncle. En route Jacob lay down to rest, placing his head against some stones. He dreamt that he saw a ladder reaching to Heaven, with angels climbing up and down. "And he saw in his sleep a ladder standing upon the earth, and the top thereof touching heaven: the angels also of God ascending and descending by it . . ." (Genesis 28: 12). This ensorcelling vision forms the central scene of the present drawing. In the right background Jacob, having recognized Rachel, removed a rock from the well so that her flock of sheep could drink; then Jacob greets his future bride with an embrace, as other shepherds look on. "And when Jacob saw her, and knew her to be his cousingerman, and that they were the sheep of Laban, his uncle: he removed the stone wherewith the well was closed. And having watered the flock, he kissed her . . ." (Genesis 29: 10, 11). In the left background Jacob is greeted at the house of Laban.

The relationship of this sheet to the Hugo van der Goes group is immediately evident in the secondary scene in the background, which depends directly on the analogous group in the Oxford *Meeting of Jacob and Rachel* (fig. 1, p. 51). The sharp delineation between foreground and background, demarcated by the hilly landscape, somewhat exaggerates, however, the disunity of spatial constructions encountered in the roundel designs of this early group. The technique, likewise, separates this drawing from others associated with the van der Goes group: Cross-hatchings are typically formed of thin parallel lines intersected by tapered hooked or comma-like strokes; the present sheet, notable for its almost total lack of cross-hatching, employs unmodulated parallel lines to define the forms and to achieve modeling.

The composition is followed faithfully in a roundel now in the Collection Frits Lugt, Institut Néerlandais, Paris (fig. 1).[1] This series devoted to

FIG. 1 After the Hugo van der Goes group. *Jacob's Dream*. Roundel. About 1490–1500. Paris, Collection Frits Lugt, Institut Néerlandais

FIG. 2 After the Hugo van der Goes group. *Rachel and Laban*. Roundel. About 1480–1500. Amsterdam, Rijksmuseum

Jacob appears to be expanded by a much-damaged roundel now in the Rijksmuseum, Amsterdam (fig. 2).[2] Jacob and his family had fled the house of Laban and pitched a tent on the mount of Galaad. In the roundel Laban has pursued his son-in-law and, when he finds him, accuses him of stealing his idols. Jacob denies this and invites Laban to search the tents. When Laban "was entered into Rachel's tent, She in haste hid the idols under the camel's furniture, and sat upon them. . . . She said: Let not my lord be angry that I cannot rise up before thee, because it has now

happened to me, according to the custom of women" (Genesis 31: 33–35). As illustrated here, Rachel adds to the deception by clasping her arms across her belly.

1. Inv. no. 8474.

2. Inv. no. RBK-14519.

BIBLIOGRAPHY: Washington, *Curtis O. Baer Collection* (exhib. cat.), 1985, p. 52, no. 22; Sander, "*Jacob and Rachel*," 1989, p. 47, fig. 11; Schade, "*Jacob and Rachel*," 1991, p. 193, fig. 5.

## 7

## Joseph Recounting His Dreams to His Father

South Lowlands, about 1520–30

Panel, 11⅝ x 6⅝ in. (29.5 x 16.8 cm)

London, Victoria and Albert Museum, 1242-1855

Perhaps the most popular as well as extensive of the Genesis cycles, to judge from the surviving drawing and roundels, was that of the story of Joseph. This panel shows the young Joseph earnestly recounting his dreams to his father as his resentful brothers listen. "I thought we were binding sheaves in the field: and my sheaf arose as it were, and stood, and your sheaves standing about, bowed down before my sheaf. . . . He dreamed also another dream, which he told his brethren, saying: I saw in a dream, as it were the sun, and the moon, and eleven stars worshipping me" (Genesis 37: 7, 9). In the middle ground at the left Joseph is seen sleeping in a hut; above, in discs, are representations of his two dreams. In the right background Joseph encounters a stranger on the plain of Sichem, who tells him that his brothers have gone to Dothain.

The composition of this rectilinear panel appears to be an adaptation of an earlier one known from a roundel now glazed into a window in the north aisle of the parish church of Saint Peter in Cassington, Oxfordshire (fig. 1).[1] The Cassington roundel, in turn, appears to rely on a design belonging to the van der Goes group. The figure of Jacob, for example, reflects the facial type and costume of Jacob in the Baer drawing (cat. no. 6). The formal organization of the composition, in which the principal subject and the ancillary scenes are separated by rocky outcroppings, is, likewise, characteristic of this early group. Jan Swart, at a later date, apparently was familiar with the same design on which the London panel depends, to judge from the similarity of the positioning of Jacob and Joseph and of the pair of figures in the background (see fig. 2); the fact that other drawings in this Joseph series by Swart (cat. no. 96) clearly rely on the van der Goes group (see cat. nos. 8 and 9) may be construed as further evidence that the present composition also derived from the same source.

The composition of this panel differs, however, from that of the Cassington roundel in several details: There is, for example, no house in the upper right behind the scene of Joseph meeting the stranger in Sichem. This may have been eliminated in an effort to have the image correspond precisely with the text: Joseph was out in a field—not near a house—when he encountered the stranger. The scene of Joseph being thrown in a pit, which appears in the upper-right background of the Cassington roundel and is clearly based on the van der Goes design (see cat. nos. 8 and 9, fig. 7), is not included in the present panel. As this was a principal scene in the van der Goes group series, the composition of the Cassington roundel is clearly a conflation. The density of the narrative—the discs with the representations of the

FIG. 1 After the Hugo van der Goes group. *Joseph Recounting His Dreams to His Father*. Roundel. About 1480–1500. Cassington, Oxfordshire, Church of Saint Peter

dreams, for example, are rather cramped in their placement—is a further indication of this. Therefore, the present panel, although of a later date—to judge from the style—appears to remain more faithful to the original composition of the van der Goes group.

This panel is crisply, if cursorily, executed in dark brown paint with yellow and dark yellow silver stain. The modeling relies more on areas articulated with stickwork than on the building up of dark tones. The play of drapery patterns is enhanced by the figure at the far right clutching his tunic, for example, but the protrusion of folds jutting out from the rear of Joseph's robe—given a richer texture by the dotting of silver stain—is not readily explicable. The feathery boughs of the trees in the background are reminiscent of those in the Affligem panels (see cat. no. 10, figs. 3 and 4). While the prominence allotted to the detailed and deeply receding background is unusual, this panel is of interest more as an example of the dissemination of a design than of stylistic accomplishment.

1. See Newton, *Oxford, CVMA*, 1979, pp. 56–57; n.II,Ic, pl. 21a; Cole, *Roundels in Britain*, 1993, p. 47, no. 405.

BIBLIOGRAPHY: Rackham, *Guide to Stained Glass*, 1936, p. 108, pl. 48.

FIG. 2 Jan Swart van Groningen. *Joseph Recounting His Dreams to His Father*. Pen and black ink, with brown wash, on paper. About 1545–55. London, British Museum

8    9

## 8

### Joseph Being Sold to the Ishmaelites

Follower of Hugo van der Goes

South Lowlands, about 1480–1500

Pen and black ink, brown wash, and white highlights, on brown prepared paper: diameter, 8¼ in. (21 cm)

Staatliche Museen zu Berlin, Preußischer Kulturbesitz, Kupferstichkabinett, KdZ 1982

## 9

### Joseph Being Sold to the Ishmaelites

South Lowlands, about 1480–90

Roundel: diameter, 8⅝ in. (21.9 cm)

University Art Gallery, University of Pittsburgh, 1140-65

In the scene represented in the Berlin drawing, Joseph, having been cast into a pit by his jealous brothers, is being pulled out to be sold to the Ishmaelites. "And when the Madianite merchants passed by, they drew him out of the pit, and sold him to the Ismaelites, for twenty pieces of silver: and they led him into Egypt" (Genesis 37: 28).

This composition apparently enjoyed enormous popularity, as it was widely reproduced in a variety of mediums over a considerable period of time. Indeed, a clearer example of the tendency in the Lowlands to copy favored compositions hardly exists. Its relationship to the Hugo van der Goes group is evident in both the compositional formula and the figural style. The brother receiv-

ing payment, seen in a three-quarter stance from the rear, is conspicuously reminiscent of the shepherd in the Oxford *Meeting of Jacob and Rachel* (fig. 1, p. 51), and the head of Joseph is remarkably close in type to that of Antonio (born about 1472), the eldest son of Tommaso Portinari, on the left wing of the *Nativity* triptych (fig. 1). These correspondences are closer here than in any other version of this composition, suggesting that the Berlin drawing is the most faithful reproduction of the original design.

The best-known—and certainly the largest—version is that in the tondo series by the Master of the Joseph Sequence, now in Berlin (fig. 2; see cat. no. 10).[1] This tondo, which is more notable for its rich palette and shimmering textures than for its narrative animation, follows the model in detail, elaborating only on elements of the landscape and the costumes. This master, who was active in Brussels about 1500, characteristically favored broad, flat, fleshy faces with rather beady eyes, in contrast to the more elongated ones with sharper noses and chins that typify those of the van der Goes group (see cat. no. 10).

The composition reappears, with emendations to accommodate the rectangular format and with alterations in costume and landscape, in the *Mayer van den Bergh Breviary* miniature introducing Psalm 68 (fig. 3).[2] The choice of this composition was probably inspired by the passages: "Draw me out of the mire, that I may not stick fast: deliver me from them that hate me, and out of the deep waters. Let not the tempest of water drown me, nor the deep swallow me up: and let not the pit shut her mouth upon me" (Psalms 68:

FIG. 1 Hugo van der Goes. *Antonio and Pigello, the Sons of Tommaso Portinari* (detail of the left wing of the *Portinari* altarpiece). Tempera and oil on panel. 1474–78. Florence, Galleria degli Uffizi

15, 16). The use of a composition from the Joseph series to illustrate one of the Psalms is curious, but it does indicate the inordinate degree to which workshops employed available designs for their immediate needs. The illuminations in the *Mayer van den Bergh Breviary*, except for several completed by Jan Provoost, are generally attributed to Simon Bening and Gheeraert Horenbout (Master of the Prayer Book of James VI of Scotland) and are dated to about 1510–15.[3] It is not clear how designs that probably originated in a workshop associated with Hugo van der Goes became available to the Bening-Horenbout workshop, although Alexander Bening, who was the father of Simon and was active in Ghent about 1470, was

FIG. 2 Master of the Joseph Sequence. *Joseph Being Sold to the Ishmaelites.* Tempera and oil on panel. 1490–1500. Staatliche Museen zu Berlin, Preußischer Kulturbesitz, Gemäldegalerie

FIG. 3 Simon Bening and Gheeraert Horenbout. *Joseph Being Sold to the Ishmaelites.* Manuscript illumination for Psalm 68, from the *Mayer van den Bergh Breviary.* About 1510–15. Antwerp, Museum Mayer van den Bergh

FIG. 4 Simon Bening and Gheeraert Horenbout. *Jacob Sends Joseph to Search for His Brothers* and *Joseph Being Sold to the Ishmaelites (bas-de-page).* Manuscript illumination from the *Grimani Breviary.* Before 1520. Venice, Biblioteca Nazionale Marciana

married to Catherine van der Goes, who may have been Hugo's sister.[4] The composition appears yet again, in a reversed and much reduced fashion, in the *bas-de-page* marginalia of the *Grimani Breviary* (fig. 4).[5] This manuscript, which is closely related to the *Mayer van den Bergh Breviary*, if not by the same hands, would have to have been completed before 1520, when Cardinal Domenico Grimani (1461–1523) acquired it.

The Berlin drawing, which is somewhat wooden in execution and shows no signs of the free, fluid line—reworking or altering a passage here and there—characteristic of an original composition, is unquestionably a copy. The precision and finish of this drawing accord it distinct appeal—qualities that are all the more apparent when it is compared with another copy (fig. 5),[6] the clumsy passages of which are exacerbated by later strengthening. The function of the present sheet is open to question. As a highly finished drawing, remarkably well preserved, it may have been intended as a collector's item that attractively recorded a much-favored composition. While difficult to establish, a fifteenth-century date does not seem unreasonable; as the model on which it is based probably dates from about 1480, the continual replication over several generations underscores a remarkably conservative and persistent aspect of design dissemination in the late fifteenth and early sixteenth century.

The composition of the roundel is very close to that of the Berlin drawing, varying only in minor details. The drapery patterns are somewhat simplified, while costumes are occasionally embellished with decorative hems and the like. The Berlin sheet depicts the robe of Joseph as marked with a single six-pointed star, the significance of which—if it holds any at all—is unclear. In the roundel version, Joseph's robe is given an allover pattern of similar stars. The motions, expressions, and general character of the figures are, however, essentially unaltered. While the drawing appears to be the work of a single hand, the roundel seems to have been painted by two hands: An accomplished artist executed the principal figures, while an assistant must have been responsible for the two groups of schematized and coarse figures in the background. As this division of labor appears to have been common workshop practice in the execution of both working drawings and glass painting, the supposition that the Berlin drawing is a copy made several decades after the original is strengthened. It is likewise probable that, in this case, the roundel predates the drawing.

The significance of the ciphers on the camels' saddlebags is unknown; a similar cipher appears on the saddlebag of the rear camel in the Berlin tondo (see fig. 2). This roundel is one of only a handful based on a design from the Joseph series by the van der Goes group that is known to survive. Of these, one represents Joseph being cast into the pit (fig. 6), and is now in the collection of Dr. William Cole;[7] the composition, excepting some changes in costume and landscape, corresponds to that of the Berlin tondo (fig. 7),[8] and there is yet another fine roundel, which depicts the meeting of Joseph and his father, Jacob ("And seeing him, he fell upon his neck, and embracing him wept" [Genesis 46: 29]), in the parish church of Saint Michael, in Begbroke, Oxfordshire (see fig. 8).[9]

1. Staatliche Museen zu Berlin, Preußischer Kulturbesitz, Gemäldegalerie, 539A.

2. Antwerp, Museum Mayer van den Bergh, 618.

3. See Nieuwdorp, *Musée Mayer van den Bergh,* 1992, p. 51.

4. See Friedländer, *Early Netherlandish Painting* 4, 1969, p. 11.

5. Venice, Biblioteca Nazionale Marciana, Ms. Lat. I, 99 (=2138), f. 65.

6. Staatliche Museen zu Berlin, Preußischer Kulturbesitz, Kupferstichkabinett, KdZ 774.

7. Cole, *Roundels in Britain,* 1993, p. 216, no. 1746.

8. Staatliche Museen zu Berlin, Preußischer Kulturbesitz, Gemäldegalerie, 539 A.

9. Newton, *Oxford, CVMA,* 1979, p. 35; Cole, *Roundels in Britain,* 1993, p. 117, no. 135. Another roundel, formerly in the Oppenheim Collection (*Oppenheim Collection* [sale cat.], 1914, p. 59, no. 155, pl. 53) but the present whereabouts of which are unknown, represents *The Beaker Is Found in Benjamin's Sack* and appears to be related to the van der Goes group.

BIBLIOGRAPHY: (8) Popham, "Notes-I," 1928, p. 179; Bock et al., *Zeichnungen,* 1930, p. 8, no. 774; Popham, "French Drawings," 1931, p. 66; Popham, "Josefslegende," 1931, p. 75, fig. 2. (9) Hovey, "Stained Glass Windows," 1953, p. 18; Husband, *Silver-Stained Roundels,* 1991, p. 212.

FIG. 7 Master of the Joseph Sequence. *Joseph Is Cast into a Pit.* Tempera and oil on panel. 1490–1500. Staatliche Museen zu Berlin, Preußischer Kulturbesitz, Gemäldegalerie

FIG. 5 After the Hugo van der Goes group. *Joseph Being Sold to the Ishmaelites.* Pen and brown ink on paper. About 1500 (?). Staatliche Museen zu Berlin, Preußischer Kulturbesitz, Kupferstichkabinett

FIG. 6 After the Hugo van der Goes group. *Joseph Is Cast into a Pit.* Roundel. About 1490–1500. Hindhead, Surrey, Collection Dr. William Cole

FIG. 8 After the Hugo van der Goes group. *The Meeting of Joseph and Jacob.* Roundel. About 1480–90. Begbroke, Oxfordshire, Church of Saint Michael

10

## Joseph Interpreting the Dreams of the Butler and the Baker

Master of the Joseph Sequence

Brussels, about 1490–1500

Tempera and oil on panel: diameter, 61 ½ in. (156.2 cm)

New York, The Metropolitan Museum of Art, Harris Brisbane Dick Fund, 1953, 53.168

The pharaoh had his chief butler and baker—both of whom had caused offense—thrown into the prison where Joseph was incarcerated after being falsely accused of raping Potiphar's wife. The butler and the baker each had a dream, which they related to Joseph, who, in turn, interpreted them, in the second of three dream-related episodes. The butler saw " . . . a vine, On which were three branches, which by little and little . . . brought forth ripe grapes . . . and I took the grapes, and pressed them into the cup which I held, and I gave the cup to Pharao. Joseph answered: . . . The three branches are yet three days: After which Pharao will remember thy service, and will restore thee . . ." (Genesis 40: 9–13). Then the baker said that he dreamt he had " . . . three baskets of meal upon my head: And that in one basket which was uppermost, I carried all meats that are made by the art of baking, and that the birds ate out of it. Joseph answered: . . . The three baskets are yet three days: After which Pharao will take thy head from thee, and hang thee on a cross, and the birds shall tear thy flesh" (Genesis 40: 16–19).

In this tondo, Joseph is shown serving the pharaoh's two fallen servants while interpreting their dreams; the representation of each dream appears above the appropriate figure. The tondo is one of a group of five representing scenes all apparently based on designs by the Hugo van der Goes group for the Story of Joseph series: The compositions of two of these, *Joseph Is Cast into the Pit* (see cat. nos. 8 and 9, fig. 7) and *Joseph Being Sold to the Ishmaelites* (cat. nos. 8 and 9, fig. 2), are otherwise known, while those of a third tondo in Berlin, *Joseph Is Introduced into the House of Potiphar* (fig. 1),[1] and another representing Joseph with the wife of Potiphar, now in Munich (fig. 2),[2] appear to preserve earlier designs of the van der Goes group. A fifth tondo, also in Berlin, in figure type and format seems to belong to this series, but the subject—perhaps Joseph with Asenath—has never been convincingly established.[3]

A series of panels originally from a polyptych at the abbey of Affligem, near Alost, is clearly by the same hand as the tondi.[4] The facial types alone establish common authorship; the face of Joseph in the Berlin *Joseph Being Sold to the Ishmaelites* (cat. nos. 8 and 9, fig. 2), for example, is virtually identical to that of Saint John in the *Crucifixion* panel from the *Affligem* altarpiece (fig. 3). Furthermore, the same gravity-defying outcropping of land seen in the background of the *Affligem Adoration* (fig. 4) is found in the background of the same Berlin tondo.

FIG. 1 Master of the Joseph Sequence. *Joseph Is Introduced into the House of Potiphar*. Tempera and oil on panel. 1490–1500. Staatliche Museen zu Berlin, Preußischer Kulturbesitz, Gemäldegalerie

The *Circumcision* panel from the Affligem polyptych is inscribed TE. BRUESELE, presumably indicating that the Master of the Joseph Sequence was active in Brussels. How the designs for the Joseph series came into this master's hands is a matter of speculation, but clearly the designs had been widely disseminated during the intervening generation between the original van der Goes group and the Master of the Joseph Sequence. A roundel based on the same composition as the present tondo is in the church of Saint Mary, Warwick.[5]

In the third and final episode involving a dream Joseph is ordered to be released from prison in order to interpret the pharaoh's disturbing dreams of the seven fat and seven lean kine and the seven ripe and seven withered ears of corn. Joseph explains, "The seven beautiful kine, and the seven full ears, are seven years of plenty. . . . And the seven lean and thin kine that came up after them, and the seven thin ears that were blasted with the burning wind, are seven years of famine to come" (Genesis 41: 26–27).

FIG. 2 Master of the Joseph Sequence. *Joseph with the Wife of Potiphar*. Tempera and oil on panel. 1490–1500. Munich, Bayerische Staatsgemäldesammlungen, Alte Pinakothek

FIG. 3 Master of the Joseph Sequence. *The Crucifixion* (detail of the *Affligem* altarpiece). Tempera and oil on panel. About 1495. Brussels, Musée d'Art Ancien

FIG. 4 Master of the Joseph Sequence. *The Adoration* (detail of the *Affligem* altarpiece). Tempera and oil on panel. About 1495. Brussels, Musée d'Art Ancien

FIG. 5 Hugo van der Goes group. *Joseph Interprets the Dreams of the Pharaoh*. Pen and brown ink on paper. 1480–90. Bayonne, Musée Bonnat

FIG. 6 Hugo van der Goes group. *Joseph with the Wife of Potiphar*. Pen and brown ink on paper. 1480–90. Oxford, Ashmolean Museum

FIG. 7 Hugo van der Goes. *The Son of James III of Scotland* (detail of the left wing of the *Trinity* altarpiece). Tempera and oil on panel. 1475–80. Edinburgh, National Gallery of Scotland

FIG. 8 After Hugo van der Goes. *The Deposition*. Tempera and oil on panel. About 1480–1500. Naples, Museo Nazionale di Capodimonte

FIG. 9 *Joseph Interprets the Dreams of the Pharaoh*. Pen and brown ink on paper. About 1500. Stuttgart, Staatsgalerie, Graphische Sammlung

FIG. 10 *Susanna in Judgment*. Roundel. About 1510–20. New York, The Metropolitan Museum of Art, The Cloisters Collection, 1984

The van der Goes group composition of this scene is preserved in a drawing now in Bayonne (fig. 5).[6] The style and the costumes depicted in this drawing suggest an early date, probably in the 1480's. Joseph's facial features, his costume, and the handling of the drapery—particularly the robe of the seated pharaoh—find very close comparison in the Oxford drawing of Joseph with the wife of Potiphar (fig. 6).[7] The Bayonne drawing, however, is more studied and meticulous in the pen work. The face of Joseph here is markedly close, for example, to van der Goes's rendering of the head of the son of James III of Scotland, the future James IV (1472/73–1513), on the left wing of the *Trinity* altarpiece in Edinburgh (fig. 7).

The treatment of the head of the figure at the upper left of the Naples *Deposition* (fig. 8)—an early copy after a lost, documented original—can be compared, furthermore, with that of the cocked head of the adviser to the pharaoh's right in the Bayonne drawing, with his jowly face, nubby chin, and long, pointed nose. This head, in turn, is analogous to that of the bareheaded man to the left of the seated pharaoh in another, and later, version of this same subject, now in Stuttgart (fig. 9).[8] This last sheet has been associated erroneously with the Joseph series by the van der Goes group, although the compositional resemblances may indicate a connection. The Stuttgart drawing, however, provides a clear example of the free use of models in developing compositions; the bareheaded figure in the far right foreground, the figure in front of him, and the recumbent dog reappear in nearly identical form in a contemporary roundel of *Susanna in Judgment* (fig. 10;

for the appearance of the same male figure in another context see cat. no. 15, fig. 4).[9] This free copying and adopting of models is characteristic of compositional formulations in the Lowlands and is symptomatic not only of the conventionalization of popular imagery but also of the artistic conservatism of large-scale roundel production.

1. Staatliche Museen zu Berlin, Preußischer Kulturbesitz, Gemäldegalerie, 539 C.

2. Bayerische Staatsgemäldesammlungen, Alte Pinakothek, 13180.

3. Staatliche Museen zu Berlin, Preußischer Kulturbesitz, Gemäldegalerie, 539 D. Friedländer (*Early Netherlandish Painting* 4, 1969, p. 64), questioning the identification of the subject as *Esther Interceding with Ahasuerus*, concluded that the tondo had nothing to do with the Joseph series. Popham, however, observed ("Josefslegende," 1931, pp. 73–74) that the seated man on the right, with the white beard, is identical to the figure of Potiphar in the tondo of *Joseph and Potiphar*, and theorized that the Berlin tondo represented Joseph and Asenath; the latter was given to Joseph as his wife, but Asenath's father, Potiphera, priest of On (or Heliopolis), was confused with Potiphar, the pharaoh's eunuch. The same scene appears in a somewhat later roundel, formerly in Berlin (see Schmitz, *Glasgemälde* 1, 1913, p. 69, fig. 116).

4. Antwerp, Koninklijk Museum voor Schone Kunsten, 345. See Friedländer, *Early Netherlandish Painting* 4, 1969, pp. 63–64, 80, plates 72–73.

5. See Cole, *Roundels in Britain*, 1993, p. 298, no. 2354.

6. Musée Bonnat, n.i 1262. See Popham, "Josefslegende," 1931, p. 75, fig. 3.

7. Ashmolean Museum. See Parker, *Drawings in the Ashmolean Museum*, 1938, pp. 4–5, no. 9, pl. 14; Winkler, *Hugo van der Goes*, 1964, p. 284, fig. 225.

8. Staatsgalerie Stuttgart, Graphische Sammlung, 1735.

9. The Metropolitan Museum of Art, The Cloisters Collection, 1984.339.

BIBLIOGRAPHY: Friedländer, "Brüsseler Tafelmalerei," 1923, p. 314; Popham, "Josefslegende," 1931, p. 75; Roosval, "Peintures des retables," 1934, p. 318; Larsen, *Primitifs flamands*, 1960, p. 121; von der Osten and Vey, *Painting and Sculpture*, 1969, p. 114; Van Roy, "Kunstschatten," 1962, pp. 226–29; Friedländer, *Early Netherlandish Painting* 4, 1969, pp. 64, 80–81, 100, pl. 71, fig. 79E.

11

## 11

### Benjamin Taking Leave of His Father

South Lowlands, about 1470–80

Pen and black ink, over brown ink, with later white fill in areas, on paper: diameter, 9 in. (22.9 cm)

Oxford, Ashmolean Museum, PI 8

When Joseph's brothers were sent into Egypt to buy grain during the famine, Benjamin, Joseph's only uterine brother, was kept at home with their father, Jacob. Upon their arrival in Egypt, Joseph accused his brothers of spying and demanded that Benjamin, the youngest, be sent for to prove the veracity of their story. Simeon was held as security and the rest of the brothers returned to their father, but only when famine forced the purchase of more grain did he allow Judah to take Benjamin back to Egypt with the other brothers: "And take also your brother, and go to the man" (Genesis 43: 13).

In the background of the present drawing, Judah takes the hand of young Benjamin and leaves his grieving father to join his nine other brothers, who are depicted in the foreground heading back to Egypt. The drawing appears to have been outlined in pen and brown ink and then completed in black ink. This overdrawing primarily models the figures and to a lesser degree fills in or completes details; there appears to be little correction or alteration of the initial composition—which, however, apparently was extended beyond the inner arc, at the top, as this outer portion is executed only in black ink. Both Parker[1]

FIG. 1 Hugo van der Goes group. *The Triumph of the Pharaoh.* Pen and brush, with brown ink, on paper. 1480–90. Oxford, Ashmolean Museum

and Popham[2] considered this probably original drawing the finest in the van der Goes group's Joseph series.

The figure of the man at the far right in the Oxford *Triumph of the Pharaoh* (fig. 1)[3] appears to have been inspired by the figure of Judah in the present drawing, which further argues for an early date. The verve and freshness of the drawing justifies Parker's and Popham's esteem. The figure of little Benjamin looking back over his shoulder at his grieving father is rendered with great poignancy. The freely expressive but economic use of line contrasts with the meticulous yet stiffer pen strokes found in both the Berlin (cat. no. 8) and the Bayonne (cat. no. 10, fig. 5) drawings, and endows this sheet with a fresh spontaneity. The treatment of the foliage as compressed hori-

zontal arcs is very similar to that found in the Brussels *Passion* panels. The occasional confusing passage—the placement of the seated Jacob in relation to the wattle fence and the steps in front of him, or the disposition of the proper left leg of the brother just behind the muzzle of the donkey relative to the section of wattle immediately before it—suggests that this drawing was preliminary to a working design in which these oddities would have been resolved.

No roundel of this composition is known, but one with *The Beaker Is Found in Benjamin's Sack* was formerly in the Oppenheim Collection.[4]

The drawing is slightly trimmed vertically at both sides.

1. *Drawings in the Ashmolean Museum,* 1938, p. 4.

2. "Josefslegende," 1931, p. 76.

3. Ashmolean Museum. See Parker, *Drawings in the Ashmolean Museum,* 1938, p. 5, no. 10.

4. *Oppenheim Collection* (sale cat.), 1914, p. 59, no. 155, pl. 53.

BIBLIOGRAPHY: Popham, "French Drawings," 1931, p. 66; Popham, "Josefslegende," 1931, p. 76, fig. 4; Parker, *Drawings in the Ashmolean Museum,* 1938, p. 4, no. 8, pl. 3; New Brunswick, *Dürer to Cézanne* (exhib. cat.), 1982, pp. 31–32, no. 25, pl. 25; Rome, *Old Master Drawings* (exhib. cat.), 1992, p. 114, no. 45.

## 12

### Tobias Drawing the Fish from the Water

South Lowlands, about 1480–90

Roundel: diameter, 7⅞ in. (20 cm)

Cambridge, King's College Chapel, 51c1

The Book of Tobit[1] tells of the trials of a devout believer's faith. Tobit was deported from Israel during the reign of Shalmaneser of Assyria, but in those difficult times he generously looked after his kinsmen, feeding and clothing them and burying them when they died, at great risk to his own life. To celebrate his deliverance, Tobit prepared a feast. When he learned from arriving guests that Jews were slain in the streets, Tobit leapt up from the table and had the bodies brought to his house to be buried, even though this was a capital offense. While resting from his labors, he suffered blindness when the dung of a swallow got in his eyes. Meanwhile, Sarah, the daughter of Raguel, was possessed by the demon Asmodeus. Tobit charged his son Tobias to collect a debt from their kinsman Gabael. En route, Tobias met the archangel Raphael disguised as a handsome young man, who agreed to accompany him on the way to Rages. Raphael instructed Tobias to catch a fish, the gall and liver of which will cure Tobit and Sarah, respectively. Asmodeus was exorcised, and Tobias married Sarah and then returned to cure his father, Tobit, whereupon Raphael revealed his identity.

In the scene depicted here, Tobias has gone to the River Tigris to wash his feet, whereupon a monstrous fish has risen up to devour him.

12

FIG. 1 Hugo van der Goes group. *Tobias Drawing the Fish from the Water*. Pen and brown ink on paper. 1480–90. Windsor Castle, Royal Library (*see plate 5*)

FIG. 2 Hugo van der Goes group. *Tobit and Tobias Praying as Raphael Departs*. Pen and brown ink on paper. 1480–90. Dresden, Staatliche Kunstsammlungen, Kupferstich-Kabinett

FIG. 3 After the Hugo van der Goes group (?). *Tobias Burning the Liver of the Fish*. Roundel. About 1500. Amsterdam, Rijksmuseum

Raphael instructs Tobias to draw the fish out of the water by its gills and then to remove the heart, liver, and gall. "Then the angel said to him: Take out the entrails of this fish, and lay up his heart, and his gall, and his liver for thee: for these are necessary for useful medicines" (Tobias 6: 5). At the right, the angel, accompanied by his dog, gives his instructions while in the background at the left Tobias, accompanied by Raphael and·by his dog, is greeted, upon his return, by his father.

The composition of the King's College roundel conforms in all but the most minute details to a drawing at Windsor Castle (fig. 1).[2] In execution this drawing is very much like both the Bayonne and Berlin drawings, relying on rather hard outlines and on modeling consisting of networks of short strokes and cross-hatching in the more shaded areas. The stiffness and lack of spontaneity likewise suggest that this is a copy, although a relatively early one, probably of the 1480s; this dating is supported by the gothic *p* watermark, according to van Puyvelde.[3] The drawing, which, particularly in the treatment of the drapery, reveals the influence of Hugo van der Goes, prompted Popham to ascribe this entire group to the Master of the Story of Tobit.[4] Another drawing from the same series—perhaps by the same hand—is now in Dresden (fig. 2);[5] it depicts the departure of Raphael, as Tobit and Tobias fall on their knees in praise: ". . . he was taken from their sight, and they could see him no more. Then they lying prostrate for three hours upon their face, blessed God . . ." (Tobias 12: 21, 22).

While the present roundel appears to be the only surviving example contemporaneous with

these early copies of the van der Goes designs, several later and rather dryly executed roundels seem to reflect the compositions of other scenes in this series. A roundel in Amsterdam shows Tobias and Sarah in fervent prayer while, in the background, Tobias burns the liver of the fish and Raphael drives out the devil (fig. 3):[6] "And Tobias remembering the angel's word, took out of his bag part of the liver, and laid it upon burning coals. Then the angel Raphael took the devil, and bound him in the desert of upper Egypt. Then Tobias exhorted the virgin, and said to her: Sara, arise, and let us pray to God to day, and to morrow, and the next day . . . and when the third night is over, we will be in our own wedlock" (Tobias 8: 2–4). Three roundels in London depict the marriage of Tobias and Sarah, the departure of Tobias and Sarah, and the healing of Tobit's blindness (figs. 4, 5, and 6);[7] the first and last retain their original borders with the appropriate biblical texts in Dutch. These roundels, which probably date to the end of the fifteenth or the beginning of the sixteenth century, are of lesser quality than the King's College example, but the facial types and the treatment of the drapery indicate that their compositions all derive from those of the Hugo van der Goes group. A fragment of a close version of the present roundel is in the Bijlokemuseum, Ghent.[8]

The composition of *Tobias Drawing the Fish from the Water*—like that of *Joseph Being Sold to the Ishmaelites* (see cat. no. 8)—reappears in the *Mayer van den Bergh Breviary* (fig. 7). While the text of Tobit does appear in the *Breviary*, beginning on the verso of folio 365, the image is used

FIG. 4 After the Hugo van der Goes group (?). *The Marriage of Tobias and Sarah*. Roundel. About 1500. London, Victoria and Albert Museum

FIG. 5 After the Hugo van der Goes group (?). *The Departure of Tobias and Sarah*. Roundel. About 1500. London, Victoria and Albert Museum

FIG. 6 After the Hugo van der Goes group (?). *The Healing of Tobit's Blindness*. Roundel. About 1500. London, Victoria and Albert Museum

FIG. 7 Simon Bening and Gheeraert Horenbout. *Tobias Drawing the Fish from the Water*. Manuscript illumination for Psalm 26, from the *Mayer van den Bergh Breviary*. About 1510–15. Antwerp, Museum Mayer van den Bergh (*see plate 6*)

not here, but, curiously, as an illustration to Psalm 26, beginning on folio 41. The correlation of this image and the text is even more obscure than that of the Joseph series and Psalm 68 (see cat. nos. 8 and 9), but the association may have been inspired by the lines: "Whilst the wicked draw near against me, to eat my flesh. My enemies that trouble me, have themselves been weakened, and have fallen" (Psalms 26: 2). (Tobias had gone to the edge of the Tigris River to wash his feet when he was attacked by the fish.) The appearance of

this scene in the *Mayer van den Bergh Breviary* further indicates not only that the illuminators relied on a large stock of models, but also that the designs for the series by the van der Goes group derived from a common source.

1. Both Tobit and Tobias are grecized forms of the Hebrew Tobiah. In the Douay Bible, Tobias is the name used for both the father and son; for the sake of clarity, the convention of calling the father Tobit and the son Tobias is used here.

2. Royal Library, 12952. See van Puyvelde, *Flemish Drawings*, 1942, p. 9, no. 2; Winkler, *Hugo van der Goes*, 1964, p. 284, fig. 226; Husband, *Silver-Stained Roundels*, 1991, p. 22, fig. 18.

3. *Flemish Drawings*, 1942, p. 9, no. 2.

4. Popham, "Notes-I," 1928, pp. 178–79.

5. Staatliche Kunstsammlungen, Kupferstich-Kabinett, C 2232.

6. Rijksmuseum, NM 12561.

7. Victoria and Albert Museum, 1245-1855, 1244-1855, and 1246-1855, respectively.

8. Inv. no. 63-9-5/37.

BIBLIOGRAPHY: Wayment, *King's College*, 1988, p. 206, no. 51C1; Husband, *Silver-Stained Roundels*, 1991, p. 141.

## 13

## The Blinding of Tobit

South Lowlands, about 1490–1500

Roundel: diameter, 8¾ in. (22.2 cm)

Brussels, Musées Royaux d'Art et d'Histoire, 560B

## 14

## Tobias Drawing the Fish from the Water

South Lowlands, about 1490–1500

Roundel: diameter, 8¾ in. (22.2 cm)

Brussels, Musées Royaux d'Art et d'Histoire, 567

These two roundels belong to the same series and appear to have been executed by the same hand. *The Blinding of Tobit* actually comprises four different scenes: In the background, through the arcade, Tobit is seated at his feast of celebration, as a servant brings him a message; Tobit goes to the door and learns from guests of the killing of Jews; Tobit buries a body in violation of the king's decree; and Tobit, resting from his labors, is blinded by the feces from a swallow's nest. In the second roundel, the sequence reads in the reverse order: Tobias draws the fish from the water with Raphael instructing him from the other side of a wattle fence; in the middle ground, again under Raphael's instructions, Tobias removes the entrails of the fish; and in the background Tobias, in the company of the angel, is welcomed home by Tobit. The composition of the latter roundel clearly derives from that of the Hugo van der Goes group (cat. no. 12); the artist merely added another background scene and, more interestingly, updated the costumes—notably, Tobias's cap and his footwear—to the fashion at the end of the fifteenth century. Specific narrative details, such as Tobias's one bare foot and his traveling kit resting against the tree in the background, are retained from the earlier version of the composition (see

13

14

FIG. 1 After the Hugo van der Goes group. *Tobias Drawing the Fish from the Water* (detail of cat. no. 14). Roundel. 1490–1500. Brussels, Musées Royaux d'Art et d'Histoire

FIG. 2 After the Hugo van der Goes group. *The Blinding of Tobit*. Roundel. About 1510. New York, The Metropolitan Museum of Art, Gift of Philip Hofer, 1937

FIG. 3 After the Hugo van der Goes group. *Tobias Drawing the Fish from the Water*. Roundel. 1500–1510. New York, The Metropolitan Museum of Art, The Cloisters Collection, 1932

cat. no. 12) and further confirm the source of the composition. It must be presumed that *The Blinding of Tobit* likewise reflects the lost van der Goes group version of this composition.

Both roundels are exceptionally well executed. Several shades of paint and hues of silver stain from light to dark golden yellow bring a richness to the images. The drawing is crisp and the modeling convincing. The painter has used stippling and fine-line etching to particular effect in indicating volumes and highlights (see fig. 1, a detail). The roundels attest to the enduring popularity of the van der Goes group compositions, yet, the

glass painter, far from producing a stiff, slavish copy, "modernized" the images and rendered the scenes with remarkable freshness. A number of later versions of these revised compositions are known, all varying in quality: A somewhat weaker, but perfectly competent version of *The Blinding of Tobit*, for example, is in The Cloisters Collection (fig. 2), while a heavy-handed variation of *Tobias Drawing the Fish from the Water* (fig. 3), in the same collection, greatly simplifies the background detail.

The Book of Tobit was accepted in the canon of the Catholic but not the Protestant Church. As

a subject it was thus conservative, but that it was favored by an individual is not necessarily to be taken as an indication of religious sentiment, for the Story of Tobit increasingly was viewed as an exemplum of patience and steadfast faith, virtues that transcend conflicts of dogma. Thus, in a time of religious foment, the Story of Tobit remained a subject of universal appeal.

BIBLIOGRAPHY: (13) Helbig, *Glasschilderkunst*, 1943, pl. 20, no. 27; Husband, *Silver-Stained Roundels*, 1991, p. 22, fig. 19. (14) Popham, "Notes-I," 1928, p. 176, fig. 2; Helbig, *Glasschilderkunst*, 1943, pl. 20, no. 27.

# 2

## Diversity of Style and Imagery: about 1480 to 1520

By the end of the fifteenth century, when roundel designs increasingly emanated from the workshops of accomplished artists, and production had escalated to a semi-industrial output, variety and quality greatly increased. By no means a representative selection, the roundels in this section do suggest the diversity of subject matter and the range of styles in currency. The Berlin *Sacrament of Baptism* (cat. no. 15) is essentially a late medieval image and clearly relies on traditional models. The drawing and the related roundel of *The Adoration of the Magi* (cat. nos. 16 and 17) are unusual in that the composition is borrowed from the center panel of an earlier and well-known triptych by Hans Memling; by the end of the fifteenth century, either individuals or glass-painting workshops generally commissioned original designs directly from leading artists, no doubt to meet the quality demands of clients but also perhaps as a way to ensure the originality of the material. Scenes from the Life and the Passion of Christ tended to be traditional in their iconography, and popular devotional subjects, such as the Agony in the Garden (cat. no. 18) and Christ led away from Herod Antipas (cat. no. 21), relied on conventional late medieval imagery that persisted in a most conservative fashion until well into the sixteenth century. The work of an anonymous North Lowlands roundel designer, called the Master of the Death of Absalom after one of his better-known drawings, now in the Louvre (cat. no. 19, fig. 1), is represented by a heretofore little-studied drawing and a roundel (cat. nos. 19 and 20) that also reflect many of the peculiarities of his style. Allegorical and secular subjects are encountered in varied guises in both designs and roundels (cat. nos. 22, 24, and 25). The brutal consequences of faith (cat. no. 23) on the one hand are counterbalanced by an equally unappealing vision of the ultimate reward for the lack of faith (cat. no. 26) on the other. The ever-present leveling force of death inspired popular imagery in the Late Middle Ages that endured into the sixteenth century (see cat. no. 27). Likewise, the progression of time, often represented in medieval calendars as the Occupations of the Months in conjunction with the signs of the zodiac, was given new forms of expression by the end of the fifteenth century (see cat. nos. 28 and 29). Responding to the conservative nature of their patrons, however, designers of roundels in this period approached stylistic innovation and broached unorthodox subject matter with great hesitancy.

## 15

### The Sacrament of Baptism

South Lowlands, about 1480

Pen and black ink, with gray wash, on paper, 9 x 7⅞ in. (22.9 x 20 cm)

Staatliche Museen zu Berlin, Preußischer Kulturbesitz, Kupferstichkabinett, KdZ 2401

Apparently from a series devoted to the Seven Sacraments, this design for a roundel represents a bishop baptizing a baby held by its mother, attended by two courtly figures, a deacon, and a monk. In a semi-circular inset below, a bishop asperges a self-mortifying penitent. The date 1517 at the bottom of the sheet, which is slightly trimmed at both sides, is in a later hand. The quality of this drawing, which Popham considered to be early but for which he did not hazard a date,[1] is high. The drawing appears to have been influenced by Rogier van der Weyden, judging from a sheet by a hand close to the master in which the basic composition is essentially the same, differing only in the reverse positioning of some of the attendant figures (fig. 1).[2] The six other sacraments by the same hand are preserved on five further sheets now divided between the Ashmolean Museum, Oxford, and the Louvre.[3]

The firm outlines clearly describe the subjects, and the use of wash in the modeling is accomplished; the spatial definition of the interior space, however, is handled somewhat clumsily. The drawing was undoubtedly a working design for a glass painter's shop; indeed, a roundel now in the Collection Frits Lugt, Paris (fig. 2),[4] representing

FIG. 2 *The Sacrament of Penance.* Roundel. About 1480–1500. Paris, Collection Frits Lugt, Institut Néerlandais

a seated bishop administering the sacrament of Penance to a kneeling female seen from behind, appears to be based on a design from the same series.[5] The figure types—notably, the broad, square face of the bishop—and the naïve perspectival rendering of the interior clearly are related. The identification of the subject is confirmed by the general correlation between the composition and the analogous sheet in the Oxford/Paris Seven Sacraments series (fig. 3).[6]

Schmitz observed the stylistic connection between this drawing and two roundels—*Alexius in School* and *The Marriage of Alexius* (fig. 4)—from a series of ten scenes from the life of Saint Alexius.[7] A Cologne provenance is indicated by the dialect of the accompanying border inscriptions and by the coat of arms of the Cologne

FIG. 3 After Rogier van der Weyden. *The Sacrament of Penance.* Pen and black ink on paper. About 1450. Oxford, Ashmolean Museum

patrician Petrus von Eychennynck found in an associated tracery light.[8] The borders of two of the roundels are inscribed with the date 1515, but—as the roundels were executed by at least three different hands and apparently at different dates—this may refer to the date that the series was installed, perhaps in the chapel of the Alexianerkloster in Cologne. The round, fleshy faces with pointed noses, the treatment of the men's long hair and the long tubular folds of the drap-

FIG. 4 *The Marriage of Alexius* (destroyed). Roundel. About 1500–1510. Formerly Berlin, Kunstgewerbemuseum

FIG. 5 *The Judgment of Susanna* (detail). Roundel. About 1510–20. New York, The Metropolitan Museum of Art, The Cloisters Collection, 1932

ery, and the flattened interior spaces manifest a commonality of style. The fleshy-faced bishop in the roundel—who holds a book in one hand and raises the other in blessing—is so close to the corresponding figure in the drawing that the two must be based on the same model. The secular costumes in the baptism scene—the pointed shoes and short tunic of the man in the foreground and the high conical hennin and veil of the woman at the far right—are characteristic of the Burgundian

Lowlands in the 1470s and 1480s, whereas the costumes in the roundel—particularly the woman's headdress and the men's long surcoats—are distinctly early sixteenth century. This suggests that the glass painter relied on earlier models, which were updated to conform to current fashion.

The latter supposition is strengthened by the fact that the male figure at the far right of the scene of Alexius's marriage (fig. 4), bareheaded and with his thumb hooked over his belt, is clearly based on a model in earlier and entirely different compositions, as, for example, *The Judgment of Susanna* (fig. 5; see also cat. no. 10, fig. 10).[9] The same figure already has been encountered in the Stuttgart *Joseph Interprets the Dreams of Pharaoh* (cat. no. 10, fig. 9), which appears to be loosely dependent on the compositions of the Hugo van der Goes group. While Schmitz saw the possibility of a Cologne or Lower Rhenish origin for the Alexius roundels, the present drawing and, at least, the designs of the related Alexius roundels are almost certainly from the South Lowlands. Whether the Alexius roundels were an import from the Lowlands, executed by a glass painter trained there, or whether they were painted after designs imported from the Lowlands remains an often-encountered but unresolved problem. The Berlin design may well be an original; in any event, it is considerably earlier in date than the roundels. The many compositional interrelationships—frequently the case in roundel production—sharply underscore both the persistent use and the wide dissemination of models as well as of compositions that selectively were based on them.

1. "Notes-II," 1929, p. 153.

2. Paris, Musée du Louvre, Département des Arts Graphiques, Collection Édmond de Rothschild, 159 DR; see Sonkes, *Dessins*, 1969, p. 163, C 39, pl. 39 a.

3. Ibid., pp. 159–67, plates 38 and 39.

4. Collection Frits Lugt, Institut Néerlandais, 546.

5. See Lugt, "Beiträge," 1931, p. 37, fig. 1.

6. Oxford, Ashmolean Museum, P 95; Sonkes, *Dessins*, 1969, pp. 159–60, pl. 38 b.

7. Formerly in the Kunstgewerbemuseum, Berlin; see Schmitz, *Glasgemälde* 1, 1913, pp. 65–67, and 2, plates 21–23.

8. Ibid., p. 66.

9. For additional versions of the composition see Husband, *Silver-Stained Roundels*, 1991, p. 147.

BIBLIOGRAPHY: Schmitz, *Glasgemälde*, 1913, p. 65, fig. 106, p. 67; Popham, "Notes-II," 1929, p. 153; Bock et al., *Zeichnungen*, 1930, p. 7, no. 2401; Berserik, "Leiden, ca. 1480–1545," 1982, fig. 59.

## 16

### The Adoration of the Magi

After Hans Memling

South Lowlands, about 1500

Pen and brown ink, with white highlights and grayish white wash, on brown prepared paper: diameter, 8⅝ in. (21.9 cm)

Paris, Musée du Louvre, Département des Arts Graphiques, 20.738

## 17

### The Adoration of the Magi

After Hans Memling

Probably South Lowlands, about 1500

Roundel: diameter, 7⅞ in. (20 cm)

New York, The Metropolitan Museum of Art, The Cloisters Collection, 1983, 1983.235

The Paris drawing relies directly on the composition of the central panel of the *Adoration* triptych painted by Hans Memling for the hospital of Saint John in Bruges in 1479 (fig. 1). Memling's composition derives, in turn, from the central panel of Rogier van der Weyden's *Saint Columba* altarpiece of 1458–59 (fig. 2)[1]—originally in the church of Saint Columba in Cologne—of which Memling, who was for a time associated with Rogier's workshop, probably had firsthand knowledge. With minor alterations, such as the elimination of the donor figure, the providing of a beard to the kneeling king, and some insignificant changes in the architecture, the drawing is faithful to its model, although lateral compression was necessary to accommodate the circular format. Directly copying from a panel painting rather than adaptively employing workshop models is uncommon for roundel production at the end of the fifteenth century. The technique of brown on brown, which provides a very soft and subtle effect that may be an attempt to emulate the

16      17

FIG. 1 Hans Memling. *The Adoration of the Magi* (central panel of the *Adoration* triptych). Tempera and oil on panel. 1479. Bruges, Hospital of Saint John

FIG. 2 Rogier van der Weyden. *The Adoration of the Magi* (central panel of the *Saint Columba* altarpiece). Tempera and oil on panel. 1458–59. Munich, Bayerische Staatsgemäldesammlungen, Alte Pinakothek

warm brown tones of matte commonly in use in the Lowlands, is also unusual. While the white highlights are skillfully employed, the grayish white wash applied to tone the sky is less effective; as the sky over the heads of the two witnesses in the window at the left is blank, it would seem that the wash may have been added later. There is a certain woodenness to this Paris sheet, which, along with its finished state, suggests that it was a copy perhaps intended for a collector rather than for use as a working design by a glass-painting workshop. The roundel—whether relying on this drawing, on a working design based on it, or on a common model—faithfully reproduces the composition with only the slightest modifications of detail; the most noticeable, other than the slight trimming of the circumference, is the addition of the paved flooring.

Lugt observed the influence of Memling as well as the Lower Rhenish qualities in the drawing, noting Dülberg's comparison of its style to

71

FIG. 3 *The Adoration of the Magi.* Painted glass panel. About 1510–20. New York, The Metropolitan Museum of Art, Purchase, Bequest of Kate Read Blacque, in memory of her husband, Valentine Alexander Blacque, Bequest of Thomas W. Lamont and Gift of J. Pierpont Morgan, by exchange, and Rogers Fund, 1982

18

FIG. 1 Jacob Cornelisz. van Oostsanen. *The Agony in the Garden.* Woodcut. 1512. New York, The Metropolitan Museum of Art, The Elisha Whittelsey Collection, The Elisha Whittelsey Fund, 1949

that of the Master of Saint Severin, and he referred to it as "mi-flamand, mi-colonais."[2] The somewhat dry and prosaic rendering of the scene has, in spirit, much in common, for example, with the *Adoration* by the Master of the Legend of Saint George, a Cologne painter active at the end of the fifteenth century who was also much influenced by Rogier van der Weyden.[3] The rays of the Christ Child's halo, the child's active focus on the gift of the Magus, and the bearded, kneeling Magus are also idiosyncracies common to Lower Rhenish interpretations of the scene and can be found in Cologne glass painting as well (see fig. 3). More typical of the Lowlands are the absence of dramatic intensity, the sculptural treatment of the complex drapery folds, and the serenity of the Virgin, whose thoughts appear focused beyond the present episode—all of which impart the sense that the scene was conceived more as a devotional image than as a recording of a historical occurrence. The melding of influences is symptomatic of economic and cultural intercourse between the Lowlands and the Lower Rhineland and underscores the difficulty in localizing many roundels and/or their designs.

The painting of the roundel—especially the skillful use of stippled mattes and stylus work in modeling the figures and the reliance on warm reddish brown tones—is also characteristic of Lowlands production: The particularly rich and dense application of paint seems to accentuate the compressed disposition of the figures. Back painting was used to darken the faces of the donkey and the black Magus. The surface disturbance at the bottom edge of the roundel was caused by

the breaking of a series of blisters after the glass was painted.

A replica of this roundel, in weathered condition, is in the chapel of Cholmondeley Castle, Cheshire.[4]

1. Munich, Bayerische Staatsgemäldesammlungen, Alte Pinakothek, WAF 1189.

2. *Dessins*, 1968, p. 39, no. 126.

3. Germanisches Nationalmuseum, Nuremberg; see Cologne, *Herbst des Mittelalters* (exhib. cat.), 1970, pp. 37–38, no. 7, fig. 7.

4. Cole, *Roundels in Britain*, 1993, p. 57, no. 482.

BIBLIOGRAPHY: (16) Besançon, *Dessins*, 1951, p. 91; Lugt, *Dessins*, 1968, p. 39, no. 126; Worcester, *Northern Renaissance Stained Glass* (exhib. cat.), 1987, pp. 62–63, no. 25, ill. (17) Husband, *Notable Acquisitions 1983–1984*, 1984, p. 19; Worcester, *Northern Renaissance Stained Glass* (exhib. cat.), 1987, pp. 62–63, no. 25, ill.; Husband, *Silver-Stained Roundels*, 1991, p. 148.

## 18

### The Agony in the Garden

North Lowlands, about 1515

Roundel: diameter, 8¾ in. (22.2 cm)

New York, The Metropolitan Museum of Art, The Cloisters Collection, 1988, 1988.304.2

After the Last Supper, Christ went to the garden of Gethsemane to pray and instructed the three disciples who accompanied him—Peter, James, and John—to keep watch. Three times Christ prayed ("Father, if it be possible, let this chalice

pass from me" [Matthew 26: 39]), and three times the disciples fell asleep. Here, Christ is shown praying, a chalice perched on a rock above him, while the disciples sleep in the foreground; in the background, Judas, holding his sack of coins, is about to lead the soldiers through the gate.

While no design for this roundel is known, its composition is close to that of *The Agony in the Garden* from the circular Passion series by Jacob Cornelisz. van Oostsanen (fig. 1; see also cat. nos. 38–42). The composition here is reversed and the figures are disposed in a slightly different manner, but their relationship to the capacious landscape is essentially the same, as is the general organization of the space. The compositional formula was conventionalized and can, in fact, be traced back

FIG. 2 Circle of Pieter Coecke van Aelst. *The Agony in the Garden*. Pen and brown ink on paper. About 1540. Amsterdam, Rijksmuseum, Rijksprentenkabinet

19

FIG. 3 Albrecht Dürer. *The Agony in the Garden*. Woodcut. About 1510. New York, The Metropolitan Museum of Art, The George Khuner Collection, Gift of Mrs. George Khuner, 1975

to Schongauer; it was followed by Dürer in all three of his graphic versions of this scene. The formula persisted and can be seen in a slightly variant form in a design attributed by Boon to the circle of Pieter Coecke van Aelst (fig. 2).[1] The designer of the Cloisters' roundel was certainly aware of versions other than that by Jacob Cornelisz.; the striking view of John in which only the top of his head can be seen may well have been inspired by the analogous scene in Dürer's Small Passion woodcut series of about 1510 (fig. 3). The figure of Peter appears to be a mere variation of his counterpart in Cornelisz.'s ver-

sion, although the latter, itself, is a variation of Peter in Dürer's 1508 engraving (*Ill. Bartsch* 10:4, p. 12), which, in turn, may have been inspired by Schongauer (*Ill. Bartsch* 8:9, p. 222). While some of Jacob Cornelisz.'s compositions from his Passion series—such as the *Taking of Christ*—are clearly dependent on Lucas van Leyden's circular Passion series, this does not seem to be the case here (*Ill. Bartsch* 12:57, p. 189).[2] All three Lowlands versions of the Agony in the Garden do, however, place the scene in a deep landscape with Christ at some distance from his disciples (least so in the roundel), while the German compositions generally tightly group the four figures and limit the spatial recession of the landscape (least so in Dürer's large woodcut [*Ill. Bartsch* 10:6, p. 101]). Jacob Cornelisz.'s version is apparently unique in representing a cave in which the souls are harrowed, below the rocky mount where Christ prays. Whether the curious crack in the earth to the right of the sleeping John in the Cloisters' roundel may be understood as a reference to this same cave is uncertain.

The skillfully painted roundel relies extensively on a fine-pointed brush to describe outlines as well as—along with the more usual stylus work and stippling—the highlights and shadows of the modeling. Gradations of matte tones and back painting are also used to good effect. The progressive lightening of the palette in the receding zones of the landscape heightens the illusion of expansive space. The colorless straight line extending from the upper left to the lower right is not a repaired break but appears to be an inadvertent scoring of the painted surface prior to firing.

1. *Netherlandish Drawings*, 1978, pp. 49–50, no. 136.

2. See Amsterdam, *Lucas van Leyden—grafiek* (exhib. cat.), 1978, pp. 62, 65.

BIBLIOGRAPHY: *European Works of Art* (sale cat.), 1988, n.p., no. 60; Husband, *Silver-Stained Roundels*, 1991, p. 136.

## 19

### The Reading of a Royal Proclamation

Master of the Death of Absalom

North Lowlands, about 1500–1510

Pen, the point of a brush, and black ink, with white and light blue highlights, on gray prepared paper: diameter, 8¼ in. (21 cm)

Staatliche Museen zu Berlin, Preußischer Kulturbesitz, Kupferstichkabinett, KdZ 13448

A small group of stylistically related drawings, many of which are designs for roundels, was first linked by Popham and attributed by him to the Master of the Death of Absalom, after a drawing of that subject now in the Louvre (see fig. 1).[1] Popham believed that this artist worked in Haarlem and, on the basis of van Mander's description of the style of Volckert Claesz., a designer of glass, reasoned that Volckert and the Master of the Death of Absalom might be one and the same.[2] Winkler, conversely, argued that he recognized the hand of Jacob Cornelisz. in these drawings;[3] returning to Popham's view, Steinbart, on the basis of a stylistic similarity to a woodcut of a club-wielding figure on horseback (Joshua or Judas Maccabaeus, one of the Nine Heroes?) that

FIG. 1 Master of the Death of Absalom. *The Death of Absalom*. Pen and brown ink, with blue wash, on paper. About 1500–1510. Paris, Musée du Louvre, Département des Arts Graphiques

FIG. 2 Master of the Death of Absalom. *A Courtly Couple with a Falcon*. Pen and brown ink, with wash, on paper. About 1500–1510. Oxford, Ashmolean Museum

FIG. 3 Master of the Death of Absalom. *Joseph's Brothers Returning to Jacob with Their Corn Money*. Brush and gray ink, with white highlights, on gray prepared paper. About 1500–1510. Dresden, Staatliche Kunstsammlungen, Kupferstich-Kabinett

is monogrammed 𝕄 and dated 1510, proposed that Popham's master apparently was identical to this Monogrammist MG.[4] In addition to the Paris *Death of Absalom*, *The Drunkenness of Noah*, *A Couple Seated before a Fire*, and *March* (cat. no. 97, fig. 1), all in the British Museum,[5] *A Courtly Couple with a Falcon* in Oxford (fig. 2),[6] *Joseph's Brothers Returning to Jacob with Their Corn Money* now in Dresden (fig. 3),[7] a *Saint George and the Dragon* in The Pierpont Morgan Library,[8] and a scene from the moralizing tale of Sorgheloos (see cat. no. 35) are additional designs for roundels that can be associated with this group. Although not a design for a roundel, perhaps the finest drawing that has been attributed to the Master of the Death of Absalom is the Amsterdam *Study with Twenty Heads* (fig. 4).[9] These sheets are executed on both prepared and unprepared paper in varying degrees of finish; there are, however, sufficient variations in both style and quality to suggest that all were not the work of a single hand, but apparently of a workshop. The finished examples were very probably intended as presentation designs rather than working drawings.

The Berlin drawing, the precise subject of which has yet to be fully elucidated, is one of the more refined of the finished examples in this group. The combined use of white and light blue highlights, applied with relatively fine and spare brushstrokes against the gray ground, gives the sheet an unusually luminous appearance. In execution, it can best be compared with the Amsterdam *Study with Twenty Heads* (fig. 4). The broad, highly individualized, and somewhat coarse fea-

FIG. 4 Master of the Death of Absalom. *Study with Twenty Heads*. Brush and gray ink, with white highlights, on dark gray prepared paper. About 1500–1510. Amsterdam, Rijksmuseum, Rijksprentenkabinet

tures of the faces in these studies find close analogies with those of the figures on and below the balcony in the Berlin sheet; similar correspondences are also quite evident in the Dresden drawing (fig. 3). Study sheets of this type must have been in wide currency and were a determinant factor in design dissemination.

1. Popham, "Dutch Designer," 1931, pp. 272–77; for the drawing (Département des Arts Graphiques, 19.218), executed in pen and brown ink, over a greenish blue wash, on paper, see Lugt, *Dessins*, 1968, p. 43, no. 138.

2. "Dutch Designer," 1931, pp. 276–77.

3. "Jacob Cornelisz," 1932, pp. 10–12.

4. *Holzschnittwerk*, 1937, pp. 24–25.

5. Inv. nos. 1927.10.10.52, 1937.2.13.1, and 1930.5.12.2, respectively; for the first and last see Popham, *Drawings in the British Museum*, 1932, p. 82, nos. 71 and 72; the domestic scene was not included.

6. Parker, *Drawings in the Ashmolean Museum*, 1938, pp. 2–3, no. 5, pl. 1.

7. Inv. no. 2732. The roundel design with a courtly hunting party (2230), contrary to Boon (*Netherlandish Drawings*, 1978, p. 192, no. 515, n. 3), appears to me to be quite different in style and technique.

8. Inv. no. PML I, 251; see Stampfle, *Netherlandish Drawings*, 1991, p. 7, pl. 8.

9. Inv. no. RP-T-1921:474; see Boon, *Netherlandish Drawings*, 1978, p. 192, no. 515.

BIBLIOGRAPHY: Bock et al., *Zeichnungen*, 1930, p. 63.

20

## 20

### The Betrayal

After the Master of the Death of Absalom (?)

North Lowlands, about 1500–1510

Roundel: diameter, 9⅛ in. (23.2 cm)

London, Victoria and Albert Museum, 393-1874

This roundel is highly idiosyncratic in both technique and composition. The sheer mass and density of the figures are as remarkable as the sharp contrasts between the darkness of the paint and the brilliance of the broad stickwork highlights amplified with the finer lines of a stylus. This highlight work is most concentrated on the upper portion of the body of Christ and on those of Saint Peter and, to a lesser degree, Malchus; the relative intensities of the resulting brilliance create a natural visual focus in the composition. The lack of facial definition of Malchus, who is about to lose his ear to the sword of Saint Peter, is truly eccentric, given that the painted surface survives in its original, intended state. The pronounced, coarse features of the faces of these highly individualized figures, the variety of bearing of their heads and bodies, and the volumetric presence imparted by the broad, hard sculptural planes of their draped forms all bring to mind the drawings of the Master of the Death of Absalom group. The emphatic lines of stickwork appear to imitate the analogous white highlights in the finished drawing by this master and his workshop. Other details, such as the open mouth of the figure directly behind the standing soldier in armor and a penchant for dark, beady eyes, emerge as

favored motifs of the Death of Absalom group. The technique of this glass painter is singularly distinguished by his system of highlighting, composed of finely etched parallel strokes with the stylus in conjunction with stickwork lines of fluctuating width, often blending into wavy passages. A stylistic idiosyncrasy is found in the curious zigzag passages of the drapery folds, as in the sleeve of Saint Peter's uplifted arm, the boot visible between the legs of the standing soldier in armor, and the sleeve of the raised arm of the gesturing man at the upper right.

A roundel in the Rijksmuseum representing *Ecce Homo*, clearly based on a design from the same series and painted in the same workshop, is probably by a different hand, as the technique is less distinctive than that of the present example (see fig. 1).[1] The same soldier in fanciful armor appearing in the *Betrayal* is seen here from the back. The open mouth and the facial expression, in general, of the soldier holding a spear are so similar to those of Absalom in the Paris drawing (cat. no. 19, fig. 1) that there can be little question of the stylistic connection.

A further roundel, now in The Cloisters Collection, can be linked to the Master of the Death of Absalom group (fig. 2).[2] This roundel, from a series of the *Nine Heroes*, is inscribed *coninck kersten artus*, although, by convention, the hero on camelback was the pagan Alexander the Great, not the Christian King Arthur. The face of the hero corresponds so closely to a face in the first row, second from the left, in the Amsterdam *Study with Twenty Heads* (cat. no. 19, fig. 4) that, again, there can be little doubt of the stylistic correlation.

The Cloisters' roundel apparently was based on a woodcut composition that is preserved as a fragment and is reproduced by Nijhoff (fig. 3).[3] This fragment appears, in turn, to belong to a series of the *Nine Heroes* of which several complete woodcuts survive. One of these, possibly representing either Joshua or Judas Maccabaeus and now in Berlin, is monogrammed M̄ and dated 1510.[4] It was on this basis that Steinbart concluded that the Master of the Death of Absalom and the Monogrammist MG were one and the same.[5] The stylistic correspondence is clear, but given the incessant use of model books, the common authorship of the woodcuts and the drawing remains unestablished.

1. Inv. no. NM 11480. See Beets, *Lucas de Leyde*, 1913, pp. 71–72; Seligman, "Roundel attributed to Lucas van Leyden," 1923, p. 13, fig. V; Popham, "Dutch Designer," 1931, p. 275; Amsterdam, *Bijbelsche Kunst* (exhib. cat.), 1939, no. 110 G; Folmer-von Oven, "Meester," Ph.D. diss., 1974, p. 14; Boon, *Netherlandish Drawings*, 1978, p. 192, no. 515. There is a pen-and-ink drawing by the Master of the Death of Absalom in the Kupferstichkabinett, Berlin (KdZ 5415), representing the same subject but there is no compositional correlation; the head of the youthful figure in the lower-left corner (see Steinbart, *Holzschnittwerk*, 1937, pl. 32), however, is nearly identical to a head in the second row, second from the left, in the Amsterdam *Study with Twenty Heads* (see cat. no. 19, fig. 4). A letter in the departmental registers of the Victoria and Albert Museum notes that the drawing in the British Museum from a series of the Occupations of the Months (cat. no. 97, fig. 1) is probably by the Master of the Death of Absalom but that the *Ecce Homo* roundel is not from the same series as the present roundel because of differences in style and dimensions. While the two roundels probably do not belong together in the same suite produced by one hand, both would seem to come from the same workshop and to rely on the same design source.

2. Inv. no. 36.24.58. See Popham, "Dutch Designer," 1931, p. 276, n. 2; Husband, *Silver-Stained Roundels*, 1991, p. 139.

3. *Nederlandsche houtsneden 1500–1550*, 1931–39, 1520 (17-B).

4. Kupferstichkabinett; see Steinbart, *Holzschnittwerk*, 1937, pp. 24–25, ill. p. 27. According to Popham ("Dutch Designer," 1931, p. 276, n. 2) there were roundels based on two of these woodcuts in the collection of F. E. Sydney at Holly Lodge, Hampstead.

5. *Holzschnittwerk*, 1937, p. 25.

BIBLIOGRAPHY: Popham, "Dutch Designer," 1931, p. 275, pl. 35; Rackham, *Guide to Stained Glass*, 1936, p. 109; Helbig, *Glasschilderkunst*, 1943, p. 210, no. 2027; Amsterdam, *Middeleeuwse kunst* (exhib. cat.), 1958, p. 176, no. 246, fig. 114; Folmer-von Oven, "Meester," Ph.D. diss., 1974, p. 13; Berserik, "Leiden, ca. 1480–1545," 1982, no. 41, fig. 65.

## 21 *see plate 7*

### Christ Being Led Away from Herod Antipas

North Lowlands, about 1515–20

Roundel: diameter (with border), 9½ in. (24.1 cm)

New York, The Metropolitan Museum of Art, The Cloisters Collection, 1932, 32.24.67

21

Inscribed (around the border): *so zalt voortgāe wat ghy bestaet ghy die volck ende lāt regert Gemīt dat recht dat onrecht haet ende des wysheits licht anthiert*

Passion cycles in the later Middle Ages were frequently expanded to include images of specific incidents that were generally omitted in earlier iconographic treatments. The present roundel appears to belong to such an extended cycle. After Christ's arrest he was first taken to the Sanhedrin, the highest Jewish court. According to the Gospel of John, there were two hearings before this court, one before Annas and the other before Caiaphas (John 18: 13, 24). While in the Early Middle Ages this first trial was generally depicted with both high priests together or with Caiaphas alone, by the end of the Middle Ages Christ's appearance before the two high priests was treated as two separate subjects. Caiaphas often can be distinguished from Annas, as he frequently is depicted tearing his clothing in indignation over Christ's avowal of being the Son of God. During this first trial, Christ was struck by a soldier and then was buffeted, spat upon, and otherwise abused by those in attendance. Christ was then taken to the procurator Pilate, but because Jews were not allowed to enter the heathen court of justice, Pilate emerged to hear out the assembled group. It is probably this first encounter with Pilate that is depicted in the background of the present roundel. As Pilate could find no reasonable

grounds for condemning Christ, he chose to evade the problem by turning him over to Herod Antipas, the tetrarch of Galilee. Herod, likewise, found no cause for prosecution, the vehement accusations of the Jews notwithstanding, and, after mockingly ordering Christ to be arrayed in a white robe, Herod then sent him back to Pilate. Because, following late medieval iconography, Pilate generally was depicted in aristocratic dress while Herod wore a crown, verification of the subject of this roundel is strengthened. It is unclear why Christ is wearing a crown of thorns in both scenes, as the actual crowning did not take place until after the second hearing before Pilate. The composition and the iconographic sequence may have been influenced by Dürer's Small Passion woodcut series of about 1508–10 in which the scene of Christ before Pilate, standing on the steps outside the temple (fig. 1), precedes that of Christ before Herod Antipas, seated and holding a scepter (fig. 2); in Dürer's sequence, this is followed by Christ at the Column, the Crowning with Thorns, Ecce Homo, and Pilate washing his hands (*Ill. Bartsch* 10:33-36, pp. 128–31).

The composition of the roundel creates an uncommon internal narrative flow: In the background Christ, moving toward the right, is brought before Pilate, while in the foreground, moving off to the left, Christ is being led away from Herod. This compositional device thus averts the frequent static quality of conventional-

FIG. 1 Albrecht Dürer. *Christ before Pilate.* Woodcut. 1508–10. New York, The Metropolitan Museum of Art, The George Khuner Collection, Gift of Mrs. George Khuner, 1975

FIG. 2 Albrecht Dürer. *Christ before Herod Antipas.* Woodcut. 1509. New York, The Metropolitan Museum of Art, The George Khuner Collection, Gift of Mrs. George Khuner, 1975

FIG. 3 *Ecce Homo.* Roundel. About 1515–20. Ghent, Bijlokemuseum

FIG. 4 *Christ Carrying the Cross.* Roundel. About 1515–20. Ghent, Bijlokemuseum

FIG. 5 Lucas van Leyden. *Ecce Homo* (detail). Engraving. 1510. New York, The Metropolitan Museum of Art, Harris Brisbane Dick Fund, 1927

ized scenes of standard devotional iconography. The text within the border here—borders are rarely preserved, as they were generally destroyed when the roundels they encircled were broken out of their original glazings—is not the appropriate passage from the Gospels, but an interpretive commentary on the event, and can be translated: Thus it will proceed, whatever you who govern land and people try to do; He loves the right, abhors the wrong, and avails Himself of the light of wisdom. The source has not been identified, but it may be one of the many popular texts and commentaries issued by the prolific Antwerp presses. The tone is somewhat polemical and seems to be an admonition to all those in a position of political power to execute their authority with righteousness, wisdom, and a love of God, following the example of Christ.

At least two other roundels from the same series have survived and are now in the Bijlokemuseum, Ghent; one represents the *Ecce Homo* (fig. 3) and the other Christ carrying the cross (fig. 4);[1] neither retains its original border. The letters *S V O*, which appear above the fringe of Herod's canopy, are repeated on the hem of the sleeve of the foreground figure in the *Ecce Homo*; their meaning, if any, is unknown. No designs for the series are known, and its origin remains obscure. The designer appears, however, to have been familiar with the work of Lucas van Leyden. The witness with the fur cap leaning on the parapet in the Cloisters' roundel, for example, is reminiscent of the analogous figure in Lucas's 1514 engraving *The Idolatry of Solomon* (*Ill. Bartsch* 12:30, p. 162), while the middle figure in the group to the right in the Ghent *Ecce Homo* finds a close double in the stout man holding a cane in the foreground of Lucas's large *Ecce Homo* (fig. 5). The present roundel is unusually painterly in technique. While the several tones of paint are occasionally worked with a badger brush, most of the modeling is achieved by extensive hatching with a fine-pointed brush or stippler amplified by etching, which produces particularly subtle textures and highlights. The extensive use of back painting adds further depth and tonality to the scene. The front surface of the glass, particularly along the lower edge, has been extensively pitted by corrosion.

1. Inv. nos. 9036 and 9039.

BIBLIOGRAPHY: Husband, *Silver-Stained Roundels,* 1991, p. 152.

## 22

### Allegory of Rout and Pillage

North Lowlands, Leiden (?), about 1515–20
Roundel: diameter, 9¾ in. (24.8 cm)
New York, The Metropolitan Museum of Art, Rogers Fund, 1912, 12.137.7

In the foreground of this dense composition a woman kneels at the side of a cradle rocking a sleeping baby. Just behind the cradle, jutting diagonally into the air, are a mast with a crow's nest

22

23

and pennant and a church spire surmounted by a cross. Directly in front and seemingly inconsistent in scale are a towered gateway, a belfry, a book next to a chalice on its side, a pouch attached to a belt, and an unidentified scalloped object. Standing to the right are two women holding a variety of metalwork vessels and flanked by a sheep and a cow. At the left, one man shoulders a coffer and another a large, lumpy sack; a third man upturns a gaming table with cards on it; and yet another drives two cattle with a switch. In the near background, a soldier wields a sword at a man, a woman throws up her arms, two men are deep in discussion, and another ignites the house behind him with a torch. In the far background, an architectural complex is in flames, while, at the left, a man drives a herd of cattle toward an approaching army preceded by a flying banner.

The meaning of this densely composed scene, massed with a curious accumulation of objects and activity, is unclear. Its apparent allegorical content seems to derive from the inherent contrasts: peace and pacifism opposing conflict and violence; the spiritual counterposing the profane; and order juxtaposing disorder. In a society whose prosperity and well-being depended heavily on prudent governance and civic harmony, allegories inveighing against economic and social disruption must have found attentive audiences.

The wide, rounded faces with high foreheads—particularly in the cases of the women—the sharp contrast of shadow to highlight, and the broad, crumpled tubular drapery folds typify the styles associated especially with Leiden and, to a lesser extent, with Amsterdam and Utrecht. The technique accords as well: The roundel shares the characteristic tones of light and dark brown paint

along with bright yellow silver stain; the forms are outlined in fine brushstrokes, often amplified with stickwork highlights; and the modeling, likewise, is achieved with stickwork and with the stylus, the point of the brush, and gradated matte tones. There is a star shatter at the base of the spire with four radiating and other breaks, now glued; grozed areas along some of these breaks have been filled and inpainted, as has a loss at the left edge.

BIBLIOGRAPHY: Drake, *English Glass-Painting*, 1912, pl. 26, fig. 1; Husband, *Silver-Stained Roundels*, 1991, p. 145.

## 23

### Saint James Intercisus

North Lowlands, Leiden (?), about 1520

Roundel: diameter, 8¾ in. (22.2 cm)

New York, The Metropolitan Museum of Art, The Cloisters Collection, 1991, 1991.291.2

Saint James Intercisus ("chopped to pieces") enjoyed the favor of the Persian king Yazdigerd I during the early fifth century. Because of his friendship with the king and the honors and wealth the latter bestowed upon him, James abandoned his Christian belief during the persecutions in about 420. When Yazdigerd died, James's mother and wife wrote to him, rebuking him for his faithlessness. Taking their admonitions to heart, James renounced all his honors and ceased to appear at court. The new king, Bahram, decided that for such ungratefulness James deserved a painful and lingering death. Unless James renounced Christ, he would be slowly dismembered, joint by joint, starting with his fingers. As James refused to re-

cant, the executioners proceeded with their work until James was a limbless trunk. He was still praising God when his head was finally severed.

Saint James, with his cap pulled over his eyes, kneels before an executioner's block awaiting the imminent cleaving of his left hand; his other hand and his feet lie in the dirt in the foreground. At the far right, another victim, secured by a rope, awaits his torment. The scene is witnessed from a window or gallery by King Bahram and two courtiers. Visible through the arch at the left are heads and various human extremities displayed on pikes from the city gate. Other prisoners peer out of the gloom behind the bars in the arched opening below the onlooking king.

The roundel is painted in unusually dark and dense tones, providing a suitably somber atmosphere for this gruesome scene. The bold stickwork of the highlighting and the deep golden-yellow hues of silver stain—largely reserved for costume elements and for the cloth on the parapet—dramatically contrast with the almost black depths of the drapery folds and the shadowy recesses of the architecture. The subtle blending of paint tones and the fine-lined etching of details, as in the hair and costumes, lend a luminous resonance to the painting. The flatter, thinner paint in the background scene through the arch; the unsure lines; and the nervous etching of the stylus suggest that this area was painted by an altogether different hand.

A replica of this roundel was formerly in the Kunstgewerbemuseum, Berlin.[1]

1. See Schmitz, *Glasgemälde* 1, 1913, pp. 69, 70, fig. 117.

BIBLIOGRAPHY: Unpublished

## An Ass Playing a Portative Organ

South Lowlands, about 1480

Pen and brown ink on paper: diameter, 8 in.
(20.3 cm)

Oxford, Ashmolean Museum, PI 1

The ass, held in a barrel chair by a safety bar, places his hooves on the keyboard as if to play the portative organ. With pince-nez perched upon his muzzle and a book of musical notation spread before him, the ass opens his maw to receive a thistle being proferred by a man in a cap and a fur-trimmed robe, probably an academic. A woman is pumping the bellows behind the organ. Although clearly a satirical subject, the precise meaning is unclear.

The image is certainly related to the oft-represented *Ass and the Lyre* based on the fable of Phaedrus: An ass found a lyre abandoned in a meadow. "I know nothing of music," he said. "If anyone else had found this lyre, he would be able to charm the ears with its divine harmonies." In other words, it is not necessarily for lack of innate ability that the ass cannot make music, but because the very circumstances of its existence preclude the possibility. Mâle, however, has suggested that it was not Phaedrus's fable but the famous comment of Philosophy in Boëthius's *De consolatione philosophiae*—required reading for every cleric—that made this a popular image: "Listen to my words, or are you like an ass before a lyre?"[1] The implication here is that the creation of music simply transcends the understanding of an ass.

The subject of the Ass and the Lyre frequently appears in Romanesque church sculpture, presumably as a reminder to young clerics to apply themselves to the teachings of the Church. A Latin poem of the fourteenth century tells of a prince who is born in the form of an ass and, nonetheless, is taught music and the arts, thus amplifying the moral;[2] circumstances therefore are overcome and the prince/ass effectively masters the lyre. In this context, the Ass and the Lyre does not refer to the animal in a deprecatory manner but uses him as a reminder of the music contained in the harp, which cannot be elicited by everyone and which knowledge and beauty can transcend. Images of the Ass and the Lyre appear on baptismal fonts and in Missals to signify that

24

FIG. 2 *Asses and Apes Singing. Bas-de-page* manuscript illumination from the *Voeux du Paon* by Jacques du Longuyon (detail). About 1350. New York, The Pierpont Morgan Library

FIG. 1 *An Ass Operating a Trebuchet. Bas-de-page* manuscript illumination from a Book of Hours (detail). About 1300. London, British Library

FIG. 3 *An Ass Playing a Cornetto and a Cat Beating a Tabor. Bas-de-page* manuscript illumination from the *Psalter of Queen Mary* (detail). About 1300–1325. London, British Library

the meek will inherit the Kingdom of Heaven; according to commentaries on Matthew 21: 5, the ass is represented among baptized carnal as opposed to spiritual man.[3]

The metaphor appears to have been extended in the later Middle Ages, as the ass is depicted in manuscript marginalia engaged in a variety of unlikely activities. An ass is seen operating a trebuchet in the *bas-de-page* illustration of a Book of Hours illuminated in Maastricht about 1300 (fig. 1),[4] but of all those activities for which he is totally unsuited, the ass is most often shown engaged in music making. In a mid-fourteenth-century Franco-Flemish copy of Jacques du Longuyon's *Voeux du Paon* two asses sing, accompanied by two apes serving as choristers, from a musical manuscript displayed on a lectern before them (fig. 2).[5] In the *Psalter of Queen Mary*, an ass blows on a cornetto while a cat beats a tabor (fig. 3).[6]

By the end of the Middle Ages, the ass was depicted engaged in human activities that seem to have become more satirical, underscoring the laughable incompetence of the beast to perform the tasks he attempts. Erasmus, in his 1533 *Adagiorum opus*, provides an explication of the saying "Asinus portans mysteria" ("an ass carrying mysteries"), which, he explains, applies to a person "who occupies a position that he does not deserve, such as an illiterate working as a librarian."[7]

The present drawing seems to take a satirical view of the Romanesque versions of the fable, and underscores the ludicrousness of an ass learning anything. The academic obviously can have no success at teaching the beast to play the portative organ. The thistle, which the academic feeds the ass, probably refers to a medieval maxim that declares that even when much better food is available the ass will eat the thistle. This would seem to reflect as much on the academic as on the ass, for it would be difficult to decide which effort is the more futile: the scholar trying to teach the ass or the ass trying to play the organ.

The drawing, which Parker has associated with the Hugo van der Goes group (the Master of the Story of Tobit),[8] is executed with linear economy and clarity. The limited modeling is achieved entirely through cross-hatching, the darkest areas rendered in a dense diamond-pane pattern. While a certain stiffness and lack of correction suggest that the drawing is an early copy, it nonetheless retains its engaging spirit and remains a rare example of satirical subject matter in roundels.

The sheet has been slightly trimmed at the left and perhaps likewise at the perimeter.

1. Mâle, *Twelfth Century*, 1978, p. 340.

2. Bolte and Polívka, *Hausmärchen der Brüder Grimm* 3, 1918, pp. 152 ff.

3. See Adolf, "The Ass and the Harp," 1950, esp. p. 52.

4. London, British Library, Stowe Ms. 17, f. 243 *v*.

5. New York, The Pierpont Morgan Library, Glazier Ms. 24, f. 48.

6. London, British Library, Ms. Royal 2 B.VII, f. 194 *v*.

7. See Veldman, "The idol on the ass," 1973, pp. 22–23.

8. Parker, *Drawings in the Ashmolean Museum*, 1938, p. 1, no. 1.

BIBLIOGRAPHY: Parker, *Drawings in the Ashmolean Museum*, 1938, no. 1, pl. 1; de Tervarent, *Attributs et Symboles*, 1958, p. 30.

## 25

### The Death of Narcissus

Master of the Joseph Series (?)

South Lowlands, about 1480

Pen and black ink on paper: diameter, 8¼ in. (21 cm)

Paris, Musée du Louvre, Département des Arts Graphiques, 20.659

The authorship of this drawing has been much discussed in the literature. Dülberg gave this amusing design for a roundel its first attribution, regarding it as the work of a follower of Geertgen tot Sint Jans, the Master of the Virgo inter Virgines, after noting the similarity of the woman at the right to the corresponding one in the Liverpool *Lamentation* (fig. 1).[1] This attribution subsequently was accepted by many critics, including Friedländer,[2] and, more recently, van Regteren Altena.[3] Popham was the first to associate this sheet with the work of the Hugo van der Goes group and with the miniatures of the putative Bruges artist Philippe de Mazerolles, later preferring the Ghent artist Lieven van Lathem.[4] The last miniaturist is said to have had two sons, of which one, Jacob, entered the service of Philippe le Beau, Duke of Burgundy; it was this Jacob van Lathem (Laethem) that Friedländer suggested

25

FIG. 1 Master of the Virgo inter Virgines. *The Lamentation*. Tempera and oil on panel. About 1480. Liverpool, Walker Art Gallery

FIG. 2 *The Death of Narcissus*. Historiated initial from a moralized Ovid manuscript. About 1475. Paris, Bibliothèque Nationale

26

FIG. 1 Dieric Bouts. *The Fall of the Damned.* Tempera and oil on panel. About 1470. Lille, Musée des Beaux-Arts

might be one and the same as the artist of the Master of the Joseph Series tondi (see cat. no. 10).[5] Lugt, while noting similarities to the style of the Master of the Turin Adoration, was tempted to go along with this suggested attribution while not discounting Popham's grouping.[6] While the stylistic comparison to the Liverpool *Lamentation* is compelling, arguments linking the present sheet with the Master of the Joseph Series group are more convincing.

Although Hoogewerff suggested that this drawing may have illustrated a contemporary book by the writer Dirk Potter entitled *Der Minnen Loop*,[7] it is now generally accepted that the drawing depicts the Death of Narcissus; a similar rendering of the subject in a miniature from a moralized Ovid manuscript would seem to confirm the identification (fig. 2).[8]

Narcissus, the beautiful son of the river-god Cephissus and the nymph Liriope, who was born at Thespis in Boetia, appears in Ovid's *Metamorphoses* (3: 341 ff.). He saw his image reflected in the waters of a fountain and became so enamored of it that he pined his life away and eventually turned into the eponymous flower. This was viewed as poetic justice for his hard-hearted attitude toward Echo and the other nymphs. In the version by Eudocia, which seems to have influenced the present representation, Narcissus became sufficiently distraught over his obsession that he threw himself into the fountain and drowned.

1. *Frühholländer* 4, n.d. [1908], pl. 5. The *Lamentation* is in the Walker Art Gallery, 37; see Friedländer, *Early Netherlandish Painting* 5, 1969, p. 39, no. 58, pl. 39.

2. See *Early Netherlandish Painting* 5, 1969, p. 44.

3. In Amsterdam, *Middeleeuwse kunst* (exhib. cat.), 1958, p. 136, no. 178, pl. 94.

4. "Notes-I," 1928, p. 179. Winkler (*Hugo van der Goes*, 1964, p. 284) considered all the drawings in Popham's group, including the present sheet, to be "von oder nach demselben Zeichner."

5. *Early Netherlandish Painting* 4, 1969, p. 64.

6. *Dessins*, 1968, p. 40, no. 127.

7. *Noord-Nederlandsche Schilderkunst* 2, 1937, p. 275, fig. 132.

8. Paris, Bibliothèque Nationale, Ms. fr. 137, fol. 37 *v*, the initial *N*.

BIBLIOGRAPHY: Dülberg, *Frühholländer* 4, n.d. [1908], pl. 5; Beets, "Schilder- en beeldhouwkunst," 1914, p. 92, fig. 5, and p. 100; Winkler, "Meister der Anna Selbdritt," 1922, p. 612; Popham, "Notes-I," 1928, pp. 178–79, fig. 7; Rotterdam, *Noord-nederlandsche Primitieven* (exhib. cat.), 1936, pp. 60–61, no. 10, pl. 9; Hoogewerff, *Noord-nederlandsche Schilderkunst* 2, 1937, pp. 274–75, fig. 132; Popham, "Flemish Miniaturists," 1938, p. 17; Amsterdam, *Middeleeuwse kunst* (exhib. cat.), 1958, pp. 136–37, no. 178, pl. 94; Lugt, *Dessins*, 1968, pp. 39–40, no. 127; Friedländer, *Early Netherlandish Painting* 5, 1969, p. 44, pl. 135 A.

## 26

### The Fall of the Damned

After Dieric Bouts

South Lowlands, Leuven (?), about 1500–1510

Roundel: diameter, 8½ in. (21.6 cm)

New York, The Metropolitan Museum of Art, The Cloisters Collection, 1990, 1990.119.2

FIG. 2 Workshop of Dieric Bouts. *The Fall of the Damned.* Pen and brown ink on paper. About 1500–1510. Paris, Musée du Louvre, Département des Arts Graphiques

The composition and style of this roundel are largely inspired by Dieric Bouts. Although the roundel does not rely on a particular work, elements of the composition are freely adapted. The three-quarter-length female figure pulling at her hair, for example, clearly quotes the analogous figure in the panel painting of the same subject by Dieric Bouts, now in the Musée des Beaux-Arts, Lille (fig. 1).[1] In this vision of hell, the glass painter, following Bouts, saw the realm of the damned as largely inhabited by the male of the species—and by demons, of course. The dependence of both compositions on common or related earlier sources is indicated by a drawing, now in the Louvre, which appears to be an early-sixteenth-century copy of a fifteenth-century original (fig. 2).[2] The man with upraised arms seen from the rear at the right in the Lille panel is nearly identical to the figure at the left in the drawing, while the standing demon with a naked victim tossed over his back is close to the analogous group in the Paris sheet; another damned soul, more prominently placed at the right in the roundel, is similarly draped over the back of an exceedingly grotesque demon. The Janus-faced monster in the Cloisters' roundel, whose head is turned back and who is about to bite down on the tonsured head of a monk, again has no direct model, but the pair certainly could have been inspired by the comparable foreground group in the Paris drawing.

The Lille panel can be paired with another panel in the same museum—the *Terrestrial Paradise* (fig. 3).[3] A painting now in Munich incorporates virtual copies of the Lille *Paradise* on the left side and of the *Fall* on the right, with a *Last Judgment* in between (fig. 4).[4] This has been used as evidence to argue that the Lille panels once served as the wings of a triptych of the Last Judgment.[5] The two foreground figures in the Munich central scene, however, are simply weak variants of two of the saved souls in the Lille panel, suggesting that the Munich canvas is a fabrication and does not preserve the composition of the lost central panel. Therefore, it is possible that the Lille panels did not, in fact, flank a *Last Judgment* but were paired with panels depicting terrestrial Paradise and hell; such an arrangement may have provided the model for the four analogous panels by Hieronymus Bosch now in the Palazzo Ducale, Venice (fig. 5).[6] This arrangement reflects the widely held belief that immediately after death each individual had to submit to a personal reckoning and was then dispatched, depending on his merits or lack thereof, to a place of torment or bliss where the Last Judgment was awaited; this doctrine was discussed, for example, in the tract written by a Carthusian entitled *Dialogue on the Particular Judgment of God*.[7] Alternatively, the two Lille panels may have formed the wings of a triptych representing *The Art of Dying Well*. A prototype of this arrangement is found, for instance, in the title miniature of the Office of the Dead in the Book of Hours of Galeazzo Maria Sforza—the so-called *Black Hours*—which shows a man on his deathbed confronting the sins of a lifetime; through the double

FIG. 6 *The Office of the Dead*. Illuminated manuscript page from the *Sforza* or *Black Hours* (detail). 1466–76. Vienna, Österreichisches Nationalbibliothek

arches at the foot of his bed, the only two alternatives of the imminent destiny of his soul are shown: either it will be condemned to the furnace of hell or led to the paradise of Heaven (fig. 6).[8]

The *Ars moriendi*, or *The Art of Dying*, inspired by the writing of Jean de Gerson (1363–1429), was one of the most popular books in the Late Middle Ages. The text, which appeared initially in Latin and later in numerous vernacular translations, tells of and usually illustrates the five evils of the devil that are visited upon a dying man in his last hours—faithlessness, despair, impatience, vainglory, and avarice—and the angelic inspiration, or *bona inspiration*, which brings spiritual recovery by countering these failings. It is, then, a text that warns of the end to come and serves as a practical guide to dying in a Christian manner. Manuscript versions appeared in the early fifteenth century and block-book versions, in which text pages alternated with full-page woodcut illustrations, were first published in the Netherlands in the 1460s.

Because of the emblematic nature of the block-book illustrations of the *Ars moriendi*, the images often were separated from the books and pinned up on the walls of bedchambers for contemplative and instructional purposes. In this context it is tempting to consider the present roundel as part of an analogous triad, along with images of Paradise and a deathbed scene, of which models abound (see fig. 7). Such a "triptych" glazed into the windows of a private chamber would form the roundel equivalent of the image in the *Sforza Hours*, serving as a daily reminder of the transience of worldly existence, which was viewed as mere preparation for eternal life after death.

FIG. 7 *Deathbed Scene*. Block-book illustration from the *Ars moriendi*. About 1496. New York, The Metropolitan Museum of Art, Harris Brisbane Dick Fund, 1923

Whatever the original context, the composition was apparently very popular, as a number of close versions exist; these include examples in Ghent[9] and Antwerp,[10] in York,[11] and another also in The Cloisters,[12] as well as one in the church of Saint Mary, Stoke d'Abernon, Surrey.[13] The present example, painted with considerable refinement, is the finest. Notable is the extensive, painterly use of the point of the brush, amplified by stippling, but with a minimal use of the stylus. The paint has been slightly rubbed in places, with some areas of loss, mostly in the rump and the hind leg of the Janus-headed dragon. A clean vertical break through the roundel has been skillfully glued.

1. Inv. no. 1808. The panel, which had previously belonged to the Musée du Louvre, was acquired by exchange.

2. See Lugt, *Dessins*, 1968, p. 23, no. 66, pl. 33.

3. Musée des Beaux-Arts, Lille, 820.

4. Bayerische Staatsgemäldesammlungen, Alte Pinakothek, 1379.

5. Châtelet, "Sur un Jugement dernier," 1965, pp. 22–24. Veronée-Verhaegen in "La Chute des Damnés," 1972, pp. 20–28, argues that the panels did form the wings of a *Last Judgment*, but in the context of Charity, and that the triptych was intended for a hospital and not as a *tableau* of Justice.

6. Châtelet, "Sur un Jugement dernier," 1965, pp. 27–28.

7. See Gibson, *Hieronymus Bosch*, 1973, pp. 61–67.

8. See Châtelet, "Sur un Jugement dernier," 1965, pp. 29–31.

9. Bijlokemuseum, 9033.

10. Museum Mayer van den Bergh, 652.

11. Formerly Collection Peter Newton.

12. The Cloisters Collection, 32.24.43 (see Husband, *Silver-Stained Roundels*, 1991, p. 142).

13. See Cole, *Roundels in Britain*, 1993, p. 265, no. 2102.

BIBLIOGRAPHY: Grosvenor Thomas Stock Book, I, p. 18, no. 172; Husband, *Silver-Stained Roundels*, 1991, p. 142.

27

## 27  *see plate 8*

### Death, with a Pope, a Prince, and a Peasant

North Lowlands, 1510–20

Roundel: diameter, 8¾ in. (22.2 cm)

New York, The Metropolitan Museum of Art, The Cloisters Collection, 1977, 1977.89

In the arresting imagery of this roundel, Death, partially draped and semi-decomposed, hovers above a peasant holding a shepherd's shovel, a prince with a crown and an ermine-trimmed mantle, and a pope wearing the triple tiara whom the grim figure is preparing to pierce with an outsized arrow. None of the estates of man nor any social stratum, no matter how privileged in life, enjoys immunity from Death, the universal leveler of all men. Indeed, all living things inevitably are harvested by Death, as, in the background, cattle, birds, and fish perish in his wake. Only the owl, the knowing witness, perched on the side of a hillock in the middle ground, seems to be spared.[1]

Death armed with an arrow has long been associated with pestilence; according to Jacobus de Voragine, Saint Gregory the Great reports that the plague of 590 in Rome was accompanied by a hail of arrows. Because Saint Sebastian survived the arrows of Diocletian's executioners the faithful believed that he could protect them from the plague.[2] Often, the plague is viewed as divine retribution and is represented by God hurling down arrows on mortal man.[3] Thus, in a fresco by Benozzo Gozzoli painted in San Gimignano in 1464 during an outbreak of plague, the citizens of the town are shown escaping the arrows raining down from Heaven by hiding under Saint Sebastian's mantle (see fig. 1).

By the end of the fifteenth century, however, a partially draped skeleton or semi-decomposed body holding an arrow or lancet was, in Northern imagery, the conventional representation of Death, with or without reference to the plague (see fig. 2). Death so represented frequently is shown encountering his unsuspecting victims as they perform their daily tasks, pursuing them as they flee in fright, or entering their chambers for the unwelcome final appointment (see fig. 3). Such portrayals are closely related to the Dance of Death, a theme that was established in the second half of the fifteenth century. In these extended series of images, Death, in a variety of positions, gestures, and expressions, is seen dancing around individuals with diverse occupations and from all classes of society.[4] In Hans Holbein the Younger's Dance of Death series, for example, some forty-odd woodcuts show Death encountering Adam and Eve followed by individuals from the ranks of royalty and the aristocracy, the Church, the military, and monasteries, as well as representatives of the professions and rural occupations, and of the three Ages of Man (see fig. 4). In all, Holbein's Dance of Death appeared in twelve editions, the last dating from 1562 and with fifty-two illustrations. Numerous other versions of this highly popular theme also were published, all underscoring the transitory nature of earthly possessions, wealth, power, and of life itself.

The present roundel, the finest surviving example of this composition, is painted in bright yellow silver stain and the brown matte tones so familiar in the Lowlands. This painter employed both the stylus and the fine point of a brush to outline and model forms to considerable effect. The cursory stylus work to highlight plant life, by contrast, is somewhat heavy-handed. Highly unusual, however, is the extensive green paint, generally yet infrequently found only in sixteenth-century German roundels. The gradation of colors achieved by skillfully mingling the hues of the silver stain with the paint is exceptional.

A variant of this roundel is in the Museum Mayer van den Bergh, Antwerp,[5] and another was formerly in the collection of James R. Herbert Boone, Baltimore (see fig. 5).[6]

1. For an extensive discussion of the negative symbolism of the owl see Vandenbroeck, "Bubo significans," 1985, pp. 19–135.

FIG. 1 Benozzo Gozzoli. *The Intercession of Saint Sebastian*. Fresco. 1464. San Gimignano, Sant'Agostino

2. See Perdrizet, *La Vierge de Miséricorde*, 1908, pp. 107–10.

3. For this theme see Hagemann, *Der göttliche Pfeilschütze*, 1982, pp. 9–47.

4. For the Dance of Death and related texts dealing with the satire of the three estates see Pleij, *Blauwe Schuit*, 1983, pp. 170–77.

5. Inv. no. 651.

6. *European Works of Art* (sale cat.), 1988, n.p., no. 63.

BIBLIOGRAPHY: Husband, *Silver-Stained Roundels*, 1991, p. 145.

FIG. 2 *The Triumph of Death*. Manuscript illumination from a North Lowlands Book of Hours. About 1500–1510. Utrecht, Rijksmuseum Het Catharijneconvent

FIG. 4 Hans Holbein the Younger. *Death Taking a Child*. Woodcut illustration from *The Dance of Death* (detail). 1538. New York, The Metropolitan Museum of Art, Rogers Fund, 1919

FIG. 3 Hieronymus Bosch. *Death and the Miser*. Tempera and oil on panel. About 1485–90. Washington, D.C., National Gallery of Art, Samuel H. Kress Collection

FIG. 5 *Death, with a Pope, a Prince, and a Peasant*. Roundel. About 1510–20. Formerly Baltimore, Collection James R. Herbert Boone

## 28

## June, and the Thirty-six Year Old: from a series of the Ages of Man and the Months

Lowlands, about 1475–1500

Roundel: diameter, 8 in. (20.3 cm)

London, Victoria and Albert Museum, 1239-1855

The subject of this roundel, referred to in the past as a "grocer,"[1] thus previously eluded incisive interpretation. A weaker and probably somewhat later version of the roundel, but clearly based on the same design, is in the Musées Royaux d'Art et d'Histoire, Brussels (fig. 1),[2] joined by a companion roundel representing a young man with hounds and a falcon (fig. 2). Both roundels have an inscription around their outer edge: That on the latter reads: *Schieloos als maerte wulpsch zonder sparen zo zijn de jonghers van xviij Jaren* (Unsettled as [the weather in] March, wanton without saving up [for the future], thus are the young men of 18 years); while the former reads: *Ten xxxvj Jaren zal men werken on proffijt zo wij de wedemaent mercken* (At the age of 36 one has to work for profits, as we typify the month of June).[3] It can now be determined that the present roundel belongs to a series devoted to the Ages of Man, linked to the months of the year.

The Ages of Man was a popular theme throughout the Middle Ages. A division into four ages, corresponding to the seasons, was common, as was a division into seven, relating as it does to the phases of the moon. Although a division into twelve would seem obvious because of the correspondence to the number of months as well as the number of apostles, it is, in fact, a rarity. The formula of man's life-span being divided into twelve units of six years each first appears in a fourteenth-century French poem, which salubriously describes the characteristics of each month, the seasons, and the nature of man at the corresponding incremental age, but in a more cynical vein it also notes that man sleeps for half his life, wastes the first fifteen years in immaturity, squanders at least five more years in illness or in prison, and, if he marries, dissipates his entire existence.[4] The popularity of the poem is evidenced by its appearance in *Le Grant Kalendrier et Compost des Bergiers*, first printed in Paris in 1491; by an enlarged edition of 1493; and by its continual inclusion in the many subsequent editions dating from the early sixteenth well into the seventeenth century. In the Netherlands, six or more editions—essentially rearrangements and abridgments of the French—were published under the title *Der Scaepherders Kalendier*, and all seem to have been printed in Antwerp.[5] A French version, much reduced in length, consisting of twelve quatrains, often appears in breviaries and Books of Hours. The following verses for March and June are found, for example, in a Book of Hours of Roman usage printed in Paris by Simon Vostre on September 16, 1498:[6]

*Mars signifie les six ans ensuivans*
*Que le temps change en produissant verdure;*
*En celluy aage s'adonnent les enfans*
*A maint esbat, sans soucy ne sans cure.*

and

*En Juing, les biens commencent à meurir;*
*Aussi fait l'homme quant a trente-six ans;*
*Pour ce en tel temps doit-il femme quérir*
*Se luy vivant veult pourveoir ses enfans.*

A similar poem by Anthonis de Roovere of Bruges, entitled *Twaelf Ouderdommen oft Tijden der Menschen/Ghecompareert teghens die tweelf Maenden vanden Jare* and written before 1482, reduces the composition to twelve triplets.[7] While the precise textual source for the inscriptions on the Brussels roundels is unknown, they clearly derive from the more terse renditions of this literary tradition. The present roundel, no doubt, originally had an inscribed border leaded around it. The Brussels roundels also include the appropriate zodiacal sign in a disc at the upper edge of the central image: Aries and Cancer, respectively. The corresponding zodiacal sign likewise may have appeared in the original border of the present roundel.

Curiously, the scale in this roundel is not properly balanced; rather than the pointer being absolutely vertical and the beam horizontal, both are askew, while the pans, which seem to focus the attention of the annotating merchant, are in equilibrium by virtue of the fact that the ropes from which they are suspended are of unequal lengths. The result of this unbalanced scale is, of course, that the merchant—presumably by intention—is consistently underweighing his goods. If putting aside the difference is this man's meaning of "work for profits," it is a cynical commentary, indeed.

The roundel is executed in brown paint with dark yellow silver stain. The control exercised in the building up of the paint tones and in the stylus work is unusually refined. While large areas of the glass are left clear, the tonalities of the composition, which show exceptional delicacy in the gradations, remain remarkably balanced. Although not emphatic, there is considerable stylus work throughout, notably in the hair, on the sacks of goods, and in the ropes of the scales to indicate the twisting of the fibers. There is also an unusually extensive amount of back painting, which creates an exceptionally effective appearance of three dimensionality; this is most evident in the

28

FIG. 1 *June, and the Thirty-six Year Old*: from a series of the Ages of Man and the Months. Roundel. About 1500. Brussels, Musées Royaux d'Art et d'Histoire

FIG. 2 *March, and the Eighteen Year Old*: from a series of the Ages of Man and the Months. Roundel. About 1500. Brussels, Musées Royaux d'Art et d'Histoire

merchant's hat, where the surface paint has been worked to such thinness, or else removed altogether, so that one can actually see through to the back-painted surface. There is a break, now skillfully glued, that runs vertically through the left leg of the merchant to the upper-right edge. There are also two pieces of frit attached to the front of the roundel that are conspicuous under surface lighting but difficult to detect when it is back lit.

Popham believed that this roundel was related stylistically to the Amsterdam Acts of Mercy series (see cat. nos. 46–48) but close comparison offers scant support for this supposition.[8]

1. Rackham, *Guide to Stained Glass*, 1936, p. 109, pl. 47 b.

2. There is, additionally, another later and weaker version of this roundel with the same inscription, in the Kikker collection, Amsterdam.

3. I am grateful to Prof. Herman Pleij, Universiteit van Amsterdam, Instituut voor Neerlandistiek, for the transcriptions and translations, as well as for directing me to the principal literature on the Ages of Man associated with the months.

4. Paris, Bibliothèque Nationale, Ms. fr. 1728. For an extensive study of the Ages of Man divided into twelve increments of six years each see Dal, *The Ages of Man*, 1980, pp. 7–27.

5. Ibid., pp. 25–27.

6. Ibid., p. 58.

7. See de Roovere, *Gedichten*, 1955, pp. 299–300. For further information on the Ages of Man and the months in Netherlandish literature see Meder, "Het leven in twaalf maanden," 1990, pp. 22–28. I am grateful to Prof. Herman Pleij for bringing both of these texts to my attention.

8. "Notes-II," 1929, p. 153.

BIBLIOGRAPHY: Popham, "Notes-II," 1929, p. 153, fig. 2; Rackham, *Guide to Stained Glass*, 1936, p. 109, pl. 47 b.

## 29

### December, Killing the Ox: from a series of the Occupations of the Months

North Lowlands, about 1510

Roundel: diameter, 9 in. (22.9 cm)

New York, The Metropolitan Museum of Art, The Cloisters Collection, 1970, 1970.323

Inscribed (on the banderoles): *Dris · Vossen · hout · vast · / · Jan · Somers · slaet · alst · past · / Mest · hebdyt · ghenoeg · ghetast*

A cycle of the Occupations of the Months is a tradition that goes back to antiquity. In the medieval world, the Occupations of the Months, often in association with the signs of the zodiac, enjoyed their richest artistic expression in the calendar pages of lavishly illuminated Books of Hours. One need only think of the famed calendar pages of the *Très Riches Heures* illuminated by the Limbourg brothers for Jean, Duc de Berry, although most *Horae*, if they illustrated the calendar pages, did so on a considerably more modest

29

level. From the Early Middle Ages, learning and labor—on however a humble scale—were associated with the redemptive process, so that by the thirteenth century Occupations of the Months appeared in the sculptural campaigns of the great cathedrals.[1] In the later Middle Ages, however, the occupations were subject to more prosaic interpretations. Because most of the population of medieval Europe was employed in or derived its wealth from agriculture, the rural occupations that marked the changing seasons were far more a part of the natural rhythm of medieval life than a modern-day city dweller might imagine. To be sure, those who enjoyed luminous visions in their Books of Hours were not the ones who actually performed the rustic work. The more genteel pursuits such as hawking, hunting, and "May-ing" were, on the other hand, the pastimes of a very privileged few. The visual conventions of the calendar pages represented, by the end of the Middle Ages, a highly idealized or romanticized view of what a largely urban middle class thought rural life and aristocratic out-of-doors pastimes— neither of which they were ever likely to experience—should be like. Indeed, at the very time that the scenes of the Occupations of the Months were at their most tranquil, idyllic, and immutable, Europe was, in fact, in a state of great economic, political, and social unrest and upheaval.

Against this background, the imagery of the present roundel is startling for its untempered earthiness. The traditional occupation for December is slaughtering (or roasting) a pig, rather than the steer shown here. The two rustics, who are given very ordinary names, set about their messy

work, while a woman at the right holds a ladle with which she intends to catch the blood. The banderoles—the first two of which are out of sequence—explain that Dris Vossen holds [the beast] tight; Jan Somers hits with all his might. The woman queries: Will you mostly catch enough [blood]? There is a *double entendre* here, however, as *mest* can mean either "mostly" or "shit."

Executed in dark brown, umber, and black paint, with a medium yellow silver stain, the roundel is unusually dark in tonality. The painter used both the stylus and the fine point of the brush to define forms. However, the clarity of outlines is blurred in places by the somewhat rubbed surface; and the painting is partially defaced by damage to the area behind the rear of the man to the left and on the belly of the steer.

1. For a discussion of the occupations in the High Middle Ages see Mâle, *Thirteenth Century*, 1984, pp. 67–79.

BIBLIOGRAPHY: Hayward, "Stained-Glass Windows," 1972, pp. 144, 145, ill.; Husband, *Silver-Stained Roundels*, 1991, p. 140.

# 3

## The Sorgheloos Series

The moralizing story of Sorgheloos (Carefree), which warns of the consequences of loose and spendthrift behavior, is a secular variation of the parable of the Prodigal Son.[1] A young man sets out into the world to indulge his wayward pursuits. So long as he has money, he is welcomed in houses of entertainment, wined and dined, and catered to by a pretty woman. Soon, however, having squandered what was not stolen, Sorgheloos is penniless and his fair-weather friends abandon him; he is stripped of his finery and driven out into the streets to live in poverty. Unlike the parable in Luke 15: 24, in which the repentant wastrel is forgiven and returned to grace— "Because this my son was dead, and is come to life again: was lost, and is found"—there is no such homecoming and forgiveness for Sorgheloos. An outcast, he is rejected forever by friends and family: "My friends and relations all turn away. Through my folly and wickedness all is quite spoiled."[2] The Sorgheloos saga conveys the simple lesson that wanton spendthriftiness, the most vitiating form of concupiscence, leads ineluctably to material ruin and a life of unremitting and relentless poverty.

The story of Sorgheloos seems to have originated with the *rederijkers kamer*, the rhetoricians' society, or amateur theatrical troupes. Every sizable town had such a group usually composed of artists, merchants, and craftsmen, and they often wrote their material and performed it publicly in festivals, processions, and at *land-juwelen*, or outdoor literary competitions.[3] The earliest known roundel design for a Sorgheloos series is stylistically related to the Master of the Death of Absalom group (cat. no. 35; see also cat. no. 19). The surviving roundels (as well as four tondi in Basel; see cat. nos. 32 and 33, fig. 2; cat. no. 34, fig. 1; cat. no. 36, fig. 2; and cat. no. 37, fig. 1) all appear to rely on a common series of designs, but the compositions are more elaborated and seem to be somewhat later

than those by the Master of the Death of Absalom. While the compositions for the complete roundel series have not survived, the narrative and a suggestion of their original appearance are provided by a later series of woodcuts by Cornelis Anthonisz. published in 1541 (cat. nos. 30 and 34).

The compositional and iconographic sources for Sorgheloos are unknown, but the narrative convention that the roundel series relied upon, like the literary sources, already was established at the beginning of the sixteenth century. Whether the designs originated, as the story itself apparently did, with the *rederijkers* is uncertain. The relationship between artists and these theatrical groups is well established, and a morality so suited to the sober and hardworking ethic of a prosperous and independent-minded society would readily have been given visual expression. The economic expansion experienced in this period brought with prosperity the concomitant evils of greed, avarice, and prodigality. Popular culture in the Lowlands quite naturally reflected the very ethical values that were much credited for the new prosperity and provided fertile ground for moralists to cultivate cautionary subjects. Sorgheloos compellingly exemplified the consequences of defying the values of an earnest, industrious people who thoroughly believed that "if a place in heaven is deemed crucial, so too is a solid position in this world."[4]

---

1. For a full discussion of this theme see Husband, "'Ick Sorgheloose,'" 1989, pp. 173–88; see also de Jong, "Sorgheloos," 1978, pp. 108 ff.

2. The text used throughout is by Jacob Jacobsz. Jonck, published by Jan Ewoutsz. in 1541 (see cat. nos. 30 and 34); the translations are by Michael Hoyle (see Husband, "'Ick Sorgheloose,'" 1989, pp. 187–88).

3. See Gibson, "Artists and *Rederijkers*," 1981, p. 435.

4. Armstrong, *Moralizing Prints*, 1990, p. 34.

## Sorgheloos Setting Out

Cornelis Anthonisz.

Amsterdam, published 1541

Woodcut, with color, 14⅞ x 7⅞ in.
(37.8 x 20 cm)

Amsterdam, Rijksmuseum, Rijksprentenkabinet,
RP-P-1932-121a

Inscribed (in the wood block): *Weelde. / Sorgeloos. / Gemack.*; (in the entablature below): *Ick sorgheloose stel my ter jacht fray ende lustisch / Met weelde mijn lief die ick beminne / Ghemack mijn pagie is oock seer rustich / Op welcke twee ick fondeer mijn hert ende sinne / Want duer haer beyder aenschouwen solaes ick vinne / Dies my gheen molestacie mach so beswaren / Als ick slechs haer beyder pays ghewinne / Want druck ende verdriet doense van my verharen / Ken achtet goet niet, al hebbent mijn ouders gaen sparen / Ick wilt verteeren / met houeeren drincken ende storten / Want minnert het goet die daghen die corten*

*Ghy jonghe ghesellen van cloecke statueren / Slacht niet den Sorgheloose maer leeft by maten / Peynsende tleven sal hier niet langhe dueren / Ende die Sorgheloose blijue by godt verwaten / Ende si en comen oock niet tot mannen van staten / Jae na een vruecht volghen wel duysentich suchten / Maer met v goet doet de armen doch charitaten / So sullen wt v wasschen die gherechte vruchten / Ende weelde en ghemack sullen daer door van v niet vluchten / Maer uwer buchten / sullē daer door vermeerē van stonden an / Dus peynst doch een weynich op den ouden man·*

30

While Sorgheloos did not appear in popular literature prior to the sixteenth century, the *topos* is frequently encountered in moralities that have similar themes of concupiscence and date back to the early fifteenth century.[1] The name Sorgheloos is first encountered in an almanac of parodic forecasts, or prognostications, compiled by "heer Sorgheloos van Kommerkercke" and printed in Amsterdam about 1540.[2] Although the Sorgheloos tale had coalesced into a conventionalized narrative, as evidenced by the roundel series, earlier in the sixteenth century, the first complete visualization to have survived is a series of woodblock prints designed by Cornelis Anthonisz., the grandson of Jacob Cornelisz. van Oostsanen (see cat. nos. 38–45); the series, with accompanying moralizing commentary by Jacob Jacobsz. Jonck, was published in Amsterdam by Jan Ewoutsz. in 1541.[3] Although the prints are not signed, they are confidently attributed to Anthonisz. not only because they were published by his longtime collaborator but also because of their unmistakable stylistic connections with autograph prints. On the basis of these prints, the roundel series that have survived in very fragmentary form can be reconstructed with some confidence.

In this first scene in the Anthonisz. series Sorgheloos, accompanied by Weelde (Luxury) who is also on horseback, sets out on his adventure,

FIG. 1 Albrecht Dürer. *The Four Horsemen of the Apocalypse*. Woodcut illustration from *The Apocalypse*. 1497–98. New York, The Metropolitan Museum of Art, The George Khuner Collection, Gift of Mrs. George Khuner, 1975

FIG. 2 Albrecht Dürer. *Knight and Landsknecht*. Woodcut. About 1496. New York, The Metropolitan Museum of Art, The George Khuner Collection, Gift of Mrs. George Khuner, 1975

FIG. 3 Cornelis Anthonisz. *The "House of Spendthrift."* Woodcut. 1541. Amsterdam, Rijksmuseum, Rijksprentenkabinet

## Sorgheloos and Weelde Dancing

North Lowlands, Leiden(?), about 1520

Roundel: diameter, 8⅞ in. (22.5 cm)

Leiden, Stedelijk Museum de Lakenhal, purchased with the support of the Rembrandt Vereniging, 1970, 7684

In the third scene in the story, Sorgheloos and Weelde leave the table to dance and enjoy themselves: "Come piper, play up, the banquet is cleared, It is time for a dance and a roundelay. . . . So come, play up, play *Folly's Delight*. . . ." In the Anthonisz. print (fig. 1) Gemack holds the train of Weelde's dress as she dances with Sorgheloos. The musicians perform in a gallery above, while another couple attended by a jester wearing a coxcomb hat are seen dancing farther back in the room; a table populated with other feasters is in the far background. The empty bedchamber to the left of the dining area presumably refers to Sorgheloos's carnal appetites.

The present roundel, usually given a general title such as *Worldly Pleasures*, only recently has been associated with the Sorgheloos story.[1] The overall arrangement of the scene with the musicians in a gallery, the appropriately extravagant costumes of the dancing couple, and the presence of the jester in a coxcomb hat all argue strongly in favor of the identification given here. Furthermore, a figure with the same facial type, wearing a similar hat with abundant plumage, and being smitten by Pouer (Poverty) and bitten by Aermoede (Indigence) in a later scene, clearly represents Sorgheloos (see cat. no. 34, fig. 1).

The roundel is exceptionally well executed, employing shades of brown to dark brown paint and yellow silver stain, enhanced with a flesh tone for faces and hands as well as for details such as shoes and hats. Contours are defined with very fine trace lines and etched lines. The modeling is achieved with stippling and extensive use of the badger brush, heightened with stylus work to pick out highlights of both the long tubular folds and the more crushed ones of the sleeves. The subtle gradations of tonalities in modeling the volumetric drapery and the stylus highlighting are particularly accomplished. No designs for this scene are known, but other weaker roundel versions are found in the chapel of Cholmondeley Castle, Cheshire,[2] and in the parish church at Dundalk, County Cork.

1. Husband, "'Ick Sorgheloose,'" 1989, p. 180.

2. Cole, *Roundels in Britain*, 1993, p. 56, no. 468.

BIBLIOGRAPHY: Amsterdam, *Middeleeuwse kunst* (exhib. cat.), 1958, p. 175, no. 244, fig. 111; Renger, *Lockere Gesellschaft*, 1970, pp. 38–39, fig. 16; Berserik, "Leiden, ca. 1480–1545," 1982, no. 43 A, fig. 71; Husband, "'Ick Sorgheloose,'" 1989, pp. 180–81, fig. 16.

while Gemack (Ease) and two dogs march alongside them. In the text below, Sorgheloos declares that he has not a care in the world and that he intends to squander in feasting and drinking all that his parents have earned through hard work. Sorgheloos on his horse clearly is based on the figure of Famine in Dürer's woodcut of the Four Horsemen of the Apocalypse (fig. 1), a visual reference that must have been employed for its ironic bite, as well as for its convenience as a model. Gemack running alongside Sorgheloos and the latter's upraised arm seem to have been inspired, on the other hand, by Dürer's *Knight and Landsknecht* (fig. 2). The present woodcut is enlivened with period color, including shades of green, brown, brick red, a vibrant orange, blue, and yellow; the frame is colored with hues of yellow, blue, and a pinkish tone. The sheet has a vertical crease near the right side of the image and is trimmed to the design on the right. The complete series to which this impression belongs is the only extant example that incorporates frames, text, and contemporary hand coloring.

In the second scene in the Anthonisz. series Sorgheloos and Weelde satisfy their appetites at the table in the "House of Spendthrift" (fig. 3); apparently with little on his mind but food,

Sorgheloos reminds his friends that he lives for the flesh, and exhorts them to "round out your bellies."

No known roundel designs or executed roundels that correspond to these initial two scenes have survived.

1. Examples, as well as analogous characters, can be found in Laurent Gallus's 1408 *Somme de roi*, known in the Netherlands as *Des Coninx Summe*, in *De Blauwe Schuit*, a poem also of the early fifteenth century, and in Sebastian Brant's *Narrenschiff*.

2. For a detailed discussion of this text see Pleij, "Sorgheloos," 1980, pp. 118 ff.

3. For a more detailed discussion of this series of prints see Armstrong, *Moralizing Prints*, 1990, pp. 26–34.

BIBLIOGRAPHY: Bolte, "Bilderbogen," 1895, pp. 122–26; Wescher, "Cornelis Teunissen," 1928, p. 35, fig. 2; Held, *Dürers Wirkung*, 1931, p. 54; Nijhoff, *Nederlandsche houtsneden 1500–1550*, 1931–39, p. 13, nos. 70–75; Dubiez, *Cornelis Anthoniszoon*, 1969, p. 113; Renger, *Lockere Gesellschaft*, 1970, p. 45, fig. 25; de Jong, "Sorgheloos," 1978, pp. 104–20; Hollstein 30, 1986, p. 30, no. 29; Amsterdam, *Kunst voor de beeldenstorm* (exhib. cat.), 1986, pp. 271–73, no. 151.1; Husband, "'Ick Sorgheloose,'" 1989, p. 178, fig. 10; Armstrong, *Moralizing Prints*, 1990, pp. 26–27, fig. 37 a.

31

FIG. 1 Cornelis Anthonisz. *Sorgheloos and Weelde Dancing*. Woodcut. 1541. Amsterdam, Rijksmuseum, Rijksprentenkabinet

32 *see plate 9*

## Sorgheloos and Lichte Fortune

North Lowlands, Leiden (?), about 1520

Roundel: diameter, with border, 10⅝ in. (27 cm)

The Toledo Museum of Art, Gift of Rosenberg & Stiebel, Inc., 1957, 57.49

## 33

## Sorgheloos and Lichte Fortune

North Lowlands, probably Leiden, about 1520

Roundel: diameter, 9 in. (22.9 cm)

New York, The Metropolitan Museum of Art, The Cloisters Collection, 1976, 1976.47

The next scene in the series represents Sorgheloos in the process of gambling away his money in a dice game with a man who has a cannister-shaped container strapped over his shoulder. In the Anthonisz. print (fig. 1), the character is called Lichte Fortune (Fickle Fortune). A man carrying cannisters of this type has been identified as a cruller man (*oblieman*), or a peddler who sold crullers, wafers, and other wares that were kept in these containers.[1] In a close version of the Toledo roundel composition executed in distemper on linen—one of a series of four, now in Basel, that share the same design as the roundels—crullers can be seen scattered about the table (fig. 2).[2] It was customary to gamble with cruller men for their wares and, as a consequence, they were considered dissolute, tavern frequenters, and ne'er-do-wells.[3] As an indication of things to come, Sorgheloos's ragtag companions-to-be, Aermoede and Pouer, have just entered the room. In the Toledo composition, Lichte Fortune points to the dice, which, no doubt, indicate a result that favors him; Sorgheloos looks on but his attentions are clearly shared with his buxom companion of the moment. The back-room tryst has arrested the attention of the other female at the table.

The Cloisters' roundel is a curious example of an altered composition that results in a confusion of subject matter. The composition clearly was inspired by the design of the Toledo roundel, as is evident from the presence of the cruller man and the pose of the seated woman who faces away from the viewer, but the crux of the narrative is removed by adding a servant figure in Lichte Fortune's place at the left of the table and by placing Lichte Fortune at the opposite side of the table where the seated woman blocks the view of the dice game. Whether this obfuscation was intentional or not is uncertain. If the glass painter had wished to transform the subject into another, such as an incident in the story of the Prodigal Son, there would have been no need to hide the gambling activity and to change the bedroom scene in the background to an innocuous outdoor one; he only would have had to replace the cruller man with a harlot to produce a serviceable depiction of the biblical parable. Such a composition is known in several versions, the best of which is in the Collection Frits Lugt, Paris (see fig. 3). As the

32

33

FIG. 2 *Sorgheloos and Lichte Fortune*. Distemper on linen. About 1520. Öffentliche Kunstsammlung Basel, Kunstmuseum

FIG. 1 Cornelis Anthonisz. *Sorgheloos and Lichte Fortune*. Woodcut. 1541. Amsterdam, Rijksmuseum, Rijksprentenkabinet

FIG. 3 *The Prodigal Son*. Roundel. About 1520. Paris, Collection Frits Lugt, Institut Néerlandais

FIG. 4 *January* (*Sorgheloos and Lichte Fortune*). Manuscript illumination from the *Hours of Jean de Mauléon* (detail). 1524. Baltimore, The Walters Art Gallery

FIG. 5 Pieter Cornelisz. Kunst. *Saint Peter Preaching and the Magician Simon*. Pen and brown ink on paper. 1515–20. Amsterdam, Rijksmuseum, Rijksprentenkabinet

FIG. 6 *Sorgheloos and Lichte Fortune*. Pen and black ink, with white highlights, on gray prepared paper. About 1510–20. Hannover, Kestner-Museum

cruller man with his cannister pack was not removed, but merely obscured with dark paint and a leather knapsack added, it would seem that the glass painter did not understand the subject matter of the composition that served as his model, but simply relied on it to produce a domestic genre scene. A variant is used, for example, to represent an indoor winter pastime in the illustration for the month of January in the calendar pages of the *Hours of Jean de Mauléon*, Bishop of Saint-Bertrand-de-Comminges, datable to 1524 (see fig. 4, detail).[4]

The Toledo roundel is executed in medium brown and black paint with yellow and dark golden yellow silver stain. The figures are described with fine black trace lines, frequently heightened with a stylus, while painted and etched lines as well as delicate stippling are skillfully employed to achieve the highly modeled forms. A fine-pointed brush is used throughout both to model, as in the bodice of the woman embracing Sorgheloos, and to provide linear detail, as in the brocade pattern of the wall hanging. Back painting enhances the illusion of depth in the scene. A loss at the upper-left edge has been restored and several breaks have been glued. A broader, less painterly technique is found in the Cloisters' roundel. The modeling relies largely on the use of gradated tones of matte washes highlighted with bold stickwork, while the stylus is restricted to a few highlights composed of either parallel or cross-hatched strokes. The forthright rendering lacks the detailed refinement and the spatial clarity of the Toledo roundel.

The substantial figure style as well as the dark tonalities of the paint and the highly contrasted modeling of the weighty drapery patterns suggest a Northern origin for these and other roundels in the Sorgheloos series. The striking pose of the seated female figure seen from the rear in the Toledo roundel resembles, for example, that of the seated figure in Pieter Cornelisz. Kunst's drawing of *Saint Peter Preaching and the Magician Simon* (fig. 5), indicating, perhaps, a Leiden origin for the former. In addition to the Basel tondo, a number of versions of this composition exist, including a highly finished drawing in Hannover (fig. 6)[5] and other roundels in Canterbury, Kent, and at Cranbrook House in Bloomfield Hills, Michigan.[6]

The figures in the Cloisters' roundel are weightier and less attenuated than those in the Toledo version, while the drapery is rendered in more abundant stiff, crumpled folds, and the modeling is more sharply contrasted. In this regard, comparison of technique can be made with the Darmstadt panel of *Delilah Cutting the Hair of Samson* (cat. no. 55), which reflects the strong influence of Lucas van Leyden, thus strengthening the connection with Leiden.

1. See Bernet Kempers, "De speler," 1973, pp. 240–42; Armstrong, *Moralizing Prints*, 1990, pp. 30–31. Bernet Kempers notes that the costume worn here is that of a soldier or mercenary, the latter often equated with a cruller man, as both were known for their dilatory and disreputable ways.

2. Basel, Kunstmuseum, 359; see Husband, "'Ick

Sorgheloose,'" 1989, p. 175, fig. 4. The four tondi that survive from this series are all about 32 inches (81.3 centimeters) in diameter.

3. See Bernet Kempers, "De speler," 1973, pp. 240–42; Armstrong, *Moralizing Prints*, 1990, pp. 30–31.

4. Baltimore, The Walters Art Gallery, Ms. W.449, fol. 2 *v.* See Wieck, in Baltimore, *Time Sanctified* (exhib. cat.), 1988, p. 50, fig. 17, p. 207, no. 77.

5. Kestner-Museum, Z 81.

6. The Canterbury fragment is glazed into a composite window in the Royal Museum and Free Library (see Pugin, *Old Dutch Windows*, 1899, pl. 11 e, entitled *Window on the Staircase*); the latter roundel belongs to the Cranbrook Educational Community, Bloomfield Hills, Michigan (1939.57); see Husband, *Silver-Stained Roundels*, 1991, p. 109.

BIBLIOGRAPHY: (32) *Sammlung des Freiherrn Adalbert von Lanna* (sale cat.), 1911, pt. 2, p. 97, no. 799, pl. 65; von Falke, *Kunstsammlung von Pannwitz*, 1925, p. 12, no. 1124; "Accessions," 1958, p. 92, ill.; "Accessions," 1960, p. 50, ill.; Bruyn, "Lucas van Leyden," 1969, pp. 44–47, ill. 263, fig. 2; Toledo, *Glass Collections*, 1969, p. 53, ill.; Husband, "'Ick Sorgheloose,'" 1989, pp. 173–75, 184, fig. 2; Husband, *Silver-Stained Roundels*, 1991, p. 202. (33) Husband, "'Ick Sorgheloose,'" 1989, p. 173, fig. 1; Husband, *Silver-Stained Roundels*, 1991, p. 154.

## 34

### Sorgheloos Is Smitten by Aermoede and Bitten by Pouer

Cornelis Anthonisz.

Amsterdam, published 1541

Woodcut, with color, 14⅞ x 7⅞ in. (37.8 x 20 cm)

Amsterdam, Rijksmuseum, Rijksprentenkabinet, RP-P-1932-121e

Inscribed (in the wood block): *Sorgheloos / Weelde. / Aermoede / Pouer / Gemack.*; (in the entablature below): *Och leyder wat staet mijn te beginnen / Weelde ende ghemack gaen mij ontlopen / Desperacie bestrijt my heel van binnen / Want op die twee stont alle mijn hopen / Sy souden niet hooren al werde van mi gheroepen / Mijn duecht die ick ghedaen heb is al verghehten / Dats om dat mijn boerse niet langher mach open / Want Pouer bijt mij ja ick worde van armoede ghesmeeten / Och had ick wat ick sout wel eeten / Daer ick onlancx nyet en wiste wat my was lustende / Nu mach ick by die schorluynen int stro zijn rustende*

*Dat eynde van blijschap is droefheyt voorwaer / Als Salemon dat seer suyverlick wt leyt / Dus elck wil hem reguleren een paer / Om mate te ghebruycken ende sinen tijt bereyt / Op dat namaels tbeginsel niet en wert beschreyt / Met den Sorgheloose als elck mach aenschouwen / Want therten der vrouwen hem so diverschelick niet / Sodatter weynich is in te betrouwen / hier / Si vullen een caproen wel duer haer woorts ontrowen / hier / Maer tende na volcht een swaer verdriet / Want het hert volcht dick die woorden niet.*

34

FIG. 1 *Sorgheloos Is Smitten by Pouer and Bitten by Aermoede.* Distemper on linen. About 1520. Öffentliche Kunstsammlung Basel, Kunstmuseum

FIG. 2 *Sorgheloos Is Smitten by Pouer and Bitten by Aermoede.* Roundel. About 1520. Lewes, East Sussex, Collection Andrew Rudebeck

35

36

Sorgheloos, experiencing his self-fulfilling prophesy, has lost all his money and is now rebuffed by his wanton companions and driven out of the "House of Spendthrift." Gemack and Weelde turn their backs and walk off as Sorgheloos suffers the all-too-real blows delivered by the allegorical figures Aermoede, wielding fire tongs, and Pouer, letting his bite be felt. Realizing the fate that has befallen him, Sorgheloos laments, "Luxury and Ease ignore me entirely / And despair is my master now. . . . Because now my purse is fast closed / For Poverty bites me, yea Indigence smites me / Oh, would that I had a morsel to eat." The figure of Gemack follows, in reverse, one of Hans Schäufelein's woodcuts of the *Wedding Dancers* (*Ill. Bartsch* 11:103-15, p. 286). The woodcut shares the same palette as the earlier one except that the walls behind the group are colored a pale salmon. There are, likewise, vertical creases near the right side of the image; the sheet is trimmed to the design at the right side. The roundel version of this scene is preserved in the Basel tondo (fig. 1)[1] as well as in two executed roundels, one in the Netherlands[2] and another in an English private collection (fig. 2).[3] For unclear reasons, however, Cornelis Anthonisz. reverses the actions of the attackers, since in the earlier versions it is Pouer who smites and Aermoede who bites.

1. Basel, Kunstmuseum, 360; see Husband, "'Ick Sorgheloose,'" 1989, p. 176, fig. 5.

2. The K. G. Boon Collection, Aerenhout.

3. This roundel was formerly in the James Rawlings Herbert Boone Collection, Oak Hill House, The Johns Hopkins University, Baltimore, and is now in the collection of Andrew Rudebeck, Lewes, East Sussex. See Husband, "'Ick Sorgheloose,'" 1989, p. 180, fig. 17; Cole, *Roundels in Britain*, 1993, p. 223, no. 1785.

BIBLIOGRAPHY: Bolte, "Bilderbogen," 1895, pp. 122–26; Held, *Dürers Wirkung*, 1931, p. 54; Nijhoff, *Nederlandsche houtsneden 1500–1550*, 1931–39, p. 13, nos. 70–75; Dubiez, *Cornelis Anthoniszoon*, 1969, p. 113, no. 59; de Jong, "Sorgheloos," 1978, pp. 104–20; Amsterdam, *Kunst voor de beeldenstorm* (exhib. cat.), 1986, pp. 271–73, no. 151.5; Hollstein 30, 1986, p. 31, no. 31; Husband, "'Ick Sorgheloose,'" 1989, p. 179, fig. 14; Armstrong, *Moralizing Prints*, 1990, pp. 31–32, fig. 37 e.

## 35

### Sorgheloos, Pouer, and Aermoede Being Rebuffed

Master of the Death of Absalom

North Lowlands, about 1500–1510

Pen and ink, with white highlights, on prepared paper: diameter, 8⅛ in. (20.6 cm)

Amsterdam, Collectie Stichting P. en N. de Boer, RM 306

## 36

### Sorgheloos and Aermoede Being Rebuffed

North Lowlands, Leiden, about 1520

Roundel: diameter, 8⅞ in. (22.5 cm)

Darmstadt, Hessisches Landesmuseum, Kg 31:35

The de Boer drawing is the earliest surviving design from the Sorgheloos series. Stylistically, it is closely related to the group of drawings ascribed to the Master of the Death of Absalom (see cat. no. 19). The variety and individualization of the faces, the animated gestures, and the technique are all characteristic of this group of drawings. Sorgheloos is now—literally—bearing the full weight of Aermoede, as clinging Pouer proves to be an added burden. The metaphor was employed in contemporary proverbs: "He who cannot support luxury must have poverty."[1] The ragtag group approaches a couple standing before a substantial abode who appear well established, but, as the man holds up his hand to halt them, it is clear that Sorgheloos will find no charity here. The composition is tightly focused on the figures, with only a portion of a pair of windows breaking the expanse of the masonry wall. The wall against which the man in the fur-lined cloak leans as he waves off the indigents also serves as a visual and symbolic barrier between the two groups. In the Cornelis Anthonisz. version, which dates to about forty years later, this scene is reduced to an inset vignette in the upper-left corner, seen through a large breach in the wall of the house that serves as the setting for the principal subject (fig. 1). The composition of the secondary scene is essentially the same as in the present drawing, except that the vantage point has expanded so that some landscape and more of the house can be seen. The absence of the wall renders the narrative line less obvious and without the accompanying text the viewer would not necessarily know that the approaching group is being spurned. The text, however, is explicit: "Indigence rides me, I shrink at the pain / While Poverty urges me onwards. / My friends and relations all turn away."

FIG. 4 *Sorgheloos and Aermoede Being Rebuffed.*
Roundel. About 1520–30. London, Victoria and
Albert Museum

The Darmstadt roundel, while consistent in
the main with both the Absalom group drawing
and the Anthonisz. woodcut, makes several
notable alterations to the composition. Pouer is
absent and the couple at the door is now a
group—perhaps representing both friends and
relatives—standing before a substantial complex
of impressive buildings, rebuffing the unfortunate
pair while appearing to discuss them. The fence is
also removed so that only an indifferent dog separates the contrasting groups. In addition to the
Basel tondo (fig. 2),[2] several executed roundels
provide close versions of this composition. There
are two replica versions at Christ Church,
Llanwarne, Hereford and Worcester (fig. 3);[3]
another is in Vienna;[4] a somewhat drier and
weaker version, with elements of its original border, is in London (fig. 4);[5] and a later version is in
a private collection at Melksham Court, Stinch-
combe, Gloucestershire.[6]

1. Armstrong, *Moralizing Prints*, 1990, p. 32.

2. Basel, Kunstmuseum, 1579.

3. These (sI 3a and sI 2c) are set in a nineteenth-
century glazing in a window on the south side of the
nave; see Husband, "'Ick Sorgheloose,'" 1989, p. 181,
fig. 18; Cole, *Roundels in Britain*, 1993, p. 132, nos.
1065 and 1066: The latter is installed backwards.

4. Österreichisches Museum für angewandte Kunst, GL
2798.

5. Victoria and Albert Museum, 66-1929.

6. Cole, *Roundels in Britain*, 1993, p. 263, no. 2090.

BIBLIOGRAPHY: (35) Laren, *Oude tekeningen* (exhib.
cat.), 1966, p. 24, no. 140; Renger, *Lockere Gesellschaft*,
1970, p. 60, fig. 38; Husband, "'Ick Sorgheloose,'"
1989, p. 183, fig. 21; Husband, *Silver-Stained Roundels*,
1991, p. 27, fig. 26. (36) Beeh-Lustenberger, *Glasmalerei
in Darmstadt*, 1973, p. 205, no. 264, fig. 173; Husband,
"'Ick Sorgheloose,'" 1989, p. 181; Husband, *Silver-
Stained Roundels*, 1991, p. 27, fig. 27.

FIG. 1 Cornelis Anthonisz. *Sorgheloos and Aermoede Being Rebuffed and
Sorgheloos in Poverty.* Woodcut. 1541. Amsterdam, Rijksmuseum,
Rijksprentenkabinet

FIG. 2 *Sorgheloos and Aermoede Being Rebuffed.*
Distemper on linen. About 1520. Öffentliche
Kunstsammlung Basel, Kunstmuseum

FIG. 3 *Sorgheloos and Aermoede Being Rebuffed.*
Roundel. About 1520. Llanwarne, Hereford and
Worcester, Christ Church

## Sorgheloos in Poverty

North Lowlands, about 1520

Roundel: diameter, 8⅝ in. (21.9 cm); with
border, 10⅞ in. (27.6 cm)

London, Victoria and Albert Museum, 65-1929

Inscribed (in the original border): *Het · ist · nu ·
te · ende* [ . . . ] *gaet · zu ·*

The roundel series ends with the scene of Sorgheloos sitting despondently on an overturned half barrel stoking a meager fire with wisps of straw. The image is compelling for the isolation of the weary Sorgheloos, who has been condemned to his marginal existence in perpetuity. Other than the dog and the cat (which still may be alive, in contrast to the nearby rat that clearly is not), his only companion is Aermoede, who can be seen through the door collecting more straw for the fire. The later Cornelis Anthonisz. woodcut elaborates on the scene, showing Sorgheloos sharing a tumbledown abode with both Pouer and Aermoede, who stirs a pot of thin brew over the fire (cat. nos. 35 and 36, fig. 1). The sheaf of straw with which Sorgheloos will fuel the fire, the cat in the bare larder, the dog licking an empty pot, and the rancid sprats and herring on the grill, as well as Sorgheloos's unshod condition, are all well-established symbols of an impoverished condition.[1] The tail of a fish sticks out of the pot here.

The roundel is executed in medium and dark brown paint with deep yellow silver stain. The painting is, in passages, rather impressionistic: The blurring of paint around the fireplace, while suggesting smoke, obscures the drawing. A companion roundel, representing Sorgheloos carrying Aermoede, again retaining its original border, is also in the Victoria and Albert Museum (cat. nos. 35 and 36, fig. 4). The same composition is found in the final tondo of the Basel series (fig. 1),[2] as well as in a drawing in Stockholm,[3] and in roundels now in a private collection in Sussex,[4] and in Christ Church, Llanwarne, Hereford and Worcester (fig. 2).[5]

1. Tuttle, "Bosch's Image of Poverty," 1981, p. 94; Armstrong, *Moralizing Prints*, 1990, pp. 32–33.

2. Basel, Kunstmuseum, 1578.

3. Ankarsvärd Collection, 432.

4. Andrew Rudebeck collection, Lewes, East Sussex; see Cole, *Roundels in Britain*, 1993, p. 222, no. 1780.

5. Set in a nineteenth-century glazing in the south side of the nave (sI 3c); see Husband, "'Ick Sorgheloose,'" 1989, p. 181, fig. 19; Cole, *Roundels in Britain*, 1993, p. 132, no. 1068.

BIBLIOGRAPHY: Rackham, *Guide to Stained Glass*, 1936, p. 109; Amsterdam, *Middeleeuwse kunst* (exhib. cat.), 1958, p. 176, no. 245; Husband, "'Ick Sorgheloose,'" 1989, p. 181.

37

FIG. 1 *Sorgheloos in Poverty*. Distemper on linen. About 1520. Öffentliche Kunstsammlung Basel, Kunstmuseum

FIG. 2 *Sorgheloos in Poverty*. Roundel. About 1520–30. Llanwarne, Hereford and Worcester, Christ Church

# 4

# Jacob Cornelisz. van Oostsanen

*Born about 1472 in Oostsanen (Oostzaan today) and active in Amsterdam from about 1500—the first recorded artist in that city—when he bought a house on the Kalverstraat, Jacob Cornelisz., with his workshop, satisfied the conservative tastes of his wealthy upper-middle-class patrons, producing small panel paintings, book illustrations, woodcuts, and designs for painted glass.¹ Nothing is known of his apprenticeship, but the linear and decorative style of his early works suggests that he was trained as a goldsmith before he took up painting. An accomplished technician but not a great innovator, Jacob was strongly influenced by Dürer, and although he never fully embraced the implications of Renaissance principles, his work, employing both traditional and unconventional themes and iconography, adopted elements of both its ornamental and thematic vocabulary in a manner that appealed to the humanist and Manneristic tastes of his urban patrician clientele. The purchase in 1520 of a second house on the Kalverstraat as well as his activity in Antwerp from 1505 to 1516, during which period he became a member of the Guild of Saint Luke, evidence the apparent success of his endeavors. His monogram, an I and an A—for Jacob of Amsterdam—flanking a cipher, appears on many of his prints and paintings. An inventory listing his possessions at the time of his death is dated October 18, 1533.*

No autograph sheets by Jacob Cornelisz. have survived and, to judge from the paucity of the extant material, designs for roundels or stained glass did not form a large part of his oeuvre. Van Mander makes no mention of his activity in this regard. The Berlin *Last Supper* (cat. no. 38) has long been attributed to Jacob² and could be a preliminary study for the corresponding scene in his circular Passion series (cat. no. 39), as the compositions are clearly related. These woodcuts, dated variously between 1511 and 1514 and clearly influenced by Dürer's Small Passion, are mentioned by van Mander. Contrary to general practices in the early sixteenth century, these wood blocks by Jacob Cornelisz. were widely used as a source of designs for varying mediums, including embroideries and reverse-glass painting (cat. nos. 39 and 40, fig. 8), as well as silver-stained roundels, whether or not the artist so intended them. There is no question, on the other hand, that the London *Messenger Telling Abraham of the Capture of Lot* (cat. no. 43), the style of which sustains its long-held attribution to Jacob Cornelisz., was intended as anything more than a design for a roundel (see cat. no. 44). While no other drawings are known to exist, a number of roundels of high quality, which clearly preserve compositions from a lost Genesis or Abraham cycle, confirm Jacob Cornelisz.'s activity as an important designer of roundels (cat. nos. 44 and 45).

1. For further biographical detail see Amsterdam, *Kunst voor de beeldenstorm* (exhib. cat.), 1986, p. 131; Washington, *Age of Bruegel* (exhib. cat.), 1986, p. 126; Carroll, "Paintings of Jacob Cornelisz.," Ph.D. diss., 1987, pp. 5–23.
2. Bock et al., *Zeichnungen*, 1930, p. 26, no. 5526, pl. 21.

FIG. 1 Jacob Cornelisz. van Oostsanen. *Christ Resurrecting the Youth of Nain*. Pen and brown ink on paper. About 1510–15. Paris, Bibliothèque Nationale

## 38

### The Last Supper

About 1510–14(?)

Pen and brown ink on paper, 9⅝ x 7⅞ in. (24.4 x 20 cm)

Staatliche Museen zu Berlin, Preußischer Kulturbesitz, Kupferstichkabinett, KdZ 5526

Jacob's style, which may have been rooted in metal engraving or in wood-block cutting prior to his training as a painter,[1] relies on long, continuous strokes that define various components of the composition; these passages are then modeled with extended, parallel, slightly curved lines, generally crossed in the darker, recessive areas. The contours of the bulky figures in the Berlin drawing are rendered with such characteristically elongated, clear strokes, while the ample drapery, accented with crumpled folds, is modeled with exceptionally controlled and delicate networks of parallel and crossed lines that become very dense in recessed areas. The foreground group is more highly finished than many drawings associated with Jacob, while the architectural background—accorded scant attention—is sketched in in the most summary fashion, suggesting the presence of a different hand altogether. Very similar treatment is encountered in the *Christ Resurrecting the Youth of Nain* (fig. 1), now in the Bibliothèque Nationale, Paris. Here, too, the background, such as it is, is cursorily indicated with minimal pen work. In the *Allegory of the Dogma of the Sacrament of the Mass* (fig. 2),[2] the architecture, similar to that in the present sheet, is rapidly sketched in,

and even the figural groups in the background, which are essential elements of the iconography, are, likewise, rendered with the utmost frugality and freedom of line. The foreground group, however, is thoroughly worked, although with somewhat more economy; increasingly, Jacob Cornelisz. would, for example, abbreviate the facial details of his figures, as can be seen in the deacon blessing a worshiper to the left of the celebrant priest. The careful rendering of the foreground figures with little evidence of reworking, and with no more than a few lines expended on the architectural or landscape settings, accords completely with the underdrawings on the panels by Jacob Cornelisz.,[3] arguing strongly for his authorship of all three drawings.[4] The present sheet, the technique of which echoes that of his earlier work and the composition of which appears to be related to the large Passion woodcut series (cat. no. 39), may date to about 1510–14.

The scene is constructed around a circular table, with Christ seated in the center on the far side and the disciples evenly distributed about him. Only Christ and the flanking saints Peter and John can be identified. John is asleep on the shoulder of Christ, who grasps a chalice with his left hand while raising his right in blessing. On the table are a paschal lamb on a large salver and two loaves of bread near the chalice. The presence of a Eucharistic chalice at the Last Supper is unusual and reflects contemporary religious thought in Amsterdam—a city that, about 1500, was dominated by a wealthy Catholic oligarchy. By the fifteenth century, there already were reformist movements in the Lowlands, most notably the

FIG. 2 Jacob Cornelisz. van Oostsanen. *Allegory of the Dogma of the Sacrament of the Mass*. Pen and brown ink on paper. About 1513. Staatliche Museen zu Berlin, Preußischer Kulturbesitz, Kupferstichkabinett

*devotio moderna*, lay followers of the contemplative lives of the Brothers of the Common Life, who taught personal piety and good works as a means to salvation, obviating the intercession of corrupt clergy. In the sixteenth century, numerous groups, such as the Sacramentarians, questioned various tenets of Catholic dogma, not the least of which was the nature of the Eucharist. The Sacramentarians, who were tolerated to varying degrees in Amsterdam up until about 1525, argued that bread and wine were merely metaphors for the body and blood of Christ; Catholic dogma, on the other hand, insisted, according to the theory of transubstantiation, that the bread and wine were, in fact, the body and blood of Christ. The Roman Church in Amsterdam was largely defended by a group known as biblical Humanists, who were among the city's intellectual elite and, on the model of Erasmus, believed in the thoughtful reevaluation of traditional doctrine rather than in wholesale reform. Most of Jacob Cornelisz.'s patrons were adherents of biblical Humanism and the imagery of many of the works that he produced reflected their convictions. For example, he provided woodcut illustrations for a 1523 anti-Sacramentarian volume by Alardus of Amsterdam, a leading defender of Catholic orthodoxy; the title page included a depiction of the Last Supper in which the paschal lamb—the sacrificial lamb as Christ himself—literally took the place of the bread, thus affording a visualization of the doctrine of transubstantiation that the tract promulgated.[5] In the present drawing the metaphor is extended by the positioning of the bread and the altar chalice alongside the paschal lamb on the salver. According to the *Speculum humanae salvationis*, the paschal lamb prefigures the Last Supper: As the Israelites ate the lamb after God delivered them from captivity, so Christ instituted the sacrament as an affirmation of the redemption of man through Christ's sacrifice on the cross. In the Berlin *Allegory of the Dogma of the Sacrament of the Mass* (fig. 2), the depiction of Christ holding his wound while supporting the cross as he tramples on the grapes in the winepress clearly is meant to equate his blood with the wine; the precious liquid is being stored by a monk and a pope for use in the celebration of the Eucharist, portrayed in the main scene, thus indicating that the blood of Christ and the Eucharistic wine are one and the same.

The compositional similarity to the corresponding woodcut (cat. no. 39) notwithstanding, the function of this drawing remains uncertain. Although the composition bleeds off at the sides, the sheet does not appear to be trimmed; the drawing is, however, slightly faded in certain areas.

1. See Carroll, "Paintings of Jacob Cornelisz.," Ph.D. diss., 1987, pp. 8–9; Washington, *Age of Bruegel* (exhib. cat.), 1986, p. 126.

2. Staatliche Museen zu Berlin, Preußischer Kulturbesitz, Kupferstichkabinett, KdZ 4404. See Washington, *Age of Bruegel* (exhib. cat.), 1986, no. 42, pp. 126–27.

3. See Carroll, "Paintings of Jacob Cornelisz.," Ph.D. diss., 1987, p. 16.

39

4. Steinbart (*Tafelgemälde des Jakob Cornelisz,* 1922, p. 162) dates the *Last Supper* to the artist's middle period—about 1519. Carroll ("Paintings of Jacob Cornelisz.," Ph.D. diss., 1987, p. 23, n. 62) considers only the *Allegory of the Sacrament of the Mass* to be by Jacob Cornelisz. and places it in his later years.

5. See Sterck, *Onder Amsterdamsche Humanisten,* 1934, p. 39; Carroll, "Paintings of Jacob Cornelisz.," Ph.D. diss., 1987, pp. 54–55.

BIBLIOGRAPHY: Bock et al., *Zeichnungen,* 1930, p. 26, pl. 21; Steinbart, *Holzschnittwerk,* 1937, p. 44, pl. 30.

## 39

### The Last Supper

1513–14; the frame is dated 1517

Woodcut, 13⅞ x 11⅜ in. (35.2 x 28.9 cm)

Amsterdam, Rijksmuseum, Rijksprentenkabinet, RP-P-B.I. 6250

Inscribed (below, in two columns):

*Quam sis egregie pietatis idoneus auctor:*
  *Nos data discipulis ultima coena docet.*
*Sordibus ablutis:famulos rex maxime regnum /*
  *Iussisti mundos semper habere pedes.*
*Quam sacra mirandae tua sunt convivia mense.*

  *Quam dulces epulae:quam sine felle dapes.*
*Ipse tuis panem et vinum largitus eorum*
  *Exatur auisti corpore corda tuo.*
*Optinam:quoties caelesti pane nutrimur /*
  *Ardenteis animos gratia maior alat.*

*Cum gratia + privilegio Car.Catho.His.Reg.*

40 *see plate 10*

### The Last Supper

Amsterdam, about 1515–20

Roundel: diameter, 8⅞ in. (22.5 cm)

The Detroit Institute of Arts, Founders Society Purchase, Octavia W. Bates Fund, 36.96

Jacob Cornelisz. executed the twelve woodcuts that comprise his round Passion series between 1511 and 1514.[1] All but one of these scenes bear, in the early impressions, a date within these years; subsequently, the dates were removed from the blocks and therefore do not appear in any of the later editions, with the exception of the unique series at Veste Coburg. In addition to early proofs (as opposed to those cut out of later impressions, which were printed with frames), the series of twelve woodcuts seems to have been printed in three different early editions, distinguished by the varying designs of the ornamental frames. The first of these editions features a narrow circular frame or border that occurs in two variations: One depicts putti and instruments of the Passion among tendrils and a cartouche with the coat of arms of Amsterdam below, and is unique to six prints from the series now in the print room at Veste Coburg (fig. 1); the other variant incorporates the busts of Old and New Testament figures in cartouches with instruments of the Passion; the coat of arms of Amsterdam, flanked by the initials A and M, below; and the word HOL / LÄT in a cartouche above (fig. 2). The woodcuts in the second edition, to which the present example belongs, feature narrow circular frames consisting of

40

FIG. 3 Jacob Cornelisz. van Oostsanen. *The Resurrection.* Woodcut. 1517. Amsterdam, Rijksmuseum, Rijksprentenkabinet

FIG. 1 Jacob Cornelisz. van Oostsanen. *The Betrayal.* Woodcut. 1514. Kunstsammlungen der Veste Coburg, Kupferstichkabinett

beaded borders enclosing a band studded at intervals with snails, shells, bells, and other designs, the crowned arms of Amsterdam at the top, and the date 1517 at the bottom. Each is, in turn, placed within a rectangular surround with fantastical creatures in the spandrels, including a dragon biting the head of a turtle in the upper right and a hen-headed creature eyeing a snail in the lower left; below is a plaque with a double column of five lines of text each. Another version of this frame with variation in the detail of the ornament also exists (fig. 3). The woodcuts in the third edition have large rectangular frames surrounding the circular scene, below which are three arched openings, those on either side occupied by Old Testament prefigurations of the Passion scene depicted in the circle above, and between these typological representations, bust-length images of two prophets (see fig. 4). The frames of the individual sheets were designed so that the sheets could be joined, making an enormous tableau measuring about 77 by over 181 centimeters.[2] The first and apparently all ensuing editions were produced in Jacob Cornelisz.'s lifetime, and were printed and published in Amsterdam by Doen Pietersz.[3] The imperial privilege referred to in the line below the two columns of text on the present sheet is, of course, an unequivocal indication that the edition was devised for a Catholic audience. The fact that Charles V ascended to the Spanish throne in 1517 may have inspired the publication of the two editions produced by Doen Pietersz. in that year.[4]

No impression of the *Last Supper* with a date is known, but the more assured cutting suggests a

FIG. 4 Jacob Cornelisz. van Oostsanen. *The Mocking of Christ.* Woodcut. 1517. Amsterdam, Rijksmuseum, Rijksprentenkabinet

later date in the chronology of the series. Although Jacob Cornelisz. used the circular format in his 1507 series of the Life of the Virgin, at least two scenes from his round Passion series seem to have been inspired by the corresponding scenes in Lucas van Leyden's 1509 circular series devoted to the same subject; in the main, however, Jacob seems to have been more influenced by Dürer, in

FIG. 2 Jacob Cornelisz. van Oostsanen. *The Flagellation.* Woodcut. 1514. Kunstsammlungen der Veste Coburg, Kupferstichkabinett

FIG. 5 Albrecht Dürer. *The Last Supper*. Woodcut. About 1508–9. New York, The Metropolitan Museum of Art, The George Khuner Collection, Gift of Mrs. George Khuner, 1975

FIG. 6 Dieric Bouts. *The Last Supper* (central panel of the *Blessed Sacrament* triptych). Tempera and oil on panel. 1464. Leuven, Church of Saint Peter

FIG. 7 After Jacob Cornelisz. van Oostsanen. *The Last Supper*. Roundel. 1515–20. Cambridge, King's College Chapel

terms of the number of scenes, the choice of subjects, and specific elements of the compositions. The present composition corresponds quite closely to the parallel scene in Dürer's Small Passion woodcut series of about 1508–10 (*Ill. Bartsch* 10:24, p. 119): Christ, nimbed with points of radiating light, sits at the head of a round table under a cloth baldachino (fig. 5); John sleeps in his arms while the remaining apostles are distributed to his left and right. Those in the foreground are seated on either of two benches with their backs to the viewer; Judas is seen in three-quarter view from the rear, holding a sack of money in his hand. The paschal lamb is set atop a large salver, and even the placement of the artist's monogram in the foreground to the left of the large-handled jug seems to have captured Jacob Cornelisz.'s attention. While Dürer's figures are compressed within the rectangular format, the circular composition adopted by Jacob Cornelisz. allows for a more commodious and evenly spaced arrangement of the figures. The prominent steps in the foreground set the scene deeper in space, heightening the illusion created by the frame that we are actually witnessing the scene through a window. In this regard, the print represents an advance over the spatial structure of the Berlin sheet (cat. no. 38). The present impression is sharp, if somewhat dry; there are some ocher spots to the right and above the head of Christ.

Jacob Cornelisz.'s composition relies heavily on traditional late medieval iconography, retaining both the identification of Judas, who betrays himself by holding up the purse of blood money, and the special status of the young John, asleep in

Christ's arms, as "he whom Jesus loved." The large jug in the foreground may be an allusion to the washing of the apostles' feet, an event that became increasingly linked, iconographically, with the Last Supper. Unlike Dürer's composition, however, that of Cornelisz. depicts Christ blessing the chalice that holds Eucharistic wafers, thus transforming the scene from an event of the Passion to the celebration of the sacrament. In this regard, the composition harks back to the central panel of Dieric Bouts's 1464 triptych of the *Blessed Sacrament*, commissioned for and preserved at the church of Saint Peter in Leuven (fig. 6)—the earliest representation of the Last Supper in the Lowlands and the first to interpret the event as a Eucharistic rite. The use of the chalice as a ciborium may refer to the subordination of the chalice to the consecration of the Host; already, in 1415, the withdrawal of the chalice from the laity had been formally sanctioned. The elevated importance of the Host—regarded as *totus Christus*—perhaps also reflects the increased prominence of the feast of Corpus Christi, the origins of which can be traced to events in Leuven some two centuries earlier.

Cornelisz.'s Passion series—whether intended or not—gave rise to a large output of roundels to judge from the numerous replicas that survive; one of the most complete series of these, comprising seven of the twelve scenes, is found in the parish church at Bradford-on-Avon.[5] There is no *Last Supper* at Bradford-on-Avon, but replicas and versions are known—to cite only a few, in addition to the fine example in King's College, Cambridge (fig. 7)[6]—in the church of Saint

Matthew, Watford, Hertfordshire,[7] and at Packwood House, Lapworth, Warwickshire.[8] The best follow Jacob Cornelisz.'s compositions faithfully but rarely slavishly, often modifying some details or introducing others.[9] The King's College version, for example, clarifying the source of light, adds a large oculus to each side wall and delineates the brick fabric (see fig. 7). The present roundel, finely painted and articulated with skillful stickwork, eliminates the foreground steps, placing the handled jug instead on a tiled floor. The painter, with apparent delight, also added a variety of colored patterns to the costumes and grains to the furniture.

The compositions of Jacob Cornelisz.'s Passion series were adapted for other mediums as well. The *Carrying of the Cross* and the *Crucifixion* inspired the corresponding scenes on the orphreys of a chasuble embroidered from about 1525 to 1530.[10] The central panel of a triptych executed in reverse-glass painting with the coats of arms of Dirck Pietersz. Spangert and his wife, Adriana van Roon (fig. 8), appears to be a loose adaptation of the present composition;[11] while the details are much altered, the general configuration of the group seated at the round table and the similarity of the foremost left figure establish the source.[12] The reverse-glass painter was not, however, exclusively dependent on Jacob Cornelisz.'s composition. Details such as the dog gnawing a bone in the foreground and the servant carrying a deep-dish pie in the right background appear to rely on the same source (reversed) as the one that inspired the glass painter responsible for a roundel representing Lazarus and Dives, now in The Cloisters

41

FIG. 8 Triptych (central panel) with *The Last Supper, Saints, and Donors*. Reverse-glass painting. About 1525. Amsterdam, Rijksmuseum

FIG. 9 *Lazarus and Dives*. Roundel. About 1520. New York, The Metropolitan Museum of Art, The Cloisters Collection, 1932

(fig. 9).[13] These recurring correspondences would seem once again to underscore the use of common models by numerous ateliers working in a variety of mediums.

1. For a more thorough discussion of this series see Steinbart, *Holzschnittwerk*, 1937, pp. 38–63, nos. 20–31; Appuhn et al., *Riesenholzschnitte*, 1976, pp. 35–39; Washington, *Lucas van Leyden* (exhib. cat.), 1983, no. 111, pp. 269–71.

2. See Appuhn et al., *Riesenholzschnitte*, 1976, pp. 35–39, fig. 27.

3. See Steinbart, *Holzschnittwerk*, 1937, p. 40.

4. Ibid., p. 41; Steinbart suggests that the Renaissance frames of 1517 may have been abandoned in favor of the more elaborate typological arrangement in honor of this event.

5. See Cole, *Roundels in Britain*, 1993, p. 31, nos. 255–59, 264, and 265. Steinbart (*Holzschnittwerk*, 1937, pp. 60–61) lists nine roundels, but two—*Christ Carrying the Cross* and *The Entombment*—are not in Bradford according to Cole.

6. See Wayment, *King's College*, 1988, pp. 172–73, 41d2.

7. See Cole, *Roundels in Britain*, 1993, p. 304, no. 2404.

8. Ibid., p. 130, no. 1049.

9. A roundel in the Stedelijk Museum Vander Kelen-Mertens, Leuven (B/III/25), which has been published on several occasions (Maes, "Inventaris," *Leuvens Brandglas*, 1987, pp. 249–50, no. 24, fig. 149; Isler-de Jongh, "Rondels de la Collection Hosmer," 1989, fig. 48), must be called into question. I have only examined this roundel installed, but the flat quality of the paint, the stiff linear outlines of the figures, the bland treatment of the faces, and the limited technique all indicate that this must be a modern copy.

10. See Amsterdam, *Kunst voor de beeldenstorm* (exhib. cat.), 1986, pp. 137–38, no. 24; see also pp. 138–39, no. 25; see also Steinbart, "Nachlese," 1929, pp. 241–42, cat. p. 260.

11. See Amsterdam, *Kunst voor de beeldenstorm* (exhib. cat.), 1986, pp. 134–35, no. 21.

12. For examples of embroideries based on lost paintings by Jacob Cornelisz. see Steinbart, "Paramente," 1921, pp. 931–37.

13. Inv. no. 32.24.37. See Husband, *Silver-Stained Roundels*, 1991, p. 144.

BIBLIOGRAPHY: (39) Steinbart, *Holzschnittwerk*, 1937, no. 20, pp. 43–44, pl. 5. (40) Grosvenor Thomas Stock Book, II, p. 74, no. 2002; Husband, *Silver-Stained Roundels*, 1991, p. 112.

## 41

### The Betrayal

About 1515–20

Roundel: diameter, 9½ in. (24.1 cm)

Amsterdam, Rijksmuseum, RBK-1966-59

Inscribed (below the sheathed sword of the figure at the right): with the cipher 𝆑

## 42

### The Crowning with Thorns

Amsterdam, about 1515–20

Roundel: diameter, 8⅞ in. (22.5 cm)

Amsterdam, Rijksmuseum, NM 12563

Inscribed (bottom left): with the cipher 𝆑

In the *Betrayal* (fig. 1)—as well as in the *Agony in the Garden* (fig. 2)—Jacob Cornelisz. seems to have been most influenced by the 1509 circular Passion series of Lucas van Leyden (*Ill. Bartsch* 12:57–65, pp. 189–97). In both instances, Jacob reversed the compositions, but the general organization of the scenes and the disposition of the figures and their placement relative to the picture plane are essentially the same (see figs. 3 and 4). In the *Betrayal* Jacob even adopts—although perhaps with less success—Lucas's device of the heavy vertical tree trunk to provide a counterweight to the massive figure of Christ. Other details, such as the position of the fallen Malchus, are more directly quoted. That Jacob's series begins in the traditional manner with the *Last*

42

*Supper* is an indication of his conservative bent, while Lucas, in keeping with sixteenth-century convention, begins his sequence with the *Agony in the Garden*.

These two roundels demonstrate how differently glass painters can treat like material based on the same series of designs. As far as the compositions are concerned, the glass painter of the *Betrayal* followed the woodcut (fig. 1) in virtually all details. The *Crowning with Thorns* generally conforms to the woodcut in all but the most minor of details, such as the omission of the masonry joints and clamps in the foreground parapet (see fig. 5). For unclear reasons, however, this glass painter has eliminated the child seated on the lower section of the parapet and blowing a horn. Moreover, he apparently objected—as did the painter of the Cambridge *Last Supper* roundel (cat. nos. 39 and 40, fig. 7)—to Jacob Cornelisz.'s unclear source of light. Here, the glass painter replaces the gallery of spectators at the left with a large quarry window admitting a flood of light that suffuses the figures from the left. In deference to the sacred nature of the subject, he has turned the head of the seated figure at the left, who holds a baton of authority, so that rather than staring out the window he now witnesses the event for which he apparently holds some responsibility. The monogram or cipher seen on the facing of the parapet where Jacob Cornelisz. placed his monogram plaque in the woodcut (fig. 5) is probably a rare instance of the glass painter identifying himself.

The *Betrayal* is executed in a medium brown, and, in the case of the tree, a dark reddish brown paint. A strong yellow silver stain is applied extensively throughout the composition: for the whole of Judas's robe, the hems and details of costumes, the gate and wall, and broadly over the landscape. Judas's money sack is painted a red to sanguine tone that appears in a less-pronounced manner in some of the faces. Dark paint and a

43

44

fine-pointed brush are used to delineate detail and outlines, as well as the hair of Christ; the hair of all the other figures is worked with a stylus. The bold range of color values and modulations of light produce a dramatic, densely painted image. The dark and tortured head of Malchus is all the more striking for the brilliant etched accents to the hair and teeth. The glass painter, who may have left his mark in the form of a small cipher just under the sheathed sword at the right, has created a rich, textured, painterly effect, which is only negligibly marred by the rubbed and abraded area at the lower left rendering this passage less than readily legible. The *Crowning with Thorns*, by contrast, is dominated by subdued tones of medium grayish brown with a dark umber-to-black paint for outlining and detailing. The pale yellow silver stain is confined almost exclusively to the hems and borders of costumes. The artist's sparing use of the stylus, and his reliance rather on a fine-pointed brush to create a sharply detailed image, gives the work the appearance of a drypoint engraving. Much of the effect relies on the contrast of the thin and relatively sparse areas of paint and the large expanses of untoned glass, but this, unfortunately, has been diminished by the extensive rubbing of the surface, particularly in the lower half. There is a horizontal break through the center that is joined by another that extends diagonally; both were glued after the removal of mending leads that have left rubbed marks.

BIBLIOGRAPHY: (42) Hudig, "Zestiende eeuwsche ruiten," 1922, pp. 42–43, fig. 5; Steinbart, "Nachlese," 1929, pp. 231–33, fig. 39.

## 43

### A Messenger Telling Abraham of the Capture of Lot

Lowlands, about 1520–25

Pen and brown ink on paper: diameter, 8⅞ in. (22.5 cm)

London, British Museum, F.f.4.91

## 44

### A Messenger Telling Abraham of the Capture of Lot

Lowlands, about 1520–25

Roundel: diameter, 8⅞ in. (22.5 cm)

Ghent, Bijlokemuseum, 9035

## 45

### Abraham Witnessing the Burning of Sodom

Lowlands, about 1520–25

Roundel: diameter, 8⅞ in. (22.5 cm)

Ghent, Bijlokemuseum, 9089

The drawing and the roundel based on it represent the incidents recounted in Genesis that immediately followed the defeat of the rebellious kings of Sodom and Gomorrah at the hands of the Elamite king Chedorlaomer. Lot, the son of Abraham's brother, was taken prisoner after the fall of Sodom: "And behold one that had escaped told Abram . . . that his brother Lot was taken"

(Genesis 14: 13–14). Abraham gathered his forces and descended upon Lot's captors: "He rushed upon them in the night: and defeated them" (Genesis 14: 15). This battle appears to be summarized by the several combatants seen in the far background. Following the battle Abraham encountered the king of Sodom: "And the king of Sodom went out to meet him, after he returned from the slaughter of Chodorlahomor" (Genesis 14: 17)—an event that takes place in the middle ground. The second roundel represents subsequent events, as retold in Genesis: In the middle ground at the right Lot is seen before the gates of Sodom greeting two angels: "And the two angels came to Sodom in the evening . . . And seeing them, he rose up and went to meet them" (Genesis 19: 1). Through the intercession of the angels, Lot and his daughters were delivered from Sodom, which by the wrath of God was then consumed in flames: "And the Lord rained upon Sodom and Gomorrha brimstone and fire" (Genesis 19: 24). The burning city dominates the background of the roundel. To these events Abraham was witness; here, with hands clasped and commanding the foreground, he views the burning city: "He looked towards Sodom and Gomorrha . . . and he saw the ashes rise up from the earth as the smoke of a furnace" (Genesis 19: 28).

Steinbart attributed the present drawing to Jacob Cornelisz. without reservation; he compared the figure of the kneeling messenger with that of the soldier to the left of Christ in the *Resurrection* woodcut (fig. 1) from the 1511 to 1514 Passion series (see cat. nos. 39–42), also noting that the small background figure of a sol-

45

dier with arm raised to deliver a mortal blow to his victim in the drawing is identical to the soldier in the background of Jacob's 1507 monogrammed woodcut, from a Marian series, of the *Miracle of the Jew Who Touched the Coffin of the Virgin* (fig. 2).[1] Popham concurred with Steinbart, citing some of the same comparisons, and amplified the close connections he saw between the drawing and the woodcut Passion series; for example, he compared the face of the messenger with that of the man raising his hand at the left in the *Ecce Homo* (fig. 3).[2] He further contended that the extremely accurate cutting of the Passion series reproduces Cornelisz.'s pen line so faithfully that a comparison between the woodcuts and the drawing is validated.[3] Popham also compared the position of the messenger's legs with those of the kneeling soldier in the *Resurrection* (fig. 1);[4] in both figures, the left and right legs, identically positioned, give the disconcerting impression of being attached to the body in the same place. Further visual support of these arguments is provided by a comparison of the messenger in the present sheet with the kneeling figure to the left of Christ in the *Crowning with Thorns* (cat. nos. 41 and 42, fig. 5).

Although not as deliberate as in the Berlin *Last Supper* (cat. no. 38), the drawing is freely but surely rendered, and there is little evidence of the artist having reworked the composition. Firm, continuous lines describe the contours, while parallel strokes model the forms and dense cross-hatching defines the shadowed areas—all characteristics of Jacob's technique. The background details are indicative if quite schematic.

Faces, for example, are often informed with no more detail than a cursory circle for an eye. Nonetheless, the treatment of the background is somewhat more comprehensive than is generally encountered in Jacob's work—a functional requirement if, as seems likely, this drawing were intended as a working design. The fact that little is left to the devices of the glass painter further supports this interpretation; a workshop or workbench drawing is more apt to reduce background elements, for example, to mere schematic indications. Details of the central figures of Abraham and the messenger are thoroughly articulated: The profile of the messenger conveys the pathos of the bearer of bad news, while Abraham's demeanor suggests reassurance and compassion. The gesticulations of the hands are particularly expressive, if somewhat difficult to read in the first instance. The present drawing appears to be somewhat trimmed at the circumference and there are several repaired tears at the edge.

The Ghent roundel is faithful in detail to the composition of the drawing, but, as is expected, many background details, such as the meeting of Abraham and the king of Sodom, have been fleshed out and brought into sharper focus. Steinbart was inclined to see the differences between the roundel and the drawing as evidence of an intermediate design.[5] Almost certainly there was such an intermediate workbench drawing but this probably would have reduced the detail, not expanded it; thus, the differences—slight as they are in this case—are likely to have occurred in spite of the intermediate drawing, not because of it. The glass painter has animated the composition

FIG. 4 *Abraham Witnessing the Burning of Sodom and Abraham and the Angels.* Roundel. 1520–25. Amsterdam, Rijksmuseum

FIG. 5 *Abraham Is Blessed by Melchizedek.* Roundel. 1520–25. Ghent, Bijlokemuseum

FIG. 6 *Abraham Praying for the Healing of Abimelech and The Oath of Bersabee.* Roundel. 1520–25. Ghent, Bijlokemuseum

FIG. 7 *The Oath of Bersabee* (detail of fig. 6)

FIG. 8 *Abraham Is Prostrate before God and The Covenant of Circumcision.* Roundel. 1520–25. London, Victoria and Albert Museum

with color and texture—notably in the costumes and details of the landscape.

The London sheet appears to be the single surviving drawing from a Genesis or Abraham cycle.[6] Other compositions from this series are preserved in several extant roundels. In addition to *A Messenger Telling Abraham of the Capture of Lot* and *Abraham Witnessing the Burning of Sodom*—a replica of which is in the Rijksmuseum, Amsterdam (fig. 4)[7]—there are two further roundels from the same series and seemingly from the same workshop.[8] One represents Abraham blessed by Melchizedek (fig. 5): "But Melchisedech the king of Salem . . . Blessed him, and said: Blessed be Abram" (Genesis 14: 18, 19). The other depicts Abraham praying for the healing of Abimelech and the oath of Bersabee (fig. 6): "And when

Abraham prayed, God healed Abimelech" (Genesis 20: 17), "And Abraham said: I will swear. . . . Thou shalt take seven ewe lambs at my hand: that they may be a testimony for me, that I dug this well" (Genesis 21: 24, 30); in the right background, a shepherd separates out the sheep, while Abraham and Melchizedek stand on a bridge over the source (fig. 7). Another roundel that appears to be based on a design from the same series although executed by a different hand or workshop represents Abraham prostrate before God and the covenant of circumcision (fig. 8): "The Lord appeared to him: . . . Abram fell flat on his face" (Genesis 17: 1, 3). "And Abraham took Ismael his son . . . and all whom he had bought, every male among the men of his house: and he circumcised the flesh of their foreskin" (Genesis 17: 23).[9] While the narratives of these compositions are very detailed, each roundel illustrates no more than two or three verses of the biblical text. Thus, if the original series covered the whole of the history of Abraham—that is to say roughly chapters twelve through twenty-four of Genesis—the cycle must have comprised an exceptionally large number of roundels.

There are certain similarities among the roundels in this series and the work of Dirick Vellert (see cat. nos. 67–80). The angle of Abraham's head and the treatment of his ear, for example, find parallels in Vellert's figural style, while the kneeling position of the messenger who tells Abraham of the capture of Lot is often echoed in the open stances of many of Vellert's figures. The central tree with the spiky, dead branches and the plantain in the foreground of *Abraham Witnessing the Burning of Sodom* are virtual hallmarks of Vellert's compositions, suggesting that Jacob must have been sufficiently familiar with Vellert's work during his period of activity in Antwerp to have incorporated in his own work elements of Vellert's vocabulary.

1. Steinbart, "Nachlese," 1929, pp. 228–29, fig. 29.

2. Popham, *Drawings in the British Museum*, 1932, p. 10.

3. Ibid.

4. Ibid.

5. Steinbart, "Nachlese," 1929, p. 229.

6. However, this may not be the only drawing by Jacob Cornelisz. related to glass painting. A sheet representing *The Refusal of Joachim's Offering*, now in the Staatliche Museen zu Berlin, Preußischer Kulturbesitz, Kupferstichkabinett (KdZ 11743), is partially circumscribed, suggesting that even though the composition was not well suited to a circular format it was at least considered for a roundel design.

7. Inv. no. NM 12564.

8. Ghent, Bijlokemuseum, 9028 and 9034.

9. London, Victoria and Albert Museum, 122-1924.

BIBLIOGRAPHY: (43) Popham, "Notes-II," 1929, pp. 156–57, fig. 7; Steinbart, "Nachlese," 1929, pp. 228–29, fig. 29; Popham, *Drawings in the British Museum*, 1932, pp. 9–10, pl. 2. (44) Steinbart, "Nachlese," 1929, pp. 229–30, fig. 32; Popham, *Drawings in the British Museum*, 1932, p. 10. (45) Steinbart, "Nachlese," 1929, pp. 229–30, fig. 33.

# 5

# Pieter Cornelisz., or the Monogrammist PC

*Pieter Cornelisz. called Kunst, born about 1489 or 1490 in Leiden, was the eldest son of the Leiden painter Cornelis Engebrechtsz. Van Mander states only that Pieter Cornelisz. was a glas-schrijver, or stained-glass painter, but it is known that he also painted pictures and designed furniture. A large group of stylistically homogeneous drawings all monogrammed with the initials PC (or DC ?)[1]—the earliest dated 1516—and, seemingly, designs for small-scale glass painting, has long been attributed to this master. For uncertain reasons, none of his works from after 1532 is dated or monogrammed. Pieter Cornelisz. apparently died in Leiden between October 1560 and July 1561.[2]*

Of the numerous extant drawings with the monogram *PC* (or *DC*), the largest group and the only one for which stained glass has survived is that devoted to the Seven Acts of Mercy. The artist treated this subject at least three times, varying the compositions. Six drawings representing six of the seven acts, all dated 1524 and all but one monogrammed *PC*, appear to preserve the compositions of a series, although they probably do not constitute an integral series themselves. This group comprises *Feeding the Hungry*,[3] *Giving Drink to the Thirsty*,[4] *Sheltering the Strangers*,[5] *Caring for the Dying* (cat. no. 48), *Freeing the Prisoners* (cat. no. 49), and *Burying the Dead*.[6] Only two drawings survive from the second series: *Feeding the Hungry*[7] and *Burying the Dead*,[8] both of which are monogrammed and dated 1531. The third series, monogrammed and dated 1532, comprises *Freeing the Prisoners*,[9] *Caring for the Dying*,[10] and *Burying the Dead*[11]—the only subject that survives in all three series. A twelfth drawing, *Giving Drink to the Thirsty*, appears to be by the Monogrammist PC but lacks a monogram or a date.[12] While only one stained-glass panel based on any of the series—the 1524 *Freeing the*

*Prisoners* (cat. no. 50)—is known to survive, another panel representing *Clothing the Naked* may, in fact, preserve a lost composition from the series (see cat. nos. 49 and 50, fig. 1). There are, however, three roundels from an Acts of Mercy series (cat. nos. 46 and 47); the designs of these roundels, clinging to late medieval conventions, are both stylistically and iconographically conservative, and must predate the Pieter Cornelisz. designs by a decade or more. Yet, in the case of *Caring for the Dying*, there are close compositional similarities between the earlier roundel and the corresponding drawing from Pieter Cornelisz.'s 1524 series (compare cat. nos. 47 and 48). In both style and technique, Pieter Cornelisz. is heavily influenced by his contemporary and studio companion Lucas van Leyden, but in this instance, at least, Cornelisz., like so many other designers for glass, relied on older models, perhaps more familiar to his conservative clientele.

1. Recently, the monogram has been read as *DC* rather than *PC* (see Amsterdam, *Kunst voor de beeldenstorm* [exhib. cat.], 1986, no. 49, pp. 167–68). Jeremy D. Bangs ("The Leiden monogramist," 1981, pp. 12–15) has attempted to demonstrate that Pieter Cornelisz. did not use the monogram *PC* because these initials do not appear with his name on a list of marks or ciphers; rather, the monogram was used by "Meester Hugenz. van Cloetinge." As Boon (*Drawings of the Frits Lugt Collection* 1, 1992, p. 236, n. 1) points out, however, ciphers and monograms cannot necessarily be equated. Boon (ibid., p. 236) states that no works were signed after 1532; Berserik (in Amsterdam, *Kunst voor de beeldenstorm* [exhib. cat.], 1986, p. 167) gives the date 1541.

2. Gibson ("Pieter Cornelisz. Kunst," 1967, p. 37) gives the bracketing dates as 1517 to 1537.

3. Staatliche Museen zu Berlin, Preußischer Kulturbesitz, Kupferstichkabinett, KdZ 1191.

4. Paris, Collection Frits Lugt, Institut Néerlandais, 5378.

5. Staatliche Museen zu Berlin, Preußischer Kulturbesitz, Kupferstichkabinett, KdZ 1193.

6. Amsterdam, Rijksmuseum, RP-T-1879 A 7.

7. Rotterdam, Museum Boymans-van Beuningen, N-5.

8. Munich, Staatliche Graphische Sammlung, 41054.

9. Formerly in the collection of the Earl of Leicester, Holkham Hall, Norfolk. See Popham and Lloyd, *Drawings at Holkham Hall*, 1986, pp. 128–29, no. 302; *Old Master Drawings from Holkham* (sale cat.), 1991, no. 62.

10. Staatliche Museen zu Berlin, Preußischer Kulturbesitz, Kupferstichkabinett, KdZ 1189.

11. Staatliche Museen zu Berlin, Preußischer Kulturbesitz, Kupferstichkabinett, KdZ 1190.

12. Frankfurt, Städelsches Kunstinstitut, 5508.

46

47

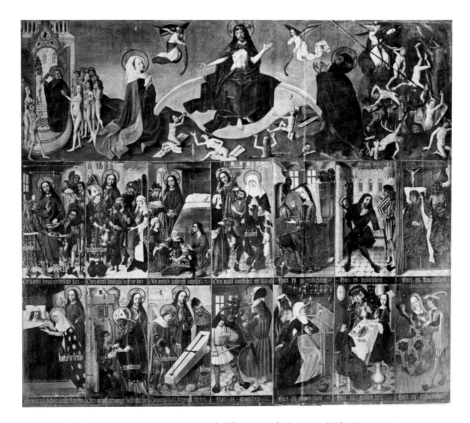

FIG. 1 *The Last Judgment* altarpiece, with *The Acts of Mercy* and *The Seven Deadly Sins*. Tempera and oil on panel. About 1500. Antwerp, Koninklijk Museum voor Schone Kunsten

46

### Feeding the Hungry

Leiden, about 1510–20

Roundel: diameter, 8⅞ in. (22.5 cm)

Amsterdam, Rijksmuseum, NM 12231 b

47 *see plate 11*

### Caring for the Dying

Leiden, about 1510–20

Roundel: diameter, 8⅞ in. (22.5 cm)

Amsterdam, Rijksmuseum, NM 12231 c

The Acts of Mercy are inspired by Christ's explanation of the Last Judgment according to Matthew: "For I was hungry, and you gave me to eat; I was thirsty, and you gave me to drink; I was a stranger, and you took me in: Naked, and you covered me: sick, and you visited me: I was in prison, and you came to me. . . . as long as you did it to one of these my least brethren, you did it to me" (Matthew 25: 35–36, 40). The seventh Act of Mercy, Burying the Dead, is first encountered in the twelfth-century *Rationale divinorum officiorum* of Johannes Beleth. Subsequently, numerology associated the Seven Acts of Mercy with the Seven Virtues and with the Seven Sacraments; in an Antwerp panel, placed below the Last Judgment, the Acts of Mercy are juxtaposed with the Seven Deadly Sins (fig. 1).

In the first quarter of the sixteenth century in the Lowlands, the Seven Acts of Mercy were generally depicted in association with the Last

FIG. 2 Master of Alkmaar. *The Seven Acts of Mercy*. Tempera and oil on panel. 1504. Amsterdam, Rijksmuseum

FIG. 3 Master of Alkmaar. *Burying the Dead and The Last Judgment* (detail of fig. 2)

Judgment. In the 1504 series by the Master of Alkmaar, for example, *Burying the Dead*,[1] which is usually at the end of the series, is placed in the middle; Christ, flanked by the Virgin and Saint John the Evangelist, is seen above, seated in judgment on a rainbow with his feet resting on an orb (figs. 2 and 3), and thus is the central focus, if not the dominant image, of the entire ensemble. In Barent van Orley's 1525 triptych from the civil hospital in Antwerp,[2] on the other hand, the central panel is devoted entirely to the Last Judgment, while the Seven Acts of Mercy are distributed over the inner and outer panels of the two shutters (figs. 4, 5, and 6). This theme remained popular in glass painting throughout the period, as evidenced by a panel dated 1556, representing *Feeding the Hungry*, which belonged to a series of the Acts of Mercy ordered by Wouter van Bylaer, head of the hospital of Saint John in Utrecht (fig. 7).[3]

The Amsterdam roundels, the compositions of which appear to have influenced Jacob Cornelisz.'s later series, follow an earlier formula in which Christ, haloed and at the back of a group of onlookers, is a witness to each of the acts—a reference to Christ's words at the Last Judgment, and a reminder to the viewer that, then, all will have to account for their earthly behavior. The moralizing image thus takes on a contemplative and rather admonitory overtone. This is evident, for example, in the illumination that serves as the frontispiece to *Benois seront les miséricordieux*, a manuscript by Dreux Jehan or a follower, commissioned for Margaret of York, wife of Charles the Bold, Duke of Burgundy, in about 1470 (fig. 8).[4] Here, the young duchess is depicted perform-

FIG. 4 Barent van Orley. *The Last Judgment* altarpiece, with *The Seven Acts of Mercy*. Tempera and oil on panel. 1525. Antwerp, Koninklijk Museum voor Schone Kunsten

FIG. 5 Barent van Orley. *The Last Judgment* altarpiece, with *The Seven Acts of Mercy* (outer left shutter). Tempera and oil on panel. 1525. Antwerp, Koninklijk Museum voor Schone Kunsten

FIG. 6 Barent van Orley. *The Last Judgment* altarpiece, with *The Seven Acts of Mercy* (outer right shutter). Tempera and oil on panel. 1525. Antwerp, Koninklijk Museum voor Schone Kunsten

FIG. 7 *Feeding the Hungry*. Painted glass panel. 1556. Utrecht, Rijksmuseum Het Catharijneconvent

FIG. 9 *Christ Healing a Blind Man*. Roundel. About 1510–20. Amsterdam, Rijksmuseum

FIG. 8 Dreux Jehan, or a Follower. *The Seven Acts of Mercy, with Margaret of York in Prayer*. Illuminated manuscript page from *Benois seront les miséricordieux* (detail). About 1470. Brussels, Bibliothèque Royale

FIG. 10 *The Miracle at Cana*. Roundel. About 1510–20. Leiden, Stedelijk Museum de Lakenhal

ing the Acts of Mercy with Christ as a witness; the final image shows the duchess in contemplative prayer, suggesting that understanding the significance of the charitable acts is of greater importance than the actual performance of them. In the roundel versions, the dense groupings of earthy, rather heavyset figures are clustered against a tightly focused background of urban architecture—a compositional arrangement that Pieter Cornelisz. adopted. In *Caring for the Dying* (cat. no. 47), the only interior scene in the group—as in the manuscript illumination—the dying man is viewed from the foot of his bed, which is centered in the composition. Christ looks over the shoulder of the priest holding a crucifix, while, at the foot of the bed, a monk reads from a book and, on the other side of the bed, a woman holds a bowl of porridge and a spoon. At the right, an opening in the wall reveals the subsequent burial of the victim, indicating that this series conformed to the biblical text, thereby limiting the acts to six.

Both roundels are executed in brown to grayish brown paint, although the tones are warmer and more reddish in *Caring for the Dying*. The pale and deeper yellow silver stain is used sparsely, confined to a few objects—the halos, the bundled bed hanging, the child's hair, and some articles of clothing—and is also used to give the ground a mottled effect. Modeling is achieved with a considerable use of the badger brush, while details such as the masonry joints and the outlining of figures are done with a fine-pointed brush and dark paint. The stylus work is particularly accomplished and effective in the rendering of such details as the cresting of the bed and the

rings of the bed hangings. It is also used to outline drapery and to highlight drapery folds, in the form of fine parallel strokes often applied in a zigzag pattern. The stylus work is especially well controlled in *Caring for the Dying*. In addition to minor inconsistencies, such as the patterned halo in this roundel but not in *Feeding the Hungry* (cat. no. 46), slight differences in style suggest different hands. The painting of *Caring for the Dying*— and that of the third and least well-preserved roundel in this series, representing *Housing the Strangers*—is a bit more refined in its execution; the facial features of the figures in *Caring for the Dying*, for example, are softer, more rounded, and delicate than those in *Feeding the Hungry*, which are broader, heavier, and more often accented with stylus work.

A fourth roundel in the Rijksmuseum, representing Christ healing a blind man (fig. 9),[5] probably by the same hand as *Feeding the Hungry*, has long and erroneously been grouped with this series when, in fact, it clearly comes from a Miracle or Public Life series. Another roundel, *The Miracle at Cana* (fig. 10), must belong to the same series as well.[6] This group of roundels has been associated stylistically with the Berlin *Sacrament of Baptism* roundel (cat. no. 15, fig. 1); Popham, furthermore, attributed two roundels of the ten devoted to the life of Saint Alexius, formerly in Berlin—*Saint Alexius at School* and *The Marriage of Saint Alexius*—to this same workshop.[7]

1. Amsterdam, Rijksmuseum, A 2815; from the church of Saint Lawrence in Alkmaar.

2. Antwerp, Museum voor Schone Kunsten, 741–745. See Friedländer, *Early Netherlandish Painting* 8, 1972, plates 84 and 85.

3. See Schmitz, *Glasgemälde* 1, 1913, p. 75. I am grateful to Zsuzsanna van Ruyven-Zeman for bringing this panel to my attention.

4. Brussels, Bibliothèque Royale, Ms. 9296, fol. 1.

5. Amsterdam, Rijksmuseum, NM 12231 d.

6. Leiden, Stedelijk Museum de Lakenhal, 7683.

7. Popham, "Notes-II," 1929, pp. 152–54. Popham believed that another roundel also in Berlin—*Christ in the House of Mary and Martha*—is by the same hand as well.

BIBLIOGRAPHY: (46) Beets, "Aanwinsten," 1911, pp. 246–47, fig. 3; Berserik, "Leiden, ca. 1480–1545," 1982, no. 37, fig. 60. (47) Beets, "Aanwinsten," 1911, pp. 246–47, fig. 5; Popham, "Notes-II," 1929, pp. 152–53, fig. 1; Berserik, "Leiden, ca. 1480–1545," 1982, no. 36, fig. 58.

## 48

### Caring for the Dying

Pen and brown ink on paper, 9⅝ x 7½ in.
(24.4 x 19.1 cm)

Amsterdam, Rijksmuseum, Rijksprentenkabinet,
RP-T-1879 A 6

Dated: 1524

Monogrammed: PC

The six Pieter Cornelisz. 1524 Acts of Mercy drawings adhere, in the main, to a late medieval formula. As in the 1470 illuminations of Margaret of York performing the Acts of Mercy (cat. nos. 46 and 47, fig. 8), the scenes are set in public among clearly ordinary folk. All the acts, excepting *Caring for the Dying*, occur out of doors against contemporary town architecture. In the Pieter Cornelisz. drawings, no single individual administers all the acts; rather, every scene would seem to involve an entirely different cast. Christ, who in medieval representations is constantly present, unobtrusively standing in the back of each group of onlookers and bearing witness, is, in Pieter's compositions, absent—at least in the physical sense—from the proceedings. In two drawings in this group, however, a haloed figure does appear; in *Giving Drink to the Thirsty* it is the man wearing a workman's vest at the back of the group (fig. 1) and in *Feeding the Hungry* it is the crippled beggar on the stairs in the background with his hand extended (fig. 2). The significance of ordinary people with halos is uncertain, but may refer to Christ's words, "As long as you did it to one of these my least brethren, you did it to me" (Matthew 25: 40).[1] That this occurs in only two of the scenes would seem to introduce an inconsistency to the series as a whole. This, and such other discrepancies as the fact that all but the Amsterdam *Burying the Dead* (fig. 3) are monogrammed and all but the Paris *Giving Drink to the Thirsty* (fig. 1) have an ancillary background scene, along with the stylistic differences—compare, for example, the relatively loose and open pen strokes of the Berlin *Feeding the Hungry* (fig. 2) with the tighter, denser, and more controlled lines of the present sheet—strongly suggest that these drawings are from several different versions of the same series.

Typical of Pieter Cornelisz.'s technique are the slightly curved and hooked strokes and the small *c*- or comma-like strokes that outline garments and cross long, defining lines, as well as the scalloped effect along the edges of hems. The reddish stains in the lower-left corner are said to be caused by a colorant in the silver-oxide solution used to produce silver stain; if so, this drawing was apparently at one time in a glass-painting workshop. This group is one of the earliest known to employ a rectilinear format.

The dependency of Pieter Cornelisz., in this sheet, on the earlier roundel design is immediately evident (see cat. no. 47). The principal differences are that Christ is not present and the bed has been moved off center to the right, blocking out the burial scene that was treated as a separate subject in the series. The resulting space at the left

48

FIG. 1 Pieter Cornelisz. Kunst. *Giving Drink to the Thirsty*. Pen and brown ink on paper. 1524. Paris, Collection Frits Lugt, Institut Néerlandais

FIG. 2 Pieter Cornelisz. Kunst. *Feeding the Hungry*. Pen and brown ink on paper. 1524. Staatliche Museen zu Berlin, Preußischer Kulturbesitz, Kupferstichkabinett

has been filled with an ancillary scene of a man and a woman in attendance at the patient's bedside. Otherwise, the composition is essentially the same. Although Cornelisz. may have been familiar with the roundel series, it is more likely that the compositions were known to him through workshop drawings.

1. Boon, *Drawings of the Frits Lugt Collection*, 1992, p. 237, in reference to the Paris drawing, suggests that this detail adds a moralizing tone, but he does not explain why, in a scene that is essentially moralizing, an ordinary man should act as a surrogate for Christ.

BIBLIOGRAPHY: Moes, *Oude teekeningen* 2, 1904–6, pl. 99; Beets, "Aanwinsten," 1911, pp. 245–46, fig. 7; Beets, "Catalogus van de tekeningen," 1913, no. 9; Beets, "Zestiende-euwsche Kunstenaars," 1935, p. 160; Hoogewerff, *Noord-Nederlandsche Schilderkunst* 3, 1939, p. 323, fig. 168; Friedländer, *Early Netherlandish Painting* 10, 1973, pl. 127 A; Boon, *Netherlandish Drawings*, 1978, p. 53, no. 147; Berserik, "Leiden, ca. 1480–1545," 1982, no. 106, fig. 167.

49

FIG. 3 Pieter Cornelisz. Kunst. *Burying the Dead*. Pen and brown ink on paper. 1524. Amsterdam, Rijksmuseum, Rijksprentenkabinet

## 49

### Freeing the Prisoners

Pen and dark brown ink on paper, 9⅞ x 7⅝ in. (25.1 x 19.4 cm)

London, British Museum, 1921.10.12.5

Dated: 1524

Monogrammed: PC

Inscribed (bottom center): *f*; (bottom center, in an eighteenth-century [?] hand): *custos decker*

## 50

### Freeing the Prisoners

Leiden, about 1525–35

Panel, 10 x 7½ in. (25.4 x 19.1 cm)

Paris, Musée du Louvre, OA 1169

Like many other drawings in this and in the other series, the present sheet is freely rendered with modeling and detailing kept to a minimum, thus providing the clearest and most readily followed design for the glass painter. The technique appears to have been characteristic of working designs for roundels in the North Lowlands during the second and third decades of the sixteenth century, in that modeling was typically indicated by the economic use of hatching and parallel lines and very rarely relied on washes. This practice may be contrasted, most notably, to the working methods of Dirick Vellert, who, characteristically, skillfully employed washes even in working tracings where

he was revising or altering the compositions (see cat. nos. 67–80).

In the present scene, the figure at the left hands some coins to an official holding a rod, symbolizing his legal authority, to secure the release of the prisoners in the background, who are being led down the stairs of the prison by the jailer holding a bunch of keys. Like many of the compositions in this series, the scene is anchored by a building in the upper-left corner, the buttress of which serves as a tablet for the artist's monogram and the date. Contrary to late medieval series, the protagonist of each scene is different.

The initial *f* at the bottom is thought to indicate the drawing's position (sixth) in the series; *custos decker* is apparently an eighteenth-century misinterpretation of the monogram *DC*.[1] Similar markings are found on other drawings in this series. The drawing appears to be trimmed just to the edge of the original composition, although portions of the original outline are visible at the left and the bottom. There are some damages along the right side and a restoration at the top-right corner.

The panel, executed in unusually heavy dark-umber-to-black matte paint, enhanced with pale yellow and dark golden silver stain, follows the drawing in detail. The modeling and shading are achieved with both stippling and stickwork, and are given depth of tone by extensive back painting. The somewhat coarse and broad strokes of the thickly painted surface produce a dry and slightly chalky effect. A second panel from the series, representing *Clothing the Naked*, also in the Louvre, is of virtually identical size and is painted in pre-

50

FIG. 1 *Clothing the Naked*. Painted glass panel. About 1525 (?). Paris, Musée du Louvre

cisely the same style and technique (fig. 1).[2] As the Pieter Cornelisz. drawing for this scene from the 1524 series has not survived, this panel—based on the precise correlation between the panel and the drawing of *Freeing the Prisoners*—may be presumed to preserve the original composition. The curious pediment capping the background structure seems somewhat out of place, as the architectural vocabulary is consistently medieval throughout all three versions of the series; yet, the shuttered and arcaded windows below and the wall and gateway are very similar to the analogous structures in *Feeding the Hungry*. The unusually thick, almost impasto-like application of matte paints, in contrast to—for example—the uniformly smooth painted surfaces of the previous two roundels (cat. nos. 46 and 47), is uncommon, but it is also encountered in two panels thought to be based on compositions by Lucas van Leyden (cat. nos. 53 and 54) and, therefore, also of Leiden origin. The glass of the present panel and of the associated one also in Paris is relatively thick, rather uneven, heavily bubbled, and very slick on the back—physical properties that are entirely characteristic, as are the undercut grozing marks, of sixteenth-century glass.

1. Popham, *Drawings in the British Museum*, 1932, p. 11.

2. See Amsterdam, *Kunst voor de beeldenstorm* (exhib. cat.), 1986, p. 168, fig. 50 a.

BIBLIOGRAPHY: (49) Beets, "Pieter Cornelisz. Kunst," 1909, pp. 12, 13; *Rodrigues Collection* (sale cat.), 1921, no. 57, pl. 21; Popham, *Drawings in the British Museum*, 1932, p. 11, pl. 3; Beets, "Zestiende-eeuwsche Kunstenaars," 1935, p. 159; Hoogewerff, *Noord-Nederlandsche Schilderkunst* 3, 1939, p. 324, fig. 169; Gibson, "Pieter Cornelisz. Kunst," 1967, p. 38; Gibson, "Two Painted Glass Panels," 1970, p. 86, fig. 9; Berserik, "Leiden, ca. 1480–1545," 1982, no. 108A, fig. 169; Amsterdam, *Kunst voor de beeldenstorm* (exhib. cat.), 1986, pp. 167–68, no. 49. (50) Beets, "Pieter Cornelisz. Kunst," 1909, pp. 13–14; Hoogewerff, *Noord-Nederlandsche Schilderkunst* 3, 1939, pp. 324, 325, fig. 170; Gibson, "Pieter Cornelisz. Kunst," 1967, p. 37; Gibson, *Paintings of Cornelis Engebrechtsz*, 1977, p. 209, no. 16; Berserik, "Leiden, ca. 1480–1545," 1982, no. 180B, fig. 170; Amsterdam, *Kunst voor de beeldenstorm* (exhib. cat.), 1986, p. 168, no. 50.

# 6

## Lucas van Leyden

*According to Karel van Mander, Lucas was born in Leiden in 1494, but some scholars have put the date at 1489.[1] He studied painting with his father, Hugo or Huych Jacobsz., and then with Cornelis Engebrechtsz. Although Lucas was primarily known as a draftsman—his drawings, engravings, and woodcuts were highly regarded and much in demand in his own lifetime—he also was apparently trained in etching by an armorer and received instruction from a goldsmith as well. In van Mander's biographical discussion, he describes Lucas as an "excellent painter, engraver, and glass painter."[2] More so than any of his forerunners, Lucas was much concerned with the individuality of his subjects and paid great attention to illuminating their psychological states through facial expression, gesture, and attitude. In 1521, he met Albrecht Dürer in Antwerp and perhaps in Leiden, and the two are said to have exchanged portrait drawings. Again according to van Mander, Lucas visited Jan Gossaert in Middelburg, although some scholars have cast doubt on this,[3] but he says that Lucas never traveled to Italy even though his work was known by Marcantonio Raimondi and others there. Van Mander recounts that Lucas had an abiding suspicion that he was poisoned in the course of his Middelburg trip and was never well afterward; he died six years later, in 1533, at the age of thirty-nine.*

Notwithstanding van Mander's testimony, no incontrovertible evidence survives documenting Lucas's activity as a glass painter. Like prints by Maarten van Heemskerck and other artists, Lucas's were used as designs for painted glass roundels whether or not they were so intended; his large *Ecce Homo* engraving (fig. 1, p. 117), for example, served as the design for an exceptionally well-painted early-sixteenth-century roundel now in the Collection Frits Lugt, Paris (fig. 2, p. 117).[4] There are references to examples of his work, but there is no way of knowing whether any of this work has survived. For instance, a box of eight rectangular glass panels depicting various subjects painted by Lucas is mentioned as having appeared in an auction in 1662 ("acht viercante glasen daerop verscheijde historiën van Lucas van Leyden geschildert").[5] Lucas engraved two series of wood blocks representing the Power of Women *topoi*, a subject that enjoyed wide popular appeal and apparently held great interest for Lucas as well. A drawing in Rotterdam representing Jael and Sisera (cat. no. 51), along with a companion sheet of *Judith with the Head of Holofernes*, now in London, has long been attributed to Lucas on the basis of style. Their subjects and format suggest that these were intended as designs for glass. The two Paris panels (cat. nos. 52 and 53), which also represent scenes from a series devoted to the Power of Women and stylistically relate to the drawings, add further evidence of Lucas's continued interest in the subject. Whether the Paris panels can be identified with these "historiën" remains a matter of speculation,[6] as does whether one or two different series are in question, but stylistic and compositional affinities to the small wood-block series, in particular, suggest that these works date from the early to the mid-1520s. A recently rediscovered drawing of *The Resurrection* (cat. no. 54)—convincingly attributed to Lucas and dating from about 1529—also appears to be a design for glass. Lucas's continued activity as a designer for painted glass is further evidenced by a panel from Darmstadt (cat. no. 55) that has much in common, both stylistically and compositionally, with the Amsterdam sheet. Representing Samson and Delilah and probably dating to the later 1520s or early 1530s, it affirms Lucas's enduring thematic fascination with the Power of Women. The question of Lucas's activity as a glass painter, so emphatically declared by van Mander, is encountered afresh in the *Triumph of David* panel in the Pinacoteca

FIG. 1 Lucas van Leyden. *Ecce Homo*. Engraving. 1510. New York,
The Metropolitan Museum of Art, Harris Brisbane Dick Fund, 1927

della Biblioteca Ambrosiana, Milan (cat. no. 56). This glass painting,
assuredly based on a composition by Lucas, is of astonishing technical virtuosity and of the highest imaginable quality; apparently
never closely studied and long assumed to be a later copy after an
engraving by Jan Saenredam, it is here argued to be an early-
sixteenth-century panel executed by a consummate artist, whether
Lucas van Leyden or not. While the design is lost, the apparently
related London *David Beheading Goliath* (cat. no. 57) could well
suggest its appearance. Stylistically, both works belong to Lucas's
earlier period. If actually painted by Lucas, the Ambrosiana panel
must be a relatively youthful work; given the extraordinary quality
and technical achievement of this panel, what he might have painted in his more mature years is intriguing to contemplate.

1. For further bibliographical information and a critical translation of van Mander's
entry on Lucas see Vos, "Life of Lucas," 1978, pp. 459–507.

2. Ibid., pp. 462–63.

3. See Boon, *Drawings of the Frits Lugt Collection*, 1992, p. 224.

4. Close examination of the iron-grozed edge and of the physical characteristics of the
glass, including the alkali-slick surface, as well as the quality of the painting, all support
a positive assessment of this often-questioned roundel. Holding the roundel against an
impression of Lucas's engraving indicates that the painter placed the glass directly over
the print and traced the composition in exact detail.

5. See "Een Kunstverzamelaar," 1882–83, pp. 303–4.

6. A letter written by Monsignor Alessandro Mazenta to Federigo Borromeo on
November 23, 1612 (see Gramatica, *Memorie*, 1919, pp. 70–71), informs the cardinal,
in regard to several paintings that are being shipped to him, that two more, one by
"Luca d'Olanda," will be sent to him in two days' time ("Se ne invieranno due altri
fra due giorni"). This may, however, refer to a painting of the Descent from the Cross
mentioned by de Brosses (*Lettres historiques* 1, 1739, p. 124) rather than to a glass
painting.

FIG. 2 Lucas van Leyden. *Ecce Homo*. Roundel. 1510–20. Paris, Collection
Frits Lugt, Institut Néerlandais

51

51 *see plate 12*

## Jael and Sisera

Leiden, after 1520

Pen and brown ink on paper, 10⅝ x 8 in.
(27 x 20.3 cm)

Rotterdam, Museum Boymans-van Beuningen,
N-13

Sisera was a Canaanite warlord who, after twenty years of oppression, was defeated by an uprising of the Israelite army under the command of Barak. Fleeing from the battlefield, Sisera sought refuge in the tent of an ally whose wife, Jael, took him in. However, because he was an enemy of the people of Israel, Jael drove a stake through his head while he slept—which is the rather gruesome scene illustrated here.[1] She "took a nail of the tent, and taking also a hammer: and going in softly, and with silence, she put the nail upon the temples of his head, and striking it with the hammer, drove it through his brain fast into the ground" (Judges 4: 21).

The drawing, executed with fine pen work to achieve a wide tonal range through the meticulous use of parallel strokes and cross-hatchings, attains an uncommonly expressive rendering of detail.[2] A drawing in the British Museum representing Judith putting the head of Holofernes in a sack (fig. 1) is so close in style, technique, and format that it is very probable that the two formed part of a series devoted to the Power of Women.[3] This was a popular theme that Lucas turned his attention to several times during his career.[4] Sometime between about 1512 and 1514 he produced a

wood-block series, in large format (41.6 x 29.2 cm), comprising six scenes (*Ill. Bartsch* 12:1, 6, 8, 10, 12, and 16, pp. 313 ff.): Adam and Eve, Delilah Cutting the Hair of Samson, the Idolatry of Solomon, Salome with the Head of John the Baptist before Herod and Herodias, Virgil Suspended in a Basket, and the Mouth of Truth. He returned to the subject between 1516 and 1519 in another wood-block series slightly smaller in format (*Ill. Bartsch* 12:2, 5, 7, 9, 11, and 13, pp. 314 ff.). Here, the scenes of Virgil were dropped while the more unusual episodes of Jael killing Sisera and Jezebel promising Naboth's vineyard to King Ahab were included; ornamental frames and inscriptions were added to these wood blocks in the second printing so that the six sheets could be joined together as a frieze.[5] Finally, there are three painted glass panels dating to about 1525–30 (cat. nos. 52, 53, and 55), also Power of Women scenes, which appear to rely on the designs of Lucas van Leyden. It is unclear, however, whether these panels depend on drawings in the same series (they are definitely not all painted by the same hand), and it is, moreover, uncertain if any of the designs for the panels are related to the present drawing, although they have much in common. It is a fact, nonetheless, that Lucas treated this subject more than any other artist of his time.

The commonly held notion that many of man's problems can be blamed on women because of the power they exert over him through their wiles, charms, beauty, cunning, or other ploys peculiar to the sex was, in the Middle Ages, given both religious and literary impetus. A great variety of writings by such figures as Geert Groote, the

founder of the *devotio moderna*, and Sebastian Brant, the moralizing author of *Das Narrenschiff*, expounded on the opprobrious nature of women. By the fifteenth century, such specific famous couples as Aristotle and Phyllis or Samson and Delilah were upheld as examples of a most respected man ultimately being dominated or humiliated by a clever or devious woman. The array of exceptional men so victimized—Adam, Solomon, Absalom, Lot, Joseph, Hercules, and Virgil, to name but a few—was large and varied. Lucas's choices of couples, often uninfluenced by literary sources, are exceptionally diversified and colorful, predicated, it seems, on no more than idiosyncratic preference. Women were, however, not always viewed so pejoratively.

In medieval typologies, such as the *Speculum humanae salvationis*, the episode of Jael killing Sisera, for example, was understood to prefigure the triumph of the Virgin Mary over the devil. Jael and Judith also were frequently paired throughout the later Middle Ages as paradigms of the power of women, extolled for their acts of valiance and their heroism. In the present scene—unusually violent for Lucas—a far dimmer view is taken and Jael is portrayed as a cunning and treacherous woman who has violated the sacred laws of hospitality. In the second printing of Lucas's small Power of Women series, the inscription at the base of the ornamental frame surrounding Jael and Sisera (fig. 2) notes that "All malice is short to the malice of a woman" (Ecclesiasticus 25: 26). The engraving, in the same direction as the drawing, was made by Jan Saenredam in 1600 (fig. 3), but the inscription here takes a more benign

FIG. 2 Lucas van Leyden. *Jael and Sisera.*
Woodcut. About 1517. New York, The
Metropolitan Museum of Art, Rogers Fund, 1922

FIG. 3 Jan Saenredam, after Lucas van Leyden.
*Jael and Sisera.* Engraving. 1600. Amsterdam,
Rijksmuseum, Rijksprentenkabinet

stance, acclaiming the valor of Jael's perfidious act.[6] Saenredam also made an engraving of *Judith with the Head of Holofernes* but, for unclear reasons, the composition here is reversed (fig. 4).[7]

The compositions of corresponding subjects differ among all the series. With the *Jael and Sisera* Lucas retained some aspects of the design of the wood block, such as the placement and arrangement of the two principal figures, who are more or less counterbalanced by the open doorway behind them. The drawing, however, is far more animated. Jael appears in a flurry of motion, her hair and drapery flying in different directions and her right leg splayed sharply outward; Sisera, in contrast, lies in calm repose, his legs akimbo. The mannered poses and the theatricality of the setting—the episode takes place before an architectural ruin—bring a sense of high drama to the scene. The woman, whose action results in a near contortion of her body, contrasts with the repose of the other figure—an effect equally apparent in the *Judith with the Head of Holofernes.*

The meticulous pen work and the fact that no prints by Lucas after these designs exist have been cited as arguments that the present sheet and the companion drawing in London were made for glass paintings.[8] While this supposition is very probably correct, the technique Lucas employed may not necessarily be taken as evidence. The present drawing, the *Resurrection* (cat. no. 54), and *David Beheading Goliath* (cat. no. 57), all thought to be designs for glass paintings, are executed in quite different techniques, yet correspondences in format, composition, and style with the extant glass panels provide more convincing evi-

dence for a commonality of function among the drawings.

1. See Kloek, "Drawings of Lucas van Leyden," 1978, pp. 444–45, no. 10. There is a copy of this drawing in the Rijksmuseum (RP-T-1912:25); see Boon, *Netherlandish Drawings,* 1978, p. 122, no. 339.

2. See Washington, *Age of Bruegel* (exhib. cat.), 1986, p. 213, no. 79.

3. Inv. no. 1854.6.28.39. See Popham, *Drawings in the British Museum,* 1932, p. 31, no. 11; Kloek, "Drawings of Lucas van Leyden," 1978, p. 445, no. 11. There is a copy of this drawing in Braunschweig, apparently by the same hand as the Amsterdam copy of the Rotterdam *Jael and Sisera.*

4. For a detailed study of the *topos* see Smith, "Power of Women," Ph.D. diss., 1978.

5. See Washington, *Lucas van Leyden* (exhib. cat.), 1983, pp. 172–74, nos. 61, 62.

6. Hollstein 23:20.

7. Hollstein 23:18.

8. See Washington, *Age of Bruegel* (exhib. cat.), 1986, p. 213; New York, *Pisanello to Cézanne* (exhib. cat.), 1990, p. 56.

BIBLIOGRAPHY: Rotterdam, *Noord-nederlandsche Primitieven* (exhib. cat.), 1936, p. 72, no. 55, pl. 37; Hoogewerff, *Noord-Nederlandsche Schilderkunst* 3, 1939, p. 288, fig. 151; Friedländer, *Lucas van Leyden,* 1963, p. 77, no. 33; Amsterdam, *Lucas van Leyden—grafiek* (exhib. cat.), 1978, pp. 58–59; Kloek, "Drawings of Lucas van Leyden," 1978, pp. 428, 432, 444–45, no. 10, p. 454; Vos, *Lucas,* 1978, p. 196, no. 237; Kloek and Filedt Kok, "De Opstanding van Christus," 1983, p. 16; Washington, *Age of Bruegel* (exhib. cat.), 1986, pp. 212–13, no. 79; New York, *Pisanello to Cézanne* (exhib. cat.), 1990, pp. 54–56, no. 15.

FIG. 4 Jan Saenredam, after Lucas van Leyden.
*Judith with the Head of Holofernes.* Engraving.
1600. Amsterdam, Rijksmuseum,
Rijksprentenkabinet

52

53

## 52

### The Idolatry of Solomon

Leiden, about 1525–30

Panel, 11 x 7½ in. (27.9 x 19.1 cm)

Paris, Musée du Louvre, OA 1191

## 53

### Jezebel Promises Naboth's Vineyard to King Ahab

Leiden, about 1525–30

Panel, 11 x 7½ in. (27.9 x 19.1 cm)

Paris, Musée du Louvre, OA 1192

Lucas van Leyden rendered the subject of the Idolatry of Solomon, as he did that of Delilah cutting the hair of Samson, twice in woodcuts and once in an engraving. In the large woodcut from the Power of Women series of about 1512–14, Solomon kneels before a statue while one of his pagan wives or concubines standing just behind him seems to urge him on (fig. 1). A number of figures in the background witness the episode and discuss it among themselves. The heart of Solomon has already been "turned away by women to follow strange gods" as the biblical text phrases it (3 Kings 11: 4)—alluded to by the figure of Cupid sitting astride the architectural element above the idol. Solomon's folly is placing love above his official duties and, as king, his seduction is not merely a private matter of the heart, but an issue of state and therefore a topic of public interest. This interpretation is reinforced

by the earnest discussion of the witnesses as well as by the severity of the public architecture against which the scene is set. In 1514 Lucas engraved the same subject. Here, the idol is a similar pagan figure holding a skull, but he now sits on a sphere that, following the late medieval model, could be an allusion to Nemesis or perhaps merely a reference to the instability or transience of earthly love (fig. 2).[1] The scene is more enclosed, and the woman, whose stance is otherwise much the same as in the earlier woodcut version, now points to the idol; by costume alone, she appears more of an exotic *voluptueuse*. In the small woodcut series of about 1516–19, the scene is set in a landscape with only a pair of witnesses (fig. 3). The idol, standing on a pedestal that, in turn, is balanced on a sphere steadied by straining putti, now dominates the composition.

The present panel brings further variation to this subject. The scene is now set in an interior with only a partial arcade providing a view to the several exterior witnesses. Here, the idol, who stands on a circular pedestal-like altar, is a naked and winged female who holds a crescent moon in one hand and with the other gestures toward the offertory fire blazing smokily before her. The presiding woman not only points to the idol, but also has one hand on the altar to indicate the immediacy of her conviction. The significance of the dwarf-like pair of figures just inside the arch, one of whom extends an arm in a broad, sweeping motion, is uncertain. No textual source for this curious configuration is known. The elements of the woman's costume, which flutter in different directions, are akin to the analogous drapery

FIG. 1 Lucas van Leyden. *The Idolatry of Solomon*. Woodcut. 1512–14. New York, The Metropolitan Museum of Art, Harris Brisbane Dick Fund, 1925

FIG. 2 Lucas van Leyden. *The Idolatry of Solomon*. Engraving. 1514. New York, The Metropolitan Museum of Art, Gift of Felix M. Warburg and his family, 1941

FIG. 3 Lucas van Leyden. *The Idolatry of Solomon*. Woodcut. About 1516–19. New York, The Metropolitan Museum of Art, Rogers Fund, 1922

FIG. 4 Lucas van Leyden. *Jezebel Promising the Vineyard of Naboth to King Ahab*. Woodcut. 1516–19. New York, The Metropolitan Museum of Art, Rogers Fund, 1922

passages in the Rotterdam *Jael and Sisera* (cat. no. 51).

The highly unusual subject of Jezebel promising Naboth's vineyards to King Ahab is treated by Lucas on only one other occasion: in his 1516–19 small Power of Women woodcut series (fig. 4). Jezebel, the wife of King Ahab of Samaria, worshiped Baal among other pagan gods and was responsible for the death of several prophets of Christ. In one of her more ruthless moments she falsely accused Naboth of treason, thus bringing about his execution, so that her husband could acquire the unfortunate neighbor's vineyards. "And it came to pass when Jezabel heard that Naboth was stoned, and dead, that she said to Achab: Arise and take possession of the vineyard of Naboth" (3 Kings 21: 15). The inclusion of this episode is the clearest indication of Lucas's increasingly pernicious reading of the subjects comprising the Power of Women series. The composition of the glass panel is the reverse of the woodcut but otherwise is quite similar. The interior setting in the panel is more elaborate, embellished with Renaissance detail, while the door is enlarged to envelop the window, revealing the stoning of Naboth in the background. The animated hand gestures and the fluttering passages of drapery again relate this panel to the Rotterdam drawing (cat. no. 51). The tranquility of this bedroom encounter belies the underlying treachery in the scene and thus creates a sense of looming drama. The rather literal contrast of activity and passivity in the Rotterdam and London drawings (see cat. no. 51) is here transposed to a psychological level.

In style and technique the two present panels are virtually identical and must be by the same hand. Both are painted in shades of dark brown to deep umber, enhanced by several hues of silver stain ranging from pale to deep golden yellow. Of exceptionally high quality, the painting is articulated with extensive use of the badger brush and stylus. Linear highlights are worked with a very fine-pointed stylus, while broader highlighted passages are achieved by the removal of mattes, creating irregular bright planes in the drapery and a series of ovoid forms in the flesh areas. The full-figured anatomies are defined by the broad planes of the drapery—specifically, by the somewhat lumpy, deeply crevassed folds—while highlights in the exuberant drapery passages are given a greater vibrancy by the skillful texturing of intermediary zones with extremely fine strokes of a needle-like stylus. Outlines of forms and other linear details are executed with the darkest tones of matte applied with the fine point of a brush. These techniques are found in their most refined form in the patterns of textiles and in the facial features. The dynamic tonalities and spatial effects are achieved without back painting.[2] In both panels the weighty, sculptural figures almost overwhelm the spaces that they occupy; the background figures, on the other hand, are slight and rather cursorily rendered, giving an impression of haziness, and appear to have been painted in by a workshop assistant. This rather blurred impression also characterizes some of the interior ornamental effects, suggesting that these details, too, may have been consigned to an assistant. Slight traces of sanguine are seen in the beard of Ahab

and in the cheeks of Jezebel. The brighter areas of the parapet in the lower-right corner of this panel, which appear to be the result of lifted paint, seem, in fact, to have been caused by an accidental marring of the unfired matte or by a flaw in the firing. The *Idolatry* panel, however, has been defaced by the numerous mending leads.

1. Master MZ represented Nemesis holding an orb in his engraved version of this rather unusual subject (*Ill. Bartsch* 9, part 1:1, p. 359); see also Washington, *Lucas van Leyden* (exhib. cat.), 1983, p. 136, no. 46.

2. A roundel in the Louvre (OA 7186) also representing the Idolatry of Solomon is painted in the very heavy matte style that appears to characterize the more ordinary Leiden production.

BIBLIOGRAPHY: (52) Amsterdam, *Kunst voor de beeldenstorm* (exhib. cat.), 1986, p. 173, no. 57. (53) Amsterdam, *Kunst voor de beeldenstorm* (exhib. cat.), 1986, p. 174, no. 58.

54

## 54

### The Resurrection

Leiden, about 1529

Black chalk, and gray and black pencil, on paper, 9⅞ x 7⅞ in. (25.1 x 20 cm)

Amsterdam, Rijksmuseum, Rijksprentenkabinet, RP-T-1982-75

This fine, late drawing by Lucas was completely unknown until it surfaced in Paris in 1980, and was subsequently acquired by the Rijksmuseum.[1] The composition, which reflects a studied familiarity with both Albrecht Dürer's 1510 large woodcut of the subject (*Ill. Bartsch* 10:15, p. 110) and the 1512 small engraved Passion series (*Ill. Bartsch* 10:17, p. 16), was known from a weak copy long in the Rijksprentenkabinet (fig. 1).[2] Kloek and Filedt Kok convincingly have argued for the attribution to Lucas, noting formal parallels such as those between the sleeping soldier in the foreground and the figure of Adam in the *Creation* engraving of 1529 (fig. 2), and between the archer looking back at Christ and the analogous figure in Lucas's 1521 version of the scene (*Ill. Bartsch* 12:56, p. 118). They note the numerous compositional alterations that speak of an authentic work, not of a copy, as well as the complex and varied techniques, particularly the use of chalk, which is found in other securely attributed works. One of the more striking aspects of the drawing is the seamless marriage of the soft expanses of the chalk, which are flawlessly contained by the fine, precise pen line. Indeed, the complicated working up of detail, rendering the work the "graphic equivalent of a painting," has

FIG. 2 Lucas van Leyden. *The Creation*. Engraving. 1529. New York, The Metropolitan Museum of Art, Harris Brisbane Dick Fund, 1933

FIG. 3 After Lucas van Leyden. *The Baptism of Christ*. Pen and black ink, with wash, on paper. About 1530. Paris, Musée du Louvre, Département des Arts Graphiques

55

FIG. 1 Lucas van Leyden. *Delilah Cutting the Hair of Samson*. Engraving. 1508. New York, The Metropolitan Museum of Art, Harris Brisbane Dick Fund, 1925

led Kloek and Filedt Kok to wonder if the drawing was not intended for another purpose. As Lucas was an engraver, and the drawing is too complex for a woodcut, they concluded that the sheet must have been made for a painted glass panel.[3] The complicated technique and the finished quality indicate that, if intended for painted glass, this sheet would have served as a design rather than as a working drawing. A sheet in the Louvre representing the Baptism of Christ (fig. 3)[4] may reflect a composition by Lucas, suggesting that he designed a series either on the Life of Christ or the Passion for painted glass. The existence of several glass panels of nearly identical format (cat. nos. 52, 53, and 55) further strengthens the association of this drawing with painted glass.

1. See Kloek and Filedt Kok, "De Opstanding van Christus," 1983, pp. 4–20.

2. Inv. no. RP-T-1900:520. See Boon, *Netherlandish Drawings*, 1978, p. 45, no. 125, where this sheet is referred to as "after Aertgen Claesz." (van Leyden).

3. Kloek and Filedt Kok, "De Opstanding van Christus," 1983, pp. 15–17.

4. Inv. no. 22.687. See Lugt, *Dessins*, 1968, p. 300, no. 86, pl. 45, pen, brush, and black ink, and gray wash, on paper. The drawing seems to be after Lucas. There is fine pen work, shading with parallel strokes, and cross-hatching in the darkest areas, combined with wash and brush drawing, but somehow the solidity of Lucas's autograph work is lacking.

BIBLIOGRAPHY: Kloek and Filedt Kok, "De Opstanding van Christus," 1983, pp. 4–20; Schapelhouman, "Lucas van Leyden, De opstanding van Christus," 1989, pp. 171–73.

## 55

### Delilah Cutting the Hair of Samson

Probably Leiden, about 1530

Panel, 11 x 7⅝ in. (27.9 x 19.4 cm)

Darmstadt, Hessisches Landesmuseum, KG 70:3

Delilah, at the instigation of the Philistine princes, attempts to inveigle Samson into divulging the secret of his strength. Three times he gives her a false explanation and three times she proves it a lie. After a campaign of haranguing and badgering, Samson finally tells her the truth; he is a Nazarite and if his head is ever shaven he will lose his great strength. "But she made him sleep upon her knees, and lay his head in her bosom. And she called a barber, and shaved his seven locks, . . . immediately his strength departed from him" (Judges 16: 19).

Lucas van Leyden first treated the subject of Delilah cutting the hair of Samson in 1508 and returned to it at least three other times over the course of his career. In his 1508 engraving the subject is approached with fresh invention (fig. 1).[1] Delilah intently goes about her treachery, leaning over Samson who, as though aware of betrayal even in his sleep, appears contorted and anguished. The group forms a powerful triangle that commands the composition. Counterbalance is provided by the weighty tree to the left and the massive rocky outcropping in the center background—elements that also serve to define pictorial spaces for further narrative details. The wary Philistines edge forward to see whether Delilah's wiles have proven effective. Lucas returned to the

FIG. 2 Lucas van Leyden. *Delilah Cutting the Hair of Samson*. Woodcut. About 1512–14. Amsterdam, Rijksmuseum, Rijksprentenkabinet

FIG. 3 Lucas van Leyden. *Delilah Cutting the Hair of Samson.* Woodcut. About 1516–19. New York, The Metropolitan Museum of Art, Rogers Fund, 1922

subject in his large series on the Power of Women of about 1512–14 (fig. 2). The basic compositional elements were retained, only here Lucas placed the scene of treachery off-center in the lower-right corner. The highlighted figures are set off against the deeply shadowed landscape, while the scene of the Philistine soldiers in the opening beyond the rocky outcropping, leading off the impotent Samson, is bathed in bright light. Delilah seems to approach her task with calm determination and Samson lies in contorted, if somewhat less anxious, repose. This formula is essentially repeated in Lucas's small Power of Women series of about 1516–19 (fig. 3), although there is now a more seductive air to Delilah.[2]

The present painted glass panel draws on elements of its several predecessors. The placement of the large tree and the central rocky outcropping is very similar to that in the engraving of about 1508, but, as in both woodcut versions, Delilah and Samson occupy the lower-right corner. The panel also expands the narrative to include both the approach of the wary soldiers, as in the engraving, and the soldiers taking away the impotent Samson; the latter scene, with the buildings behind, is a fairly direct quote from the corresponding version in the large Power of Women series. The addition of the *Morgenstern* placed at a diagonal in the lower-left corner quotes with equal frankness from the corresponding scene in the small woodcut series. Contrary to the biblical text, Lucas—in keeping with the increasingly pernicious slant of his Power of Women scenes—has Delilah herself, not a barber, perform the treacherous task. Any possibility of a sympathetic read-

ing of Delilah's actions is removed here. Having just cut off the last of Samson's hair, Delilah displays her trophy in an upheld hand to the onlooking soldiers as an all-clear signal. All danger removed, the soldiers then come forward to take the betrayed warrior prisoner and, in the left background, to lead him off in captivity in what is the very image of treachery triumphant.

It is not inconceivable that the present panel preserves the composition of another sheet in the Power of Women series known from the *Jael and Sisera* and *Judith and Holofernes* drawings (cat. no. 51, fig. 1), but the narrative complexity and the more forthright expression of Delilah's betrayal would seem to separate this from the earlier Power of Women scenes. In both the London and Rotterdam drawings the emphasis is distinctly on the act of treachery, as though a historical episode were frozen in time. Jael is caught in a frenzy of activity, her right arm fully raised and wielding the mallet, her right leg splayed out, and her drapery aflutter, in the moment just before she drives the peg through Sisera's skull. Judith's body seems to twist in different directions partly to counterbalance the weight of the head she is about to deposit in the sack and partly in revulsion toward the object she holds. The agitated movement of the two women is in contrast to the mannered repose of Sisera and the firm solidity of the handmaiden. In the *Delilah* panel, however, the focus is shifted to the impact of Delilah's treachery. The only motion is implied by her raised hand displaying the hair of the betrayed Samson to the Philistine soldiers. The earlier printed versions focused on the action of cutting the hair; although the betrayal is alluded to in the backgrounds, Delilah's intense concentration on her act allows the viewer to see her as a heroine willing to undertake a distasteful task for the greater benefit of her people. This is disallowed in the imagery of the painted glass panel. In these regards, then, it appears that the panel depends on yet another, otherwise unknown series on the immensely popular Power of Women theme.

Boon noticed the stylistic affinity of this panel with the drawing of *The Resurrection*, after Lucas, in the Rijksprentenkabinet (cat. no. 54, fig. 1),[3] although comparison is more striking with the Rijksmuseum's recently acquired original (cat. no. 54). The compositions, each anchored by a strong triangularly configured group—Christ and the foreground soldiers in the drawing and Delilah, Samson, and the rocky projection in the present panel—and each with a background spatially defined by a single dominant tree and rocky outcroppings, are essentially the same. The figures have a similar weightiness and presence: The sleeping soldier with his elbow on the tomb and the slumbering figure of Samson share a common conception. Such close correlations cannot be found in the Rotterdam *Judith* and the London *Jael* drawings, which probably date to the early 1520s. The drapery style in both the Amsterdam drawing and the panel is more sculptural, with deep angled folds surrounding the smooth highlighted surfaces defining the underlying anatomy, characteristics that suggest that they date well

toward the close of Lucas's career. This strengthens the supposition that Lucas, indeed, created yet another Power of Women series, which must date from the end of his life. The present panel most probably was painted by a workshop associated with Lucas or that, at the very least, had access to his designs; it can be reasonably dated to about 1530.

1. See Washington, *Lucas van Leyden* (exhib. cat.), 1983, p. 58, no. 10.

2. Ibid., p. 176, no. 63.

3. See Boon, *Netherlandish Drawings*, 1978, p. 45, no. 125.

BIBLIOGRAPHY: Kloek and Filedt Kok, "De Opstanding van Christus," 1983, pp. 16–17; Amsterdam, *Kunst voor de beeldenstorm* (exhib. cat.), 1986, pp. 172–73, no. 56.

## 56 *see plate 13*

### The Triumph of David

Leiden (?), about 1510–30

Panel, 9¼ x 7⅜ in. (23.5 x 18.7 cm)

Milan, Pinacoteca della Biblioteca Ambrosiana, 343

After the young David slew Goliath, he faithfully continued to serve Saul. "Now when David returned, after he slew the Philistine, the women came out of all the cities of Israel, singing and dancing, to meet king Saul, with timbrels of joy, and cornets. And the women sung as they played, and they said: Saul slew his thousands, and David his ten thousands" (1 Kings 18: 6–7). As represented here, David is the sole beneficiary of the women's adulation, standing rather passively and holding up, with improbable ease, the gigantic head of Goliath impaled on the end of his outsized sword.

Van Mander, in writing of Lucas van Leyden, notes that: "One also comes across his glass paintings once in a while, which are well worth collecting. One for instance belongs to Goltzius, who is very fond of Lucas' work: the women dancing out to greet David, done with amazing technique ["dat wonder fraey is ghehandelt"]; a print has been made after it also, very well engraved by Jan Saenredam."[1] In 1625, Cardinal Federigo Borromeo published a guide to his collection at the Ambrosiana in which he describes a work on glass ("crystallini operis"), next to miniatures by Marchesini and Decio, and which, he says, is rendered monochromatically, and in its subtle delicacy is superior to any other art work ("monochromate pictum est, et molli subtilitate artificium omne vincit").[2]

Unfortunately, Borromeo neglects to indicate the subject of the *cristallo* panel he describes, nor was there any mention of a glass painting—or of any other work by Lucas van Leyden, for that matter—in Borromeo's donation of his collection to the Ambrosiana in 1618.[3] Only in the nineteenth century are the glass painting described by van Mander, the *crystallini operis* discussed by Borromeo, and the present panel all accepted as

56

FIG. 1 Jan Saenredam, after Lucas van Leyden. *The Triumph of David*. Engraving. 1600. New York, The Metropolitan Museum of Art, Harris Brisbane Dick Fund, 1917

FIG. 2 Pieter Fierens, after Lucas van Leyden. *The Triumph of David*. Engraving. About 1600. Amsterdam, Rijksmuseum, Rijksprentenkabinet

being one and the same.[4] Both Hymans[5] and Bredius[6] accepted the attribution of the panel to Lucas; the fact that Lucas was known as a glass painter, the exceptional quality of the panel, and the lack of evidence to the contrary compelled Stiassny to at least tacitly support the attribution as well.[7] Ensuing scholars by and large have questioned whether the present panel is the one referred to by van Mander and they generally were inclined to see it not as a work by Lucas but rather as a copy after the Jan Saenredam engraving of 1600 (fig. 1).[8] Hoogewerff, on the other hand, believed the composition of the glass panel and the somewhat altered one of Saenredam's engraving were independent of each other, but must have depended on an earlier lost work of Lucas's, probably a drawing.[9] While Gibson thought the panel was a copy after Lucas,[10] Vos returns to the view that it is most likely copied from the Saenredam engraving, which, in turn, was based on a lost composition by Lucas.[11] Kloek and Filedt Kok, while doubting that the Milan panel can be the same one described by van Mander, concur with this assessment, noting the stiff quality of the painting.[12] Luijten's comments suggest that Saenredam's engraving and, by implication, the present panel were the result of the revival of interest in Lucas's work, the enkindling of which was largely due to Goltzius.[13] Smith believes that it is the work of a copyist and suggests that van Mander may have seen this copy in Goltzius's collection, mistakenly identifying it with the original.[14] Finally, Jones suggests that as no other paintings on glass by Lucas survive with which to compare the Ambrosiana panel, the attribution to Lucas perhaps should not be ruled out altogether.[15]

The negative estimations notwithstanding, the extraordinary technique and the outstanding quality of the panel have given several authors pause, if not bewildered them outright. Stiassny, for example, comments that the evident perfection of the panel, which cannot be obscured even by the appallingly poor photograph of it that was made available to him for study, argues for Lucas's hand, particularly as he was said to have been a glass painter.[16] Hoogewerff, likewise, notes that the panel, in an unusual grisaille technique, is worked with exceptional care, attains a pinnacle of refinement, and is executed with such precision and control that the glass painter must have been an accomplished engraver as well.[17] The reluctance to accept this panel as the one described by van Mander becomes less surprising, however, with the realization that, like Stiassny, evidently none of these authors has actually examined the panel and they know it only through poor reproductions.

As several critics have noted, in addition to its more compact format (23.4 x 18.8 cm, as opposed to the engraving, which measures 28 x 19.1 cm) the panel differs from the engraving in numerous compositional details. In the panel, the hilly background rises well above the head of David and is surmounted by a walled town. David is placed toward the foreground, closer to the plane occupied by the woman seen from behind; the

FIG. 3 Lucas van Leyden. *Joseph Recounting His Dreams to His Father*. Engraving. 1512. New York, The Metropolitan Museum of Art, Rogers Fund, 1931

FIG. 4 Lucas van Leyden. *The Adoration of the Magi*. Engraving. 1513. New York, The Metropolitan Museum of Art, Harris Brisbane Dick Fund, 1935

increased space between him and the woman with the sheet of music is filled with plant life, which recedes to the middle ground. The foreground is shallower and, although devoid of stones—including the rock with the date—also contains an abundance of flora. Attention to botanical detail is again evident in the sprigs of oak growing out of the masonry wall in the upper-left corner. There are numerous subtle differences in the drapery folds, generating greater fluidity in these voluminous passages. The head of Goliath is considerably larger, so that it has a more imposing presence. The tighter focus of the composition underscores the brooding, almost foreboding, atmosphere of this curiously unjoyous episode; the menacing wrath of the unseen Saul seems to loom over the scene.

What is not evident in reproductions of the Milan *Triumph of David* is that it is mounted backwards in its frame and, until now, always has appeared as such in photographs and reproductions. Since a glass panel, unlike a print, would not necessitate reversing the image that it was taken from, the Milan panel logically cannot be based on the Saenredam engraving.[18] There are two contemporary engraved copies after Saenredam, published by Pieter de Jode and Pieter Fierens,[19] which, of course, reverse the original composition, but otherwise—with the exception of substituting the letter *L* for the date 1600 on the rock in the foreground—follow their model in slavish detail (see fig. 2). Because glass painters likewise faithfully followed the compositions of prints they used as designs (see figs. 1 and 2, p. 117), it is highly unlikely that either of these engraved copies served as the model for the Milan panel. One is led to Hoogewerff's conclusion that both the panel and the engraving must depend on an earlier design by Lucas, undoubtedly a drawing (or a copy, in the case of the print). Lucas, indeed, appears to have executed a series of drawings representing episodes from the Story of David, and

the similarity of the figural style and of the compositions suggests a close relationship with this panel (see cat. no. 57).

The physical and material properties of both the glass and the paint of the Milan *Triumph of David* speak of an origin in the first half of the sixteenth century. For the size of the panel, the glass is relatively thin (about .3 cm)—thinner than that of the two Paris panels (cat. nos. 52 and 53), but about the same as the one in Darmstadt (cat. no. 55). The *Triumph of David* has convincing lateral undulation, while the back has the alkali-slick surface characteristic of sixteenth-century glass. The glass itself is exceptionally fine, with little or no bubbles or impurities. The perimeter of the panel is iron grozed all around, leaving a beveled edge, the chipping of which has been summarily smoothed; a narrow border was then painted in black matte, producing a finished edge that is utterly typical of early-sixteenth-century technique. Curiously, however, the bevel angles toward rather than away from the painted surface, which is unusual.

The painting is executed, like the *Triumph* roundels of Dirick Vellert (cat. nos. 67 and 68), entirely in grisaille with matte tones in subtle gradations ranging from a soft, pale gray to black. Laid down in remarkably thin layers, the paint has an almost dusty feel to it, indicating that it was lightly fired at a relatively low temperature. The resulting lack of fusion preserved the intended tonal gradations but has allowed the paint to flake off in spots; in other areas, such as the blade of the sword, the extremely thin layers of matte have been rubbed away completely.

While the material properties are thoroughly typical of Lucas's time, the technique and quality of the painting are simply unparalleled in any period. The thinness of the mattes, the infinitely subtle gradations in the modeling, the absolute control of the brush, and the wide dynamic range from deep shadow to brilliant highlight produce

uncommonly rich pictorial and textural effects. So subtle is the painting that the panel is actually difficult to view; a delicate adjustment of back and surface light is required, for if either is too strong the painterly effects seem to dissolve. With optimum illumination the panel ignites in a luminous and silvery brilliance that is nothing short of astonishing. One can hardly imagine that such incomparable virtuosity could be forthcoming from an early-seventeenth-century copyist at a time when the art of glass painting was at a nadir, following the traumatic period of iconoclasm and Reformation, but, on the other hand, one can well imagine how de Brosse, having never seen such a painting, could refer to this panel in the eighteenth century as "le Triomphe de David,

FIG. 5 Lucas van Leyden. *The Triumph of David*. Engraving. 1513. Amsterdam, Rijksmuseum, Rijksprentenkabinet

excellent dessin de clair obscur"[20]—for so it might well have appeared, reversed, as it is, in its frame. Nor can one be surprised that Borromeo expresses wonderment that "upon its examination the doubt is raised as to whether use was made of the burin or the paint brush" ("in cuius contemplatione haret animus, dubitatq; scalprone, an pencillo Artifex usus fuerit").[21]

What is more difficult to understand is why in his description Borromeo states, "I could not discover who painted it nor how it was that painting on crystal came about. What is certain is this is a new invention" ("Sed neque quis pinxerit, neq; quomodo pingi crystallum coeptum sit, inuenire potui. Nouitium certe inuentum").[22] If Borromeo acquired the panel between 1618 and 1625 (Goltzius died in 1620), its omission from the act of donation is understandable, but it is hard to comprehend Borromeo's failure to associate this exceptional object—a work that "artificium omne vincit"—with van Mander's description, published in 1604, even if the panel Borromeo was discussing is an altogether different one. Surely, if it literally represented a recent—rather than a heretofore unencountered—technical innovation, Borromeo and his many agents hardly could have been at a loss to explain its origins.

However perplexing the several references that seem to pertain to the Ambrosiana panel, it remains a singular achievement of glass painting that almost certainly dates to the early decades of the sixteenth century. The rather elongated figure style in the tightly composed group—one member of which has a vine-leaf wreath about her head—finds close comparison in the group clustered around the father in Lucas's 1512 engraving of *Joseph Recounting His Dreams to His Father* (fig. 3). The vine wreaths and extravagant feathers in the dagged headdresses appear frequently in Lucas's graphic works dating between 1510 and 1515, as can be seen in his 1513 *Adoration* engraving (fig. 4). Furthermore, there is much in common between the woman at the right in the Ambrosiana panel and the analogous figure in Lucas's 1513 engraving of the same subject (fig. 5), particularly her stance, the gathering of drapery at her feet, and the passivity of her expression. Lucas, no doubt, produced the design for this glass painting during his early period. A remarkable conceit, the Ambrosiana panel—certainly never intended to be installed in a window—is a true *Kabinettscheibe*, and was so viewed from its inception. There appears to be no compelling reason to doubt the identification of the work with the one described by van Mander. The question of whether or not Lucas painted the panel remains a matter of speculation, but so crediting him can only bring added luster to his name.

1. See Vos, "Life of Lucas," 1978, pp. 474, 475.

2. See *Musaeum*, 1625, p. 19.

3. See Jones, *Ambrosiana*, 1993, pp. 347–57.

4. See Stiassny, "Oberitalienischen Sammlungen," 1888, p. 390.

5. See *Livre des peintres*, 1884, p. 147.

6. Ibid. See also Beets, *Lucas de Leyde*, 1913, p. 72.

57

7. See Stiassny, "Oberitalienischen Sammlungen," 1888, p. 390.

8. See Dülberg, *Frühholländer* 3, n.d. [1907], pp. 10, 25; Beets, *Lucas de Leyde*, 1913, p. 72; Hirschmann, *Hendrick Goltzius als Maler*, 1916, p. 41, n. 2; and von Frimmel, "Davidbildern," 1921, p. 149.

9. See Hoogewerff, *Noord-Nederlandsche Schilderkunst* 3, 1939, pp. 314–15. Galbiati (*Itinerario*, 1951, p. 170) attributed the panel to Lucas.

10. See Gibson, "Two Painted Glass Panels," 1970, p. 86, n. 17.

11. See Vos, "Life of Lucas," 1978, pp. 503–4, n. 117.

12. Kloek and Filedt Kok, "De Opstanding van Christus," 1983, p. 16.

13. See New York, *Pisanello to Cézanne* (exhib. cat.), 1990, p. 56.

14. See Smith, *Lucas Catalogue Raisonné*, 1992, p. 98.

15. See Jones, *Ambrosiana*, 1993, p. 248.

16. See Stiassny, "Oberitalienischen Sammlungen," 1888, p. 390.

17. See Hoogewerff, *Noord-Nederlandsche Schilderkunst* 3, 1939, p. 314.

18. Hoogewerff (ibid., p. 317) has argued, based on the use of the right and left hands, that Lucas's original composition must have shown David on the left, as he is in the Ambrosiana panel.

19. See Hollstein 23: 14, B and C.

20. See *Lettres historiques* 1, 1739, p. 129.

21. See *Musaeum*, 1625, p. 19.

22. Ibid.

BIBLIOGRAPHY: Stiassny, "Oberitalienischen Sammlungen," 1888, p. 390; Beets, *Lucas de Leyde*, 1913, p. 72; von Frimmel, "Davidbildern," 1921, p. 149; Hoogewerff, *Noord-Nederlandsche Schilderkunst* 3, 1939, pp. 314–15, fig. 166; Vos, "Life of Lucas," 1978, pp. 503–4, notes 117, 118; Kloek and Filedt Kok, "De Opstanding van Christus," 1983, p. 16, n. 31; Smith, *Lucas Catalogue Raisonné*, 1992, pp. 95–98, fig. 41; Jones, *Ambrosiana*, 1993, p. 248.

57

## David Beheading Goliath

Leiden, about 1511–14

Brush and gray-black ink, with gray wash, on paper, 10¼ x 7⅝ in. (26 x 19.4 cm)

London, British Museum, 1892.8.4.18

The attribution of this unsigned drawing to Lucas has long been accepted on the strength of stylistic and compositional grounds.[1] The composition—with the supine figure of Goliath dominating the foreground; the balancing weight of the tree; the rocky outcroppings separating the middle ground from the background; along with the several groups of figures, architecture, and rugged topography in the distance—displays Lucas's quintessential style. The similarity of the composition to that of the artist's large *Samson and Delilah* of about 1512–14, for example, is particularly striking (see cat. no. 55, fig. 2). This drawing, in fact, has been associated with Lucas's printmaking efforts, the broad, contoured lines suitable for a wood-block design that required cutting along both sides of a line. While little is known of Lucas's methods, designs were often drawn directly on the block, or in the process of transferring the design onto it the drawing was destroyed.[2] The scale and linear clarity of this sheet, on the other hand, make it eminently serviceable as a design or a working drawing for a stained-glass panel. The dynamic range of tonalities, from dense black to white, is particularly well conveyed by the technique, and, in this regard, the drawing is most instructively compared to the Ambrosiana panel (cat. no. 56): The rapid but carefully modulated transition from the dense black at David's waist to the brilliant highlights of his left arm and shoulder, for instance, is achieved with analogous power in both compositions.

A close relationship between the present drawing and the Milan panel is more specifically evidenced in the individualization of the figure of David, which carries from one composition to the other. David's hair, with curls at the brow and temples, for example, is the same, as is his dress, including the large pouch hanging from his waist, and his footwear. The enormous sword with the bifurcated termini of the hilt is also essentially identical. The formal devices are likewise very similar, with the weight of the figures drawn toward the foreground, anchored by a strong vertical in the upper-left corner and by the deeply receding landscape at the upper right—characteristics of many of Lucas's compositions.

Luijten ventures that Saenredam's *Triumph of David* can be associated with two other engravings after Lucas, one representing Jael and Sisera

FIG. 1 Lucas van Leyden. *David before Saul.*
Engraving. About 1508. New York, The
Metropolitan Museum of Art, Rogers Fund, 1917

(cat. no. 52, fig. 1) and the other Judith with the Head of Holofernes (cat. no. 52, fig. 2), and that the three formed part of a series of the "deeds of biblical heroes and heroines."[3] This is unlikely, however, as the *Jael* and *Judith* scenes clearly belong to a Power of Women series in which particular women use their cunning—or treachery, as in both instances here—to get the better of particular men. The *Triumph of David*, on the other hand, represents the hero enjoying the praise of a multitude of women, and therefore most probably belongs to an altogether different series depicting the Story of David. Lucas revisited the subject of David in his engraved works on numerous occasions: *David and Abigail* (*Ill. Bartsch* 12:24, p. 156) dates to about 1507, *David in Prayer* (*Ill. Bartsch* 12: 28, p. 160) to about the same year, and another version of *David in Triumph* (see cat. no. 56, fig. 5) to about 1513; the brooding figure of Saul in *David before Saul* clearly conveys the seething rage and jealousy brought on by David's triumph (see fig. 1). The engraved inscriptions below the images support this distinction, as that below the scene of David quotes the appropriate biblical passage from 1 Kings 18, while those on the other two engravings make specific reference to the woes brought upon men by the wiles of women.[4] In addition, the *Jael* and *Judith* plates are nearly the same size (about 28.5 x 21.1 cm), while the *David* plate is somewhat smaller (28 x 19.1 cm).

Besides the correspondence of the figures of David here and in the Ambrosiana panel, the format and the background composition of the present sheet, with its groups of figures from ancillary scenes placed in the dramatic topography, are characteristics of Lucas's narrative series. Whether the drawing upon which the Ambrosiana panel is based once formed part of a David series with the present sheet is a matter of speculation, but it remains, certainly, a reasonable possibility. Kloek considers the use of wash in this drawing illogical in areas, and wonders whether it is original.[5] Filedt Kok, on the other hand, notes Lucas's exceptional use of wash in the underdrawing of his *Last Judgment* triptych, and quite rightly sees the careful application of wash here as an enhancement of light and shade indicated by the hatching.[6]

1. See Popham, *Drawings in the British Museum*, 1932, pp. 28–29.

2. For an example of a brush drawing executed directly on a wood block see Winzinger, *Altdorfer—Graphik*, 1963, app. 8, and Regensburg, *Altdorfer* (exhib. cat.), 1988, pp. 150–51, no. 72.

3. New York, *Pisanello to Cézanne* (exhib. cat.), 1990, p. 97.

4. The inscriptions also state that when the engravings were made the original sheets were still in Leiden where an anonymous artist copied them, which perhaps accounts for the drawings now in Amsterdam and Braunschweig (see cat. no. 51, notes 1, 3).

5. See Kloek, "Drawings of Lucas van Leyden," 1978, p. 443, no. 8; Washington, *Lucas van Leyden* (exhib. cat.), 1983, p. 124, no. 40.

6. Filedt Kok, "Underdrawing and other technical aspects," 1978, p. 97.

BIBLIOGRAPHY: Colvin, "Handzeichnungen des Lukas van Leyden," 1893, p. 170, fig. 9; Popham, *Drawings in the British Museum*, 1932, pp. 28–29, no. 4; Friedländer, *Lucas van Leyden*, 1963, p. 74, no. 8; Amsterdam, *Lucas van Leyden—grafiek* (exhib. cat.), 1978, pp. 86–88; Filedt Kok, "Underdrawing and other technical aspects," 1978, pp. 37, 39, fig. 34, and pp. 97–98; Kloek, "Drawings of Lucas van Leyden," 1978, p. 443, no. 8; Washington, *Lucas van Leyden* (exhib. cat.), 1983, p. 124, no. 40.

# 7

# Jan Gossaert

*Jan (Jennyn) Gossaert was born in Maubeuge—and, hence, was also known as Mabuse (Malbodius)—in the province of Hainaut, about 1478. He entered the Antwerp Guild of Saint Luke in 1503 and became a Free Master in 1505. A panel painter as well as a designer of furniture and stained glass, Gossaert was employed in 1508 by Philip of Burgundy and, in the same year, accompanied him to Rome. Returning to the Lowlands in 1509, he worked for Philip at the castle of Souburg in Middelburg. Gossaert was greatly influenced by the antique, and specifically by the work of Luca Signorelli and Jacopo de' Barbari, and, like most of his contemporaries, especially by Albrecht Dürer. In 1517, Philip became bishop of Utrecht and moved to the nearby bishop's palace at Wijk bij Duurstede, probably bringing Gossaert with him. Jan van Scorel became his student in 1518, and in 1520 Gossaert rented a studio in Utrecht. In 1523, he worked at Mechelen in the service of Margaret of Austria, regent of the Lowlands. After his patron Philip died in 1524, Gossaert returned to Middelburg and entered the service of Adolph of Burgundy. Toward the end of his life Gossaert worked for several other aristocratic patrons. He introduced the Mannerist style to the Lowlands, strongly influencing Pieter Coecke van Aelst, among other younger artists. He died in 1532, probably in Breda.*

Unlike most of the artists who produced designs for silver-stained roundels, Jan Gossaert spent the better part of his career as a court artist in the service of aristocratic or royal patrons. The first of the Lowlands Romanists, Gossaert, whose style basically falls somewhere between that of the flamboyant Late Gothic and the Renaissance, was one of the first artists in the North to introduce new canons of form and beauty into his work, based on an imitation of antiquity. The intellectual circles at the courts that he served, populated with Humanist thinkers, scholars, writers, and other artists, proved fertile ground for developing these ideals. Unfortunately, little is known of his workshop methods. Only one drawing related to roundel production (cat. no. 58) can, beyond any doubt, be attributed to Gossaert; numerous others are close in style (cat. no. 59), but whether these are workshop efforts or the work of protégés or other artists influenced by but independent of him cannot be said. That all these drawings are finished designs, that no working drawings are known, and that no roundels based on these designs are extant may leave open the possibility that these drawings were intended as objects for a collector's cabinet and were never meant to be executed as roundels. There are, on the other hand, extremely high-quality roundels that are so close to his work in subject matter, composition, and style that the possibility of Gossaert providing designs to glass-painting workshops cannot be ruled out (see cat. no. 60). Gossaert's style, in any case, was certainly known well beyond his rarefied circles, and—no doubt to his great dismay—was emulated by glass painters in a manner that was utterly oblivious to its sources and implications (see cat. no. 61).

58

59

58 *see plate 14*

## The Beheading of John the Baptist

South Lowlands, about 1509–10

Pen and umber ink, with brown wash and white highlights, on brown prepared paper: diameter, 9⅝ in. (24.4 cm)

Paris, École Nationale Supérieure des Beaux-Arts, M.487

Inscribed (upper right): GENNIN + GOSSART + DE + M

This signed drawing is the only project for painted glass roundels, among a group of finished designs, that can be attributed unquestionably to Jan Gossaert. In the foreground, the Baptist kneels, blindfolded and with hands tied before him, moments before his decollation at the hands of the spirally posed swordsman behind him. To the left, atop two steps, a bountifully endowed Salome, enveloped in swirls of crumpled drapery, holds the salver on which she will collect the Baptist's head. Behind her another woman and a man who rests his head disinterestedly on his right hand (Herodias and Herod Antipas ?) look on. Another figure, in classically inspired parade armor, stands in a doorway at the right.

Executed after Gossaert's return from Italy, the drawing reflects the interest in the antique inspired by his stay in Rome, which remained a profound influence throughout his career. Well-proportioned classical architecture dominates the middle ground and the background of the scene. The mixture of monumental structures with crumbling ruins provides a fantastical and highly imaginative architectural setting, characteristic of many of Gossaert's compositions. The influence of Mannerism, which was soon to become the pervasive style in the North, is also abundantly evident in the large statuesque figures, whose articulated full-bodied forms respond to the ordered verticals of the architectural background.

The weighty muscular figures are masterpieces of draftsmanship, swathed in extravagant drapery, which swirls about their limbs and is punctuated by extensive passages of small, agitated crumples. The forms are outlined with crisp, fluid lines, while modeling and shading are achieved by small modulated parallel strokes and by cross-hatching in only the darkest areas. The white highlights are used extremely sparingly and bring a subtle luster to the composition, thus augmenting the gentle reflected light that bathes the entire scene with a luminous warmth that is underscored by the subdued tone of the prepared paper.

Whether or not a roundel evolved from this finished design is unknown. The fact that no working designs or workshop drawings in Gossaert's style exist may suggest that this sheet and other related finished designs (see cat. no. 59) were intended solely for a collector's cabinet. The use of a brown prepared ground for a roundel design appears to be unique to this drawing.

BIBLIOGRAPHY: Winkler, "Anfänge Jan Gossarts," 1921, pp. 5, 8; Popham, *Drawings of the Early Flemish School*, 1926, p. 34, pl. 62; Popham, "Notes-II," 1929, p. 155; Krönig, "Frühzeit Jan Gossarts," 1934, pp. 165–68, 176, pl. 1; Krönig, *Der italienische Einfluß*, 1936, pp. 66–67, 130–31; Rotterdam, *Noord-nederlandsche Primitieven* (exhib. cat.), 1936, p. 69, no. 40, fig. 53; Folie, "Les Dessins de Jean Gossart," 1951, p. 90, no. 10; Ghent, *Charles-Quint et son temps* (exhib. cat.), 1955, p. 139, no. 175; Winkler, "Aus der ersten Schaffenszeit des Jan Gossaert," 1962, pp. 150–51, notes 2, 13, and 14, fig. 4; Rotterdam, *Jan Gossaert genaamd Mabuse* (exhib. cat.), 1965, p. 279, no. 54; Friedländer, *Early Netherlandish Painting* 8, 1972, pl. 67, no. 16; Florence, *L'Époque de Lucas de Leyde* (exhib. cat.), 1981, p. 126; Paris, *Renaissance et Maniérisme* (exhib. cat.), 1985, p. 90, no. 42, ill.; Husband, *Silver-Stained Roundels*, 1991, p. 22, fig. 17.

59

## The Judgment of Paris

South Lowlands, about 1510–20

Pen and ink, heightened with body color, on dark gray prepared paper: diameter, 9¼ in. (23.5 cm)

Edinburgh, National Gallery of Scotland, D652

Inscribed (at the bottom): *Nicasius van Mabuÿse*

At the marriage of Peleus and Thetis, Eris, the goddess of Discord, who had not been invited to the nuptial celebrations, expressed her irritation by tossing into the assembled company a golden apple on which were engraved the words: "Let the most beautiful of you pick me up." Juno, Minerva, and Venus laid claim to the apple, and Jove, unable to decide which of the three was the most meritorious, instructed Mercury to lead the three goddesses to Mount Ida and to defer the decision to Paris, who was then a brave shepherd. The goddesses confront Paris with their

FIG. 1 *The Judgment of Paris*. Pen and brown ink on paper. About 1520. Boston, Museum of Fine Arts, H. D. Parker Fund

FIG. 2 *Aegisthus Killing Agamemnon in the Presence of Clytemnestra*. Pen and brush, with black ink and white highlights, on blue-gray prepared paper. Before 1517. Paris, Collection Frits Lugt, Institut Néerlandais

FIG. 3 *Justice*. Pen and black ink, with chalk and white highlights, on gray prepared paper. About 1520. Vienna, Graphische Sammlung Albertina

respective cases. Each attempts to sway his judgment with tempting inducements: Minerva offers the gifts of intellectual superiority and martial renown, Juno offers a kingdom, and Venus, the most beautiful woman in the world. Paris awards the apple to Venus, a choice that eventually conjoins him with Helen and precipitates the Trojan War.

The present drawing reflects a medieval version of the episode in the form of a rationalized romance in which Paris, arrayed in fine armor rather than in the garb of a shepherd, rests under a tree after traveling or hunting and dreams the entire incident. Following late medieval tradition in the North, Mercury is portrayed as a bearded old man with a winged hat, holding the apple of discord in one hand and the caduceus in the other. Andrews suggests that this representation is a fusion of the stories of Paris and of King Alfred of Mercia, who was forced by William Albonac of Grantham to choose a wife from among William's three daughters.[1] The compositional similarities in a slightly later treatment of the same episode (fig. 1)[2] indicate a conventionalization of the subject.

The Edinburgh drawing is one of seven finished designs on dark gray prepared paper for painted glass roundels that relate to the style of Gossaert. In addition to the present example, there are *The Feast of Esther and Ahasuerus* in Rotterdam;[3] *Aegisthus Killing Agamemnon in the Presence of Clytemnestra* (fig. 2) and *A Woman Beheading Three Sleeping Persons*, both in Paris;[4] *Fortuna* in Hamburg;[5] *Justice* (fig. 3) in Vienna;[6] and *Jezebel Abandoning Ahab* (?) in Cambridge.[7] A number of hands appear responsible for these drawings: The ones in Cambridge, Paris, and Rotterdam may be by one artist, while the Hamburg and Vienna drawings, as well as the present sheet, seem to be by different hands.[8] None, upon close comparison with the Paris *Beheading of John the Baptist* (cat. no. 58), can be regarded as the work of Gossaert himself.[9] The present drawing, however, exhibits the closest stylistic affinities with Gossaert, of the group, but the difficulty in distinguishing among his works and those attributed to his workshop already has been pointed out.[10] The similarity of Paris's helmet to that depicted in the upper portion of the Rotterdam *Studies from the Antique* (fig. 4) indicates a close connection to Gossaert's work. Likewise, the three nude goddesses here are simply variations on the three standing nude figures in Gossaert's drawing of *The Women's Bathhouse* (fig. 5)—if, indeed, this last is an original.[11] These female nudes ultimately recall the figure of Amphitrite in Gossaert's 1516 *Neptune and Amphitrite* now in Berlin (fig. 6).[12] The technique of the present drawing is, nonetheless, quite different from that of the Paris *Beheading of John the Baptist*, and is particularly noticeable in the rather mechanical strokes of the shading, the more emphatic application of highlights, and the harsher light, which lacks the gentle reflective values that characteristically suffuse Gossaert's compositions. Whether the present drawing is by workshop assistants or independent protégés can-

FIG. 4 Jan Gossaert. *Studies from the Antique*. Pen and gray-brown ink on paper. 1508–9. Rotterdam, Museum Boymans-van Beuningen

not be established. Unfortunately, almost nothing is known of the working methods of Gossaert—as noted, a court artist for most of his career—or how these may have differed from the practices of his peers, in the employ of urban mercantilistic patrons.

Nicasius Gossaert, whose name is inscribed at the bottom of the Edinburgh drawing, was Jan's brother and an architect; it is thought that this design may have belonged to him.[13]

1. *Catalogue of Netherlandish Drawings*, 1985, p. 33.

2. Boston, Museum of Fine Arts, 97.705.

3. Museum Boymans-van Beuningen, 139.

4. Collection Frits Lugt, Institut Néerlandais, 5498 and 1978-T.4, respectively.

5. Kunsthalle, 23908.

6. Graphische Sammlung Albertina, 7834.

7. Fitzwilliam Museum, PD 356-1963.

8. Bruyn ("Jan Gossaert Exhibition," 1965, p. 467) saw four different hands at work among the five drawings shown in the 1965 Rotterdam and Bruges exhibition, as well, but he does not specify which two drawings he thought by the same hand.

9. Bruyn (ibid.) and Folie ("Les Dessins de Jean Gossart," 1951, pp. 77 ff.) are likewise of the opinion that only the Paris *Beheading* is unquestionably by Gossaert; Boon (*Drawings of the Frits Lugt Collection*, 1992, p. 208) considers the exclusion of all but the latter design for a roundel from the work of Gossaert to be a "radical view."

10. See von der Osten, "Studien zu Jan Gossaert," 1961, p. 463.

11. London, British Museum, 1924.5.12.1. See Popham, *Drawings in the British Museum*, 1932, pp. 18–19.

FIG. 5 Jan Gossaert. *The Women's Bathhouse*. Pen and black ink, with chalk, on paper. London, British Museum

FIG. 6 Jan Gossaert. *Neptune and Amphitrite*. Tempera and oil on panel. About 1516. Staatliche Museen zu Berlin, Preußischer Kulturbesitz, Gemäldegalerie

12. Staatliche Museen zu Berlin, Preußischer Kulturbesitz, Gemäldegalerie, 1/727.

13. See Washington, *Old Master Drawings* (exhib. cat.), 1990, p. 114.

BIBLIOGRAPHY: van Gelder, "Jan Gossaert in Rome," 1942, p. 10; Folie, "Les Dessins de Jean Gossart," 1951, p. 96, no. 14; Andrews, *Fifty Master Drawings*, 1961, no. 10; Rotterdam, *Verzameling van Sir Bruce en Lady Ingram* (exhib. cat.), 1961, p. 43, no. 42, pl. 1; Rotterdam, *Jan Gossaert genaamd Mabuse* (exhib. cat.), 1965, pp. 287–88, no. 56; Andrews, *Catalogue of Netherlandish Drawings*, 1985, p. 33; Washington, *Age of Bruegel* (exhib. cat.), 1986, p. 181, no. 65; Washington, *Old Master Drawings* (exhib. cat.), 1990, p. 114, no. 47.

60

FIG. 1 Jan Gossaert. *Saint Luke Painting the Virgin* (detail). Tempera and oil on panel. About 1520. Vienna, Kunsthistorisches Museum

## 60

### The Judgment of Paris

Lowlands, 1520–30

Roundel: diameter, 8¾ in. (22.2 cm)

Cleveland Museum of Art, John L. Severance Fund, 85.148

Paris has fallen asleep near a spring and Mercury, contrary to convention, is shown here as a youth rather than as an old man. While in the Edinburgh drawing all three goddesses are presented as nudes, out of an interest in antique forms, in this roundel only Venus reveals her charms, perhaps to further influence Paris's decision. Lacking the more defined musculature of the Edinburgh figures, the nude Venus is especially close to the standing woman combing her hair in the London *Women's Bathhouse* (cat. no. 59, fig. 5). The curly-haired Paris, with high, slightly hollowed cheeks, and the cherubic Mercury clearly evidence the influence of Gossaert, recalling the facial types of the angel and the putti in his *Saint Luke Painting the Virgin* of about 1520 (fig. 1).

BIBLIOGRAPHY: New York, *Form and Light* (exhib. cat.), 1985, no. 2; Husband, *Silver-Stained Roundels*, 1991, p. 201.

61

## 61

### Woman Supporting a Heraldic Shield

Lowlands, about 1520–30

Roundel: diameter, 9½ in. (24.1 cm)

New York, The Metropolitan Museum of Art, The Cloisters Collection, 1932, 32.24.32

Arms: A sword in pale argent hilted or between two mullets of six points

The weighty and well-muscled form of this female supporter, as well as her long flowing tresses, distinctly reflects the influence of Gossaert. However, his efforts to kindle a spirit of classical revival and to bring a new standard of beauty to art, expressed through a mannered but heroic plasticity, are all but lost on the designer of this roundel. While lip service is paid to the form, the composition basically relies on the late medieval formula of wild men and wild women cast as heraldic supporters, as in Martin Schongauer's *Wild Woman and Child with a Shield* (fig. 1). Rather than extolling the idealized beauty of the antique form—much of which is concealed here by the shield—the glass painter has adapted current fashion to serve a traditional role in which the supporter of a heraldic shield symbolizes strength, fecundity, and the perpetuation of the lineage.[1] While Gossaert often underscores the monumentality of his nude figures by establishing a low viewpoint (see cat. no. 59, fig. 6), here we have a raised view. There is no setting of carefully observed classical architecture; the figure is set, like her wild forebear, in a verdant landscape redolent of the wild folk's woodland idyll. A nod to contemporary tastes and a deep bow to tradition manifest the conservatism of this glass painter's clientele.

The roundel is executed in tones of reddish to dark brown paint, with hues of deep to golden yellow silver stain. The forms are outlined in umber paint, while the modeling of the female figure is largely executed with a badger brush. The landscape is articulated with considerable stickwork. Three breaks have been reglued and, along with a loss, have been restored.

The arms are unidentified.

1. See New York, *The Wild Man* (exhib. cat.), 1980, pp. 185–89.

BIBLIOGRAPHY: Grosvenor Thomas Stock Book, I, p. 172, no. 1050; Husband, *Silver-Stained Roundels*, 1991, p. 155.

FIG. 1 Martin Schongauer. *A Wild Woman and Child with a Shield*. Engraving. About 1480–90. New York, The Metropolitan Museum of Art, Harris Brisbane Dick Fund, 1928

# 8

## The Pseudo-Ortkens Group

*Aert van Ort, or Ortkens, who was mentioned in 1522 by the Humanist Gerard Geldenhauer as a designer of stained glass,[1] was born in Nijmegen and was active in Antwerp from about 1513 to 1538. Over the years, designs for stained-glass windows in Rouen, Tournai, and Antwerp; designs for tapestries; and a large group of stylistically distinctive designs for roundels and small-scale glass have all been attributed to him. The identity of the artist—or more probably of the workshop—is highly problematic and has long been the subject of considerable debate and speculation.*

In 1917, M. J. Friedländer identified the artist of a group of drawings in Leipzig as the glass painter Aerdt van Ort, or Ortkens, on the basis of the name "Adam van Ort," which occurs on a design for a tapestry in the British Museum representing Venus and scenes of the Rape of Helen of Troy (fig. 1, p. 135) and which Friedländer considered a later misreading of "Aerdt."[2] Popham mentions a series of tapestries at Hampton Court that are stylistically related to this tapestry design and suggests that Aert van Ort was a designer of both glass and tapestries.[3] Lafond, on the other hand, demonstrated rather convincingly that Aert (Arnoult) van Ort, born in Nijmegen, produced only monumental pot-metal glass windows;[4] van der Boom rebutted this thesis by introducing an assistant who may have executed some of the works attributed to Aert Ortkens.[5] However, the issue remained obfuscated by the natural confusion between Friedländer's Aerdt Ortkens and Lafond's Arnoult de Nimègue (Aert van Ort); they are two very distinct artistic personalities, even though both van der Boom and Helbig before him saw certain stylistic connections among some of the small-scale works and some of the scenes in the Tournai windows.[6] To distinguish the author of the small-scale designs and roundels discussed by Friedländer from

Lafond's monumental stained-glass painter, the eponym "Pseudo-Ortkens" has long been employed.

Wayment attempted to establish the identity of this rather stylistically eccentric master; believing that a glass painter could have produced designs for tapestries as well as for roundels, he associated the letters *A M* found on one of the Tournai windows and on some tapestries with the workshop of the Mechelen glass painter Adriaen van den Houte (about 1459–1521) and his son Pieter van den Houte.[7] Numerous flaws, however, have been found in his thesis,[8] although Wayment did observe that some works by the Pseudo-Ortkens group have a close affinity to the style of the young Barent van Orley (about 1488–1541).[9] Boon cited the Amsterdam drawing *A Tournament for a Princely Marriage* (fig. 2, p. 135), the London design for a tapestry with scenes of the Trojan War (fig. 1, p. 135), and the Hampton Court *History of Aeneas* tapestries to underscore this relationship, and concluded that the Pseudo-Ortkens must have been active in Brussels and may well have been working with, or related to, Barent van Orley.[10]

Evers saw the affinities, but recognized that the work of the Pseudo-Ortkens lacks the vigorous and inventive qualities apparent even in the youthful efforts of Barent van Orley. Thus, she argued that the artist's father, Valentijn van Orley (1466–1532), who had founded a workshop that he and other family members—particularly Barent's younger brother, Everaert (born about 1491)—as well as assistants ran for at least two generations, had produced the large body of work collectively given to the Pseudo-Ortkens group.[11] Valentijn and Everaert were registered as masters in the Antwerp guild, but as neither enrolled apprentices after 1517, it is assumed that they returned to Brussels, where they were documented in 1527.[12] To explain the individual stylistic variations within an essen-

FIG. 1 Pseudo-Ortkens group. *The Judgment of Paris, The Rape of Helen of Troy, and Priam in Council*. Pen and brown ink on paper. About 1520. London, British Museum

FIG. 2 Pseudo-Ortkens group. *A Tournament for a Princely Marriage*. Pen and brown ink on paper. About 1520. Amsterdam, Rijksmuseum, Rijksprentenkabinet

FIG. 3 Valentijn (?) van Orley. The *Saint Joseph* (or Saluzzo) altarpiece (detail of the inner right shutter). Tempera and oil on panel. About 1500–1515. Brussels, Musée d'Art Ancien

FIG. 4 *David and Bathsheba* (detail). Tapestry. About 1520. Château d'Écouen

tially homogeneous body of work, as well as the numerous close and contemporaneous versions of popular designs (see cat. nos. 62 and 63), Evers proposed that the large and successful workshop of painters, who became increasingly active as designers of roundels and especially of tapestries, must have made extensive use of model books. For example, the kneeling bearded figure seen in three-quarter view from the rear, in the left foreground of the Lugt *Samuel Anointing David* (cat. no. 62), is indisputably a close relative of the figure standing at the left edge on the inner right shutter of the *Saint Joseph* (or Saluzzo) altarpiece (fig. 3, above), which is signed *ORLEI* (Valentijn van Orley ?) and can be dated about 1500–1515.[13] The ladies in the right section of the *David and Bathsheba* tapestry, now at Écouen (fig. 4, above), with their characteristic headdresses over hair parted in the middle and their hands holding up the abundant cascading drapery of their dresses, find numerous close analogies in roundel designs (see cat. nos. 63 and 64, fig. 2). Likewise, the hooded doctors, with their curiously crossed arms, found on one of the shutters from the 1514 altarpiece now in Jäder, Sweden (fig. 5, p. 137), representing the twelve-year-old Christ in the Temple and signed by Jan van Coninxloo (about 1489–after 1546)—related by marriage to the van Orleys, and perhaps apprenticed in the family workshop—appear in remarkably similar form in the many working designs and roundels of *Susanna and the Elders* (see cat. nos. 63, 64, and 65). Evers also attempted to establish a stylistic chronology in the Pseudo-Ortkens group. Therefore, she would attribute the Amsterdam design for a window with the *Ascension of Christ, with Donors* (fig. 6, p. 137)—the figures characterized by peculiar pupilless circles for eyes—as a work of Valentijn in the 1480s,[14] while the Lugt *Samuel Anointing David* (cat. no. 62), for example, is seen as a later workshop design of about 1520. Evers's reading of the Pseudo-

Ortkens group thus takes into account the earlier and later groupings of the material that Benesch already had recognized in 1928,[15] and that Boon reinforced fifty years later.[16]

It appears that Evers's Valentijn van Orley or Pseudo-Ortkens-group workshop produced large numbers of designs for glass as well as for tapestries, but did not execute them. The workshop styles are, nonetheless, reflected in the glass production. The windows of the church at Llanwellwyffo (fig. 7, p. 137), for example, convey the calmer, more archaic style of the early Valentijn van Orley workshop, readily differentiated from the later roundel production. The glass generally fails, however, to capture either the nervous tension of the drawings or the eccentricities of their style. Additionally, the varied quality of painting suggests that the designs of the Pseudo-Ortkens-group workshop were widely disseminated throughout the first three decades of the sixteenth century.

1. Geldenhauer, *Collectanea* 16, pp. 72–73.

2. Friedländer, "Aerdt Ortkens," 1917, cols. 161 ff.

3. Popham, *Drawings in the British Museum*, 1932, p. 37.

4. Lafond, "Arnoult de Nimègue," 1939, p. 28, and "Le peintre-verrier Arnoult de Nimègue," 1952, pp. 333–34.

5. Van der Boom, "Aerdt Ortkens," 1949, pp. 79 ff.

6. Ibid.; Helbig, "Arnould de Nimègue," 1937, pp. 279–91.

7. Wayment, "A Rediscovered Master—I," 1967, pp. 172–202; "A Rediscovered Master—II," 1968, pp. 71–94; "A Rediscovered Master—III," 1969, pp. 257–69.

8. See Boon, *Drawings of the Frits Lugt Collection*, 1992, p. 293.

9. Wayment, "A Rediscovered Master—III," 1969, pp. 257–69, esp. pp. 266–69.

10. See Boon, *Netherlandish Drawings*, 1978, pp. 137–38; Boon, *Drawings of the Frits Lugt Collection*, 1992, p. 293.

11. See Evers, "Valentijn van Orley en zijn atelier," thesis, 1986.

12. See Friedländer, *Early Netherlandish Painting* 8, 1972, p. 51.

FIG. 5 Jan van Coninxloo. *Christ in the Temple* (detail of a shutter from the Jäder altarpiece). Tempera and oil on panel. 1514. Jäder, Sweden

13. On the other hand, the beard, facial features, and bent posture of Samuel in the Lugt drawing also correspond very closely to the figure approaching Lazarus on the outer left shutter of Barent van Orley's 1521 *Virtue of Patience* triptych now in Brussels (Musée d'Art Ancien, 335). For the attribution of the *Saint Joseph* altarpiece to Valentijn see De Coo, "Twee Orley-retabels," 1979, pp. 67–80.

14. See Boon, *Netherlandish Drawings*, 1978, p. 7, no. 13. The early date of this drawing—the paper bears watermarks datable to 1470–77—precluded, in Boon's opinion, any connection with the Pseudo-Ortkens drawings of the 1520s.

15. See Benesch, *Albertina Katalog*, 1928, pp. 5–6, no. 27. Because of the stylistic differences among the Albertina *Entry into Jerusalem* and the later Pseudo-Ortkens drawings that resemble the early style of Barent van Orley, Benesch was disinclined to attribute the Vienna sheet to Ortkens.

16. See Boon, *Netherlandish Drawings*, 1978, pp. 137–38. Boon tends to recognize "one or two later periods."

FIG. 6 Valentijn (?) van Orley. *The Ascension of Christ, with Donors*. Pen and black ink on paper. About 1480–90. Amsterdam, Rijksmuseum, Rijksprentenkabinet

FIG. 7 *Christ and His Disciples*. Stained-glass window (detail). About 1500. Wales, Church at Llanwellwyffo

62

FIG. 1 Simon Bening and Gheeraert Horenbout. *Samuel Anointing David.* Manuscript illumination for Psalms, from the *Grimani Breviary.* Before 1520. Venice, Biblioteca Nazionale Marciana

## 62

### Samuel Anointing David

Brussels, about 1520–25

Pen and brown ink, with some later strengthening in darker ink, on paper: diameter, 8⅝ in. (21.9 cm)

Paris, Collection Frits Lugt, Institut Néerlandais, 5377

After the Lord rejected Saul, Samuel was ordered to go to the house of Jesse in Bethlehem where he would be told which of his sons would be anointed as the next king of Israel. Since seven sons were brought forth and rejected Samuel asked Jesse if he had yet another son. Jesse replied that there was one other, the youngest, unfavored son, who was shepherding. Samuel instructed him to be brought forward. "And the Lord said: Arise, and anoint him, for this is he. Then Samuel took the horn of oil, and anointed him in the midst of his brethren: and the spirit of the Lord came upon David . . ." (1 Kings 16: 12–13).

The composition of this drawing, unusual for the Pseudo-Ortkens group—here abandoning, for example, its otherwise unerring preference for masonry architecture—appears to be a reversed adaptation of the illumination accompanying the text of Psalms in the *Grimani Breviary* (fig. 1). In the drawing, the anointing of David is brought closer to the foreground, and one of the kneeling brothers has been shifted farther back and to the right side. The house, with the similar detail of the half-timbering, has been moved to the right background, giving greater prominence to the gate and stave fence. The roundel design, apparently in-

spired by the illumination, must, therefore, postdate the famed breviary, generally thought to have been completed within a few years on either side of 1515. Quite how or in what form the composition was transmitted to the Pseudo-Ortkens workshop is not clear, but it is not the only instance of a connection between roundel designs and the illuminations in the *Grimani Breviary*: For example, border vignettes on one folio of the manuscript were adapted from two of the designs in the Story of Joseph series by the van der Goes group workshop (see cat. nos. 8 and 9, fig. 4). We are thus able to trace the dissemination of a model book or group of designs originating in a Ghent or Bruges workshop closely associated with Hugo van der Goes in the 1470s or 1480s, to a workshop producing roundel designs in the 1490s, to one of the illuminators of the *Grimani Breviary* between 1510 and 1520, and ultimately to the van Orley–Pseudo-Ortkens workshop in Brussels about 1520 or slightly later.

The Lugt drawing, executed in a firm hand, is a competent working design that conveys many of the stylistic eccentricities of the workshop. The eyes of the figures, for example, are heavily underlined and, characteristically, look virtually closed. The hands, rendered with disregard for anatomical correctness, are often considerably ill proportioned and the spread, undulating fingers almost appear unjointed. All but the youngest figures are given puffy cheeks, jowls, and heavy chins. The pen work seems unstudied, if a little mechanical at times, particularly in the short strokes of the cross-hatching. There are two other close versions of this drawing: The one in a Swiss private collec-

FIG. 2 *Samuel Anointing David.* Pen and brown ink on paper. 1520. Oxford, Ashmolean Museum

tion is generally held to be the best, while the other, now in the Ashmolean Museum, Oxford (fig. 2), is deemed to be somewhat weaker.[1]

The present drawing, formerly in the collections of the Staatliche Museen zu Berlin, Preußischer Kulturbesitz, Kupferstichkabinett,[2] is trimmed just outside of the circumference. There is a tear from the top edge to the center, as well as a small loss at the bottom edge and another near the center in Samuel's robe, all of which have been restored.

1. See Boon, *Drawings of the Frits Lugt Collection,* 1992, p. 295.

2. See Bock et al., *Zeichnungen,* 1930, p. 46, no. 4425, pl. 41.

BIBLIOGRAPHY: Friedländer, "Aerdt Ortkens," 1917, col. 162; Bock et al., *Zeichnungen*, 1930, p. 46, no. 4425, pl. 41; Wayment, "A Rediscovered Master—I," 1967, pp. 179–80, n. 34, fig. 9; Stampfle, *Netherlandish Drawings*, 1991, p. 51, no. 81; Boon, *Drawings of the Frits Lugt Collection*, 1992, pp. 295–96, no. 162.

## 63

### Susanna and the Elders

About 1520

Pen and brown ink, with traces of black chalk, on buff-colored paper: diameter, 8⅞ in. (22.5 cm)

Paris, Collection Frits Lugt, Institut Néerlandais, 6612

## 64

### Susanna and the Elders

Lowlands, about 1520–40

Roundel: diameter, 8⅞ in. (22.5 cm)

London, Victoria and Albert Museum, 5636-1859

The apocryphal story of Susanna and the Elders, an addition to the Book of Daniel (13: 15–25), tells of the Babylonian beauty who, while cooling herself at the fountain in her garden, was sexually accosted by two elders. They had recently been appointed to judgeships and, although she knew they would attempt to besmirch her reputation, she cried out. One of the elders ran to the garden gate and opened it; meanwhile the servants came running in response to their mistress's cries, whereupon the judges falsely accused Susanna of committing adultery with a young man in the garden. The next day the spiteful judges condemned Susanna and sought to have her put to death. By separating the elders and then cross-examining them, however, the young Daniel uncovered their treachery and sentenced the false accusers to be stoned to death. This story, perhaps the most ancient to contrast the corrupt and false application of law with its wise and just administration, clearly held great resonance for a people whose social and economic well-being depended on just governance. The theme assumed greater importance for Humanist thinkers with the increasing inability of religious authority to maintain social tranquility.

There are more surviving drawings and roundels from the Story of Susanna than from any other series—of which the Pseudo-Ortkens version, to judge from the exceptionally large number of extant replicas, versions, and variants, seems to have enjoyed the greatest currency.[1] The story appears to have been conveyed in four scenes—Susanna approached by the elders, Susanna accused before a judge, the elders cross-examined by Daniel, and the stoning of the elders—making it a relatively small series and

63

64

FIG. 1 *Susanna and the Elders*. Pen and brown ink on paper. About 1520–25. Cambridge, Harvard University Art Museums, Fogg Art Museum

FIG. 2 *Susanna and the Elders before the Judge*. Pen and brown ink on paper. About 1520–25. Cambridge, Harvard University Art Museums, Fogg Art Museum

FIG. 3 *The Stoning of the Elders*. Pen and brown ink on paper. About 1520–25. Cambridge, Harvard University Art Museums, Fogg Art Museum

therefore, presumably, cheaper to obtain and thus available to a wider market.

The Lugt drawing is probably the finest on this subject in the Pseudo-Ortkens series to survive. A variant composition (fig. 1), one of three from the most complete series of the group (see figs. 2 and 3), is much simplified and rather coarsely drawn. The present sheet is executed in a fine dry line, worked in a series of parallel strokes and cross-hatchings. The hands of the figures, characteristically, have splayed fingers, rendered in nervous wavy lines. The drapery consists of predominantly long folds terminating in sharply angled crumpled patterns. The small-featured faces are punctuated with rather beady eyes. The tall tree in the foreground establishes spatial depth while visually separating the elders from Susanna. The elaborate masonry architecture in the background is articulated with barrel-arched apertures set with two narrow lights surmounted by a small oculus—seemingly a hallmark of the Pseudo-Ortkens compositions. The sheet is trimmed just to the circumference. Small losses on both the left and right sides have been restored.

Of all the surviving roundels based on this composition, the Victoria and Albert example most closely follows the Lugt design.[2] There are minor variations in the treatment of the garden wall, the ornament of the fountain, and details of the landscape. The technique, however, suggests that the roundel was painted at a later date. Exceptional are the range of the palette—umber, brown, and a brownish red that is close to sanguine, as well as yellow and golden yellow tones of silver stain—and the total opacity of the umber paint; the stickwork in the foliage of the trees, creating an emission of light that, in combination with the dense umber paint, imparts a greenish visual effect; and the use of gradations of thinly applied silver stain, which lightens as the composition recedes into the background, to indicate the ground. While such techniques may well be the efforts of a precociously inventive painter, they are not generally encountered until the 1530s. Further effects are achieved by the use of dabbled paint on the masonry garden wall, darker tones of silver stain to pick out ornamental details, and bold stickwork to indicate highlights, intensified by the relative lack of intermediary tonalities in the modeling. The dynamic range of textures and hues lends both coloristic appeal and clearer spatial definition to the composition. The fountain waters in which Susanna washes her hands are rendered entirely in stickwork, giving them a sparkling effect. Far from succumbing to tired and lifeless formulas, the glass painter brings fresh visual interest to an exceptionally enduring composition.

1. See Husband, *Silver-Stained Roundels*, 1991, pp. 156–57.

2. Apparently an even closer version was formerly in the Kaiser-Friedrich-Museum, Berlin. A photograph of it can be found in Popham's research notes, now housed in the RKD, The Hague. Another version is in the collection of William Cole (*Roundels in Britain*, 1993, p. 212, no. 1721).

BIBLIOGRAPHY: (63) Wayment, "The Dido and Aeneas Tapestries," 1969, p. 372, n. 4; Florence, *L'Époque de Lucas de Leyde* (exhib. cat.), 1981, pp. 169–70, no. 115, pl. 19; Isler-de Jongh, "Rondels de la Collection Hosmer," 1989, p. 36, n. 15, p. 89, fig. 57; Husband, *Silver-Stained Roundels*, 1991, p. 156; Stampfle, *Netherlandish Drawings*, 1991, p. 51, nos. 82, 83; Boon, *Drawings of the Frits Lugt Collection*, 1992, pp. 293–95, no. 161. (64) Amsterdam, *Middeleeuwse kunst* (exhib. cat.), 1958, pp. 177–78, no. 248; Florence, *L'Époque de Lucas de Leyde* (exhib. cat.), 1981, p. 169; Isler-de Jongh, "Rondels de la Collection Hosmer," 1989, p. 36, n. 15, p. 89, fig. 56; Husband, *Silver-Stained Roundels*, 1991, p. 156; Boon, *Drawings of the Frits Lugt Collection*, 1992, p. 294.

65  *see cover*

## Susanna and the Elders

About 1520–25

Roundel: diameter, 9½ in. (24.1 cm), with border, 13 in. (33 cm)

New York, The Metropolitan Museum of Art, The Cloisters Collection, 1990, 1990.119.1

Inscribed (around the border): *Susanna et · / Exarserūt senes / in cōcupiscentiā / declinaverūt ocu / los suos ut nō vidē / rēt celū daniel 13*

The design of this roundel is clearly influenced by that of the Pseudo-Ortkens group but exhibits considerable differences, the most obvious of which is the reversed composition. Additionally, the elders are accosting Susanna rather than merely approaching from the background (although one wonders how they can possibly move with the superfluity of trailing drapery about their feet), and Susanna reacts accordingly by throwing her arms up in horror. Responding to her cries, two servants in the right background are running into the garden. The massing of the towers and other structures in the distance provides a rather stronger architectural statement than the Pseudo-Ortkens group is normally wont to prefer. This roundel is exceptional in that it retains its original border with the appropriate Latin biblical inscription. The text, however, is rather truncated; the passage would read: "ingrediebatur Susanna, et deambulabat in pomario viri sui . . . et exarserunt [senes] in concupiscentiam eius . . . et declinaverunt oculos suos ut non viderent caelum . . ." ("Susanna went in, and walked in her husband's orchard. . . . and they [the elders] were inflamed with lust towards her . . . and turned away their eyes that they might not look unto heaven . . .") (Daniel 13: 7–9). While there is little question that all roundels were originally set within borders—whether inscribed, ornamented, or of undecorated colored glass—very few have survived, as they were inevitably destroyed when the roundels were removed from their original glazings.

The present roundel is executed in tones of medium to dark brown paint, with hues of light to rich, deep yellow silver stain. The forms are edged with painted lines and stickwork, while the modeling of the drapery is achieved largely with a badger brush. The foliage is given volume and

65

66

texture with the point of a brush as well as with the stylus, while the waters of the fountain, worked entirely with a stylus, have a shimmering appearance. The ornamental band surrounding the inscription is an unusual elaboration.

BIBLIOGRAPHY: Husband, *Silver-Stained Roundels*, 1991, pp. 156–57.

## 66

### Scene from Virgil's Second *Eclogue*

Lowlands, about 1520

Pen and brown ink on paper: diameter, 9 in. (22.9 cm)

Oxford, Ashmolean Museum, PI65

Inscribed (upper left): CORIDŌ; (upper right): ALEXIS; (lower left): TESTILIS; (lower right): NIMPHA

The subject is drawn from the second poem in Virgil's *Eclogues*, or *Bucolica*, in which the shepherd Corydon expresses his obsessive passion for a handsome youth named Alexis. "Corydon, the shepherd, was aflame for the fair Alexis, his master's pet, nor knew he what to hope. As his one solace, he would day by day come among the thick beeches with their shady summits, and there alone in fruitless passion fling these artless strains to the hills and woods: O cruel Alexis, care you naught for my songs? Have you no pity for me? You will drive me at last to death" (*Eclogue* 2: 1–7). Without the benefit of the identifying *tituli*, one would hardly be able to recognize the scene. The Pseudo-Ortkens group makes no attempt to

portray the pastoral idyll in classical vocabulary; rather, all the figures are dressed in contemporary costume. Nor is there the slightest indication of the fervent drama being played out in an Arcadian landscape. Curiously, the ancillary figures are given greater prominence than the principals. A nymph sits on a small knoll in the foreground, making a floral wreath. "See for you the Nymphs bring lilies in heaped-up baskets; for you the fair Naiad, plucking pale violets and poppy-heads, blends narcissus and sweet-scented fennel flower; then, twining them with cassia and other sweet herbs, sets off the delicate hyacinth with the golden marigold" (*Eclogue* 2: 45). The peasant maid Thestylis stands behind, and to the left, in front of a herd of goats; she carries a flask and a handled pot, while balancing a flat, circular pan on her head that perhaps holds *moretum*—a cheese, flour, salt, oil, and herb concoction. In the middle ground, Corydon sits beneath a tree with his bagpipes at his side, idly pushing about a shepherd's shovel, while, one assumes, he moons over his unrequited love. The object of his obsession, Alexis, is removed to the background, fashionably dressed, and standing with open arms.

The *Eclogues* were appreciated throughout most of the Middle Ages; as early as the fourth century, writers had viewed the fourth *Eclogue* as a prophecy of the coming of Christ. This drawing seeks to promote no such Christian values, but evidences a broad interest in the literature of the ancients; indeed, the Pseudo-Ortkens group appears to be among the earliest workshops to provide classical subjects on a large scale. Whether a particular interpretation of the subject inspired

the curious composition of the present drawing is unclear. The pen work is summary and unstudied, yet retains the hallmarks of the Pseudo-Ortkens-group style, particularly in the treatment of the eyes, which generally appear shut or blank; in the expansive and angularly crumpled drapery of the seated figures; and in the minimal modeling. The figures are provided with individual spaces defined by topographical features, which indicates that they are meant to be perceived as at a greater remove than their actual distance from each other would suggest. In this regard the composition is more typical of tapestry rather than of roundel designs of the period. This, however, is not surprising, for the drawing emanated from a workshop that produced many designs for both mediums.

There are a number of repaired tears and fills, particularly around the edges.

BIBLIOGRAPHY: Parker, *Drawings in the Ashmolean Museum*, 1938, pp. 26–27, no. 65, pl. 13; van der Boom, "Aerdt Ortkens," 1949, pp. 85–86, fig. 11; Wayment, "A Rediscovered Master—I," 1967, p. 182, fig. 17.

# 9

## The Roundel Series of Dirick Vellert

*Dirick Jacobsz. Vellert probably was born about 1480–85 in Amsterdam, but nothing is known of him before his inscription as a master in the Antwerp painters' guild in 1511. He was already a mature artist when he executed his earliest certain works, the two glass roundels of the* Trionfi *(cat. nos. 67 and 68), dated six years after he enrolled in the guild. Few documents record his activity. Vellert served as dean of the guild twice (in 1518 and 1526) and registered six apprentices between 1512 and 1530.[1] He was awarded a contract to produce a window for the altar of Saint Nicholas in the Antwerp Cathedral between 1516 and 1517, and his assistants were paid a tip for setting up another window in the cathedral, this time above the pulpit, in 1539–40.[2] Both windows are now lost. The city of Leiden paid the artist in 1532 for a window, also lost, which was a gift to the president of the Grand Council in Mechelen.[3] In December 1547, Vellert granted power of attorney to two lawyers in Amsterdam to manage his business affairs there.[4] It is presumed that he died shortly after.*

Dirick Vellert's contemporaries recognized him as one of the foremost glass designers in the Lowlands. Guicciardini named him and Aert Ortkens as the leading glass painters in Antwerp, and praised Vellert as an "excellent master of great invention."[5] Vellert's prominence was such that he served as host to the great German artist Albrecht Dürer during the latter's visit to Antwerp; Dürer recorded in his diary a lavish banquet that Vellert held in his honor.[6] Vellert's international reputation won him one of the major commissions of sixteenth-century stained glass, the cycle of monumental windows at King's College Chapel, Cambridge.[7]

Vellert's fame as a glass painter was short-lived. By the early seventeenth century his identity already was forgotten, and his prints and drawings appeared in catalogues and inventories ascribed to the Master Dirk van Staren (or the Maître de l'Étoile), so-named after the artist's monogram, which was composed of a five-pointed star flanked by his initials. It was not until 1901 that Gustav Glück identified the glazier Dirick Vellert, then known only from documents, as the engraver and draftsman Dirk van Staren.[8] Glück was able to reconstruct a corpus of drawings, prints, and one painted glass roundel by the artist, an *oeuvre* that was expanded by later writers.

Vellert produced designs for large-scale windows and he executed engravings, etchings, and woodcuts, but the majority of his surviving works are roundel designs.[9] The artist's chronology is relatively easy to follow since he dated works throughout his career. The panels and drawings included here are representative of his development as a designer of small-scale glass. Vellert is one of the few sixteenth-century glass designers who painted roundels himself, and his first and last dated panels are by his own hand: the *Trionfi* of 1517 (cat. no. 67) and the *Judgment of Cambyses* of 1542 (cat. no. 80). In early works such as the *Trionfi*, compositions tend to be crowded and spatial relationships are sometimes unclear. The *Judgment of Cambyses* displays the accomplishment of the artist's later works, in which he skillfully adapts the compositions to the circular shape by placing figures to the sides and by using empty spaces and juxtapositions in scale to heighten the dynamic rhythm of the curve of the roundel. Most of Vellert's roundel designs represent traditional religious themes such as the Life of the Virgin (cat. nos. 74 and 75) and the Apocalypse (cat. no. 71). As in the works seen here, Vellert's roundel designs participated in the artistic trends current in panel painting, and his designs incorporate aspects of the fashionable Antwerp Mannerist style, the contemporary taste for Italianate ornament, and the muscular, heroic figure types of the so-called Romanist artists such as Barent van Orley and Pieter Coecke van Aelst. Vellert occasionally borrowed compositional models—notably, from Dürer's woodcuts—but his designs are always highly imaginative and individual, presenting new combinations of massive figures in vigorous arrangements that exploit the roundel's circular format.

1. See Rombouts and van Lerius, *Antwerpsche Sint-Lucasgilde*, 1961, pp. 75, 77, 82, 105–6, 111, 115.

2. Ibid., p. 75, n. 3.

3. See Bangs, *Documentary Studies*, 1976, p. 117.

4. Published in Wayment, *Windows of King's College*, 1972, p. 127, Appendix G.

5. Guicciardini, *Descrittione*, 1567, p. 100. Guicciardini's remarks about Vellert were repeated by Vasari (*Vite*, 1881, p. 588).

6. See Rupprich, *Dürer Schriftlicher Nachlass* 1, 1956, p. 169, entry for 12.5.1521.

7. For this commission see Wayment, *Windows of King's College*, 1972; Konowitz, "Vellert," Ph.D. diss., 1992. These are the only large-scale windows by Vellert that survive.

8. Glück ("Name des Meisters D*V," 1901, pp. 10–11) discovered that a woodcut device of the Antwerp painters' guild, signed with the monogram and dated 1526, is referred to in the guild ledgers as having been produced by Vellert the year he was dean for the second time (1526).

9. For Vellert's engravings, etchings, and woodcuts see Popham, "Engravings and Woodcuts of Vellert," 1925, pp. 343–68. Baldass ("Dirk Vellert als Tafelmaler," 1922, pp. 162–67) and Friedländer (*Early Netherlandish Painting* 12, 1975) ascribed a group of panel paintings to Vellert, but in the opinion of this writer these panels are not by the artist (see Konowitz, "Vellert," Ph.D. diss., 1992, pp. 117–28).

67

68

## 67

### The Triumph of Time

Roundel, without silver stain: diameter, 7⅞ in. (20 cm)

Brussels, Musées Royaux d'Art et d'Histoire, 5956

Signed (on the legs of the figure at the right): DIRICK/VELLE; dated (on the plaque, bottom right): · 1 · 5 · 1 · 7 · / APR 21

## 68  *see frontispiece*

### The Triumph of Faith

Roundel: diameter, 8¾ in. (22.2 cm)

Amsterdam, Rijksmuseum, RBK-1966-58

Signed (below the angel's left foot): D * V; dated (on the plaque, bottom center): 1517 / MEI

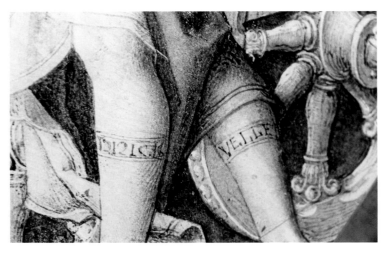

FIG. 1 Dirick Vellert. *The Triumph of Time* (detail of cat. no. 67)

These two grisaille roundels, the earliest dated works by Vellert, are also his earliest signed works. The roundel in Brussels has the further distinction of being the only work that bears his full name (see fig. 1). The recent discovery of the monogram on the Amsterdam panel is particularly significant.[1] The fact that this monogrammed roundel can be ascribed on the basis of style to the same hand that painted the Brussels panel, signed with Vellert's name, confirms Glück's identification of the artist with the engraver known since the early seventeenth century as the monogrammist Dirk van Staren.[2]

These roundels undoubtedly were part of a larger cycle illustrating Petrarch's famous poem *I trionfi*. The completed series would have included four additional scenes of the Triumph of Chastity, Love, Death, and Fame. Vellert follows the standard formula for representations of the Triumphs. Time, portrayed as a bearded old man with crutches and wings, rides on a wagon furnished with hourglasses and pulled by two deer. His entourage includes a child and a young man—symbolic of the three Ages of Man. Faith, represented as the Trinity, appears on a wagon drawn by the symbols of the Evangelists and is accompanied by a multitude of saints.

In the Brussels roundel the artist borrowed motifs from several Italian prints. The figure of Time is copied in reverse from a fifteenth-century

Florentine engraving from a series of Petrarch's *I trionfi* (fig. 2), and the boy holding the jug and the helmeted figure at the right derive from two engravings after Mantegna's *Triumph of Caesar* (figs. 3 and 4).[3] The Amsterdam roundel does not employ borrowed motifs.

The site for which Vellert's panels were intended is unknown, but they were most likely designed for the private home of a patron interested in humanistic themes. Contemporary documents mention houses decorated with glass windows whose subjects were the *Trionfi*. The Humanist Jerome de Busleyden had the dining-room windows of his home in Mechelen—built and furnished after his return from Italy in 1506—

FIG. 2 *The Triumph of Time*. Engraving. 15th century. London, British Museum

FIG. 5 A. Onghena. *The Triumph of Fame* (detail of plate 22 from Joan. d'Huyvetter, *Zeldaaheden*). Etching. 1829. The Hague, Koninklijk Huisarchief

FIG. 6 *The Triumph of Fame*. Pen and brown ink, with wash, on paper. About 1515–20. Bremen, Kunsthalle

FIGS. 3 and 4 Giovanni Antonio da Brescia, after Mantegna. *The Triumph of Caesar* (details). Engravings. About 1500. Staatliche Museen zu Berlin, Preußischer Kulturbesitz, Kupferstichkabinett

adorned with glass panels representing the *Trionfi*, along with portraits of Petrarch and Saint Jerome.[4] Another example is a series of small windows depicting Petrarch's *Trionfi* as parallels to the Sacraments, executed in 1517 for a home in Bruges.[5] In Vellert's *Triumph of Faith*, Saint Bartholomew, with his knife, is prominent at the far right—perhaps a distant but tantalizing clue to the patron of Vellert's series, although who this Bartholomew may be is impossible to say.

A lost glass roundel of the *Triumph of Fame*, formerly in the collection of Joan. d'Huyvetter in Ghent, repeatedly has been considered to have been part of Vellert's series.[6] This roundel, known only from an etching published in the nineteenth century (fig. 5), follows the formula of the corresponding engraving in the same Florentine series from which Vellert quoted in his *Triumph of Time*. However, this attribution must remain conjecture, especially since no signature is recorded on the roundel. Moreover, a design for a glass roundel in Bremen, almost identical in composition to the d'Huyvetter roundel, casts doubt on the connection to Vellert (fig. 6).[7] The drawing has no stylistic similarities to Vellert's work and can be ascribed to an anonymous artist associated with the Antwerp Mannerists. The relationship between drawing and roundel is unclear, but if the drawing was, indeed, the model for the roundel, this would demonstrate that the d'Huyvetter *Triumph of Fame* came not from Vellert but from a different shop.

Both roundels are painted in tones of pale grayish to rich deep brown, and they are unique in Vellert's work for the complete absence of silver stain. The technique, which seems to have been used earlier by Lucas van Leyden (see cat. no. 56), is highly painterly; Vellert defines and models the forms by applying deeper tones of paint with a fine-pointed brush over paler shades of mattes. Only occasionally does Vellert employ the stylus to indicate extreme highlights, as in the drapery fluttering behind the angel, or to indicate textures and fine detail, as in the wings and hair of the same figure. In some areas both techniques are combined with such finesse that, without magnification, it is difficult to distinguish them.

1. First noted by Konowitz, "Glass Designer Dierick Vellert," in Worcester, *Northern Renaissance Stained Glass* (exhib. cat.), 1987, pp. 22–23.
2. Glück, "Name des Meisters D*V," 1901.
3. Ibid., pp. 12–16. Vellert borrowed the figure of the young man from Mantegna, but changed his plain headband to a winged helmet. Glück's identification of this figure as Mercury has been accepted by subsequent writers, as has his suggestion that the young woman at the left wearing a jeweled diadem and clasp personifies Fame, even though she does not display any of the attributes associated with Fame, and she is shown accompanying the chariot rather than being trampled by it. Perhaps this figure is Venus. In a Flemish tapestry of the *Triumph of Time* produced about 1510–20, now in the Keresztény Múzeum, Esztergom, classical gods and goddesses accompany Time's chariot—among them a figure labeled *Mercury* and a jeweled and crowned young woman labeled *Venus* (László, *Flemish and French Tapestries in Hungary*, 1981, p. 41, pl. 3, no. 25).

4. See De Vocht, *Jerome de Busleyden*, 1950, pp. 246–48. These windows are also mentioned by Vanden Bemden, "Rondels représentant les Triomphes de Pétrarque," 1977, p. 21.

69                 70

5. The document concerning these windows is published in "Pierre de Dappere," 1866–70, pp. 288–91.

6. See Beets, "Dirick Jacobsz. Vellert," 1922, pp. 90–91; Helbig, *Glasschilderkunst*, 1943, p. 19; Ramaix, in Brussels, *Le siècle de Bruegel* (exhib. cat.), 1963, p. 243, no. 466; Helbig and Vanden Bemden, *Vitraux 3*, 1974, p. 275, fig. 201, p. 277; Vanden Bemden, "Rondels représentant les Triomphes de Pétrarque," 1977, p. 21.

7. See Busch and Keller, *Meisterwerke der Kunsthalle Bremen*, 1959, no. 17, ill.: *A Triumphal Procession*, attributed to Cornelis Engebrechtsz.; brush and brown ink, heightened with white, on brownish gray prepared paper; diameter, 25 cm; provenance, Benno Geiger, Vienna, A. Grahl, Dresden (L. 1199). Boon (*Netherlandish Drawings*, 1978, under no. 541, pp. 204–5: *Triumph of Fame*, Geiger Collection) believes that the drawing is by the same hand as a glass design in the Rijksprentenkabinet, Amsterdam, which he ascribes to an anonymous artist of the Antwerp Mannerist school. The Bremen drawing is abraded and was heavily retouched by a later hand, especially in the areas of the shadows. Its poor condition makes a precise attribution extremely difficult.

BIBLIOGRAPHY: (67) Glück, "Name des Meisters D*V," 1901, pp. 12–16, pl. 1; Rooses, "De Romanisten," 1902, p. 170; Beets, "Dirick Jacobsz. Vellert," 1908, pp. 165–66, 175; Beets, "Dirick Jacobsz. Vellert," 1922, pp. 85–87; Beets, "Verres Peints," 1925, p. 116, fig. 1; Laurent, "Le Vitrail de Dirick Vellert," 1925, pp. 81–84; Popham, "Engravings and Woodcuts of Vellert," 1925, pp. 346–47; Helbig, *Glasschilderkunst*, 1943, pp. 29, 100, fig. 195; Brussels, *Le siècle de Bruegel* (exhib. cat.), 1963, p. 243, no. 466, ill.; Helbig and Vanden Bemden, *Vitraux 3*, 1974, pp. 275–81, fig. 202; Friedländer, *Early Netherlandish Painting 12*, 1975, p. 157, pl. 70 A; Brussels, *Dürer aux Pays-Bas* (exhib. cat.), 1977, p. 144, no. 195, ill.; Bourg-en-Bresse, *Van Orley* (exhib. cat.), 1981, p. 114, no. 93, ill. p. 115; Konowitz, "Glass Designer Dierick Vellert," in Worcester, *Northern Renaissance Stained Glass* (exhib. cat.), 1987, pp. 22–23, fig. 5. (68) "Verschillende verzamelingen," 1969, p. 59, ill. p. 57; Konowitz, "Glass Designer Dierick Vellert," in Worcester, *Northern Renaissance Stained Glass* (exhib. cat.), 1987, pp. 22–23, fig. 4; Wayment, *King's College*, 1988, p. 90, n. 40; Antwerp, *Antwerp* (exhib. cat.), 1993, no. 50 A, pp. 195–96, ill.

## 69

### Moses and the Burning Bush

Pen and brown ink, with gray wash over black chalk, on paper: diameter, 11¼ in. (28.6 cm)

Staatliche Museen zu Berlin, Preußischer Kulturbesitz, Kupferstichkabinett, KdZ 3364

Signed and dated (top center): 1523 MERT 31 / D * V

## 70

### The Return of the Holy Family from Egypt

Pen and brown and dark brown ink, with light and medium gray wash, over black chalk, on paper: diameter, 11¼ in. (28.6 cm)

London, British Museum, 1923.1.13.3

Signed and dated (top center): 1523 IVLI 11 / D * V

Vellert inscribed fourteen designs for glass roundels with the date 1523. Most of these sheets also indicate the day and the month as well as the year, as do the present two drawings. On the basis of style, four undated sheets by the artist and, very likely, a painted glass roundel can also be placed at the same time and should be considered part of the group.[1] These all most likely formed a single set of designs for a series of roundels representing parallel incidents from the Old and the New Testament. All eighteen drawings are about the same size and employ the same technique, and all depict Old and New Testament subjects. Moreover, many of the subjects are extremely rare in Netherlandish art except in typological programs.[2]

Glück had already suggested that the Berlin *Moses and the Burning Bush* may have been part of an incomplete cycle designed by Vellert juxtaposing the Story of Moses with the Life of Christ, although Glück could not name a specific surviving sheet that would have been paired with this particular scene.[3] It is probable, however, that this proposed series was not limited to scenes of Christ and Moses but also included such Old Testament types as David and Elisha, among others. Therefore, *Moses and the Burning Bush* may have been paired with Vellert's design of *Gideon and the Miracle of the Fleece* in Berlin (fig. 1), dated the same day (March 31, 1523).[4] Both scenes were traditional types for Marian subjects such as the Nativity, the Annunciation, and the Immaculate Conception, since Mary's virginity was thought to have been prefigured by the fleece that absorbed the divine dew while the ground remained dry, and by the bush that burned but was not con-

FIG. 1 Dirick Vellert. *Gideon and the Miracle of the Fleece*. Pen and ink, with gray-brown wash, on paper. 1523. Staatliche Museen zu Berlin, Preußischer Kulturbesitz, Kupferstichkabinett

FIG. 2 After Dirick Vellert. *Gideon and the Miracle of the Fleece*. Roundel. About 1523–30. Paris, Collection Frits Lugt, Institut Néerlandais

FIG. 3 Dirick Vellert. *The Massacre of the Innocents*. Pen and brown ink, with gray wash, on paper. 1523. London, British Museum

sumed. It is likely that one or more lost drawings of Marian themes were intended to accompany these designs.

The drawings of Gideon and Moses are similar in composition and in the scale of the figures. Both depict a man kneeling in the foreground, a shoe or helmet at his feet to the left, with a rocky-mountain landscape at the right. Vellert may have intentionally strengthened the visual link between the two designs. After he completed the landscape in the drawing of *Gideon and the Miracle of the Fleece*, the artist sketched the outline of a tree to the left of Gideon, which corresponds to the tree in the center of the scene to the left of Moses. Fortunately, a painted glass roundel from the workshop survives that records the final formulation (fig. 2). Here the artist did, indeed, add the tree, making the composition even closer to that of *Moses and the Burning Bush*.[5] In the *Return of the Holy Family from Egypt* Vellert made some minor adjustments—notably, the addition of the tree at the right, which appears to be an extension of the original trunk, and the alteration of Christ's right foot. There is a curious statuesque solidity to the Virgin and in the forward movement of Christ and Joseph. In a parallel variance of emotional content, the Virgin seems remote while the eye contact between Christ and Joseph creates a touching intimacy. Joseph's prominence recalls his particular importance in popular devotion in the fifteenth and sixteenth centuries.[6]

The relationship between the drawing and the roundel of Gideon offers some insights into the roles of the designer and the glass painter in the series proposed here. The drawing appears to be detailed, but a comparison with the roundel re-

veals that Vellert employed shorthand techniques in the pattern. For instance, he indicated plain bands shaded with wash in areas such as the hem of Gideon's cloak, the top of his boots, and the horse's bridle, which in the roundel the glass painter filled with intricate patterns of studs and arabesques. Vellert employed summary sketchy pen lines for the decoration of the soldiers' armor, which was elaborated with ornament in the roundel.

In addition, the painter introduced descriptive detail and naturalistic motifs—such as the nails on the horse's shoes and the shrubs and stones along the riverbank—to areas that are simply shaded in the drawing. We can surmise from the relationship between this drawing and the roundel that in indicating other patterns in the series of 1523 Vellert also made use of timesaving devices and that the glass painter was expected to add a variety of details and rich surface textures in the final stage of the design. Thus we can imagine that in the completed roundels after the present drawings the wide collar of Moses' coat and the cuffs and borders of Joseph's cloak and robe would be embellished with a decorative pattern or with the texture of fur. Further, we can assume that all of the designs from 1523 were intended to be dense with abundant detail in the finished, painted stage. Clearly, the glass painter was not considered a mere mechanical copyist but was entrusted to make his own contribution to the design.

The *Return of the Holy Family from Egypt* is more difficult to relate to the known drawings of 1523. The theme is rare in Northern art. It is usually not shown as an independent subject, but either as part of a narrative cycle of the Life of

Christ or in typological programs paired with scenes of the return from a journey or from exile. Moreover, in execution and figure type the drawing is similar to sheets in the 1523 series such as the *Massacre of the Innocents* (fig. 3), further suggesting that it is not an autonomous design but rather belonged to the group.[7] Perhaps it was paired with a design of an appropriate Old Testament type, now lost.

Although it is impossible with the present evidence to determine the original site for which Vellert's cycle may have been planned, our knowledge of the intended context of other typological series of roundels suggests that it may have been designed for windows in a chapel, or for glazing in a cloister. The unusually large number of scenes makes the latter possibility particularly attractive, since the arcades and chapels of cloisters frequently contained extensive cycles of glass roundels, and typological programs of painted windows were extremely common in cloisters.[8]

The proposed series of 1523 is the only set of designs by Vellert for glass roundels that represents a didactic rather than a narrative sequence. This is, however, the formula employed for the artist's greatest commission for stained glass, the monumental windows at King's College Chapel, Cambridge. Whereas the scenes at King's College conform to standard formulas set by the medieval typological handbooks, in the roundel designs Vellert's choice of subjects includes many scenes that are rare in the typological tradition, and he seems to have employed unusual pairings, thus suggesting the comparative freedom enjoyed by the artist in this small-scale and more intimate medium.[9]

1. The drawings in the group with the date 1523 include: *The Crossing of the Red Sea* (Weimar, Kunstsammlungen); *Moses Sweetening the Bitter Waters at Mara* (Hamburg, Kunsthalle; dated November 29); *Moses Displaying the Tablets of the Law* (Weimar, Kunstsammlungen; dated November 25); *David's Flight from Saul* (Vienna, Graphische Sammlung Albertina); *Hannah Presenting Samuel to the Priest Eli* (Vienna, Graphische Sammlung Albertina; dated August 28); *Elisha and the Shunammite Woman* (Hamburg, Kunsthalle); *Naaman Bathing in the Jordan* (London, British Museum; dated November 26); *The Massacre of the Innocents* (London, British Museum); *The Marriage at Cana* (London, British Museum; dated November 25); *The Sermon on the Mount* (Weimar, Kunstsammlungen; dated November 25); *Christ and the Centurion of Capernaum* (Weimar, Kunstsammlungen; dated November 29). The undated drawings are *Balaam and the Ass* (Braunschweig, Herzog Anton Ulrich-Museum); *David Beheading Goliath* (Vienna, Graphische Sammlung Albertina); *Saul Ordering the Slaughter of Ahimelech and the Priests of Nob* (Frankfurt, Städelsches Kunstinstitut); *The Temptation of Christ* (Weimar, Kunstsammlungen). In addition, a destroyed roundel of *The First Day of Creation*, painted by Vellert himself, may have served as the first scene in the cycle (dated 152[?] and signed with the artist's monogram; formerly Berlin, Kunstgewerbemuseum; ill. in Baldass, "Dirk Vellert als Tafelmaler," 1922, pl. 83). The present writer has also proposed that a painted glass roundel of *The Creation of Eve* in a private collection in Rotterdam records a lost design by Vellert for this series: see Konowitz, "Vellert," Ph.D. diss., 1992, pp. 37–38.

2. For the reconstruction of the series of 1523 see Konowitz, "Vellert," Ph.D. diss., 1992, pp. 28–39. See also Konowitz, "Glass Designer Dierick Vellert," in Worcester, *Northern Renaissance Stained Glass* (exhib. cat.), 1987, pp. 24–26; Washington, *Age of Bruegel* (exhib. cat.), 1986, p. 291, under no. 114.

3. Glück, "Name des Meisters D*V," 1901, p. 20.

4. For the drawing of Gideon see Bock et al., *Zeichnungen*, 1930, no. 4346.

5. The artist continued to use the device of dividing space with a tree in subsequent drawings in 1523. See Konowitz, "Vellert," Ph.D. diss., 1992, p. 32.

6. For the cult of Saint Joseph see Schwartz, "Iconography of the Rest on the Flight," Ph.D. diss., 1975, pp. 48–51. See also Ainsworth, in New York, *Petrus Christus* (exhib. cat.), 1994, no. 20, pp. 170–76.

7. See Popham, *Drawings in the British Museum*, 1932, no. 3, p. 50.

8. See Konowitz, "Vellert," Ph.D. diss., 1992, p. 39. For cloister glazing in general see Hayward, "Glazed Cloisters," 1973, pp. 93–109, esp. p. 107, notes 1–5. Lillich has proposed that typological glazing programs were particularly characteristic of monastic patronage, although not limited to it. She notes that an emphasis on Old Testament themes and esoteric types frequently marks monastic art, a preference she explains as reflecting the need not for instruction but for stimulation to encourage the interpretation and meditation of the monks ("Monastic Stained Glass," 1984, pp. 207–54, esp. pp. 208–9).

9. The unusual scenes and pairings are discussed in Konowitz, "Vellert," Ph.D. diss., 1992, pp. 28–39.

BIBLIOGRAPHY: (69) Glück, "Name des Meisters D*V," 1901, p. 8, fig. 5; Rooses, "De Romanisten," 1902, p. 170; Wurzbach, *Künstler-Lexicon*, 1910, p. 747; Beets, *De houtsneden*, 1915, p. 20; Bock et al., *Zeichnungen*, 1930, p. 55, 2, pl. 48; Washington, *Age*

·IOANNES DIE APOS / TEL GODS WTVERCORE / MITS DES KEYSERS DO / MITIANVS THOREN · / WORDT HIER OM DWOIRD / GODS AEN DE PORTE LATINE / IN HEETE OLIE GESODE · / SONDER PIJNE ·

71

of Bruegel (exhib. cat.), 1986, under no. 114, n. 3, p. 291; Konowitz, "Glass Designer Dierick Vellert," in Worcester, *Northern Renaissance Stained Glass* (exhib. cat.), 1987, p. 26, fig. 11. (70) Beets, "Dirick Jacobsz. Vellert," 1912, p. 152, n. 2; Vasari Society, 1912–13, no. 19, ill.; Popham, "Teekeningen," 1925, p. 205; Popham, *Drawings in the British Museum*, 1932, p. 50, no. 2; Faggin, *La pittura*, 1968, fig. 39; Tümpel, *Rembrandt*, 1970, under no. 68; Washington, *Age of Bruegel* (exhib. cat.), 1986, under no. 114, n. 3, p. 291.

## 71

### Saint John in a Cauldron of Boiling Oil

About 1522–30

Pen and black and brown ink, with gray-brown wash over black chalk, on paper: diameter, 11⅛ in. (28.3 cm); size of sheet, 12⅝ x 10⅞ in. (32.1 x 27.6 cm)

Staatliche Museen zu Berlin, Preußischer Kulturbesitz, Kupferstichkabinett, KdZ 3363

Signed (bottom center): D * V

Inscribed: (on the city gate) P L (for *Porta Latina*); (below the scene) · IOANNES DIE APOS / TEL GODS WTVERCORE[N], / MITS DES KEYSERS DO / MITIANVS THOREN, / WORDT HIER OM DWOIRD / GODS AEN DE PORTE LATINE / IN HEETE OLIE GESODE[N], / SONDER PIJNE ·

This drawing is the first in a series of eighteen designs by Vellert for a cycle of the Apocalypse; the remaining seventeen drawings are in Paris (Musée du Louvre, Rothschild Collection). Each

scene in the series is drawn on a rectangular sheet within a circular enframing line. At the bottom of each page the artist inscribed two columns of text of four lines each, commenting on the scene in Flemish. The text on the present drawing may be translated: "John the Apostle, the chosen one of God, by the anger of Emperor Domitian is here because of the word of God by the *Porta Latina* boiled in hot oil without pain." The source of the inscription is unknown.

Many compositions in the series are derived from Dürer's famous Apocalypse woodcuts of 1498, which Vellert had received as a gift from Dürer himself in January 1521.[1] Vellert included all of the subjects in the first half of Dürer's series, but his cycle ends after the trumpeting of the fourth angel following the breaking of the seventh seal (Apocalypse 8: 12–13). We can speculate that Vellert may have planned more drawings, now lost or never executed, corresponding in theme to Dürer's last seven woodcuts. None of Vellert's drawings has been executed in glass.

The subject of the present sheet, not in the Apocalypse, is described in apocryphal texts such as *The Golden Legend*. According to these sources, during the persecutions of Emperor Domitian, John was submerged in a vat of boiling oil in front of the city gate in Rome known as the *Porta Latina*. Miraculously, the saint did not suffer any pain from this ordeal, and emerged unharmed. He was afterward expelled to Patmos, where he experienced the apocalyptic visions.

John's torture is also the first scene in Dürer's Apocalypse (fig. 1). Vellert's design, however, is the only sheet in his series that refers to a visual

FIG. 1 Albrecht Dürer. *The Torture of Saint John the Evangelist*. Woodcut. 1497–98. New York, The Metropolitan Museum of Art, Bequest of Grace M. Pugh, 1985

FIG. 2 Quentin Massys. *Saint John Boiled in Oil* (detail of the right wing of the *Lamentation* altarpiece). Tempera and oil on panel. 1511. Antwerp, Koninklijk Museum voor Schone Kunsten

source other than Dürer. In fact, the drawing is unusual in Vellert's *oeuvre* of roundel designs in that it paraphrases not a print but a large-scale panel painting: the right wing, representing John boiled in oil, of Quentin Massys's great *Lamentation* altarpiece, which had been on view in the Antwerp Cathedral since 1511 (fig. 2).[2] Similar to Massys's painting are Vellert's representation of the emperor on horseback, the placement of the *Porta Latina*, and the figure of the crouching man feeding the fire in the foreground. However, Vellert avoids the trappings of the fashionable Mannerist style adopted by Massys. He exploits the circular format by creating a rhythmic movement from the towering equestrian figures of Domitian and the soldiers at the right, to the lunge of the crouching muscular man stoking the fire in the lower center, and finally to the smooth curves of the upraised arms of the saint and of the man holding the bellows at the left. Whereas Massys heightened the sense of violence by surrounding the saint with grotesque Leonardesque heads, Vellert avoided showing John's tormentors as physically deformed and created instead massive heroic types and restrained poses that underscore the ritualistic nature of the event.

Vellert's drawings of the Apocalypse are all signed with his monogram but none is dated. Although the series is usually placed about 1521, the year Vellert received the woodcuts from Dürer, the large bulky figures (see fig. 3) and naturalistic landscapes in these sheets (see fig. 4) are markedly different from Vellert's drawing of *The Trinity, Flanked by Saint Peter and Moses* (his only dated work of 1520), with its slender figures and ornamental

architectural setting (fig. 5), and suggest a date in the mid- to late 1520s.[3] Moreover, the last drawing in the series—*The Trumpeting of the Fourth Angel* (fig. 6)—provides a *terminus post quem* of late 1522. The Vulgate text states that a lamenting eagle appeared in the sky at the sounding of the fourth trumpet (Apocalypse 8: 13). This scene is common in medieval Apocalypse cycles, and is included by Dürer. Instead of this eagle, however, Vellert shows an angel crying in the sky, surely illustrating the "angel" that Luther substituted for the "eagle" in his Bible translation published in September 1522: Luther's Bible included woodcut illustrations from Lucas Cranach's shop, and in this cycle, otherwise largely dependent on Dürer, the Vulgate eagle was replaced with an angel. Since numerous subsequent illustrations of the Apocalypse, both Protestant and Catholic, did the same, on the basis of this drawing alone it is impossible to say if such a choice indicates specific sympathies of either the patron or Vellert himself.

Vellert's series is one of a great number of illustrations of the Apocalypse produced in the Lowlands and Germany in the 1520s and 1530s. These images were undoubtedly made as a response to the renewed preoccupation with eschatology that intensified during the first decades of the sixteenth century. As this writer has discussed elsewhere, some of the inscriptions on Vellert's drawings from the series suggest a relationship with the reform movement that was increasingly widespread in the Lowlands in the 1520s.[4] For instance, throughout the series there is a repetition of the term "the word"—a concept central to the reform writers. Even the text of the

present drawing contains such a reference, describing this scene of John's persecution and deliverance because of "the word of God" (an allusion to Apocalypse 1: 9). In light of the texts inscribed on Vellert's drawings, along with the use of Lutheran imagery in the scene of *The Trumpeting of the Fourth Angel*, the question of Vellert's intended audience is particularly intriguing.[5]

1. For Dürer's journal entries describing his contact with Vellert see Rupprich, *Dürer Schriftlicher Nachlass* 1, 1956, pp. 157, 164, 169.

2. For Massys's altarpiece see Silver, *Paintings of Quinten Massys*, 1984, pp. 45–52, no. 11, pl. 15.

3. The date 1521 was suggested by Beets ("Dirick Jacobsz. Vellert," 1912, pp. 134–35). On the basis of style, Glück ("Name des Meisters D*V," 1901, p. 23) and Held (*Dürers Wirkung*, 1931, p. 88, n. 3) suggested a date of the mid-1520s for the series.

4. Konowitz, "Vellert," Ph.D. diss., 1992, pp. 43–47.

5. Eisler (*Master of the Unicorn*, 1979, p. 61) has suggested that the reason such large numbers of Apocalypse illustrations were produced in the sixteenth century may be that the subject itself provided, on the one hand, an expression of reform sentiments without fear of persecution. On the other hand, as he points out, the Apocalypse held special meaning in a Catholic context, since it could be read as censoring the heretic ideas of the reformers.

BIBLIOGRAPHY: Glück, "Name des Meisters D*V," 1901, p. 23, pl. V; Beets, "Dirick Jacobsz. Vellert," 1908, p. 188, no. 1; Beets, "Dirick Jacobsz. Vellert," 1912, pp. 141, 142; Bock et al., *Zeichnungen*, 1930, pp. 55–56, pl. 47; Isler-de Jongh, "Rondels de la Collection Hosmer," 1989, p. 32, under no. 1, fig. 34.

FIG. 3 Dirick Vellert. *Saint John and the Vision of Heaven*. Pen and black and traces of brown ink, with gray-brown wash, over chalk, on paper. About 1522–30. Paris, Musée du Louvre, Département des Arts Graphiques, Collection Édmond de Rothschild

FIG. 4 Dirick Vellert. *The Opening of the Sixth Seal and the Great Earthquake*. Pen and black and traces of brown ink, with gray-brown wash, over chalk, on paper. About 1522–30. Paris, Musée du Louvre, Département des Arts Graphiques, Collection Édmond de Rothschild

FIG. 5 Dirick Vellert. *The Trinity, Flanked by Saint Peter and Moses*. Pen and brown ink, with brown-gray wash, on paper. 1520. Paris, Musée du Louvre, Département des Arts Graphiques, Collection Édmond de Rothschild

FIG. 6 Dirick Vellert. *The Trumpeting of the Fourth Angel*. Pen and black and traces of brown ink, with gray-brown wash, over chalk, on paper. Late 1522. Paris, Musée du Louvre, Département des Arts Graphiques, Collection Édmond de Rothschild

72

73

FIG. 1 Dirick Vellert. *The Birth of the Virgin*. Pen and dark brown ink, with brown wash, on paper. 1532. Weimar, Staatliche Kunstsammlungen

FIG. 2 Dirick Vellert. *The Adoration of the Shepherds*. Pen and dark brown ink, with brown wash, on paper. 1532. Weimar, Staatliche Kunstsammlungen

## 72

### The Adoration of the Magi

Pen and dark brown ink, with light brown wash over black chalk, on paper: diameter, 11⅛ in. (28.3 cm)

Vienna, Graphische Sammlung Albertina, 7802

Signed and dated (bottom right): D * V / 1532

Inscribed (at the upper left in graphite, in a modern hand): 2

## 73

### The Adoration of the Magi

1532 or later

Roundel: diameter, 11⅜ in. (28.9 cm)

Darmstadt, Hessisches Landesmuseum, Kg 31:33

Vellert designed a series of roundels illustrating events in the Life of the Virgin, seven scenes of which are preserved in drawings or painted glass. Three of the scenes are included here: the present drawing and the roundel of *The Adoration of the Magi*, the two sheets of *The Presentation in the Temple* (cat. nos. 74 and 75), and the roundel of *The Flight into Egypt* (cat. no. 76). Also part of this cycle are two drawings in Weimar of *The Birth of the Virgin* (fig. 1) and *The Adoration of the Shepherds* (fig. 2), a drawing of *The Marriage of the Virgin* (British Museum), and several workshop copies of *The Presentation of the Virgin*.[1] We can presume that the entire series was made in 1532 on the basis of the drawing in Vienna, which

is dated that year. Each composition derives from the corresponding woodcut in Dürer's series of the Life of the Virgin; since Dürer's series consists of nineteen sheets plus a title page, we can speculate that Vellert's cycle included more scenes than the seven that we know.

The designs are creative variations of Dürer's woodcuts rather than literal copies. For instance, in *The Adoration of the Magi*, the architecture—a thatched shed, a tower, and a stone arch—clearly pays homage to Dürer, but the entire structure has been reduced in scale to adapt the composition to a circular format and to make the figures more prominent (see fig. 3): The slanted wooden roof on the side of the building has been flattened and elongated to adjust to the roundel's more planar design. Vellert also reversed the pose of the Virgin

and Child and made the composition more symmetrical by placing them in the center rather than to the right, as in Dürer's scene, creating a more dynamic arrangement for the circular scheme. Moreover, Vellert "modernized" the figures with elegantly twisting poses, flamboyant costumes, and fluttering drapery reminiscent of the fashionable Antwerp Mannerist style of the 1520s and 1530s. The addition of a crowd of figures also underscores the similarity to the work of the Mannerists.

The roundel follows the drawing but with numerous minor changes, including the trimming of the entire perimeter, which cuts off details seen along the edge of the drawing. Some of the motifs were eliminated: for instance, the bird on the roof, the dog at the left, and the angel above the black

Magus's head. The cellar grate, prominent in the lower left of the drawing, has been shifted farther left in the glass panel and only the top of its arch is indicated.

Thus, the glass panel is not a mere simplified copy of the drawing, but demonstrates the creative variations and alterations of the glass painter. Some of the imagery has been changed: For example, the angel in the drawing, silhouetted before the tower at the crossing of the beams at the center right, was replaced by a ruined stone slab, from which a plantain sprouts. The ruined building is a long-standing reference to the Old Law, which was superseded by the New Law brought by Christ. The introduction of the plantain further underscores the significance of the scene, since this medicinal weed, used for the stanching of blood, was a common reference to the path of salvation.[2]

The glass painter freely changed numerous details of the design, including the military boot of the Magus at the left in the drawing, which, in the roundel, became a soft leather boot with slits, spurs, and cuffs. The links in the chain worn by the kneeling Magus are changed from rectangles to disks, and the ornament of his hat consists of swirls instead of fleur-de-lis shapes. Moreover, the glass painter added elaborate surface patterns to areas that the draftsman left plain. Textures are more differentiated in the roundel: The Magi's coats are painted as rich brocade, the collars and the edges of their robes are trimmed with thick fur, and the Virgin's dress is edged with an ornamental band. In the drawing the wall behind Joseph is indicated by perfunctory ruled lines, whereas in the roundel it is painted as individual

74

FIG. 3 Albrecht Dürer. *The Adoration of the Magi*, from the Life of the Virgin series. Woodcut. About 1502. New York, The Metropolitan Museum of Art, The George Khuner Collection, Gift of Mrs. George Khuner, 1975

blocks of heavy stone slabs, and the roof above the wall is divided into wooden slats fastened with tiny nails. The brickwork of the arches and towers is made more specific and detailed and the staff leaning against the arch has the knobby texture of bark. Clearly, the finished painted roundel was considered a work of art that was worthy of imaginative interpretation of the master's more cursory design.

1. See Glück, "Name des Meisters D*V," 1901, plates III, IV; Popham, *Drawings in the British Museum*, 1932, p. 51, no. 7; Kloek, *Beknopte catalogus*, 1975, no. 302.

2. See Ferguson, *Signs and Symbols in Christian Art*, 1976, p. 36. For plantains in scenes from the Life of Christ see Mundy, "Gerard David's *Rest on the Flight into Egypt*, 1982, esp. pp. 213–14.

BIBLIOGRAPHY: (72) Weigel, *Werke der Maler*, 1865, p. 694 (as by Dirk van Staren); Schönbrunner and Meder, *Handzeichnungen*, 1896, p. 312 (as by Dirk van Staren); Glück, "Name des Meisters D*V," 1901, pp. 21–22; Wurzbach, *Künstler-Lexicon*, 1910, p. 747; Schmitz, *Glasgemälde* I, 1913, p. 70, fig. 19; Meder, *Die Handzeichnung*, 1923, pp. 620–21; Benesch, *Albertina Katalog*, 1928, p. 7, no. 41; Held, *Dürers Wirkung*, 1931, p. 91; Popham, *Drawings in the British Museum*, 1932, p. 51; Frodl-Kraft, *Die Glasmalerei*, 1970, p. 64, no. 22, pl. 22; Wayment, *Windows of King's College*, 1972, p. 19; Beeh-Lustenberger, *Glasmalerei in Darmstadt*, 1973, p. 230, under no. 295; Brussels, *Dürer aux Pays-Bas* (exhib. cat.), 1977, p. 168, no. 357, ill. p. 120; Washington, *Age of Bruegel* (exhib. cat.), 1986, p. 293, fig. 2; Konowitz, "Glass Designer Dierick Vellert," in Worcester, *Northern Renaissance Stained Glass* (exhib. cat.), 1987, pp. 23–24, fig. 6; Husband, *Silver-Stained Roundels*, 1991, p. 19, fig. 11; Konowitz, "Drawings as intermediary stages," 1991, p. 143, fig. 1.

(73) Schmitz, *Glasgemälde* I, 1913, p. 70, fig. 188; Beets, "Dirick Jacobsz. Vellert," 1922, p. 91, n. 1; Benesch, *Albertina Katalog*, 1928, p. 7, under no. 41, pl. 12; von der Osten, "Blick in die Geburtshöhle," 1967, p. 113; Frodl-Kraft, *Die Glasmalerei*, 1970, p. 64, no. 23, pl. 23; Beeh-Lustenberger, *Glasmalerei in Darmstadt*, 1973, p. 230, no. 295, pl. 198; Konowitz, "Glass Designer Dierick Vellert," in Worcester, *Northern Renaissance Stained Glass* (exhib. cat.), 1987, p. 24, fig. 8; Husband, *Silver-Stained Roundels*, 1991, p. 20, fig. 12; Konowitz, "Drawings as intermediary stages," 1991, p. 143, n. 2.

## 74

### The Presentation in the Temple

About 1532

Brush and dark brown ink with white highlights, over black chalk, on gray-green prepared paper: diameter, 9⅜ in. (23.8 cm)

London, British Museum, 1952.1.21.85

## 75

### The Presentation in the Temple

About 1532

Pen and brown and dark brown ink, with brown wash, over a tracing in brown ink and grid lines in black chalk, on paper: diameter, 10⅞ in. (27.6 cm)

London, British Museum, 1923.4.17.4

Inscribed: (at the bottom left) with an arrow and a crescent; (on the back, in ink, in a seventeenth-century [?] hand) *teekening antijck 1 patacon*

Saint Luke relates how the Virgin and Joseph, following Jewish law, brought the Christ Child to the Temple in Jerusalem to consecrate him to the Lord (Luke 2: 22–39). Luke's account also refers to the rite of Purification of the Mother, which required the sacrifice of two turtledoves or pigeons. As is common in Northern depictions of the Presentation, here the subject is combined with the recognition of Christ as the Messiah by Simeon, who is shown lifting the child over the altar (Luke 2: 25–35). Vellert includes a woman at the right holding a cage with the sacrificial birds. The birds and the presence of candles—as, for example, the one held by Joseph—allude to the feast of the Purification of the Virgin (Candlemas), a Christian festival in which candles are carried in procession; references to this feast are often found in Northern scenes of the Presentation in the Temple.

In these scenes Vellert reinterprets Dürer's woodcut of the same subject (fig. 1). He borrowed several figures from Dürer but rearranged them in space, placing them to the far left and right in order to leave the center empty and thus to exploit the rhythmic movement of the circular format. The setting has been changed from Dürer's severe, unadorned classical portico to a barrel-vaulted structure lavishly decorated with garlands, putti, bucrania, and other antique motifs. Whereas the architecture towers over the figures in Dürer's print, Vellert reduced the relative scale of the building to make the figures more prominent. He changed the mood of the scene from Dürer's somber austerity to one of energy and flamboyant exuberance.

These drawings, representing two stages in the evolution of the design, offer a rare glimpse into Vellert's working method.[1] The drawings survive in two stages of completion. In the version on white paper, the composition was first indicated with black-chalk outlines and thin, rigid lines drawn with a pen and light brown ink. These hesitant lines are tracings, as several scholars have suggested.[2] Over the traced lines the artist made compositional changes with thicker, more fluid strokes in a darker brown ink and wash. The version on prepared paper is highly finished, executed in the chiaroscuro technique typical of designs for glass roundels. One might assume that the sketchy, reworked drawing is a preliminary study for the finished sheet but, in fact, the relationship is reversed. Pentimenti in the sketchy version show that the traced lines correspond to the chiaroscuro drawing and that the darker, more fluid lines are later revisions. The boy seated on the altar steps, for example, was first drawn in profile, as in the chiaroscuro drawing, but Vellert adopted a three-quarter view for the boy's head at the later stage. The fingers of the boy's raised hand were partly closed in the underdrawing, as they are in the colored sheet; in the later version his hand was opened to show the palm. The dog's head was first depicted from the back as in the finished drawing, then was altered to a profile view, with a layer of mane around the neck.

The size of the design was expanded from the stage represented by the chiaroscuro drawing

75

(diameter, 23.8 cm) to the reworked drawing (27.6 cm) without changing the actual size of the figures. The architectural backdrop was made taller and was redrawn to include the entire lunette and to add a coffered arch flanked by putti. A lamb was placed on the altar steps. New figures were added to the right and left and the space was widened in the center to contain a boy with a bird in the foreground, a view of a landscape through an arch, and two soldiers entering in the background, one holding a candle. (The latter soldier refers back to Vellert's model, Dürer's woodcut, in which a man holds a candle in the center background.) With these changes Vellert made the scene more dynamic. The conception of the design becomes more grand, and the shifting of the figures away from the center intensifies the circular rhythm of the scene.

As the revised drawing includes large traced areas that are not in the chiaroscuro version, we can surmise that there was an intermediary stage from which the reworked sheet was traced. In this intermediary step, an earlier design was probably cut down the center and a new section presumably inserted on which the revised scene was drawn. It is also likely that Vellert or an assistant produced another, clean version incorporating the changes, from which a glass roundel would have been painted. Thus the composition must have undergone at least three or four different stages of preparation before its final formulation.

Although we know of few such examples in Lowlands art, Vellert's drawings present a working method that was probably common in the sixteenth century. To satisfy commissions for

FIG. 1 Albrecht Dürer. *The Presentation in the Temple*, from the Life of the Virgin series. Woodcut. About 1505. New York, The Metropolitan Museum of Art, The George Khuner Collection, Gift of Mrs. George Khuner, 1975

images of popular subjects such as the Life of the Virgin, sample designs of compositions were evidently kept in stock in the shop. Clients could make their selections among the stock models and, from these, glass paintings could then be produced relatively easily and quickly.[3] The patterns could also be reworked for various reasons, as, for instance, to personalize or update a com-

76

FIG. 1 Albrecht Dürer. *The Flight into Egypt*, from the Life of the Virgin series. Woodcut. About 1503. New York, The Metropolitan Museum of Art, The George Khuner Collection, Gift of Mrs. George Khuner, 1975

mission or to increase the artist's repertoire of scenes. Vellert's *Presentation in the Temple* on white paper can be categorized as this type of revised design. The chiaroscuro drawing, more-over, may well have been a stock model, created for presentation to prospective clients. That it was considered a completed version in itself is shown by the fact that the composition was utilized for a painted glass roundel.[4]

The arrow and crescent inscribed at the bot-tom left of the sketchy drawing is also found on *The Marriage of the Virgin* from the series,[5] and on a drawing by Jean Cousin, all from the same album formerly owned by the Earl of Essex.[6] The significance of the motif has not been explained.

1. The following discussion is based on this author's analysis of Vellert's technique ("Drawings as intermedi-ary stages," 1991), in which similarities are observed between Vellert's execution of this series and Albrecht Dürer's production of the Green Passion.

2. See Konowitz, "Drawings as intermediary stages," 1991; see also Popham, *Drawings in the British Museum*, 1932, p. 51, no. 7, and Robinson and Wolff, in Washington, *Age of Bruegel* (exhib. cat.), 1986, p. 34.

3. This practice is discussed by Konowitz, "Drawings as intermediary stages," 1991, p. 152, and Husband, *Silver-Stained Roundels*, 1991, pp. 19–20.

4. The roundel is preserved in the Church of the Holy Trinity, Berwick-upon-Tweed (Northumberland), En-gland. (For an illustration see Cole, *Roundels in Britain*, 1993, p. 18, no. 146. The roundel follows the composi-tion of the chiaroscuro drawing, not the sketchy one as Cole states.)

5. British Museum, 1923.4.17.3. Popham, *Drawings in the British Museum*, 1932, p. 51, no. 7.

6. Popham, *Drawings in the British Museum*, 1932, p. 51, no. 6, pl. 19.

BIBLIOGRAPHY: (74) *National Art-Collections Fund*, 1952, p. 30, no. 1642; Rowlands, *Master Drawings*, 1984, p. 91, no. 78, colorpl.; Konowitz, "Drawings as intermediary stages," 1991, pp. 144, 149–50, fig. 5. (75) Popham, "Teekeningen," 1925, p. 208; Popham, *Drawings in the British Museum*, 1932, p. 51, no. 6, pl. 19; *National Art-Collections Fund*, 1952, p. 30, under no. 1642; Rowlands, *Master Drawings*, 1984, p. 91, under no. 78; Washington, *Age of Bruegel* (exhib. cat.), 1986, p. 293, under no. 115, n. 5; Konowitz, "Drawings as intermediary stages," 1991, pp. 144, 149–50, fig. 4.

## 76

### The Flight into Egypt

1532 or later

Roundel: diameter, 10¾ in. (27.3 cm)

Amsterdam, Rijksmuseum, NM 12969

Although technically accomplished, the execution of this roundel is not as fine as that of Vellert's drawings and signed glass paintings, and the panel should be considered as a studio work after a lost design by the artist. The scene is derived from Dürer's woodcut of *The Flight into Egypt*, with numerous changes (see fig. 1): The Virgin is now shown from the front, the setting is a townscape rather than a wood, and two narrative episodes are added—the Massacre of the Innocents in the background and the Miracle of the Falling Idol in the center. The first scene shows the fate escaped by the Christ Child, as the children of Bethlehem are slaughtered following Herod's orders

(Matthew 2: 16). The second story, told in the apocryphal Gospel of Pseudo-Matthew, relates how the pagan idols of Egypt miraculously fell to the ground and were broken when the Christ Child came before them.

Pale grayish brown, medium to rich brown, thin reddish brown, and umber are among the varied tones of the palette used here. The silver stain is limited to hues of pale and medium yel-low. Again, the technique is very painterly. Con-tours and forms are defined and the description of detail is achieved with a fine brush, which is most obvious in the rendering of the mane and the coat of the ass. The stylus is used more liberally here, but in a fine and subtle manner. It is employed so delicately, for example, in the rump of the steer and the near foreleg of the ass that without care-ful scrutiny it would go undetected, but is used with greater boldness in the beard and the hat of Joseph and in the stones in the foreground.

In addition to the present panel, another roundel after this design is known; it is now in the Church of the Holy Trinity, Bradford-on-Avon, Wiltshire.[1]

1. See Cole, *Roundels in Britain*, 1993, p. 32, no. 269; Schmitz, *Rund- und Kabinettscheiben*, 1923, fig. 71.

BIBLIOGRAPHY: Beets, "Dirick Jacobsz. Vellert," 1922, p. 91, no. 1; Schmitz, *Rund- und Kabinett-scheiben*, 1923, p. 12, fig. 71 (as by Dirick Vellert); Held, *Dürers Wirkung*, 1931, pp. 66–67, 91; Scharf, in Glück, *Malerei*, 1933, p. 329; Beeh-Lustenberger, *Glasmalerei in Darmstadt*, 1973, p. 230, under no. 295; Brussels, *Dürer aux Pays-Bas* (exhib. cat.), 1977, no. 358, pp. 168–69, ill. p. 121; Konowitz, "Drawings as intermediary stages," 1991, p. 143, n. 2.

77

78

## 77

### Abraham and the Pharaoh (?)

About 1535–40

Pen and brown and dark brown ink, with grayish brown wash, over black chalk, on paper: diameter, 10⅝ in. (27 cm)

London, British Museum, 1923.4.17.1

Inscribed: (on the tablet, bottom center) · 11 · ; (at the lower-left edge) ♉. [a bull's head]; (on the back) *teckening antijck 5 schellingen*

## 78

### God Appearing to Abraham and Abraham Entertaining the Three Angels

About 1535–40

Pen and brown ink, with grayish brown wash, over black chalk, on paper: diameter, 10⅝ in. (27 cm)

London, British Museum, 5226-184

Inscribed: (lower center, in brown ink, in a later hand) GENES 18; (bottom center, in black ink, in a later hand) 0008

## 79

### Abraham and the Covenant of Circumcision

About 1535–40

Roundel: diameter, 11 in. (27.9 cm)

Amsterdam, Rijksmuseum, NM 3154

Signed (etched in just below the point of God's toe): D * V

This glass panel probably formed part of a cycle of roundels representing scenes from the Life of Abraham. Since, as the roundel and the two present drawings indicate, each design would have included three or more episodes in the story, the cycle was very likely densely illustrated. Many of the scenes are rare in the art of the Lowlands, which suggests that the series was intended to be extensive.

Neither the drawings nor the roundel is dated, but on the basis of style they can be placed in the second half of the 1530s. The densely populated compositions and the animated poses of the figures recall those of Vellert's Life of the Virgin series of 1532. Moreover, this increased dynamism and a new, deeper recession in space in these designs are comparable to late works by the artist—such as his monumental engraving of *The Deluge* of 1544 (fig. 1)—which show the influence of Pieter Coecke van Aelst and Barent van Orley. In *Abraham and the Pharaoh (?)*, for example, the strong spiral movement of figures and animals radiating forward from the background to the center and the sides recalls the powerful central panel of Barent van Orley's *Virtue of Patience* altarpiece of 1521 (fig. 2). In the drawings of Abraham, Vellert now shades with parallel lines and uses hatching more extensively than in his earlier sheets, such as the series of 1523, in which he employs the tonal effects of wash (see cat. nos. 69 and 70). This more linear approach may be related to Vellert's interest in Dürer's woodcuts, to which he began to turn for compositional models during this period in the designs for his Apocalypse and Life of the Virgin series.

Vellert's technique in the two drawings resembles the one he employed in *The Presentation in the Temple* (cat. nos. 74 and 75). The compositions were first traced with black chalk, then carefully reinforced with pen and light brown ink, and finally reworked freehand with a darker brown ink and with wash. The revisions in these drawings are more radical than in the sheets from the Life of the Virgin series. In *Abraham and the Pharaoh (?)*, all the figures were extensively redrawn, the placement of the shepherd and the animals was shifted slightly, and a tree was added at the left to help define the middle space—a device familiar from Vellert's drawings of 1523 (see cat. nos. 69 and 70). Other notable changes are the appearance of God in the clouds at the upper left, the figure in the bed in the background, and the positions of the foremost sheep, the steer's head at the left, and the shepherd's arm and staff in the center, as well as alterations to Abraham's drapery.

In the drawing of *God Appearing to Abraham and Abraham Entertaining the Three Angels* the alterations are even more dramatic. The initial traced figure of God standing at the left center was not incorporated into the subsequent stage; instead, God was completely redrawn in a smaller scale at the upper left, descending in a cloud rather than standing. This revision creates a strong diagonal movement from the upper left to the lower right—a fundamental change from Vellert's earlier designs, which tend to be more planar in conception. The position of Abraham's head was changed from a three-quarter to a profile view, raised slightly in the direction of God in

79

FIG. 1 Dirick Vellert. *The Deluge*. Engraving. 1544. New York, The Metropolitan Museum of Art, Harris Brisbane Dick Fund, 1925

FIG. 2 Barent van Orley. *The Destruction of the Children of Job* (central panel of the *Virtue of Patience* altarpiece). Tempera and oil on panel. 1521. Brussels, Musée d'Art Ancien

the sky. The horizon was lowered, the landscape was redrawn, and many of the buildings were replaced with hills. New columns as well as arches were added to the portico with heavy ruled lines, and the decoration of the pediment of this structure was changed from narrow rectangular openings to wide swirls.[1]

The subject of the drawing identified here as *Abraham and the Pharaoh (?)* is in fact not clear. The sheet probably illustrates the twelfth chapter of Genesis, as Popham and later Hand tentatively suggested, or the twentieth. Both stories are similar in detail. According to Genesis 12, Abraham pretended that Sarah was his sister, fearing that the pharaoh would harm him if he knew that she was his wife. The pharaoh added Sarah to his harem, but when he discovered her true relationship to Abraham, he returned her to her husband. Later, Abraham likewise misled King Abimelech into believing that Sarah was his sister. The Lord appeared to Abimelech in a dream, warning him to return Sarah to Abraham, which he subsequently did. Both the pharaoh and the king presented Abraham with gifts of sheep, oxen, and servants, which would explain the presence of all three in the drawing. A small figure of God at the upper left descends in a cloud, perhaps addressing the figures in the background. The numeral 11 inscribed on the step in the foreground does not correspond to either of these biblical texts, but may perhaps refer to the sequence of the scene in the series.[2]

The drawing of *God Appearing to Abraham and Abraham Entertaining the Three Angels* illustrates Genesis 18: 1–15, which tells of three men who appeared at the aged Abraham's house. Abraham welcomed the strangers and gave them water and his best food. The strangers, who were angels, revealed to Abraham that his wife, Sarah, would bear a son. Sarah was standing at the tent door nearby and laughed when she overheard this prediction since she was then a very old woman. The Lord reprimanded Abraham for Sarah's laughter, repeating that she would, indeed, have a son. In the foreground of the drawing, God appears to Abraham. This meeting is most likely the one described in Genesis 18: 17–33, when God revealed to Abraham his plan to destroy the sinful cities of Sodom and Gomorrah. Abraham tried to bargain with God to save the cities, until

God finally agreed that he would not destroy them completely if ten righteous people could be found living there.

In addition to the main scenes in the foreground, several incidents were drawn in the preliminary outline stage that Vellert later omitted by sketching over them with heavier strokes of darker ink and wash. The Lord initially was shown in the sky appearing before Abraham in the background at the center right, and at the far right the Lord was depicted reprimanding Sarah, while Abraham watched from behind (Genesis 18: 15). Vellert deleted the latter scene by drawing a curtain and a column over it and by introducing the figures of the three angels in the background.

FIG. 3 Dirick Vellert. *Biblical Subject (Abraham's Soldiers Rescuing Lot ?).* Pen and brown ink, with light brown wash, on paper. 1535–40. London, British Museum

With darker ink the artist also added the three angels walking in the landscape in the left background and the three angels flying in the sky at the right.

Both drawings have been trimmed significantly along the perimeter, cutting off the circumference, parts of the foliage, and some of the figures. In the scene of Abraham entertaining the angels, the third angel has been almost completely cut away: Only part of his face and his hand at the far left remain. Thus, originally there were three angels at the table, in accordance with the biblical text, not only two, as was thought by Popham.[3]

A third sheet by Vellert, also drawn in successive stages with different inks, may have belonged to this series as well (see fig. 3).[4] The broad figure types resemble those in the present sheets, as does the artist's extensive use of hatching and the costume worn by the man seen from the back, which is similar to that of Abraham. In this third drawing a troop of soldiers surrounds a group of buildings and two soldiers look up at a tower. An identification of the subject has never been offered, but perhaps it represents the battle between Abraham and the Oriental kings described in Genesis 14:14–16: When Abraham learned that his nephew Lot was taken captive he armed his servants and rescued him.

The roundel illustrates God's covenant with Abraham as recounted in Genesis 17. God appeared before Abraham and promised that he would be the father of many nations and that Abraham and his descendants would own all the lands of Canaan; Abraham, for his part, would see that all males born thereafter would be circumcised. This scene is depicted in the right background of the roundel. Abraham was then one hundred years old, his wife, Sarah, was ninety, and they had no issue. Nonetheless, God declared that Abraham would be blessed with a son born of Sarah. Upon hearing this extraordinary news, Abraham prostrated himself before God—the foreground scene in the roundel. Then Abraham "took Ismael his son, and all that were born in his

house: and all whom he had bought, every male among the men of his house: and he circumcised the flesh of their foreskin forthwith the very same day, as God had commanded him" (Genesis 17: 23). This is the episode shown in the left background.

The monogram etched in just below the foot of God leaves no doubt as to the authorship of this roundel. No drawing for it has survived, but it clearly relates to the same series, as do the present drawings. The standing figure of God in the foreground wearing a papal tiara is extremely close to that of the standing God traced in the center of the sheet marked GENES 18 (cat. no. 78); only the position of God's right hand—lifting his robe in the drawing and raised in blessing in the roundel—is altered. It is possible that a series of roundels was executed by Vellert, and that later, dissatisfied with the results, he traced the designs and began to rework the compositions.

The roundel is painted in varying tones from pale brown to medium umber, enhanced with yellow and deep golden yellow silver stain. The technique is freer and more assured than that encountered in the *Flight into Egypt.* Both the fine-pointed brush and the stylus are employed but in more equal balance. For the first time we see the stylus used to model forms—most noticeably in the robes of God. The distribution and balance of tonalities is more harmonic, providing a richer, more atmospheric effect.

Numerous breaks have been glued with fills where necessary; the fills and chips along the break lines, however, have not been restored.

1. Wayment (*Windows of King's College,* 1972, p. 19, pl. 6.3) suggests that the initial design dates about fifteen to twenty years earlier than the reworked stage, but I agree with Hand (Washington, *Age of Bruegel* [exhib. cat.], 1986, p. 293) that there is no evidence for this in the style of the initial drawing.

2. As suggested by Hand (ibid.). Hand points out that the astrological symbol for Taurus inscribed on the drawing is similar to symbols that appear on other sheets by Vellert and other artists from the collection of the Earl of Essex (Popham, *Drawings in the British Museum,* 1932, p. 51, no. 6 [*The Presentation in the Temple,* cat. no. 75] and p. 51, no. 7 [*The Marriage of the Virgin*].

3. See Popham, *Drawings in the British Museum,* 1932, p. 52, no. 9.

4. London, British Museum, 1923.4.17.2. Pen and brown ink, with brown wash, on paper: diameter, 26 cm. See Popham, *Drawings in the British Museum,* 1932, p. 52, no. 10, pl. 19 (as Unknown Biblical Subject).

BIBLIOGRAPHY: (77) Popham, "Teekeningen," 1925, pp. 206–8, ill. p. 6; Popham, *Drawings in the British Museum,* 1932, pp. 51–52, pl. 19; Helbig, *Glasschilderkunst,* 1943, no. 2002; Wayment, *Windows of King's College,* 1972, pp. 19–20, pl. 6.3; Washington, *Age of Bruegel* (exhib. cat.), 1986, pp. 292–93; Husband, *Silver-Stained Roundels,* 1991, p. 29, n. 21. (78) Popham, "Teekeningen," 1925, p. 207; Popham, "Notes-II," 1929, p. 157, fig. 8; Popham, *Drawings in the British Museum,* 1932, p. 52, no. 9; Helbig, *Glasschilderkunst,* 1943, no. 2002; Wayment, *Windows of King's College,* 1972, pl. 6.3; Wayment, "'Vidimus,'" 1980, p. 60, n. 11; Washington, *Age of Bruegel* (exhib. cat.), 1986, p. 293, under no. 115. (79) Beets, "Dirick Jacobsz. Vellert," 1922, pp. 87–89, fig. 4; Hudig, "Quelques Vitraux," 1923, p. 103; Popham, "Teekeningen," 1925, p. 207; Popham, "Notes-II," 1929, p. 156, fig. 6; Scharf, in Glück, *Malerei,* 1933, p. 329; Helbig, *Glasschilderkunst,* 1943, p. 29; Washington, *Age of Bruegel* (exhib. cat.), 1986, p. 293, no. 115, fig. 1; Antwerp, *Antwerp* (exhib. cat.), 1993, pp. 195–96, no. 50 B, ill.

80

FIG. 1 Gerard David. *The Judgment of Cambyses: The Arrest of Sisamnes*. Tempera and oil on panel. 1498. Bruges, Groeningemuseum

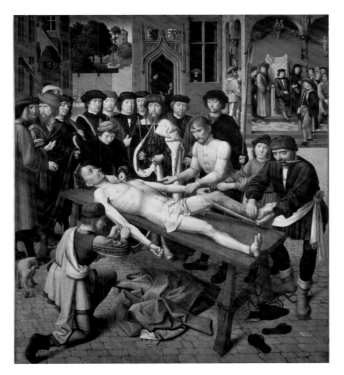

FIG. 2 Gerard David. *The Judgment of Cambyses: The Flaying of Sisamnes*. Tempera and oil on panel. 1498. Bruges, Groeningemuseum

80 *see plate 15*

## The Judgment of Cambyses

Roundel: diameter, 11 in. (27.9 cm)

Amsterdam, Rijksmuseum, RBK-14517

Signed (etched into the lower part of the parapet): D * V, and dated (etched into the plaque above the head of the flayed skin over the throne): 1542

Vellert himself painted this exquisite panel, his last known roundel design. Until the recent discovery of the date 1542 on the plaque above the throne in the left background, the roundel was generally placed about a decade earlier, circa 1530.[1] The composition and the figure types are, indeed, more restrained than those of the only other known work from the artist's last decade of activity, the monumental engraved *Deluge* of 1544, with its vast panoramic vista filled with turbulent crowds of massive figures twisted in anguish (cat. nos. 77–79, fig. 1). However, the substantial figures in the present roundel are consistent with the works of Vellert's later career, as is the dynamic conception of space. The flatness of medieval stained glass has now been completely transformed to an aesthetic of complex spatial depth comparable to that of contemporary panel painting. Within the small-scale format of the roundel Vellert created a monumental scene, with the sharply foreshortened reclining figure in the foreground, the spacious room that recedes to the judgment seat in the left background, the archway at the right through which the observers look on, and the distant city view beyond. To reinforce the

dynamic circular movement of the roundel shape, Vellert placed the tightly packed group of figures in the flaying scene slightly off-center. This dense figure group is juxtaposed with a void area to the left, separating the moment of punishment from its consequence—the background scene with the flayed skin draped over the throne.

The subject, an episode taken from ancient history, was well known in the Lowlands in the fifteenth and sixteenth centuries as an exemplum of Justice and Virtue. The story, related by Herodotus and later by Valerius Maximus, tells how the Persian king Cambyses punished the corrupt judge Sisamnes for accepting bribes. The story was also retold in the fourteenth-century *Gesta Romanorum*. In the foreground Vellert represents the gruesome punishment, as Sisamnes is flayed alive. At the left we see Sisamnes's son and successor, Otanes, seated on the throne of judgment, over the back of which his father's flayed skin is draped as a brutal reminder. Panel paintings and tapestries of such judgment scenes were commonly placed in the courtrooms of town halls in the Lowlands to serve as a moral lesson and a harsh warning to contemporary judges; perhaps the best-known examples are the *Judgment of Cambyses* panels painted by Gerard David for the town hall of Bruges (figs. 1 and 2).[2] The large number of surviving roundel designs representing classical and Old Testament Justice themes suggests that windows of these subjects also must have played an important role in the decoration of town halls.

Vellert here uses a relatively limited palette of medium to dark brown in conjunction with ar-

resting hues of golden yellow and dark coppery yellow silver stain. Reverting to a more painterly technique, he employs the stylus only sparsely; other than in the costume of the kneeling figure seen from the back, it is largely reserved for giving highlights and texture to hair. Vellert combines a perspective scheme of dramatic recession in space, indicated by the tiled pavement, with the optical effect of the recessive appearance of the dark silver stain on the back of the glass. As the angle of view is shifted, the silver stain and the painted surface can be seen to move in relation to each other. The combined effect is one of remarkable dimensionality. The use of increasingly deeper tones as the composition recedes only heightens this effect. Likewise, the balanced distribution of light and of color values brings a binding harmony to the scene.

There are two diagonal breaks that converge at the lower right; the lower one was grozed, requiring a fill that has not been toned in, leaving the white line.

1. For the date of circa 1530 see Wayment, *Windows of King's College*, 1972, pp. 19, 70.

2. For Judgment scenes in city halls see de Ridder, "Gerechtigheidstaferelen," 1980, pp. 42–62. As de Ridder points out, courtrooms frequently contained an image of the ultimate Judgment scene—that of the Last Judgment.

BIBLIOGRAPHY: Wayment, *Windows of King's College*, 1972, pp. 19, 70, pl. 6.2; Raguin, in Worcester, *Northern Renaissance Stained Glass* (exhib. cat.), 1987, p. 11.

# 10

## Pieter Coecke van Aelst and His Circle

FIG. 1 Pieter Coecke van Aelst. *Allegorical Scene, with Gambling*. Pen and brown ink, with wash and white highlights, on paper. 1529 (?). Rotterdam, Museum Boymans-van Beuningen

*Born in Aelst in 1502, Pieter Coecke, according to van Mander, apprenticed in the atelier of Barent van Orley in Brussels, although he later studied with and worked in the studio of his father-in-law, Jan Dornicke. He had probably traveled to Italy by 1525 or 1526. Shortly thereafter, in 1527, he became a member of the Antwerp guild of Saint Luke. He traveled to Constantinople in 1533–34 at the request of the Van der Moyen family, weavers in Brussels. Coecke became dean of the guild in 1537, and enjoyed the patronage of Mary of Hungary, regent of the Lowlands, whose principal palace was in Brussels. He was primarily a painter and a designer of tapestries and stained glass, and it is said that he introduced the art of painting tapestry cartoons to Antwerp in 1541–42. He had a large and prolific studio, which also produced paintings, sculpture, and architectural designs, as well as the decorations for Charles V's Entry into Antwerp in 1549. Pieter Coecke moved to Brussels in 1546 or 1549, where he died in December 1550.*

Although considerable examples of his workshop production survive, only a small number of drawings can be attributed with assurance to the hand of Pieter Coecke van Aelst. Friedländer lists five signed drawings, including the Rotterdam allegorical scene with gambling (fig. 1, above)[1] and a series of five tapestry designs for the Story of David, now in the British Museum.[2] These drawings, nonetheless, reveal a distinctive and innovative style that favored tall, elegant figures characterized by mannered proportions, extravagant gestures, and exaggerated anatomical detail, set in broad but ambiguous space, and embellished with elaborate decoration. They move about sinuously on exceptionally small feet, their bodies draped in swirls of material that often appears more like smoke than fabric. The horror of a static effect in Coecke's work propels the fig-

ures far beyond any motion required by the narrative, driving them to a state Friedländer described as "an almost inebriate hypermania."[3] Coecke's technique stressed the use of varied tones of washes—usually at least three—which has the look of, and may have been inspired by, Italian chiaroscuro prints (see fig. 1, above).

Pieter Coecke, like Barent van Orley, was better known as a designer and painter of tapestry cartoons than of stained glass and roundels. There is no documentary evidence linking him to any large-scale glazing project, although he seems to have inspired the 1532–35 *Last Supper* in the *States of Holland* window in the church of Saint Catharine at Hoogstraten,[4] and was apparently responsible for the now lost 1536–37 Saint Nicholas windows in Antwerp Cathedral.[5] No signed design for a roundel by Pieter Coecke is known, and it is unlikely that either sheet here is by his hand; the four other known drawings for the *Trionfi* series also appear to be workshop copies of high quality, executed by several different hands. The frenetic Mannerism referred to by Friedländer is most evident not in the drawings but in the roundels of the John the Baptist series, the finest and most extensive to survive (see cat. nos. 85–90). The modeling of forms and the development of tonal values are achieved with a more restrained use of washes in both drawings shown here, but the *Triumph of Divinity* roundel (cat. no. 84), in particular, with its broad range of paint and silver-stain hues, conveys a chiaroscuro effect. At least one other series of roundels designed by Pieter Coecke is evidenced by three derivative workshop copies of indifferent quality representing *The Miracle of the Loaves and Fishes*, *Christ in the House of Simon the Leper*, and *Christ at Emmaus* (figs. 2–4, p. 159).[6] Several roundels based on both the first (see fig. 5, p. 159) and the last of these are known, but, like the drawings, they appear to be the product of an undistinguished workshop using copies of Pieter Coecke's designs.[7]

FIG. 2 After Pieter Coecke van Aelst. *The Miracle of the Loaves and Fishes.* Pen and brown ink, with gray wash, on paper. About 1535–40. London, British Museum

FIG. 3 After Pieter Coecke van Aelst. *Christ in the House of Simon the Leper.* Pen and brown ink, with gray wash, on paper. About 1535–40. London, British Museum

FIG. 4 After Pieter Coecke van Aelst. *Christ at Emmaus.* Pen and brown ink, with gray wash, on paper. 1535–40. London, British Museum

FIG. 5 After Pieter Coecke van Aelst. *The Miracle of the Loaves and Fishes.* Roundel. About 1530–40. Brussels, Musées Royaux d'Art et d'Histoire

1. New York, *Pisanello to Cézanne* (exhib. cat.), 1990, pp. 57–59, no. 16.

2. *Early Netherlandish Painting* 12, 1975, pp. 34–35. A drawing in Paris in the Collection Frits Lugt of *The Capture of the City of Ai*, a design for a tapestry from a series representing the Story of Joshua, bears the monogram (?) *A P*, reversed, perhaps, to compensate for the reversal of the weaving process (see Boon, *Drawings of the Frits Lugt Collection*, 1992, pp. 92–95, n. 1). For the Rotterdam drawing see Marlier, *Pierre Coeck*, 1966, pp. 88–90; for the British Museum drawings see Popham, *Drawings in the British Museum*, 1932, pp. 22–23, nos. 3–7.

3. *Early Netherlandish Painting* 12, 1975, p. 39.

4. See Helbig, *Vitraux* 2, 1968, pp. 135, 220–21. Boon (*Drawings of the Frits Lugt Collection*, 1992, p. 92) likewise credits Coecke with the 1537 windows of Antwerp Cathedral.

5. See Helbig, *Glasschilderkunst*, 1943, p. 64.

6. London, British Museum, 5226-182, 5226-181, and 5226-183, respectively. See Popham, *Drawings in the British Museum*, 1932, pp. 25–26, nos. 13–15, and Marlier, *Pierre Coeck*, 1966, pp. 370–72, figs. 320–322.

7. A roundel after *The Miracle of the Loaves and Fishes* is in the Musées Royaux d'Art et d'Histoire, Brussels (556; see Marlier, *Pierre Coeck*, 1966, p. 371, fig. 323), and another was formerly in the collection of Maurice Drake (see Popham, *Drawings in the British Museum*, 1932, p. 25, no. 13). A roundel after the *Christ at Emmaus* was also formerly in the collection of Maurice Drake; whether this is the same roundel once in a Westchester collection is uncertain (see Husband, *Silver-Stained Roundels*, 1991, p. 189). Another roundel, rectangular in format, is in the church of Saint Mary, Boyton, Wiltshire (Cole, *Roundels in Britain*, 1993, p. 30, no. 245).

81                          82

## 81

### The Triumph of Fame

Antwerp, about 1530–40

Pen and black and brown-gray ink, gray wash,
and white body color, on paper: diameter,
11⅛ in. (28.3 cm)

Amsterdam, Rijksmuseum, Rijksprentenkabinet,
RP-T-1992-3

## 82

### The Triumph of Fame

Lowlands, about 1530–40

Roundel: diameter, 10¼ in. (26 cm)

Cambridge, Fitzwilliam Museum, C.38-1983

This drawing is one of a series of six designs for
roundels by Pieter Coecke van Aelst representing
Francesco Petrarch's *I trionfi*, an extended allegorical poem. The series begins with Love, who is
vanquished by Chastity; Chastity succumbs to
Death, and Death is defeated by Fame. Time over-
comes Fame, and, finally, Divinity prevails over
all. Drawings for the entire series, although not all
by the same hand, survive. Those of Love and
Chastity (figs. 1 and 3) are in the École Nationale
Supérieure des Beaux-Arts, Paris;[1] corresponding
roundels (figs. 2 and 4) are in the Kunsthaus
Heylshof, Worms,[2] and the Fitzwilliam Museum,
Cambridge,[3] respectively. The design for Death
(fig. 5) is in the Graphische Sammlung Albertina,

Vienna;[4] no roundel based on it, however, is
known. The drawing for Time (fig. 6) is also in the
École Nationale Supérieure des Beaux-Arts,[5] while
a corresponding roundel (fig. 7) is in the collection
of the Rijksmuseum, Amsterdam.[6] The remaining
two designs, for Fame and Divinity, and the corresponding roundels, are presented here. Bruyn
considered the drawings for this series the work of
a foreman (*meesterknecht*) in the atelier of Pieter
Coecke van Aelst, produced toward the end of the
1530s;[7] undoubtedly workshop copies, they are
not, however, all by the same hand.

Standing upon her triumphal wagon, drawn
by two lions, the winged Fame blows two long
trumpets, one representing Fame and the other
Infamy. Bound volumes on a four-sided lectern in
front of her list all her past deeds. The wagon is
preceded by assorted heroes of antiquity—most
conspicuously, by Samson, carrying two enormous columns. Just behind Fame are two histori-
ans; the one nearest to the foreground records
his chronicles in an open book. Expired on the
ground before the wagon are the three Fates, but
in the drawing of Death on his triumphal wagon
(fig. 5), the Fates, with distaff and spindle, are
shown spinning out their vicissitudes behind
Death.

The present drawing was unpublished until it
appeared on the art market in 1992;[8] it was subsequently acquired by the Rijksmuseum.[9] More so
than any other drawing in this series, the densely
populated composition, relieved only by a glimpse
of a deep landscape at the upper right, concen-
trates the figures on a shallow foreground plane.
In the scenes of Chastity and of Love, for exam-

ple, a line of figures heads off along a diagonal
through the middle ground, while a landscape
receding in space dominates the upper zones of
the picture plane. Such expansive spatial constructions are of less concern in the present composition. The technique, however, seems fairly
consistent in all the drawings; the figures and
forms are clearly outlined with fine black trace
lines and skillfully modeled with wash and body
color. The extensive use of wash gives added plasticity and torsion to the contrapposto of the mannered figures. A sense of motion is heightened by
the eccentric flutters of drapery and the exaggerated gestures. The relationship of the component
elements nonetheless remains clear, and contrib-
utes to a narrative unity.

The roundel faithfully follows the composition of the drawing, although it deletes some of
the ancillary figures: The second historian and
several figures from the group preceding Samson
are missing. This figural editing may have been
necessary to accommodate the relatively large figure scale within the size of the roundel. Unfortunately, this sense of overcrowding is exacerbated
by the apparent trimming of the circumference of
the roundel, further editing the figures around the
periphery. The painter has not been able to repro-
duce the effect of the wash and body color with
the mattes and silver stain; the figures, as a result,
are sculpturally less compelling and the visual
effect, as a whole, is less dimensional.

Another version of this roundel is in the castle
chapel at Endingen (Enghien), but like most of the
roundels in this chapel it is a nineteenth-century
reproduction.[10]

1. Inv. nos. M. 623 and 624. See Paris, *Renaissance et Maniérisme* (exhib. cat.), 1985, pp. 102–4, nos. 49, 50. Marlier, *Pierre Coeck*, 1966, pp. 368–70, discusses this series but appears to be aware of only four of the drawings.

2. See Swarzenski, *Stiftungkunsthaus Heylshof*, 1927, no. 229; Benesch, *Albertina Katalog*, 1928, p. 9, no. 55.

3. Inv. no. C.37-1983.

4. Inv. no. 7965; see Benesch, *Albertina Katalog*, 1928, p. 9, no. 55.

5. Inv. no. M. 625; see Paris, *Renaissance et Maniérisme* (exhib. cat.), 1985, pp. 105–6, no. 51.

6. Inv. no. RBK-1961-102. Another version of this roundel is in the castle of Héverlé, near Leuven, but this is said to be a nineteenth-century copy (see Bruyn, "Tekeningen uit de werkplaats van Pieter Coecke," 1988, p. 75, n. 12.

7. Ibid., pp. 73–86, fig. 6.

8. See *Master Drawings 1500–1900* (exhib. cat.), 1992, no. 2, where it was ascribed to the early period of Pieter Coecke.

9. See "Keuze uit de aanwinsten," *Bulletin van het Rijksmuseum* 41, no. 1, 1993, pp. 31–32.

10. See Bruyn, "Tekeningen uit de werkplaats van Pieter Coecke," 1988, p. 75, fig. 6, notes 12, 26. For the roundels in the chapel at Endingen see Maes, "De vroege neogotik te Leuven en de namaakmedaillons van de 19de eeuw," *Leuvens Brandglas*, 1987, pp. 102–48, fig. 64.

BIBLIOGRAPHY: (81) *Master Drawings 1500–1900* (exhib. cat.), 1992, pp. 8–9; "Keuze uit de aanwinsten," *Bulletin van het Rijksmuseum* 41, no. 1, 1993, pp. 31–32. (82) Wayment, "Six Netherlandish Roundels," 1983, pp. 387–88; Bruyn, "Tekeningen uit de werkplaats van Pieter Coecke," 1988, p. 75, n. 14.

FIG. 1 Pieter Coecke van Aelst. *The Triumph of Love*. Pen and black and gray-brown ink, with gray wash and traces of white body color, on paper. About 1530–40. Paris, École Nationale Supérieure des Beaux-Arts

FIG. 2 After Pieter Coecke van Aelst. *The Triumph of Love*. Roundel. About 1530–40. Worms, Kunsthaus Heylshof

FIG. 3 Pieter Coecke van Aelst. *The Triumph of Chastity*. Pen and brown and gray-brown ink, with gray wash, on paper. About 1530–40. Paris, École Nationale Supérieure des Beaux-Arts

FIG. 4 After Pieter Coecke van Aelst. *The Triumph of Chastity*. Roundel. About 1530–40. Cambridge, Fitzwilliam Museum

FIG. 5 Pieter Coecke van Aelst. *The Triumph of Death*. Pen and black ink, with gray-black wash, on paper. About 1530–40. Vienna, Graphische Sammlung Albertina

FIG. 6 Pieter Coecke van Aelst. *The Triumph of Time*. Pen and brown ink, with gray-black wash, on paper. About 1530–40. Paris, École Nationale Supérieure des Beaux-Arts

FIG. 7 Pieter Coecke van Aelst. *The Triumph of Time*. Roundel. About 1530–40. Amsterdam, Rijksmuseum

83      84

## 83

### The Triumph of Divinity

Antwerp, about 1530–40

Pen and brown ink, and gray washes, on paper: diameter, 11¼ in. (28.6 cm)

Paris, École Nationale Supérieure des Beaux-Arts, M. 626

## 84

### The Triumph of Divinity

Antwerp, about 1530–40

Roundel: diameter, 11 in. (27.9 cm)

Amsterdam, Rijksmuseum, RBK-1961-103

Divinity is represented by Christ enthroned on a triumphal wagon, drawn by the lion and the ox, the symbols of the Evangelists Mark and Luke, respectively, and accompanied by the eagle and the angel, the symbols of John and Matthew. Christ holds a scepter in his right hand and with his left hand he steadies an orb against his left thigh. The entire group is borne aloft on a trailing bank of clouds. Below, in the earthly realm, Fame, Time, Chastity, and Love lie vanquished upon the ground, while Death, at the far left, tumbles from the clouds above them. Also to the left is a devil, at the fiery entrance to hell. The whole of the dense landscape appears to be aflame. In the heavenly zone above the level occupied by Christ as intercessor, hosts of saved souls wander through Paradise. Higher above them, in the clouds, God, with angels hovering before him, surveys the

panorama below. As the orb held by Christ shows the world divided into three parts, according to medieval tradition, so Coecke presents a tripartite vision of the universe.

This representation of *The Triumph of Divinity*, in which the picture plane is divided into three distinct zones, is compositionally the most complex of the series. The extensive use of washes of varying densities, which leave very little of the paper untouched, brings to this drawing a complex and luminous balance of tonalities and forms. These forms are outlined with a fine pen line, with a sureness and an economy that lend a mannered tension to the figures. The drama of this triumphant procession is heightened by the agitated drapery patterns and by the varied formations of the clouds. More than any of the other compositions in the series this one conveys a feeling of motion, avoiding any sense of the static.

The roundel faithfully follows the design, but, as in *The Triumph of Fame* (cat. no. 82), the glass painter appears to have had difficulty reconciling figure scale, which resulted in compositional adjustments; the angels, for example, are here reduced to winged putti heads. This glass painter is rather more successful than the painter of *Fame* at developing a broader range of tonalities, which he uses to greater effect in expressing volumes and spatial relationships. The figures are more convincingly modeled and the recessive spaces of the lateral zones are clearly defined. The extremely dark, brown tones are effectively employed to suggest the earth slipping off into the regions of hell. This is more explicit in the vision of hell, where the glass painter adds a figure who appears

FIG. 1 *The Triumph of Chastity*. Roundel. About 1530–40. Paris, Collection Frits Lugt, Institut Néerlandais

to be attempting to crawl away from the clutches of the devil onto the earthly area occupied by the vanquished Triumphs.

The *Trionfi* were executed as a series of engravings by Philips Galle after designs by Maarten van Heemskerck (*Ill. Bartsch* 56:5601); there are also *Trionfi* designs for a tapestry series by Michiel Coxie.[1] A simplified series of the *Trionfi*, in which a single personification rides upon a beast (see fig. 1), was widely replicated in silver-stained roundels.[2]

1. Budapest, Szépművészeti Museum, 1386, 2842, 2498, 2841, and 1332, respectively.

2. See Vanden Bemden, "Rondels représentant les Triomphes de Pétrarque," 1977, pp. 5–22.

BIBLIOGRAPHY: (83) Wescher, "Pieter Coecke van Aelst," 1938, pp. 58–59; Mechelen, *Margareta van Oostenrijk* (exhib. cat.), 1958, no. 175; Marlier, *Pierre Coeck*, 1966, pp. 368–69, fig. 316; Huvenne, "Pieter Pourbus," 1980, p. 25, fig. 14; Bourg-en-Bresse, *Van Orley* (exhib. cat.), 1981, no. 22; Bruges, *Pierre Pourbus* (exhib. cat.), 1984, pp. 252–53, fig. 115; Paris, *Renaissance et Maniérisme* (exhib. cat.), 1985, p. 106, no. 52; Bruyn, "Tekeningen uit de werkplaats van Pieter Coecke," 1988, p. 75, fig. 9. (84) "Keuze uit de aanwinsten," *Bulletin van het Rijksmuseum* 10, no. 1, 1962, p. 43; Bruyn, "Tekeningen uit de werkplaats van Pieter Coecke," 1988, pp. 75, 81, fig. 10, n. 13; s'Hertogenbosch, *Maria van Hongarije* (exhib. cat.), 1993, p. 268, no. 205 b.

85

## 85–90 *see plate 16*

### The Birth of John the Baptist; The Departure of John the Baptist; The Preaching in the Wilderness; The Baptism of Christ; The Feast of Herod; The Dance of Salome

Antwerp, about 1540

Roundels: diameter, each, approximately 11 in. (27.9 cm)

Amsterdam, Rijksmuseum, NM 12567–12572

No designs for this unusually large series have survived, but the mannered style, which seems to relish contrapuntal figures teetering in contorted poses engulfed in eccentric flurries of drapery, conveys the idiosyncracies of Pieter Coecke's most expansive style. The six roundels that comprise this series—now undoubtedly incomplete, as major episodes, such as the Martyrdom, are missing—appear to have been painted by two different hands. The less skillful painter, who used paler tones of brown and lighter yellow silver stain, is responsible for *The Birth of John the Baptist, The Departure of John the Baptist,* and *The Dance of Salome.* The trace lines and modeling are not as incisive, the defining of hands and faces not as accomplished, and the less assured control of light and tonalities flattens the dimensionality of the compositions. To the second, more accomplished hand may be attributed *The Preaching in the Wilderness, The Baptism of Christ,* and *The Feast of Herod*; this artist employs more contrasting tones of paint and denser hues of silver stain. He articulates forms, contours, and details with

86

87

88

89

90

FIG. 1 Follower of Pieter Coecke van Aelst. *Justice and Wisdom*. Pen and black ink, with black wash, on paper. About 1530. Paris, Musée du Louvre, Département des Arts Graphiques

greater assurance and heightens the effects with contrasting tonalities. On the whole, the forms are more volumetric, the spaces more convincingly defined, and the renderings thereby more compelling. The style of these roundels generally is similar to that of the close follower or associate of Pieter Coecke who produced the drawing in Paris of *Justice and Wisdom* (fig. 1).[1]

The figure style, typified by extremely elongated bodies—excepting the all-too-short lower legs—and by emphatic contrapposto, as well as the angled heads with downcast eyes, finds close comparison in the Paris sheet. For example, the figure of Herodias in *The Feast of Herod* and in *The Dance of Salome* is very similar to that of Justice, and striking analogies in the rendering of the male figures can likewise be found. The painterly technique of the drawing, most probably a design for a painted glass panel,[2] relies entirely on washes for modeling and for indicating values of light and dark. In this regard, it accords with the technique of the *Trionfi* designs (cat. nos. 81 and 83), and generally seems to be characteristic of Antwerp and Brussels work, reflecting, no doubt, the influence of Dirick Vellert.

1. Musée du Louvre, Département des Arts Graphiques, 22,642. Lugt (*Dessins*, 1968, p. 63, no. 211) believed this sheet to be by Pieter Coecke.

2. See Marlier, *Pierre Coeck*, 1966, p. 299.

BIBLIOGRAPHY: Hudig, "Zestiende eeuwsche ruiten," 1922, pp. 43–52, figs. 4, 9, and 10; Marlier, *Pierre Coeck*, 1966, pp. 373–75, figs. 325–330; Bruyn, "Tekeningen uit de werkplaats van Pieter Coecke," 1988, p. 85, n. 24.

# 11

## Jan Swart van Groningen

*Little documented information exists regarding Jan Swart, although Karel van Mander relates that Swart was born in Groningen, worked in Gouda about 1522–23, was much influenced by Jan van Scorel, and traveled to Venice probably before 1526 or, at the latest, 1530. As Swart appears to have been a master by about 1525, he was probably born about 1500. He was an accomplished woodcut artist, and he produced numerous woodcut illustrations for the Vorsterman Bible, which was published in Antwerp where he lived and worked from about 1524 to 1528; there he was influenced by the Antwerp Mannerists and particularly by both Dirick Vellert and Pieter Coecke van Aelst. He was also, like so many artists of his time, greatly affected by the work of Albrecht Dürer. Swart was a prolific designer of glass roundels and panels and many drawings in his hand or in his style have survived. His work was much valued by the Crabeth brothers in Gouda, and Adriaen Pietersz. Crabeth was perhaps his foremost student. The influence of Jan van Scorel is most conspicuous in Swart's later years. His death date is not certain, but it is likely that he died in Gouda in or about 1558.*

To judge from the large numbers of sheets in his style that survive, Jan Swart must have had a prolific workshop specializing mainly in designs for glass; the homogeneity and longevity of its output suggest the successful marketing of this recognizable and enduring style. As a consequence, the identification of Swart's own hand and the establishment of a stylistic chronology are difficult. The few works that are or can be dated accurately include the series of woodcuts representing Süleyman the Magnificent and his entourage dated 1526 (cat. no. 91); three woodcuts printed in Basel in 1528; the woodcut illustrations in the Vorsterman Bible, printed in Antwerp in the same year;[1] the drawing of *The Descent of the Holy Spirit* dated 1533,

now in the British Museum (fig. 1, p. 167);[2] and the series of ten iron-plate etchings representing scenes from the Life of Saint John the Baptist, one of which is dated 1553 (fig. 2, p. 167).[3] Most of Swart's *oeuvre* seems to date from after the Italian trip (and possibly a continuing journey to Constantinople) and shows no marked shifts in style from that produced about 1526 to 1530 and the late work of the 1550s. In Boon's view, however, the early influence of the Gothic Mannerists in Leiden gave way to that of the Antwerp Mannerists—particularly Dirick Vellert and Pieter Coecke van Aelst—and then of Dürer. In the 1540s, the style of Italian High Renaissance art began to make an impression, and the final phase of Swart's production clearly was under the sway of Jan van Scorel, as well as of Marcantonio Raimondi and his followers.[4] It appears that the mannered style of Maarten van Heemskerck also influenced Swart's later work (see cat. no. 96). These transitions, however, seem more a response to changes in popular taste than inherent stylistic developments; the distinctive style of Swart's workshop remains unmistakable throughout. The conservative—and commercial—nature of the workshop is evident not only in the formulation of and adherence to a particular style, but also in the adaptation of familiar imagery borrowed from earlier generations of artists (see cat. no. 96). The Swart workshop, like many others in the first half of the sixteenth century, also quoted freely from well-known artists of the period; the Berlin *Prodigal Son as a Swineherd*, for example, clearly reflects Dürer's engraved composition of the same subject (figs. 3 and 4, p. 167).[5] One of the more striking aspects of the designs produced by Swart's workshop is the distinct preference for a relatively large-scale rectangular format (frequently they are fourteen or more inches high), often terminating in a hemicyclic arch; designs for roundels, on the other hand, are a rarity. Swart's influence on the Crabeth brothers of Gouda was apparently not limited to style alone, as their designs for small-scale glass were also exclusively rectangular (see cat. nos. 117–122, 126, and 127). Whether this preference was occasioned by changing fashion or architectural context is unknown. Increasingly, toward the end of Swart's career, however, his figures became more massive and monumental, effectively making his scenes legible at a greater distance.

1. See Beets, *De houtsneden*, 1915.

2. Inv. no. 1860.6.16.55; see Popham, *Drawings in the British Museum*, 1932, p. 44, no. 9. This is not an autograph sheet and its authorship is uncertain.

3. For a discussion of Swart's chronology see Dodgson, "Holzschnitten Jan Swarts," 1910, p. 33; Beets, "Jan Swart," 1914, pp. 1–19; Popham, *Drawings in the British Museum*, 1932, p. 41.

4. See Boon, *Drawings of the Frits Lugt Collection*, 1992, p. 361.

5. Staatliche Museen zu Berlin, Preußischer Kulturbesitz, Kupferstichkabinett, KdZ 5636.

FIG. 1 Jan Swart van Groningen. *The Descent of the Holy Spirit*. Pen and black ink, with gray wash, on paper. 1533. London, British Museum

FIG. 2 After Jan Swart van Groningen. *Saint John the Baptist Pointing to the Hatchet at the Foot of the Tree*. Iron-plate etching. 1553. Amsterdam, Rijksmuseum, Rijksprentenkabinet

FIG. 3 Jan Swart van Groningen. *The Prodigal Son as a Swineherd*. Pen and black ink, with gray wash, on paper. About 1530–40. Staatliche Museen zu Berlin, Preußischer Kulturbesitz, Kupferstichkabinett

FIG. 4 Albrecht Dürer. *The Prodigal Son as a Swineherd*. Engraving. About 1496. New York, The Metropolitan Museum of Art, The George Khuner Collection, Gift of Mrs. George Khuner, 1975

91 92

## 91

### "Mamalucke," from a Procession of Turkish Riders

Published by Willem Liefrinck, Antwerp, 1526

Woodcut, 12¾ x 10 in. (32.4 x 25.4 cm)

Amsterdam, Rijksmuseum, Rijksprentenkabinet, RP-P-1950-409b

## 92

### Turkish Warrior Supporting a Heraldic Shield

Lowlands, about 1530

Roundel: diameter, 9 in. (22.9 cm)

New York, The Metropolitan Museum of Art, The Cloisters Collection, 1932, 32.24.29

The five woodcuts that comprise this Procession of Turkish Riders series were published by Willem Liefrinck in Antwerp in 1526, the same year that Süleyman's army overran Hungary after the battle of Mohács, heightening the European fear of the Turkish threat; three years later, the Turkish army laid siege to Vienna. Swart was one of many artists at this time who depicted these exotically arrayed figures. Although not signed, the wood blocks possess the linear clarity, bold figure style, and firm control of line that distinguish Swart's monogrammed and slightly earlier *Christ Preaching from a Ship* (fig. 1). The broad popularity of this series of prints is attested to by those it inspired, such as the etching by Daniel Hopfer (fig. 2); three compositions in the series, including the

present one, were copied at a later date, perhaps by Melchior Lorch (fig. 3).[1] Erhard Schön borrowed from the series for his illustrations of participants in the 1529 siege of Vienna; the near "Mamalucke" rider now leads off two bound prisoners, his horse has been given the head of that of Swart's middle rider, and the back rider is eliminated altogether (fig. 4).

The glass painter of the present roundel made even more liberal use of Swart's composition: The foreground rider in the woodcut has become, in reversed direction, a standing figure supporting a heraldic shield. Little of the detail has been altered; even the position of the hand, which originally held the reins, remains the same, making its function here unclear. Instead of a bannered spear, the figure now holds an outsized arrow, understood in late medieval imagery as a symbol of death, in general, and of the plague, in particular (see cat. no. 27). The warrior stands on a grassy knoll in the foreground; just behind, pigs feed from a trough against a background of village buildings—a setting that is ordinarily associated with scenes of the Prodigal Son as a swineherd. The elaborate shield is emblazoned with an unidentified cipher. The significance of the imagery is unclear. Conventionally, wild men, naked women (see cat. no. 61), imposing beasts, and the like served as heraldic supporters. Perhaps the "Mamalucke" was simply seen as an exotic type, but this seems unlikely given the curious combination of the pestilential arrow and the feeding swine. A reference to the Turkish threat, with which central Europe was much preoccupied at this time, related somehow to the identity of the

cipher, would seem a more probable avenue of interpretation.

Although not intended as designs, these prints evidently were used as such; three woodcuts from this series now in the Rijksmuseum, for example, are pricked for transfer. The reversal of the heraldic supporter in the roundel would suggest an intermediate copy. The roundel, while competently executed in medium tones of brown paint with pale and medium yellow hues of silver stain and highlighted with deliberate stickwork, is certainly not of the quality of the *Banquet before an Enthroned King* (cat. no. 95). The circular format, apparently rarely, if ever, used by Swart's workshop, further suggests the appropriation of Swart's compositions by a lesser workshop.

1. Kunsthalle, Hamburg, 29336. Two other compositions by the same hand appear on the recto and verso of another sheet in the same print room (29337).

BIBLIOGRAPHY: (91) Nijhoff, *Nederlandsche houtsneden 1500–1550*, 1931–39, nos. 25–29; Henkel, "Nederlandsche houtsneden," 1936, pp. 99–100; Vienna, *Kunst der Graphik* (exhib. cat.), 1964, no. 375; Amsterdam, *Vorstenportretten* (exhib. cat.), 1972, pp. 11–12, no. 5; Hollstein 29, 1984, pp. 111–13, no. 9; Amsterdam, *Kunst voor de beeldenstorm* (exhib. cat.), 1986, pp. 175–77, no. 59, fig. 59.2. (92) Grosvenor Thomas Stock Book, I, p. 98, no. 1047; Husband, *Silver-Stained Roundels*, 1991, p. 154.

FIG. 1  Jan Swart van Groningen. *Christ Preaching from a Ship*. Woodcut.
About 1525. New York, The Metropolitan Museum of Art, Harris Brisbane
Dick Fund, 1926

FIG. 2  Daniel Hopfer. *Three Mamluks*. Etching.
About 1530–35. New York, The Metropolitan
Museum of Art, The Elisha Whittelsey Collection,
The Elisha Whittelsey Fund, 1951

FIG. 3  Probably Melchior Lorch. *Three Mamluks*.
Pen and black ink on paper. About 1550–60.
Hamburg, Kunsthalle, Kupferstichkabinett

FIG. 4  Erhard Schön. *Two Janissaries with Two
Prisoners*: from a series of The Participants in the
1529 Siege of Vienna. Woodcut. 1530. Erlangen-
Nürnberg Universität, Graphische Sammlung

93

## The Feast of Ahasuerus

About 1530–35

Pen and black ink, with brown wash, on paper, 10⅛ x 7¾ in. (25.7 x 19.7 cm)

Amsterdam, Rijksmuseum, Rijksprentenkabinet, RP-T-1919-57

Inscribed (upper center, above the mirror): *gulde laken*

The composition of this drawing harks back to that of *The Last Supper* by Jacob Cornelisz. (cat. no. 38), and has much in common with the iron-plate etching of *The Marriage Feast at Cana* after Swart (fig. 1). Ahasuerus, slightly to the right of center, is seated before a cloth of honor. The guests are distributed to the left and the right around the table, which leaves the near end empty. The female seated on a stool and seen from the back is placed sufficiently to the left to counterbalance Ahasuerus. The servant entering at the upper right establishes a strong diagonal, which comfortably resolves the asymmetrical composition. The drawing is firm but fluid and shows little evidence of altering or reworking. Wash alone is used for the modeling. Sufficient indication of the ornamental detailing in the cloth of honor and the architrave is given for the glass painter, but is left incomplete. The inscription, which Boon considers to be in Swart's hand,[1] notes that the hanging should be silver stained.

A close copy of this drawing is also in the Rijksprentenkabinet (fig. 2).[2] The composition is copied with exactitude but the line is weaker and the effect comparatively stiff and mechanical. The wash in this version of the composition is denser in tone, and the sharp contrast of light and shadow is closer to that found in the panels executed

FIG. 1 After Jan Swart van Groningen. *The Marriage Feast at Cana*. Iron-plate etching. About 1540–60. Amsterdam, Rijksmuseum, Rijksprentenkabinet

FIG. 2 After Jan Swart van Groningen. *The Feast of Ahasuerus*. Pen and umber ink, with dark brown wash, on paper. About 1535–40. Amsterdam, Rijksmuseum, Rijksprentenkabinet

FIG. 3 After Jan Swart van Groningen. *Esther before Ahasuerus*. Painted glass panel. About 1550–60. Amsterdam, Rijksmuseum

after Swart's designs (see cat. no. 95). Boon's assertion that the present drawing is the original is supported not only in terms of the quality of its execution, but also by the fact that the paper of the copy has a later watermark. With two such close versions of the same composition, the question of function arises. As there is no reworking or alteration in either sheet, it seems probable that both are workshop drawings after the original design; if the present one is, indeed, by the master's own hand, Swart would seem to have followed Dirick Vellert's practice of producing workshop drawings from his own designs. The somewhat later copy may have been executed in the interest of preserving the master version as well as of satisfying ongoing demand; it is also perfectly likely that, in a large workshop, a popular series was executed simultaneously at two or more glass-painters' benches. In any event, these two drawings clearly demonstrate the difficulty in distinguishing both the authorship and function of drawings produced by workshops as large and productive as Swart's apparently was. No executed panels based on this composition have survived, but another panel of indifferent quality, now in the Rijksmuseum, representing Esther before Ahasuerus (fig. 3),[3] may preserve, in a debased fashion, another composition from the same series.[4]

1. See Boon, *Netherlandish Drawings*, 1978, p. 162, nos. 441, 442.

2. Inv. no. A 3479.

3. Inv. no. NM 10180 B.

4. See Boon, *Netherlandish Drawings*, 1978, p. 162, no. 442.

BIBLIOGRAPHY: Hudig, "Zestiende eeuwsche ruiten," 1922, pp. 44–45, 50, fig. 11; Boon, *Netherlandish Drawings*, 1978, p. 162, no. 441.

## 94

### A Banquet before an Enthroned King

About 1540–45

Pen and brown ink, with pencil, on paper, 14¼ x 12 in. (36.2 x 30.5 cm)

London, British Museum, 1863.5.9.941

Inscribed (on the back): *f*

## 95 *see plate 17*

### A Banquet before an Enthroned King

About 1540–45

Panel, 9⅜ x 7¼ in. (23.8 x 18.4 cm)

Amsterdam, Rijksmuseum, RBK-1984-42

A king, holding a staff or scepter, is enthroned on a raised dais sheltered by a circular tent. Before him a group of seven men sits around a table feasting while engaged in animated discussion; in the background, armies are massed, while in the distance at the far right a city burns. The subject has yet to be satisfactorily identified. Baldass suggested that the drawing could be paired with one

94

95

FIG. 1 Jan Swart van Groningen. *A Banquet before an Enthroned King.* Pen and brown ink, with dark brown wash, on paper. About 1540–45. Staatliche Museen zu Berlin, Preußischer Kulturbesitz, Kupferstichkabinett

in Dresden representing the son of Cambyses sitting in judgment on the flayed skin of his father—a popular Judgment scene in the Lowlands (see cat. no. 80);[1] Popham agreed that the compositions are very similar but rightly concluded that the present drawing does not appear to be a complementary scene of wise and unjust judgment.[2] More recent suggestions include the sacking of Jerusalem by Nebuchadnezzar, as recounted in 4 Kings 24 and 25, and the prophecy of the event according to Jeremias 13: 13, 14, and 27:[3] "Behold I will fill all the inhabitants of this land, and the kings of the race of David that sit upon his throne, and the priests, and the prophets, and all the inhabitants of Jerusalem, with drunkenness. . . . I will not spare, and I will not pardon: nor will I have mercy, but to destroy them. . . . Woe to thee, Jerusalem, wilt thou not be made clean after me: how long yet?"

The present drawing is executed with a free and expressive but controlled line, while the modeling is achieved entirely with washes. There is a fluid range of tonal values from highlights to deep shadow; the artist has used the wash to exceptional effect in creating shadows. The full-bodied figures have varied and animated expressions, their bodies and hands engaged in spirited poses and gestures. The penchant for Renaissance ornament and Italianate influence suggest a date in the 1540s. Like the previous drawing (cat. no. 93), there is a close copy of the London sheet, now in

Berlin (fig. 1).[4] This drawing, rendered in a more erratic and nervous line, is modeled in a rather denser, monochromatic wash that tends to flatten the composition. The faces are less well articulated and details such as decorative elements and drapery patterns are more stiffly composed. A horizontal line indicates the lead line between the central panel and the surmounting lunette.

The glass panel, which is without the upper lunette, follows the design in detail although it is slightly trimmed at the bottom and compressed laterally; for example, the man at the right with the high hat remains unedited but the figure to his right has been pushed forward so that he is hidden behind the seated man in the foreground. The glass painter employed an unusual and varied palette of gray, reddish gray, reddish brown, and deep reddish brown; the silver stain ranges from a pale to a deep golden yellow. The modeling has been achieved almost exclusively with a badger brush, which worked away the mattes in finely graded transitions from dense colors to expanses of colorless glass. The stylus is only rarely used to articulate and lend brilliant highlights to select areas; it can be observed at its best effect in the hair and feathered hat of the figure at the left seen from the back. The painter's draftsmanship is well demonstrated by the foreshortened arm of the gesturing man seated at the far right side of the table. The uncommon control and balance of a dynamic range of light and tonal values establish this painter as an exceptional artist with an unusual command of technique.

1. See Baldass, "Jan Swart," 1918, p. 18, no. 21. The drawing is in the Staatliche Kunstsammlungen, Dresden, 673. Baldass identifies the subject as Sisamnes.

2. *Drawings in the British Museum*, 1932, p. 44, no. 10.

3. See Amsterdam, *Kunst voor de beeldenstorm* (exhib. cat.), 1986, p. 250, no. 131.

4. Staatliche Museen zu Berlin, Preußischer Kulturbesitz, Kupferstichkabinett, KdZ 9588.

BIBLIOGRAPHY: (94) Baldass, "Jan Swart," 1918, p. 11, no. 55; Popham, *Drawings in the British Museum*, 1932, p. 44, no. 10; Amsterdam, *Kunst voor de beeldenstorm* (exhib. cat.), 1986, p. 131 a. (95) Rotterdam, *Noord-nederlandsche Primitieven* (exhib. cat.), 1936, p. 116, no. 12; Bogtman, *Nederlandsche Glasschilders*, 1944, p. 32, pl. 4; "Keuze uit de aanwinsten," *Bulletin van het Rijksmuseum* 33, no. 2, 1985, p. 125, no. 7, ill.; Amsterdam, *Kunst voor de beeldenstorm* (exhib. cat.), 1986, p. 250, no. 131; Bruyn, "Oude en nieuwe elementen," 1987, pp. 153–55, fig. 17.

## 96

## Joseph Being Sold to the Ishmaelites

About 1545–55

Pen and black ink, with brown wash, on paper, 10¾ x 7¼ in. (27.3 x 18.4 cm)

London, British Museum, 1923.1.13.8

The story of the Egyptian Joseph, an extended metaphor of the just and unjust, enjoyed enduring popularity in the Lowlands throughout the period in which roundel production flourished. Swart alone appears to have based at least three different

series of designs for glass on this subject. Of particular interest in the series represented by the present drawing is the fact that Swart, in his compositions, referred back to the corresponding designs by the Hugo van der Goes group dating nearly eighty years earlier (cat. nos. 7–11). In the drawing here, for example, Swart follows the composition in general and directly quotes specific passages of the van der Goes group's *Joseph Being Sold to the Ishmaelites* (fig. 1). The disposition of the figures—Joseph being lifted out of the well at the lower left and his brothers consummating the transaction with the Ishmaelite merchant diagonally behind—remains the same, and the counterbalancing diagonal of the camel procession and the shepherds resting on the background promontory are virtually direct quotations. The three other surviving compositions by Swart from this series—*Joseph Recounting His Dreams to His Father* (fig. 2), *Joseph Is Cast into a Pit* (fig. 3), and *Joseph Being Sold to Potiphar*—also reflect, in varying degrees, the compositions of the van der Goes group's series.[1] The principal cluster of three figures in *Joseph Is Cast into a Pit*, for example, reflects the same compositional arrangement as in the scene by the van der Goes group (fig. 3 and cat. nos. 8 and 9, fig. 7).[2]

No panel based on these designs is known to have survived. A roundel, on the other hand, adapted from the design for *Joseph Recounting His Dreams to His Father*, but of a later date, is now in the Victoria and Albert Museum (fig. 4);[3] the design, however, is not well suited to the circular format, and, as a result, some details—including the visual shorthand of the representations of the dreams—had to be expurgated, while the incidental shrubbery to the right was added in.[4] A later circular design for a scene with the same subject, from yet another series of the Story of Joseph, may be a copy after one by Swart; as he rarely produced designs for roundels, it probably represents a more successful adaptation of a Swart composition to the circular format (fig. 5). The Joseph series was not an isolated instance of Swart referring to the compositions of the van der Goes group. A design in the Collection Frits Lugt, Paris, for example, for a panel representing Tobias burning the liver and heart of the fish and praying in thanks with Sarah, reveals that Swart clearly was aware of the fifteenth-century Tobit series; although the composition is essentially reversed, with the praying Sarah and Tobias moved to the rear of the room, the grouping of the couple at the bed, the burning of the innards in the fireplace, and the fleeing demon all hark back to the van der Goes group composition (fig. 6 and cat. no. 12, fig. 3).[5]

The figures in the present drawing, and in Swart's later work in general, are massive and are densely grouped in the foreground. The animated and varied postures and gestures focus the central action, and the increased figure scale relative to the overall composition enhances the narrative drama. The exaggeration of anatomical forms, the mannering of poses, and the monumentalizing of the figures may reflect the influence of Maarten van Heemskerck, whose work enjoyed increasing

96

FIG. 1 Master of the Joseph Sequence. *Joseph Being Sold to the Ishmaelites.* Tempera and oil on panel. 1490–1500. Staatliche Museen zu Berlin, Preußischer Kulturbesitz, Gemäldegalerie

FIG. 2 Jan Swart van Groningen. *Joseph Recounting His Dreams to His Father.* Pen and black ink, with brown wash, on paper. 1545–55. London, British Museum

FIG. 3 Jan Swart van Groningen. *Joseph Is Cast into a Pit.* Pen and black ink, with brown wash, on paper. 1545–55. London, British Museum

FIG. 4 After Jan Swart van Groningen. *Joseph Recounting His Dreams to His Father*. Roundel. About 1545–55. London, Victoria and Albert Museum

FIG. 5 After Jan Swart van Groningen. *Joseph Recounting His Dreams to His Father*. Pen and black ink, with brown wash, on paper. About 1545–55. Staatliche Museen zu Berlin, Preußischer Kulturbesitz, Kupferstichkabinett

popularity in the 1550s. For example, the substantial forms, the shifting of weight from one to the other leg, and the expressive hand gestures in Swart's *Joseph Recounting His Dreams to His Father* (fig. 2; see also fig. 5) have much in common with Heemskerck's engraving of the same subject (fig. 7). The forms in the present sheet, defined with firm, fluid lines showing little evidence of alteration or reworking, are then modeled with the skillful, painterly use of wash. The graphic clarity of the composition is characteristic of Swart's later work.

1. These drawings are also in the British Museum, 1923.1.13.6, 7, and 9, respectively.

2. Four further drawings by Swart of the Story of Joseph, also in the British Museum (1923.1.13.10–13), belong to an altogether different series of designs; yet, at least one from this series, *The Cup Is Found in Benjamin's Sack*, again quotes heavily from the corresponding van der Goes group composition.

3. Inv. no. C65-1926.

4. Another roundel based on the design for *Joseph Being Sold to Potiphar* was formerly in the F. E. Sidney collection, Hampstead; this design, too, was not well suited to the circular format. See Popham, *Drawings in the British Museum*, 1932, p. 46, no. 20.

5. Inv. no. 4541. See Boon, *Drawings of the Frits Lugt Collection*, 1992, pp. 362–63, no. 204. There is a later panel in the Collection Frits Lugt (8573) that, in turn, seems to quote the figure of Tobias burning the heart and liver in this composition; see Boon, *Drawings of the Frits Lugt Collection 2*, 1992, p. 302, fig. 118.

BIBLIOGRAPHY: Popham, *Drawings in the British Museum*, 1932, pp. 45–46, no. 19.

FIG. 6 Jan Swart van Groningen. *Tobias and Sarah*. Pen and brown ink on paper. About 1545–50. Paris, Collection Frits Lugt, Institut Néerlandais

FIG. 7 Dirck Volckertsz. Coornhert, after Maarten van Heemskerck. *Joseph Recounting His Dreams to His Father*. Engraving. 1549–50. Amsterdam, Rijksmuseum, Rijksprentenkabinet

# 12

## Diversity of Style and Imagery: about 1520 to 1560

The four decades that this section encompasses undoubtedly witnessed the most prolific and creative roundel production in the Lowlands. While Dirick Vellert, Pieter Coecke van Aelst, Jan Swart, Lambert van Noort, and the Crabeth brothers—to name just some of the more prominent artists involved—produced large numbers of designs for glass and either headed up or collaborated with glass-painting workshops that executed them, numerous others produced roundels of the highest quality that cannot be stylistically associated with a particular artistic personality. Traditional medieval subjects endured; *March*, from a series representing the Occupations of the Months (cat. no. 97), at first glance could be taken for a work by the Master of the Death of Absalom. A comparison of the two versions of *The Adulterous Woman Washing the Feet of Christ* (cat. nos. 98 and 99) exemplifies the transition from the enduring late medieval narrative tradition to a more complex and personal response to the written words of faith. Conventional Old Testament subjects appeared in new typological arrangements, often imbued with unprecedented dramatic intensity (see cat. no. 101). Heightened interest in textual sources, fostered by Humanist thought, stimulated a proliferation of Old Testament narratives; Maarten van Heemskerck alone produced designs for nearly thirty such series, many of which illustrated relatively arcane subjects that heretofore had rarely, if ever, been represented in art. Innovative compositions brought novelty to familiar subjects (see cat. no. 109); traditional imagery was invigorated by consummate technical achievement. Stylistic diversity flourished, embracing the mannered and eccentric (cat. nos. 105 and 106) along with the established (cat. no. 102). Yet, in a period in which artistic creativity was greatly stimulated by humanistic thought and religious divergence, there were constants; the evanescent quality of worldly concerns and the transitory nature of life itself remained as abiding a theme in this period as it had throughout the later Middle Ages and as it would in the coming Golden Age (see cat. no. 110).

<u>97</u>

## 98

### The Adulterous Woman Washing the Feet of Christ

South Lowlands, Leuven, about 1520

Roundel: diameter, 9 in. (22.9 cm)

Leuven, Stedelijk Museum Vander Kelen-Mertens, B/III/13

## 99

### The Adulterous Woman Washing the Feet of Christ

North Lowlands, about 1520–30

Roundel: diameter, 9 in. (22.9 cm)

London, Victoria and Albert Museum, 5634-1859

While a guest at the table of the Pharisee Simon, Christ was approached by an adulterous woman who proceeded to wash his feet with her tears, dry them with her hair, and then anoint them with ointment she had brought with her. Simon expressed dismay that Christ would suffer a woman whose reputation had been so tarnished by her sins. In response Christ said: "Many sins are forgiven her, because she hath loved much. But to whom less is forgiven, he loveth less" (Luke 7: 47). Although the recounting of this incident, which appears only in the Gospel according to Saint Luke (7: 36–50), does not name the woman, she is traditionally believed to be Mary Magdalene, recognizable by her attribute, the jar of ointment. The Leuven roundel leaves little doubt as to her identity, as three principal events in this penitent saint's life are depicted in the background. At the far right, an angel tells the Three Maries at the tomb that Christ has risen (Matthew 28: 1–6); in the near background, Mary Magdalene, having returned to the tomb after telling the disciples what had transpired, sees a man whom she at first takes to be a gardener, but when she realizes that he is Christ and reaches out to him, she is admonished not to touch him (*Noli me tangere*) (John 20: 14–17); and in the left background, the Maries on their way to find the disciples are met by the resurrected Christ (Matthew 28: 8–10).

The Leuven roundel is among the finest of a group traditionally attributed to that city, and the characteristics that these roundels have in common are exceptionally well represented here.[1] This roundel is composed with a clear sense of the dramatic narrative. Christ, as the central figure, is strikingly silhouetted against a cloth of honor. The seated man at the right considerably lifts up the edge of the tablecloth so that the spectator can witness the Magdalene kneeling in the foreground and performing her penitential ritual. The three background scenes are viewed through an arch, which effectively serves as a proscenium; this architectural barrier sets the viewer apart both in space and time so that future events depicted simultaneously appear—in contrast to the immediate reality of the principal scene—as visions rather than historical record.

## 97

### March: Pruners, from a Series of the Occupations of the Months

North Lowlands, about 1525–35

Roundel: diameter, 9 in. (22.9 cm)

Amsterdam, Rijksmuseum, RBK-1984-41

Inscribed (on the banderole): MARCIVS

The conservative nature of the subject matter is matched by that of the style. The stocky figures pruning stylized trees and vines have much in common with those in an analogous composition by the Master of the Death of Absalom some decades earlier in date (fig. 1; see also cat. no. 20); only the costumes indicate a date well into the second quarter of the sixteenth century. The ram, the zodiacal sign for Aries, is seen not in its usual airborne aureole, but as an earthbound witness to the labor associated with March. A close version of this roundel, differing only in the more elegant cut of the foreground figure, is found in the Museum Willet-Holthuysen, Amsterdam.[1] In the same collection there are three more roundels extending the sequence and preserving further compositions upon which both series depended: One, inscribed *aprilis* on a banderole, represents two gallants falconing, with Taurus looking on in the background; another, inscribed *mayus*, portrays an elegant couple falconing on horseback, with Gemini disporting in the background; and the third, inscribed *junius*, depicts a couple—overdressed for the occasion—shearing sheep, with Cancer in the foreground. The mingling of peasant and courtly occupations in a rural idyll

FIG. 1 Master of the Death of Absalom. *March: Pruners*, from a series of the Occupations of the Months. Brush and black ink, with light blue highlights, on gray prepared paper. 1500–1510. London, British Museum

quite devoid of the harsh realities of agrarian life is thoroughly rooted in late medieval imagery. The heavyset figures in the present roundel as well as the dense tonalities worked with a badger brush suggest an origin in the North Lowlands. The roundel is executed in brown paint with pale yellow and yellow silver stain. Stickwork is extensively used, particularly around the edges of garments.

1. See Berserik, "Leiden, ca. 1480–1545," 1982, nos. 58–61, figs. 96, 98–100.

BIBLIOGRAPHY: Rotterdam, *Noord-nederlandsche Primitieven* (exhib. cat.), 1936, pp. 115–16, no. 11, pl. 10; Bogtman, *Nederlandsche Glasschilders*, 1944, pl. 3; "Keuze uit de aanwinsten," *Bulletin van het Rijksmuseum* 33, no. 2, 1985, pp. 124–25, fig. 6.

The figures are youthful in appearance even when individuals, such as the man to Christ's right, are intended to be considerably aged. There is little sense of anatomy, as the figures are draped in loose, flowing robes with broad, smooth planes interrupted by or terminating in long tubular folds and extended deep, crevasse-like linear passages. The physiognomies are placid and unfurrowed, punctuated by small dark eyes, neat noses, and narrow mouths, all framed by silken, often wavy hair. While the Master of the Death of Absalom group (see cat. no. 20), for example, brings dramatic impact to its compositions by defining the nature of the participants through varied physical features and motions, the Leuven roundels are pervaded by a serenity that encourages contemplation of the significance of the events portrayed.

The same subject is represented in the contemporary—or somewhat later—London roundel. The traditional composition, which incorporates several ancillary exterior scenes of perspectival and spatial ambiguity, is abandoned in favor of one that emphasizes the principal scene, set in a rational interior space. The individualization of the participants and the animated gestures and poses enliven Christ's unfolding disputation; increased Humanist textual interest is seemingly blended with medieval devotional imagery. In contrast to the Leuven roundel, this example focuses less on the event represented than on the lesson revealed through Christ's teachings. The roundel is finely executed in brown paint and a golden yellow silver stain. The refined painterly style is enhanced by the use of both an extraordinarily fine and subtle stylus and the point of a brush, with the most arresting achievement the capturing of the textures in the passages of hair and fur. The roundel appears to be related to those produced in Leiden, as well as stylistically influenced by the graphic work of Lucas van Leyden of about 1510–20. While several close versions of the Vander Kelen-Mertens Museum roundels are known,[2] the Victoria and Albert Museum roundel seems unique.

The surrounds are of nineteenth-century fabrication.

1. For a recent and extended discussion of Leuven roundel production see Maes, *Leuvens Brandglas*, 1987.

2. A reversed variant is in the parish church of Saint Mary at Fawlsey, Northamptonshire (see Cole, *Roundels in Britain*, 1993, p. 80, no. 668). Another variant, also in reverse, is now in the Musées Royaux d'Art et d'Histoire, Brussels; it was apparently fabricated by Jan de Caumont between 1634 and 1636 for the Alexius Cloister in Leuven (see Maes, *Leuvens Brandglas*, 1987, p. 229, fig. 136).

BIBLIOGRAPHY: (98) Helbig, *Glasschilderkunst*, 1943, pl. 82, no. 182; Maes, "Leuvense brandglasmedaillons," 1976, p. 324, fig. 7; Vanden Bemden, "Fichier du Rondel," 1979, p. 158, fig. 6; Maes, *Leuvens Brandglas*, 1987, pp. 226–29, no. 12, pl. 7. (99) Popham, "Notes-II," 1929, p. 154; Rackham, *Guide to Stained Glass*, 1936, p. 109, pl. 44 B.

98

99

100         101

## 100

**A Murder Scene**

North Lowlands, about 1520

Roundel: diameter, 9¼ in. (23.5 cm)

Cambridge, Fitzwilliam Museum, C.17-1984

## 101

**Joab Murdering Abner**

North Lowlands, about 1520

Roundel: diameter, 8½ in. (21.6 cm)

New York, The Metropolitan Museum of Art,
The Cloisters Collection, 1984, 1984.206

Scenes of violence are by no means uncommon in the roundel repertoire. In both examples here the assailant dispatches his victim with a sword—in one in a passageway and in the other at the dining table. Neither scene, separated from its presumed series, can be identified with certainty. It has been suggested that the Fitzwilliam roundel represents Absalom murdering Amnon in revenge for Amnon's incestuous behavior with Tamar, but according to the biblical text Absalom's servants carried out the murderous act, whereas here a dinner guest appears to be the aggressor. Contrary to the text, Absalom does not appear to be present to give the order to attack, nor can any textual basis be found—assuming that this is, in fact, a biblical scene—for the group in the right background. A roundel in the Victoria and Albert Museum corresponds more closely to the biblical account of Absalom's murder of Amnon (fig. 1).[1]

The subject of the Cloisters' roundel, likewise, remains unestablished. It was thought to represent Joab murdering Amasa, as recounted in 2 Kings 20: 9, 10: "And Joab said to Amasa: God save thee, my brother. And he took Amasa by the chin with his right hand to kiss him. But Amasa did not take notice of the sword, which Joab had, and he struck him in the side, and shed out his bowels . . . and he died." As this scene was frequently understood as a prefiguration of Christ's betrayal, the roundel may have belonged to an extended typological series. Jacob Cornelisz. van Oostsanen, for example, employed this subject as one of two prefigurations of the Betrayal, in the third edition of his circular Passion series (fig. 2; see cat. nos. 39–42). This episode, however, took place in open country, and, furthermore, much emphasis is placed on the pulling of the beard. The treacherous act is depicted as well in a fine drawing executed with accurate detail in blue washes, now in the École Nationale Supérieure des Beaux-Arts, Paris (fig. 3).[2] The particulars of the present scene accord more closely with Joab murdering Abner, as related in 2 Kings 3: 27: "And when Abner was returned to Hebron, Joab took him aside to the middle of the gate, to speak to him treacherously: and he stabbed him there in the groin, and he died." This scene, too, was frequently viewed as an antitype to the Betrayal, and it appears, for instance, in the *Biblia pauperum* block book, first published in the Lowlands about 1460 (fig. 4).

While both roundels are of exceptional quality, the techniques employed and the resulting effects are quite different. The Fitzwilliam roundel is the more archaic composition; the constricted space is overfilled with figures, while the outstretched arms and the ancillary background scenes add to the sense of frenetic activity. The action is given substance by the bold outlining of the figures and by the modeling of the matte areas, which are carefully modulated with stippling. Stickwork provides emphatic highlights to the edges of garments and to architectural elements; silver stain, used primarily to lend decorative effect to costumes, brings greater narrative weight to the foreground group.

The Cloisters' roundel is painted with dark, varying tones of matte in broad planes, worked with a brush and extensively with a stylus. The fur trim of the costumes and the details of the faces and hair assume a silvery brilliance that dramatically contrasts with the somber tonalities of paint. The action is reduced to the two looming figures in the foreground, set off by the broad angular planes of the architectural setting; the group at the rear left and the glimpse of the architecture through the window seem no more than incidental details punctuating the scene. The impact of the Fitzwilliam composition is generated by the dramatic exaggeration of the violence of the murderous act. In the Cloisters' roundel, on the other hand, the beady, deliberate gaze of Joab and the uplifted head and desperate hand gestures of Abner, all rendered in brooding tones, give the scene a psychological intensity that underscores the moral repugnancy of the treacherous murder, rather than the horror of the act itself. This raises the possibility that, while the Cambridge roundel perhaps belonged to a narrative or typological

FIG. 1 *Absalom Murdering Amnon*. Roundel. About 1520. London, Victoria and Albert Museum

FIG. 3 *Joab Murdering Amasa*. Pen and brush and blue ink, with wash, on paper. About 1560. Paris, École Nationale Supérieure des Beaux-Arts

sequence, the Cloisters' roundel may reflect Humanist influence in the development of exempla iconography, which, through a reassessment of the biblical texts, sought to incite a personal, contemplative response to specific Christological imagery, thereby engendering a form of devotionalism that emphasized a more direct relationship between the faithful and God.[3]

1. Inv. no. 5647-1859. Wayment ("Six Netherlandish Roundels," 1983, p. 388) considers this roundel the work of Pieter van den Houte of Mechelen.

2. Inv. no. M 673.

3. See Marrow, "Symbol and meaning," 1986, pp. 150–69.

BIBLIOGRAPHY: (100) Wayment, "Six Netherlandish Roundels," 1983, pp. 387–88, pl. 66. (101) Rackham, "Stained Glass in the Collection of Mr. F. E. Sidney," 1929, p. 14, fig. 2; *Collection formed by F. E. Sidney* (sale cat.), 1937, p. 10 or 12, no. 52, 53, or 75; Worcester, *Northern Renaissance Stained Glass* (exhib. cat.), 1987, p. 65, no. 26; Husband, *Silver-Stained Roundels*, 1991, p. 144.

FIG. 2 Jacob Cornelisz. van Oostsanen. *The Betrayal*. Woodcut. 1517. New York, The Metropolitan Museum of Art, The Elisha Whittelsey Collection, The Elisha Whittelsey Fund, 1949

FIG. 4 *Joab Murdering Abner*, *The Betrayal*, and *Tryphon Betraying Jonathan*. Block-book illustration from the *Biblia pauperum*. About 1460. Paris, Musée du Louvre, Département des Arts Graphiques, Collection Édmond de Rothschild

102

FIG. 1 Jan de Beer. *Studies of Heads*. Brush and black ink, with black chalk, on lilac prepared paper. About 1520. London, British Museum

FIG. 2 Jan de Beer. *Saint Luke Painting the Virgin*. Brush and black ink, with white highlights, on gray prepared paper. About 1520–25. London, British Museum

FIG. 3 Jan de Beer. *Saint Luke and the Vision of Zacharias*. Brush and black ink, with white highlights, on gray prepared paper. About 1520–25. Lille, Musée des Beaux-Arts

102 *see plate 18*

### Christ at Emmaus

Jan de Beer

South Lowlands, Antwerp, about 1520

Pen and dark gray ink and gray wash, with white highlights, on blue-gray prepared paper: diameter, 7 in. (17.8 cm)

Amsterdam, Rijksmuseum, Rijksprentenkabinet, RP-T-1939-7

Jan de Beer was registered as a pupil in the Antwerp guild of Saint Luke in 1490, became a master in 1504, and is mentioned as dean in 1515. He appears to have spent his entire career in Antwerp, where he died sometime before 1536.

In this fine rendering, Christ is flanked by two apostles; the one to the left, seen from behind, turns and looks back over his shoulder and the other, at the right, is shown in three-quarter view from the front, bending toward the center, the curve of his back echoing the circular format of the design. In the left background, the Supper at Emmaus takes place in an open, arcaded loggia. The arrangement of the figures, which suggests a clockwise movement, successfully contrives a sense of motion comfortably disposed in a circular space. The closely placed, piercing eyes and sharp-featured faces lend a nervous intensity to the figures, heightened by the agitated clusters of the drapery folds. The modeling is limited to short parallel strokes, crossed in the denser areas, apposed by the white highlights. The unusual, saturated tonalities are rarely encountered in roundel designs. The sheet has been pricked for transfer, presumably to convert the presentation sheet easily into a model or working drawing.

Very few drawings can be convincingly associated with Jan de Beer. The sheet with studies of heads, in the British Museum, inscribed *Jan de Beer* (fig. 1),[1] and the present sheet and two other drawings, one of *Saint Luke Painting the Virgin* (fig. 2) and the other of *Saint Luke and the Vision of Zacharias* (fig. 3),[2] both of which are designs for roundels on gray prepared paper, are almost certainly by the same hand.[3] Friedländer attributed two other finished drawings for roundels to de Beer: a *Martyrdom of Saint Andrew*, in Dresden, and a scene with Saints Crispin and Crispinian, in the Graphische Sammlung Albertina, Vienna.[4] A large drawing of *The Tree of Jesse* seems to be a design for a stained-glass window.[5] No working designs by Jan de Beer, or roundels based on them, appear to have survived, once again raising the question of the relationship of finished drawings to roundel production.

1. See Popham, *Drawings in the British Museum*, 1932, p. 4, no. 1.

2. The drawings are in the British Museum (1860.6.16.57; see Popham, *Drawings in the British Museum*, 1932, pp. 69–70, no. 22) and the Musée des Beaux-Arts, Lille, respectively.

3. See Boon, *Netherlandish Drawings*, 1978, p. 15, no. 27.

4. See *Early Netherlandish Painting* 11, 1974, pp. 18–19, pl. 206 A, C.

5. Ibid., p. 18, pl. 206 D.

BIBLIOGRAPHY: Boon, *Netherlandish Drawings*, 1978, p. 15, no. 27.

## 103

### The Mystical Mass of Saint Gregory

Lowlands, about 1520–25

Roundel: diameter, 8¾ in. (22.2 cm)

London, Victoria and Albert Museum,
1015-1905

The legend of the Mass of the pope and church father Saint Gregory the Great, which originated only in the fifteenth century, is related to a venerated devotional image in the church of Santa Croce in Gerusalemme, Rome. In the course of celebrating the Mass, Saint Gregory besought God to dispel his doubts concerning the true nature of the sacramental wine and the Eucharist. In response, Gregory had a vision in which Christ as the Man of Sorrows appeared on the altar surrounded by the instruments of the Passion. Exemplifying the doctrine of transubstantiation, depictions of the event—as is the case here—often show Christ's blood spurting from his wound into a chalice, demonstrating that the blood of Christ and the sacramental wine are one and the same. In wide currency at the end of the Middle Ages, the imagery of the Mass of Saint Gregory was much favored by Counter-Reformationists and adherents of Catholic dogma and tradition.[1] The inscription below an engraving by Israel van Meckenem that supposedly reproduces the Santa Croce image (fig. 1) records the popular misbelief that the original image was given to the church by Gregory in commemoration of his visionary Mass.[2]

The dramatic intensity of this scene is enhanced by the inventive use of light and shadow. The large window in the background of the church bathes the interior with light, but the central subject, Saint Gregory's mystical vision of Christ the Redeemer, is set in the dimness of the altar area shielded from the light by a curtain, which perhaps is intended to underscore the belief that only Gregory could see the vision. The diminutive standing Christ supports the cross—of proportionate scale—under his left arm, while his right hand indicates the wound from which the blood of redemption is pouring into the chalice. Interestingly, the other instruments of the Passion are depicted in full scale. Gregory, in contrast, is flooded with light coming from the opposite direction, through the gap in the curtain at the far left pushed back by the kneeling monk. In the right background, a witness points out this miraculous scene to his companion.

Rendered in rich brown tones with pale yellow silver stain, this roundel is exceptional for its painterly execution. The tonal gradations in the modeling are almost entirely built up with the application of varying densities of paint, while details are defined with a fine-pointed brush. Although there is stylus work, notably in the intrados of the window, the edges of the altar cloth, and the sleeve of the pointing witness, there is almost no working away of the matte areas, or any stickwork. The technique, like that of the Ambrosiana panel (cat. no. 56), requires a balance of surface and back lighting; under full, back light,

103

FIG. 1 Israel van Meckenem. *The Man of Sorrows*. Engraving. About 1470–80. Staatliche Museen zu Berlin, Preußischer Kulturbesitz, Kupferstichkabinett

FIG. 2 Lucas van Leyden. *David in Prayer*. Engraving. 1520. New York, The Metropolitan Museum of Art, Harris Brisbane Dick Fund, 1933

the painting takes on a rather grainy appearance that diffuses somewhat the effect of the fine brushwork. The uncommon skill of the painter can be seen in the subtle handling of the drapery folds on Gregory's left arm and on the foreshortened arm of the witness—to cite but two notable passages in this accomplished glass painting.

Wayment considered this roundel to be by Jacob Cornelisz. van Oostsanen largely because it follows the composition of a panel painting also attributed to this artist[3]—which would seem, however, to have more to do with iconographic convention than with style. The style, in general, appears to be more related to Leiden than to Amsterdam, and details, such as the fine facial features, the curious treatment of the ears, the drapery patterns of small, crinkled folds countered by broad, smooth planes, and the somber tonalities with brilliant highlights all reflect an awareness of Lucas van Leyden's engravings of the 1520s (fig. 2).

1. For a full discussion of the theme see Cologne, *Die Messe Gregors des Grossen* (exhib. cat.), 1982.

2. For a study of the Santa Croce image and Israel van Meckenem's engraving see Bertelli, "*Image of Pity,*" 1967, pp. 40–55.

3. See *King's College*, 1988, p. 62. See also Wayment, "Mass of Saint Gregory Roundel," 1989, pp. 61–62.

BIBLIOGRAPHY: Popham, "Notes-II," 1929, p. 154, fig. 3; Rackham, *Guide to Stained Glass*, 1936, p. 109; Wayment, *King's College*, 1988, pp. 62, 66, n. 25, fig. 14; Wayment, "Mass of Saint Gregory Roundel," 1989, pp. 61–62, fig. 1.

104

## 104

### Susanna Accused by the Elders

South Lowlands, about 1530

Roundel: diameter, 8⅛ in. (20.6 cm)

London, Victoria and Albert Museum, 5637-1859

Inscribed (on the decorative bands of the elder's robe): PATHR [ . . . ] / SE W CANN / VTIOVE

Brilliant surface light and subtle coloristic and textural effects are the most immediately striking qualities of this roundel. It is executed in black and reddish brown paint with deep golden silver stain. Luminosity is achieved largely through the skillful use of stickwork to indicate highlights, which are then meticulously blended into the darker recesses with the delicate use of the badger brush to work away the surface paint in gentle gradations. This deft but precise stickwork brings a silvery quality to the illuminated image. The marbleizing of the column and the use of dots of silver stain on the costume of the male figure second from the right, to suggest a silken fabric, are unusually inventive and effective applications of technique. The composition, while not dependent on the Pseudo-Ortkens designs (see cat. nos. 63–65), seems to reveal an awareness of them. The small, dark, and recessed eyes of the figures, along with the proportionately small heads relative to body height, are certainly reminiscent of

FIG. 1 After the Pseudo-Ortkens group. *Susanna Accused by the Elders.* Roundel. About 1520–30. Paris, Collection Frits Lugt, Institut Néerlandais

FIG. 2 Pseudo-Ortkens group. *Susanna and the Elders.* Pen and brown ink, with traces of black chalk, on paper. About 1520. Paris, Collection Frits Lugt, Institut Néerlandais

105

the Pseudo-Ortkens figure style. The disposition of the figures, as well as their number—which is reduced by half—is considerably altered (see fig. 1). The judge here no longer occupies his seat, backed with a cloth of honor; standing and holding the baton signifying the authority of his office, he unceremoniously leads Susanna by the skirt of her dress. The dominating presence of the column recalls the emphatic verticality of the tree trunk in the Pseudo-Ortkens composition that separates the innocence of Susanna kneeling at the fountain from the lasciviousness of the approaching elders (fig. 2). As the turbaned man at the left is the only obvious candidate for an elder, the second one would seem to be missing from this version altogether. Rather than emphasizing the confrontation between the accused and the accusers, as did the Pseudo-Ortkens painter, by grouping the two parties on opposite sides of the seated judge, the artist here emphasizes the grossly prejudicial nature of the case with the egregious behavior of the judge. The severity of the architectural setting, unrelieved by so much as a hint of landscape, adds to the harsh overtones of the scene. The two tears glistening on the cheek of the woman at the extreme left further underscore the poignancy of the unfolding drama.

An inadvertent trail of glass extends horizontally across the lower portion of the roundel. Surrounded by whorls, a large piece of frit is conspicuous just to the left of the brim of the judge holding the baton. These defects in the glass were apparently inconsequential to the glass painter, whose exceptional skill revived the narrative and visual impact of this persistently popular subject

for an audience that placed considerable value on the virtues of faith, patience, and civic justice.

The inscription on the decorative bands of the elder's robe has no apparent meaning. The surrounds are of nineteenth-century fabrication.

BIBLIOGRAPHY: Rackham, *Guide to Stained Glass,* 1936, p. 111.

105  *see plate 19*

## God Saving the Infant Jerusalem

After the Master of the Miracles of the Apostles

North Lowlands, possibly Leiden, about 1525–30

Panel, 10⅞ x 8¼ in. (27.6 x 21 cm)

Amsterdam, Rijksmuseum, NM 10175

Inscribed (at the center): vive · vive ·

Although this curious scene has never convincingly been identified, it has been suggested that it represents the infant Samuel, who was brought by his mother to the high priest Eli.[1] A more probable identification, however, which would correlate with the inscription, is with the prophecy of Ezekiel, in which he likens Jerusalem to a child abandoned at birth, but saved and lovingly reared by God: " . . . and I said to thee when thou wast in thy blood: Live: I have said to thee: Live in thy blood" ("Vive; dixi, inquam, tibi: In sanguine tuo vive") (Ezechiel 16: 6). Another panel, clearly belonging to the same series and now in the Centraal Museum, Utrecht (fig. 1),[2] shows the

child, bathed and seated on a cushion, being anointed by God, who prepares to clothe her; above is an inscription that reads, "*feci · tecū · pactum.*" " . . . and I entered into a covenant with thee . . . and I anointed thee with oil. And I clothed thee . . . " (" . . . et ingressus sum pactum tecum . . . ") (Ezechiel 16: 8–10).

The arresting composition well exemplifies the stylistic diversity, not to say eccentricity, of later roundel production. The high priest, enveloped in extravagantly patterned robes, bends over to lift up the small child, who reaches out to her protector. The preposterous proportions of this figure—accentuated all the more by his disproportionately small head—are fully revealed in the companion panel. The scene is set within a peristyle of fantastical conception, against an elaborate architectural background also of classical inspiration. The style has been associated with an anonymous draftsman known as the Master of the Miracles of the Apostles, after a series devoted to that subject from which two sheets survive: *Sapphira before the Apostles* and *Saints Peter and Paul Curing a Cripple before the Temple of Jerusalem* (fig. 2).[3] Stylistic affinities are evident, but the excesses of our glass painter are lacking. In the Oxford drawing of *Raphael Leaving the House of Tobit* (fig. 3), for example, the figures are less elongated, heads and bodies are more satisfactorily proportioned, and the architectural spaces are more rational. The intimation that the Master of the Miracles of the Apostles and this glass painter are one and the same would seem, therefore, difficult to support.[4]

The panel is painted in varying tones of dark brown and umber with trace lines of black; a rich

FIG. 2 Master of the Miracles of the Apostles. *Saints Peter and Paul Curing a Cripple before the Temple of Jerusalem.* Pen and brown ink, with brown wash, on paper. About 1530. Staatliche Museen zu Berlin, Preußischer Kulturbesitz, Kupferstichkabinett

106

FIG. 3 Master of the Miracles of the Apostles. *Raphael Leaving the House of Tobit.* Pen and brown ink, with brown wash, on paper. About 1530. Oxford, Ashmolean Museum

yellow silver stain is used mostly in the robes of the high priest and in the architectural ornament. Stickwork and the stylus were employed to lighten large areas of the pavement. The contrasting of silver stain and mattes against clear glass with black trace lines on a completely silver-stained area to suggest robes of two different fabrics achieves an arresting effect. Both surface and back painting have been used to create varied textures in the architecture. The dark and somewhat brooding nature of both the architecture and the

figures is given greater drama set, as they are, against the light paving and the bright open sky.

1. See Amsterdam, *Kunst voor de beeldenstorm* (exhib. cat.), 1986, pp. 171–72, no. 55.

2. Inv. no. 4316.

3. Paris, Musée du Louvre, Département des Arts Graphiques, 18.891, and Staatliche Museen zu Berlin, Preußischer Kulturbesitz, Kupferstichkabinett, KdZ 11993, respectively. For the Master of the Miracles of the Apostles see Amsterdam, *Kunst voor de beeldenstorm* (exhib. cat.), 1986, p. 171, no. 54.

4. Ibid., pp. 171–72, no. 55.

BIBLIOGRAPHY: Berserik, "Leiden, ca. 1480–1545," 1982, no. 159, fig. 226; Amsterdam, *Kunst voor de beeldenstorm* (exhib. cat.), 1986, pp. 171–72, no. 55.

## 106

### Followers of Christ Each Bearing His Cross

South Lowlands, possibly Antwerp, about 1560

Panel, 9⅜ x 7¼ in. (23.8 x 18.4 cm)

Amsterdam, Rijksmuseum, RBK-1992-4

The subject of this panel, Followers of Christ Each Bearing His Cross, is not from the Passion, as one might initially think, but rather is a representation of Christ's words as recounted in the Gospel according to Saint Matthew: "If any man will come after me, let him deny himself, and take up his cross, and follow me" (Matthew 16: 24). Christ is accompanied here not by Roman soldiers, tormentors, and adherents, but by a throng

of believers of all ranks, from the fashionably dressed gentleman on his left to the ragtag cripple on the ground directly behind him. All are bound together by a faith in the redemption of mankind through Christ's suffering—the identification with which is symbolized by the smaller crosses all his followers hold. Christ, carrying an almost T-shaped cross, the crossbar of which has extensively scooped-out termini, reaches out his hand beseechingly and gazes beyond the picture plane with an agonized expression, as though calling to all those who look on to join the faithful.

The painter of this roundel appears to have adopted several popular styles of Antwerp origin, mingling them in a rather eclectic fashion. The influence of Jan Swart can be seen in the facial types, with their beady eyes and their woolly hair swept forward, while the man with the high hat recalls the foreground figure in the woodcut of *Christ Preaching from a Ship* (see cat. nos. 91 and 92, fig. 1). The contorted figure of Christ, on the other hand, draped in a clinging robe accentuated by agitated tubular folds, relates more to the eccentrically mannered style of the workshop of Pieter Coecke van Aelst, such as that of the Saint John the Baptist series (cat. nos. 85–90). The grotesque misproportions of Christ's feet and lower limbs, however, exceed even the most exaggerated figures by Coecke van Aelst's workshop. If such mingled (and mangled) stylistic plagiarisms were the stock-in-trade of less creative commercial workshops, this panel is a rare example of the practice.

The present work is executed in tones of reddish brown to umber paint, enhanced with silver stain ranging in hue from pale to deep golden yellow. With minimal outlining, the figures are modeled with considerable stickwork, used not only to highlight edges and to define hair and beards but also to texture the landscape, Christ's cross, and other elements of the composition.

BIBLIOGRAPHY: "Keuze uit recente schenkingen en legaten," *Bulletin van het Rijksmuseum* 40, no. 3, 1992, p. 304, fig. 18.

## 107

### Saint Anthony Abbot and a Kneeling Donor

Lowlands, about 1530

Panel, 11½ x 14½ in. (29.2 x 36.8 cm)

Boston, Museum of Fine Arts, 56.44

107

This panel is part of a larger ensemble, now lost, which probably consisted of a central panel with a devotional image and perhaps another flanking patron saint and donor on the opposite side. Scale and subject matter make it likely that the panel originally came either from a church—perhaps connected to an Antonite or affiliate foundation—or from a private chapel. The figures are placed in an undefined space against a parapet, beyond which an expansive landscape and seascape, punctuated with rocky outcroppings and a distant town, are visible.

Comparison has been made to the donor figures in Jan van Scorel's altarpiece commissioned by the van Lockhorst family (fig. 1);[1] the faces here, however, are more individualized. More recently, Wayment has associated this panel with the work of Cornelis Jacobsz., the second son of Jacob Cornelisz. van Oostsanen;[2] as little can be attributed to him, this is a highly speculative supposition. The smooth, broad planes of the youthful, untroubled faces as well as the technique recall the style of Leuven glass painting (see cat. no. 98); the general composition and details in the treatment of the ears, hair, and drapery folds can be compared, for example, with those of a roundel representing Saint Egidius and a donor (fig. 2).[3]

The present panel is executed in shades of brown and dark brown paint and varying hues of silver stain; the modeling is achieved almost entirely by badger-brush work in the matte areas, although fine stickwork is evident in the highlighting of hair and the edges of the folds of the garments, and in the landscape. The silver stain is used sparingly, confined to the halo, landscape, and ornament. Unipartite panels rarely exceed the dimensions of this panel.

1. See Cambridge, *Medieval and Renaissance Stained Glass* (exhib. cat.), 1978, p. 84.

2. *King's College*, 1988, p. 62.

3. Leuven, Stedelijk Museum Vander Kelen-Mertens, 5.

BIBLIOGRAPHY: Cambridge, *Medieval and Renaissance Stained Glass* (exhib. cat.), 1978, pp. 83–84, no. 41; Wayment, *King's College*, 1988, pp. 62, 66, n. 24; Wayment, "Mass of Saint Gregory Roundel," 1989, pp. 62–63, fig. 3; Husband, *Silver-Stained Roundels*, 1991, p. 99.

FIG. 1 Jan van Scorel. *Saints and Donor Figures* (detail of the *van Lockhorst* altarpiece). Tempera and oil on panel. About 1526. Utrecht, Centraal Museum

FIG. 2 *Saint Egidius and a Donor*. Roundel. About 1520. Leuven, Stedelijk Museum Vander Kelen-Mertens

108

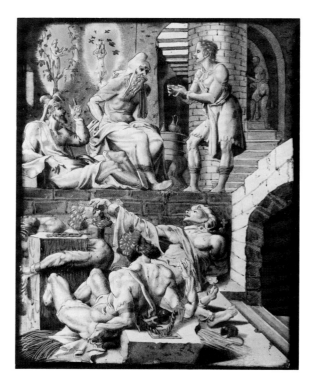

109

## 108

### Joseph Interpreting the Dreams of the Butler and the Baker

Dirck Volckertsz. Coornhert, after Maarten van Heemskerck

North Lowlands, Amsterdam, 1549

Engraving, 9⅝ x 7⅝ in. (24.4 x 19.4 cm)

Rotterdam, Museum Boymans-van Beuningen, L.1966.36

Inscribed (bottom center): *M. Hemskerck inventor. 4 / Dv Cuerenhert fecit* 1549

## 109

### Joseph Interpreting the Dreams of the Butler and the Baker

After Dirck Volckertsz. Coornhert, based on a design by Maarten van Heemskerck

North Lowlands, Amsterdam, 1550–60

Panel, 9⅝ x 7⅝ in. (24.4 x 19.4 cm)

Ghent, Bijlokemuseum, 9018

Maarten van Heemskerck was born in 1498. He worked in Haarlem with Jan van Scorel, leaving in 1532 for an extended trip through Italy, the influence of which was evident throughout his long career, spent mostly in Haarlem, where he died in 1574. The largest part of his prodigious *oeuvre* was his numerous series of prints, which were widely circulated in his own lifetime and initially were devoted to conventional biblical subjects and the lives of the saints. His later work,

influenced by Humanist writings, embraced more arcane Old Testament subjects, which were often given trenchant theological and polemical interpretation. Heemskerck at first executed his own prints but later in his career relied on professional engravers. He designed some stained-glass windows, notably those of the Carmelite church in Haarlem, for which he was paid in 1544,[1] but there is no evidence that he produced designs for silver-stained roundels. On the other hand, although there is no indication that his prints were so intended, many were used as designs for small-scale glass in both circular and rectangular formats, as the present example demonstrates.

Heemskerck executed the drawings for his Joseph series in 1549;[2] six from the original series of eight have survived, although two are fragmentary:[3] *Joseph Recounting His Dreams to His Father, Joseph Seeking His Brothers in the Plain of Sichem, Joseph Interpreting the Dreams of the Butler and the Baker, Joseph Interpreting the Dreams of the Pharaoh, Joseph's Cup Is Found in Benjamin's Sack*, and *Joseph Hosting a Banquet for His Brothers*. Dirck Volckertsz. Coornhert (1522–1590), who enjoyed a fruitful collaboration with Heemskerck, executed the engravings in 1549 and 1550.[4] Impressions of all eight numbered scenes survive, thereby preserving the compositions of the fragmentary and lost drawings;[5] the episodes missing from the series of designs are *Joseph Fleeing Potiphar's Wife* and *Joseph Embracing His Father, Isaac*—scenes three and eight, respectively.

Heemskerck, himself a master engraver, provided designs of linear clarity that the engraver

could readily follow. The engravings necessarily reverse the Heemskerck compositions, but Coornhert otherwise remained extremely faithful to the originals, frequently following the designs line for line without imparting a sense of slavish copying. In *Joseph Seeking His Brothers in the Plain of Sichem* (fig. 1), for example, the systematic hatchings of gradated densities express the tonal values of the modeling with such lucidity that Coornhert's engraving (fig. 2) is able to convey both the strength of Heemskerck's line and the powerful modeling of his muscular and volumetric figure style.

Six rectangular unipartite panels based on Coornhert's engravings are preserved in Ghent: *Joseph Recounting His Dreams to His Father; Joseph Seeking His Brothers in the Plain of Sichem*; the present scene; *Joseph Interpreting the Dreams of the Pharaoh; Joseph Hosting a Banquet for His Brothers*; and *Joseph's Cup Is Found in Benjamin's Sack*.[6] The Ghent panels are slightly increased in both dimensions. The glass painter, who appears to have copied directly from the prints, was obliged to expand the compositions somewhat by adding minor detail. In the case of *Joseph Seeking His Brothers in the Plain of Sichem*, the figures at the right side, cut off in the print, have been extended, and at the top merely open sky is added (figs. 2 and 3). As for the present examples, the architecture at the top and the right side is expanded in the panel. This simple expediency works to the detriment of *Joseph Recounting His Dreams to His Father*, where the foreground of the panel is considerably enlarged by dead space in the form of risers and landings,

FIG. 1 Maarten van Heemskerck. *Joseph Seeking His Brothers in the Plain of Sichem*. Pen and brown ink on paper. 1549. Copenhagen, Statens Museum for Kunst

FIG. 2 Dirck Volckertsz. Coornhert, after Maarten van Heemskerck. *Joseph Seeking His Brothers in the Plain of Sichem*. Engraving. 1549–50. Amsterdam, Rijksmuseum, Rijksprentenkabinet

FIG. 3 After Maarten van Heemskerck. *Joseph Seeking His Brothers in the Plain of Sichem*. Painted glass panel. 1550–60. Ghent, Bijlokemuseum

FIG. 4 Dirck Volckertsz. Coornhert, after Maarten van Heemskerck. *Joseph Recounting His Dreams to His Father*. Engraving. 1549–50. Amsterdam, Rijksmuseum, Rijksprentenkabinet

FIG. 5 After Maarten van Heemskerck. *Joseph Recounting His Dreams to His Father*. Painted glass panel. 1550–60. Ghent, Bijlokemuseum

thus compromising the balance of Heemskerck's composition (figs. 4 and 5). Beyond altering the format, the Ghent painter closely followed the engravings, but the medium imparts a very different effect. Systematic passages of parallel lines and hatchings that rigorously articulate the engraved figures are replaced, in the panels, by planes of varying tonalities of mattes that model the figures in a looser, more painterly fashion. Thin, pale mattes are juxtaposed with dense, saturated ones, while touches of sanguine, sparing but emphatic use of silver stain, stickwork highlights, and considerable areas of unpainted glass bring an exceptional tonal range to the panels that enhances their legibility and compensates for the sometimes imperfect draftsmanship.

In addition to the Ghent panels, there is also a series of roundels, based on the same series of engravings, which have been set into the centers of rectilinear windows glazed with an elaborate ornamental perspectival strapwork of Renaissance inspiration—the so-called *floris* style (see fig. 6)—that was popularized by and was characteristic of Antwerp decorative work at about the middle of the sixteenth century. Above each roundel is a device identifying the donor of the window and below is a cartouche inscribed with the corresponding biblical text in Dutch. These windows, now in Brussels, were once installed in the former convent hospital of Saint Elisabeth in Lier (Lierre), southeast of Antwerp.[7] In an effort to reconcile the different formats, the glass painter generally reduced the height of the compositions and added to the width. In *Joseph Interpreting the Dreams of the Butler and the Baker*, for example, the scene is cut down to the top of Joseph's head and the visualizations of the dreams are slightly cropped (fig. 7). In *Joseph Seeking His Brothers in the Plain of Sichem*, on the other hand, an arched opening has been added at the left (fig. 8)—a detail possibly inspired by the opening at the lower right of the present composition. The Brussels roundels are painted with greater control and precision than the Ghent panels; while tonal range in mattes and silver stain is less pronounced, the painting is enhanced with sanguine, along with a sparing use of an unusual green enamel and skillful highlighting with stickwork.

The striking rendering of this popular Old Testament story, the clarity of the compositions, and the economy of the narrative made the designs appealing to glass painters and their clients. Whether Heemskerck or his publishers provided glass painters with sets of prints on some commercial basis or whether the glass painters simply pirated the compositions is unclear. In either case, Heemskerck's prints enjoyed enduring popularity among glass painters; a series based on his Triumphs of Patience, for example, was commissioned for a house in Deventer by a namesake in 1611, sixty years after the prints were engraved.[8] The two painted glass versions of the Joseph series discussed here, however, both appear to have been executed shortly after their engraved sources.[9]

1. Veldman, *Heemskerck*, 1977, p. 13.

2. *Joseph Hosting a Banquet for His Brothers* is signed and is dated 1549, and *Joseph's Cup Is Found in Benjamin's Sack* is dated 1549 and monogrammed M.H.; *Joseph Seeking His Brothers in the Plain of Sichem* is signed.

3. Copenhagen, Statens Museum for Kunst. See Garff, *Tegninger af Maerten van Heemskerck*, 1971, nos. 28–31. For a detailed discussion of the Joseph series and the glass based on the engravings see Vanden Bemden, "Histoire de Jóseph," 1976, pp. 85–100.

4. See Veldman, New Hollstein, *Heemskerck*, part 1, 1993, pp. 54–56, nos. 43–50, and *Ill. Bartsch* 55: .007.1–8, pp. 34–41.

5. Even though popular scenes such as *Joseph Presenting Jacob to the Pharaoh* and *Joseph Buying the Stores of Grain* are wanting, the Joseph series is assuredly complete, as Heemskerck's Old Testament narrative cycles never comprise more than eight scenes.

6. Bijlokemuseum, 9013, 9014, 9018, 9015, 9019, and 9012, respectively.

7. See Helbig and Vanden Bemden, *Vitraux 3*, 1974, pp. 148–64. In anticipation of the demolition of the foundation, the glass was sold to the Musée d'Armures et d'Antiquités, then located in the Porte de Hal in Brussels; it ultimately was transferred to the Musées Royaux d'Art et d'Histoire (2017 II, III, IIII, VIIII, XI, and XII), where it remains today. Only the roundel of *Joseph Recounting His Dreams to His Father* and the text cartouches for *Joseph Fleeing the Wife of Potiphar* and *Joseph Hosting a Banquet for His Brothers* survive; these all have the inventory number 2017 D.

8. The glass was excavated in Deventer.

9. See Vanden Bemden, "Histoire de Joseph," 1976, pp. 89–90.

FIG. 6 After Maarten van Heemskerck. *Joseph's Cup Is Found in Benjamin's Sack* (detail of a leaded stained-glass window). About 1550. Brussels, Musées Royaux d'Art et d'Histoire

FIG. 7 After Maarten van Heemskerck. *Joseph Interpreting the Dreams of the Butler and the Baker* (detail of a leaded stained-glass window). About 1550. Brussels, Musées Royaux d'Art et d'Histoire

FIG. 8 After Maarten van Heemskerck. *Joseph Seeking His Brothers in the Plain of Sichem* (detail of a leaded stained-glass window). About 1550. Brussels, Musées Royaux d'Art et d'Histoire

BIBLIOGRAPHY: (108) Kerrich, *Catalogue of prints*, 1829, pp. 13–14; Veldman, New Hollstein, *Heemskerck*, part 1, 1993, p. 54, no. 46. (109) Vanden Bemden, "Histoire de Joseph," 1976, pp. 87–88, fig. 11.

## 110

### *Memento mori*

North Lowlands, about 1530

Roundel: diameter, 8¾ in. (22.2 cm)

Ghent, Bijlokemuseum, 9041

Inscribed (on the banderole): *Besiet · ons · wael · te · recht / Wer · ist · hÿr · meister · of · knecht*

The rather gruesome subject matter of this roundel addresses the transitory nature of life and the leveling effect of death. Such *Vanitas* and *Memento mori* images were common throughout the later Middle Ages, persisting through the sixteenth and seventeenth centuries. The literal reading of the inscription, "Look at us carefully and choose right / Who is called master or servant," may be rendered more poetically and closer to the flavor of the original: "Look at us and tell me which / Once was poor and once was rich."[1] While personifications of Death are fairly common in roundel iconography, *Memento mori* images are surprisingly rare. The reasons for this are unclear; by way of explanation, one might surmise that while most would not doubt the veracity of the message, perhaps far fewer would wish to have a daily visual reminder.

1. I am grateful to Tor Seidler for rendering my literal translation into a couplet that captures the sense of the rhyme.

BIBLIOGRAPHY: Vanden Bemden, "Fichier du Rondel," 1979, p. 157, fig. 7.

## 111

### The Encounter of the Marchese of Saluzzo and Griselda

Cornelis Anthonisz.

North Lowlands, Amsterdam, about 1530–50

Pen and brown ink, with black wash, on paper: diameter, 9⅝ in. (24.4 cm)

Paris, École Nationale Supérieure des Beaux-Arts, M. 1498

Cornelis Anthonisz. (commonly abbreviated Thonisz., hence his monogram CT), the son of one of Jacob Cornelisz.'s two daughters, was born about 1505, probably in Amsterdam. His earliest signed work, a portrait of a civic guard, is dated 1533. He was best known as a map maker, his most famous work the 1538 map of Amsterdam; he produced a second version in 1544. He also executed a large number of woodcuts, both princely portraits and moralizing subjects accompanied by texts—of which the Sorgheloos series is one of the better known (cat. no. 34); these were published largely in Amsterdam by Doen Pietersz. and then Jan Ewoutsz. He developed a style, much influenced by Jan van Scorel, that was char-

110

111

FIG. 1 Cornelis Anthonisz. *Gualtieri Asking Griselda for Her Hand*. Pen and brown ink, with black wash, on paper. About 1530–40. Paris, École Nationale Supérieure des Beaux-Arts

FIG. 2 Cornelis Anthonisz. *Allegorical Figure of Ill Fortune*. Pen and brown ink, with gray wash, on paper. About 1530–40. London, British Museum

acterized by a relaxed, fluid line. The attribution to him of several drawings for roundels is made purely on a stylistic basis; there is no documentary evidence to establish Cornelis Anthonisz.'s activity as a designer of glass.

The present sheet represents a scene in the story of Gualtieri, the marchese of Saluzzo, and Griselda, the peasant girl he married, as recounted in book ten of Boccaccio's *Decameron*. Uncertain of his wife's faithfulness and constancy, Gualtieri contrives a number of dreadful trials to test Griselda, including giving her the impression that he has murdered their two children, shamming a divorce and a new marriage, and reducing her to rags with the intention of sending her back to her peasant hovel. All this Griselda endures with patience and utter faithfulness to her husband. Finally convinced of her unfailing merits, Gualtieri reveals his ruse, restores her to honor, and the two live on in great contentment. In the scene here, Gualtieri has set out with his riding party; happening upon the beautiful Griselda washing her father's laundry, he determines to marry her. In another drawing from the same series, Griselda has been led out of her house, and, in front of his assembled company, Gualtieri asks Griselda if she will marry him (fig. 1).[1]

The composition is organized in much the same way as Cornelis's opening scene in his 1541 Sorgheloos series (cat. no. 30), but this in itself is insufficient to support an attribution to Cornelis. The inclination to monumentalize the figures, the penchant for open-handed gestures, and the tendency to terminate folds of drapery in small right angles or hooks all appear to be stylistic charac-

teristics of Cornelis. The precise but fluid pen strokes are without alteration, and the washes are applied with complete assurance. The distinctive technique, in which the forms are outlined in pen and ink and modeled with brushstrokes of different washes, recalls that of Vellert in the 1520s (see cat. nos. 69–71). Several other drawings by the same hand are known, and all, including a rectilinear drawing in the British Museum representing the allegorical figure of Ill Fortune, appear to be designs for glass (fig. 2).[2]

1. Paris, École Nationale Supérieure des Beaux-Arts, M. 1499.

2. Inv. no. 1921.10.8.19. See Popham, *Drawings in the British Museum*, 1932, pp. 48–49, no. 1. A further drawing for a roundel, representing a birth scene, perhaps the birth of Saint John the Baptist, is now in the Staatliche Graphische Sammlung, Munich, 982.

BIBLIOGRAPHY: Wescher, "Cornelis Teunissen," 1928, pp. 34–35, fig. 1; Wegner, *Niederländischen Handzeichnungen*, 1973, p. 10; Paris, *Renaissance et Maniérisme* (exhib. cat.), 1985, p. 112, no. 55; Munich, *Niederländische Zeichnungen* (exhib. cat.), 1989, pp. 11–12, no. 3, fig. 3.

# 13

# Lambert van Noort

*Lambert van Noort was born about 1520 in Amersfoort, near Utrecht, in the North Lowlands. He probably received his training in the workshop of Jan van Scorel in Utrecht. In 1549 he joined the Antwerp guild of Saint Luke, and the following year he became a citizen of Antwerp. From that time on he is frequently recorded in the documents of that city. In March 1561 he rented a house from the Church of Our Lady in the Cammerstraat in the center of Antwerp, where his five children, including the painter Adam van Noort, were born. Van Noort's wife, Katelijne van Broeckhuysen, died before September 1, 1570, and the artist's death followed hers within a year—sometime before June 24, 1571—perhaps as a result of the plague.*

Van Noort, like many other artists in the first half of the sixteenth century, was trained as a painter, but a sizable portion of his *oeuvre* consisted of designs for works of art to be executed by other artists. This separation between design and execution was based on the theoretical importance of *inventio*, as compared with the material realization of a concept. Van Noort's *oeuvre* includes some paintings and comprises drawings for prints and architectural projects, but, above all, the production consists of working designs for stained glass, varying from roundels and larger panels to monumental church windows. A small number of drawings served as designs for other branches of the decorative arts, such as goldsmiths' work and tapestries.

Van Noort's designing activity for roundels is concentrated in the decade of the 1550s and is, therefore, representative of the very last phase of the blossoming of roundel production in the Lowlands. His designs continue in a way the characteristics of Jan Swart's approach.[1] The main literal source of his narrative material is the Bible—generally, the Old Testament. The choice of the subjects is often determined by their moralistic undertones. His close adherence to the texts made him invent extensive series, like the Story of Noah, which comprises twelve sheets. The scenes correspond closely to the biblical descriptions, but are often embellished with architecture in the Renaissance style. Considering the large number of van Noort's drawings for roundels and unipartite panels—some forty altogether—it is surprising to find today no more than seven of his designs realized in small-scale glass and none of these was made from an existing drawing. The sheet with *The Healing of Tobit* in Munich (cat. no. 113) and the associated roundel (cat. no. 114) provide the closest parallel between a drawing by van Noort and an executed glass panel. In addition to the different format and the reversed composition, however, the several sketches below the main scene indicate that the Munich drawing was intended as a study for van Noort's own use, not as a working design for the roundel. *The Disembarking of the Animals* (cat. no. 112), on the other hand, was certainly executed as a working design, but no corresponding roundel for this or any other scene from the series has survived. That van Noort's designs were also indirectly used by glass painters may be proved by the Nebuchadnezzar panels (cat. nos. 115 and 116). The engraved series dated 1558, made from his designs, was copied within some fifty years by at least three different glass painters.

About 1558–59, van Noort made a trip to Italy, and after his return he rarely produced any more designs for roundels. The diminishing demand for these works of art must have played a role in focusing his attention on monumental stained glass from then on; the best of these specimens are the three still-extant Gouda windows executed from his designs. There is no proof in the archives of an affiliation with any glass painter other than with the workshop of Digman Meynaert in Antwerp, which included his nephew Hans Scrivers. It was responsible for the Gouda windows and also might have painted roundels from van Noort's designs, together with a certain Gerrit, who scratched his name in a panel (cat. no. 115).

1. For a discussion of the influence of Jan Swart on van Noort see van Ruyven-Zeman, "Lambert van Noort Inventor," Ph.D. diss., 1990, pp. 118–19.

112

## 112

### The Disembarking of the Animals

Pen and brown ink, with blue wash, on light brownish paper: diameter, 10⅜ in. (26.4 cm)

Paris, Collection Frits Lugt, Institut Néerlandais, 8881

Signed and dated (bottom center): *Lambert. a. / Noort. de. amorsfo / Inven= / 1557*

This is the tenth sheet in a series consisting of twelve drawings and comprising one of the most detailed illustrations of the Story of Noah in the art of the Lowlands. The series starts with *Building the Ark* and ends with *The Sacrifice of Noah* (Genesis 6: 13–9: 17). The ten scenes in between depict *The Embarking of the Animals*, *The Embarking of Noah and His Family*, *The Deluge* (fig. 1), *Noah Sending Off a Raven*, *Noah Sending Off the First Dove*, *Noah Sending Off the Second Dove* (fig. 2), *The Second Dove Returning with an Olive Leaf*, *Noah Sending Off the Third Dove*, *The Disembarking of the Animals*, and *Building the Altar* (fig. 3). The series, divided among three museums and a private collection, appears to have survived in its entirety.[1] Another extensive treatment of the subject is the series of prints by Cornelis Cort after designs by Maarten van Heemskerck of 1558–59, which consists of six sheets. Only the third, *The Deluge*, seems to have been preserved in the form of an oval panel now in a Maastricht private collection.

As the twelve images seem to make a complete series, it is unlikely that the ensuing episode, the Drunkenness of Noah, was also included in the sequence. Only the present sheet and *Building the Altar* (fig. 3) are signed in full; the others are monogrammed. All the drawings are dated and include the word "Inventor." This refers to the fact that van Noort was responsible only for the designs, which then served as working drawings for the glass painter who executed the roundels.

Noah, seen from the back, occupies the foreground of the present drawing; his wife stands next to him. Two of his three sons, Shem, Ham, and Japheth, are depicted with their wives, to the left and right of Noah. The third couple is situated close to the gangplank of the ark, from which pairs of various kinds of animals are disembarking.

Van Noort follows the structural details of the ark given in Genesis: It has three stories and a roof. Furthermore, to suggest a structure from antiquity, this ark is fashioned in Renaissance style, with a pediment and a barrel vault, and is decorated with pilasters and sculpture. Van Noort's view of the bow of the ark is equally impressive (fig. 4). The use of pen with brown ink and blue wash is characteristic of the artist's roundel designs. Unlike some of van Noort's cartoons for church windows, roundel designs never include color indications, for it was up to the glass painter to enliven the design with the relatively narrow choice of colors available at that time; other than the brown and black matte vitreous paints, the artist was limited to varying shades of silver stain and sanguine. The sheet is trimmed within the perimeter of the circumference, leaving only traces of the ink line, and is foxed throughout.

In keeping with the moralizing tendencies of sixteenth-century art in the Lowlands, van Noort's

FIG. 4 Lambert van Noort. *The Return of the Second Dove with an Olive Leaf*. Pen and brown ink, with blue wash, on paper. 1557. Amersfoort, Museum Flehite

113

Noah series no doubt conveyed more to the contemporary viewer than the mere chronicling of events as recounted in Genesis. A paragon of faith and righteousness, Noah was spared the fate suffered by the rest of mankind, as the faithlessness and wickedness of the old world was destroyed and replaced by the progeny of Noah in a new one. The role of Noah as the virtuous progenitor of the new order may have been seen in terms of political allegory. For example, a series of ten tapestries representing the Story of Noah, commissioned by King Philip II and executed from 1563 to 1566,[2] perhaps was meant as an allusion to the king's role as the just and noble protector of the New World. A series of roundels as extensive as that designed by van Noort might well have been intended for a civic setting as an admonition against unjust or unrighteous behavior.

1. *The Embarking of the Animals* belongs to R. C. Noortman, Maastricht, and *The Deluge* to the Rijksmuseum, Amsterdam (RP-T-19:54). Excepting the present drawing, those remaining in the series—nine in all—are in the Museum Flehite, Amersfoort (S 11–S 19).

2. See Junquera de Vega, "'L'Histoire de Noé,'" 1973, pp. 143–71.

BIBLIOGRAPHY: Anzelewsky et al., *Zeichnungen im Berliner Kupferstichkabinett*, 1973, pp. 48–49, no. 66; Boon, *Netherlandish Drawings*, 1978, p. 133, no. 378, n. 2; Florence, *L'Époque de Lucas de Leyde* (exhib. cat.), 1981, pp. 163–64, no. 113, pl. 37; Munich, *Niederländische Zeichnungen* (exhib. cat.), 1989, p. 57; van Ruyven-Zeman, "Lambert van Noort Inventor," Ph.D. diss., 1990, pp. 166–68, T.9.10; Boon, *Drawings of the Frits Lugt Collection*, 1992, pp. 279–80, no. 155, pl. 68.

## 113

## The Healing of Tobit

Antwerp, about 1555

Pen and grayish brown ink, with brown and gray wash and white highlights, on paper, 10 x 10⅜ in. (25.4 x 26.4 cm)

Munich, Staatliche Graphische Sammlung, 21147

Inscribed (on the column, in another hand): *N*

The subject of this drawing is taken from the perennially popular apocryphal Book of Tobit (see cat. nos. 12–14).[1]

The present sheet, which might have been part of a series, depicts the climax of the story. Tobias, accompanied, as ever, by his dog as well as by the archangel Raphael, whose real identity is still not known to him, restores his father's sight by applying the gall of the fish caught in the River Tigris to his eyes. Behind Tobit is his wife, Anna, and probably the young bride, Sarah, with a servant. The Story of Tobit, a paradigm of unflagging patience and faith in the face of persistent tribulation finally being rewarded, struck a responsive chord in a broad audience. The apotropaic role played by the guardian angel Raphael, whose name means "God heals," also contributed to the appeal of the story. Van Noort seems to have departed from an older design generally attributed to Jan Swart, preserved via a late copy by Rubens (1577–1640) in the Musée du Louvre, Paris (fig. 1).[2] The figures on the left in the present drawing are arranged more effectively in the space, although the composition of the architecture in the background is not clear.

FIG. 1 Peter Paul Rubens, after Jan Swart van Groningen. *The Healing of Tobit*. Pen and brown ink, with brown wash, on paper. End of the 16th century. Paris, Musée du Louvre, Département des Arts Graphiques

FIG. 2 Lambert van Noort. *The Marriage of Tobias and Sarah*. Pen and light brown ink on paper. 1562. Amsterdam, Rijksmuseum, Rijksprentenkabinet

114

FIG. 3 Lambert van Noort. *The Entombment*. Pen and brown ink, with blue wash, over black chalk on paper. Before 1555. Brussels, Musée d'Art Ancien

The drawing is executed on an almost square sheet of paper; a circle was circumscribed by the artist over the finished design. The right feet of Sarah and of Raphael fall outside the circle, just like the minuscule heads at the bottom of the page; these appear to be the remains of sketches of two young women and of Tobit and Raphael that probably once were part of a preparatory drawing on the same sheet before it was trimmed. The Munich drawing also shows traces of white where corrections were made, and thus represents a stage in the genesis of a roundel or print design. A roundel in Leuven (cat. no. 114) may reflect a subsequent composition by van Noort of this same subject. There is another drawing of *The Marriage*

of *Tobias and Sarah*, monogrammed and dated 1562, which is similar in format and also has a circle superimposed over the composition (fig. 2);[3] whether this linear drawing, very likely intended as a working design, relates to the same series as the present sheet or to an altogether different and later series with this subject is uncertain.

The present sheet is neither signed nor does the monogram appear to be autograph, but it most likely was made for Lambert van Noort's own studio use, and the attribution to him by Wegner is fully convincing on the basis of the figure style.[4] Similar women occur in *The Entombment* (fig. 3)—among other compositions—a drawing from an extensive monogrammed series of the Passion of Christ; probably all these works are designs for glass panels dating from shortly before 1555.[5]

1. Cole (*Roundels in Britain*, 1993, p. 334), for example, indexed over seventy roundels depicting scenes from the Story of Tobit.

2. Département des Arts Graphiques, 20282. The drawing is one in a series of eight sheets illustrating the events from the moment that Anna receives a goat until the benediction of old Tobit on his deathbed. See Paris, *Rubens, ses maîtres, ses élèves* (exhib. cat.), 1978, pp. 71–72, nos. 63–70. For two sixteenth-century roundels that closely follow the Paris composition of *The Healing of Tobit* see Cole, *Roundels in Britain*, 1993, p. 4, no. 24, p. 145, no. 1166.

3. Amsterdam, Rijksmuseum, Rijksprentenkabinet, RP-T-11:86. See also van Ruyven-Zeman, "Lambert van Noort Inventor," Ph.D. diss., 1990, p. 169, T.12, fig. 111.

4. *Niederländischen Handzeichnungen*, 1973, p. 22.

5. van Ruyven-Zeman, "Lambert van Noort Inventor," Ph.D. diss., 1990, pp. 175–78, T.19.12, fig. 22.

BIBLIOGRAPHY: Wegner, *Niederländischen Handzeichnungen*, 1973, p. 22, no. 80, 2, fig. 28; Munich, *Niederländische Zeichnungen* (exhib. cat.), 1989, pp. 57–58, pl. 32; van Ruyven-Zeman, "Lambert van Noort Inventor," Ph.D. diss., 1990, p. 170, T.13, fig. 10.

## 114

### The Healing of Tobit

South Lowlands, about 1555–60

Roundel: diameter, 10¼ in. (26 cm) [without modern border]

Leuven, Katholieke Universiteit, Kunstpatrimonium, ARG 4

Van Noort's compositional effort for *The Healing of Tobit* did not stop with the Munich sheet, as the design of this roundel evidences. Essentially a reversed image of the Munich composition, with slight alterations, it differs primarily in the shifting aside of the central group of Tobit and Tobias, whereby the representation of the protagonists in three-quarter view and in profile is inverted. The background wall has the same elevation as in the Munich drawing, but is shown in a clearer and more spacious arrangement reminiscent of the Louvre sheet (cat. no. 113, fig. 1). The landscape view to the left gives greater depth to the composition.

The design of this roundel only recently has been considered to be by van Noort. It certainly

115

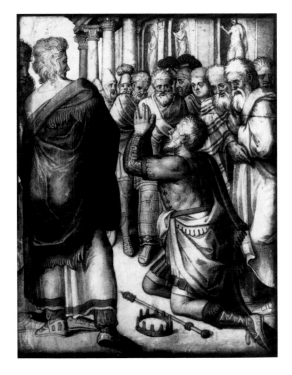

116

did not form a pair with the fragment in the Stedelijk Museum Vander Kelen-Mertens in Leuven, since the style and execution are wholly different.[1] The mannered figure of Tobias and the improvement in composition make this design slightly posterior to the Munich drawing, suggesting a date of about 1555 or somewhat later.

The execution of the roundel has been ascribed to the Leuven glass painter Pieter Boels—a most hypothetical attribution for lack of clear indications and any signed work by him.[2] He is recorded to have executed a series depicting the Story of Tobit in 1564 for the winter refectory of Park Abbey near Leuven. In view of the reversed composition, as compared to the Munich sheet, and the fact that Tobias anoints his father with his left hand, the anonymous glass painter may have worked from a van Noort design for a print. The technique of execution and the close adherence to the designer's style suggest a date immediately after 1555 for the roundel. Painted with touches of sanguine, it has a horizontal break and a vertical break below, both of which have been glued and restored.

1. Inv. no. 49; stylistic similarities seen by Maes, *Leuvens Brandglas,* 1987, pp. 295–96, no. 49, fig. 185.

2. Leuven, *Ars sacra antiqua* (exhib. cat.), 1962, G.26.

BIBLIOGRAPHY: Helbig, *Glasschilderkunst,* 1943, no. 1704; Leuven, *Ars sacra antiqua* (exhib. cat.), 1962, G.26; Maes, *Leuvens Brandglas,* 1987, pp. 296–98, fig. 187; Munich, *Niederländische Zeichnungen* (exhib. cat.), 1989, pp. 57–58, fig. 45; van Ruyven-Zeman, "Lambert van Noort Inventor," Ph.D. diss., 1990, pp. 214–15, G.IX.

## 115

### The Crowning of Nebuchadnezzar

After Hans Liefrinck, based on a design by Lambert van Noort

Antwerp (?), about 1558–75

Panel, 10⅛ x 7⅝ in. (25.7 x 19.4 cm)

Cambridge, King's College Chapel, 27g2

Incised (in the drapery around the neck of the figure at the left): *Gerrit*

## 116

### Nebuchadnezzar Kneeling to Praise God

After Hans Liefrinck, based on a design by Lambert van Noort

Antwerp (?), about 1558–75

Panel, 10 x 7⅝ in. (25.4 x 19.4 cm)

Cambridge, King's College Chapel, 27f2

The subjects of these two panels are from the rarely illustrated story of the second dream of King Nebuchadnezzar and its interpretation, taken from the Book of Daniel (4: 1–13), one of the four great Old Testament prophets. The glass panels follow the seventh and eighth numbered iron-plate etchings, respectively, in a series of eight by Hans Liefrinck (about 1518–1573), published by him in 1558 in Antwerp (figs. 1 and 2).[1] The subjects of the six previous scenes from the full cycle represent Nebuchadnezzar, King of Babylon, dreaming of a tree that has to be cut down; Nebuchadnezzar consulting the wise men of his country about the dream; Daniel interpreting the dream and foretelling the king's downfall and possible restoration to power; a voice from Heaven revealing to the king his punishment; the king, overcome by madness, being stripped of his crown and sent into exile; and, finally, the king, on hands and knees, eating grass, among the beasts of the field (fig. 3).

The designs of the etchings have been attributed until recently to Maarten van Heemskerck on the authority of Kerrich, to whom only the fifth and sixth sheets in the series were known.[2] The figure style, however, is so close to that of signed drawings by Lambert van Noort from 1555 on that he must be considered the designer.[3] In both panels, a strong diagonal is established by the placement of the principal figures—a characteristic of van Noort's compositional arrangements. In the first panel, the diagonal disposition of the courtiers and the king suggests depth in a space otherwise lacking clear definition. Also typical of van Noort is the use of elaborate Renaissance architecture for backgrounds, the splendor of which, in the second panel, has been somewhat diminished by the trimming of the top. The glass painter edited out some compositional elements of the etchings, such as—again in the second panel—the figure at the far right and the house in the upper-left background; he also simplified the anatomy of the king, revealed through his garments. The etchings thus served as models for the glass painter, who, to judge from the incised name, was called Gerrit. It is not a frequently occurring name among the artists inscribed in the Ligger, or guild register, of Antwerp.[4]

FIG. 1 Hans Liefrinck, after Lambert van Noort. *The Crowning of Nebuchadnezzar.* Etching. 1558. Antwerp, Stedelijk Prentenkabinet

FIG. 2 Hans Liefrinck, after Lambert van Noort. *Nebuchadnezzar Kneeling to Praise God.* Etching. 1558. Antwerp, Stedelijk Prentenkabinet

Only the two last panels of this series seem to have been preserved. The corresponding widths of the glass panels and the prints indicate that the latter were used as cartoons; both panels, however, appear to have been trimmed on the top. The glass painter reworked the designs in a simplified but more decorative manner, embellishing the gowns of some figures with stripes. He employed the point of the brush in a skillful, painterly manner, most evident in his treatment of the hair and the facial features (fig. 4). His ample use of silver stain and sanguine in two hues renders him a special place among the glass painters of the third quarter of the century and gives his work a liveliness of expression.[5]

Another version of *Nebuchadnezzar Kneeling to Praise God*, trimmed more extensively at the top, is at Strawberry Hill (fig. 5).[6] It is executed solely in black paint, the highlights etched with a stylus, and it adheres more closely to van Noort's design. This glass painter went to great lengths to emulate the monochromatic effects of light and shadow of the etching, while his probably older colleague Gerrit paid less attention to these, aiming instead for a most colorful result, letting the sanguine paint, originally meant for flesh color, counterbalance the silver stain.

An oval panel from a third series based on van Noort's series of designs is in a private collection in Hillsborough, California, and represents the sixth scene: Nebuchadnezzar, in a mad state, grazes on his hands and knees among the beasts of the field (fig. 6).[7] The popularity of the series was no doubt due in large measure to the moralizing nature of the story, warning against the per-ils of hubris. The choice of this subject, for which no earlier parallels are found, is all the more remarkable, since it is the Babylonian king—the enemy of the Jews—who is restored to power. With the Story of Nebuchadnezzar, Daniel—the personification of Justice (his name means "God judges")—promises mercy to all who show penitence. It was perhaps this reassuring aspect of the story, in a period of religious turbulence, that accounts for the sudden interest it evoked.

1. See van Ruyven-Zeman, "Lambert van Noort Inventor," Ph.D. diss., 1990, pp. 203–4, P.II.

2. See Kerrich, *Catalogue of prints*, 1829, pp. 32–33; also Hollstein 8, p. 247, nos. 506–511.

3. For further detail see van Ruyven-Zeman, "Lambert van Noort Inventor," Ph.D. diss., 1990, pp. 63, 203–4, P.II.6, fig. 70.

4. If the execution is, indeed, by an Antwerp artist, Geert de Perre or Geeraert Potter could be possible candidates. The former is documented in 1549 as a pupil of the glazier Cornelis van Houte, and the latter in 1557 as a master glass painter. See Rombouts and Lerius, *Antwerpsche Sint-Lucasgilde* 1, 1872, pp. 168, 200.

5. For a dating in the third quarter of the sixteenth century see Wayment, *King's College*, 1988, p. 84. Cole (*Roundels in Britain*, 1993, p. 42, no. 355) dates the panel too late, in my opinion, placing it at the end of the sixteenth or the beginning of the seventeenth century. If, however, the execution was this late, colored enamel surely would have been added. Another late-sixteenth- to early-seventeenth-century current in Haarlem shows a preference for black paint only. See, for example, Husband, *Silver-Stained Roundels*, 1991, p. 21, colorplates 13 and 14.

6. See Cole, *Roundels in Britain*, 1993, p. 283, no. 2242.

7. See Husband, *Silver-Stained Roundels*, 1991, p. 51, Inv. no. 968. This glass panel is also a simplified version of the etching, omitting the architectural view and high hills in the background.

BIBLIOGRAPHY: (115) Wayment, *King's College*, 1988, p. 87, no. 27g2; van Ruyven-Zeman, "Lambert van Noort Inventor," Ph.D. diss., 1990, pp. 215–16, G.X.1, fig. 73; Cole, *Roundels in Britain*, 1993, p. 42, no. 355. (116) Wayment, *King's College*, 1988, p. 84, 27f2; van Ruyven-Zeman, "Lambert van Noort Inventor," Ph.D. diss., 1990, pp. 215–16, G.X.2, fig. 74; Cole, *Roundels in Britain*, 1993, p. 41, no. 352.

FIG. 4 *The Crowning of Nebuchadnezzar* (detail of cat. no. 115)

FIG. 3 Hans Liefrinck, after Lambert van Noort.
*Nebuchadnezzar Eating Grass*. Etching. 1558.
Antwerp, Stedelijk Prentenkabinet

FIG. 5 After Lambert van Noort. *Nebuchadnezzar
Kneeling to Praise God*. Painted glass panel. 1558–75.
Twickenham, Middlesex, Strawberry Hill

FIG. 6 After Lambert van Noort. *Nebuchadnezzar Eating
Grass*. Painted glass panel. 1558–75. Hillsborough,
California, Private collection

# 14

## Dirck Pietersz. Crabeth

*Dirck Pietersz. Crabeth, the son of Pieter Dircxsz., must have been born in Gouda about 1520. He is mentioned in the archives of that city from 1545 until his death in 1574, and was the most accomplished of the several stained-glass painters with the surname Crabeth. Little is known of his training, although the influence of Jan Swart van Groningen is evident in his earlier works and that of Frans Floris in those of his later years. He is known by document to have supplied a window for the Catharijneconvent in Utrecht in 1540 and, subsequently, he executed other windows for churches in The Hague, Delft, and Amsterdam. From 1555 he worked almost exclusively on the windows of the church of Saint John in Gouda, finishing the last one in 1570, four years before his death.*

Although the roundel "industry" was sustained largely by secular clients, virtually no glass has remained in its original setting, and the provenance of displaced glass is rarely known. A series of eight panels with richly ornamental architectural surrounds, now belonging to the Musée des Arts Décoratifs, Paris (cat. nos. 117–120), is an eye-arresting exception: These windows came from the still-extant house at Pieterskerkgracht 9 in Leiden, and were almost certainly commissioned by Adriaen Dircxz. van Crimpen from Dirck Crabeth in, or slightly before, 1543. Further informing us of the original context of this remarkable glass are two of the original mullioned windows embellished with caryatid stiles (see cat. no. 124) and three mid-nineteenth-century watercolors, which illustrate the glass panels and their window frames still *in situ* (see cat. no. 125). Adding to our understanding of the creative process are several original designs for narrative scenes (cat. nos. 121 and 122) that show Crabeth, best known for his monumental windows for the church of Saint John in Gouda begun in 1555 (fig. 1, p. 199), already as an accomplished and

innovative draftsman early in his career. The Leiden windows appose Old and New Testament scenes, reminiscent of early typological arrangements, but the choice of subjects—Samuel and the apostle Paul—has little to do with the Christological medieval models and the significance is not well understood today. Crabeth and other artists of his era, reflecting the tensions of Catholic and reformist thought, created numerous works that explored all aspects of Christian doctrine. Even though the resulting images were largely intended for private use, overt or strident postulations were not without risks. As a result, religious imagery of the period is frequently eclectic, mingling old ideas with new and eschewing controversial doctrinal forms. Catholic and Protestant sympathies were, as a consequence, not always easy to detect.[1] Only as reformist activity inexorably drifted toward violence, which, in the Lowlands, erupted in the iconoclastic rampages beginning in 1566, did roundel imagery become polarized and polemical. A series of roundel designs devised by Crabeth in the 1560s (cat. nos. 126–128), for example, evidently inspired by Spiritualist writings, flagrantly attacks one of the fundamental tenets of the Catholic faith, the doctrine of Good Works. This series, produced at the dawn of iconoclasm, thus stands as a harbinger of the religious conflict that effectively brought the flowering of roundel production in the Lowlands to a precipitous close.

1. For discussions of the artistic and intellectual climate in the Lowlands during the period of Reformation and its effects on art and iconography see Parshall, "Kunst en reformatie," 1987, pp. 164–75, and Zijp, "De iconografie van de reformatie," 1987, pp. 176–92.

FIG. 1 Dirck Pietersz. Crabeth. *The Expulsion of Heliodorus from the Temple.* Window. 1555. Gouda, Church of Saint John

117

118

119

120

117–120   *see plate 21*

## Samuel Is Brought to the High Priest Eli; The Banquet of Samuel and Saul; The Preaching of Paul; The Blinding of Elymas

Four windows from the house at Pieterskerkgracht 9, Leiden

Panels, with leaded ornamental surrounds, 117 and 118: 43⅛ x 25½ in. (109.5 x 64.8 cm); 119 and 120: 39⅛ x 25½ in. (99.4 x 64.8 cm)

Paris, Musée des Arts Décoratifs, 46517 C, 46517 D, 46518 C, and 46518 D

Inscribed (on the pediments of the upper panels): 1543

Perhaps the only documented examples of a secular provenance, these windows came from the large town house known as the *Pax Huic Domui*, at Pieterskerkgracht 9 in Leiden.[1] The owner of the house, and presumably the commissioner of the windows, was Adriaen Dircxz. van Crimpen, bailiff and *dykgraaf* of Rijnland from 1537 on.[2] Three drawings made by Gerardus Johannes Bos in 1846 of the windows in their original frames establish that initially at least twelve paired panels, pedimented scenes over arcaded ones—two pairs each—were glazed into three separate mullioned windows (fig. 1).[3] These windows each consist of a central unipartite panel leaded into elaborate and highly decorative architectural surrounds complemented with swags, putti, birds, and animals. The architectural settings, composed of parapeted arcades, colonnades, aediculae, ped-

imented *tempietti*, friezes, and entablatures, un-abashedly follow classical Italianate models; there is not a hint of the *floris*-style strapwork ornament that was the vogue among the Antwerp Mannerists (see cat. nos. 108 and 109, fig. 6). The upper panels, with the pedimented central scenes, each have, in the upper corners, a pair of coats of arms, two of which have been identified as those of the van der Does and Burnier families, while the others are more tentatively thought to be the arms of the van Crimpen, van Rosendael, Erasmus, van Oudewater, Cant, Pauw, and Loen families.[4]

The house was sold in 1844, and although the glass was still there in 1846 it must have been sold shortly thereafter by the new owners, who ordered its removal, perhaps out of recognition of the importance of the glass (in 1856, the house was in use as a school). The panels were included in the 1861 Soltykoff sale in Paris, by which time the original twelve had been reduced to eight; these eight panels appeared again in the 1890 sale of the collection of Baron Achille Seillière. They were then acquired by the stained-glass painter Georges Néret through whose daughter they came to the Musée des Arts Décoratifs.[5]

In addition to the eight panels now in the Musée des Arts Décoratifs, the Bos drawings (fig. 1) inform us of two other Old Testament scenes. To these may be added two further scenes—one from the Old and one from the New Testament—which do not appear in the Bos drawings but are known from Crabeth's original designs (see cat. nos. 121–123, figs. 1 and 3). Seven of these scenes are from the first Book of

Samuel (Kings 1 and 2) and five from the Acts of the Apostle Paul; in correct narrative order they are: 1. *Samuel Is Brought to the High Priest Eli by His Parents*: ". . . with three calves, and three bushels of flour . . . she brought him to the house of the Lord . . . and offered the child to Heli" (1 Kings 1: 24–25).; 2. *God Calling Samuel*: " . . . Samuel slept in the temple of the Lord . . . And the Lord called Samuel" (1 Kings 3: 3–4).; 3. *The Battle for the Ark of the Covenant* (fig. 2; see also cat. no. 121): "So the Philistines fought, and Israel was overthrown . . . And the ark of God was taken: and the two sons of Heli, Ophni and Phinees, were slain" (1 Kings 4: 10–11).; 4. *The Philistines Taking the Ark of the Covenant to the Temple of Dagon*: "And the Philistines took the ark of God, and carried it from the Stone of help into Azotus" (1 Kings 5: 1).; 5. *Samuel Offering a Sacrificial Lamb to Yahweh and the Israelites Defeating the Philistines*: "And Samuel took a sucking lamb, and offered it whole for a holocaust to the Lord . . . when Samuel was offering the holocaust, the Philistines began the battle against Israel: but the Lord thundered . . . And the men of Israel . . . made slaughter of them" (1 Kings 7: 9–11).; 6. *The Banquet of Samuel and Saul*: ". . . And Samuel said: . . . set it before thee, and eat: because it was kept of purpose for thee, when I invited the people. And Saul ate with Samuel that day" (1 Kings 9: 24).; 7. *Samuel Anointing Saul* (fig. 3): "And Samuel took a little vial of oil, and poured it upon his head" (1 Kings 10: 1).; 8. *The Vision of Saint Paul* (see cat. nos. 121, 122, and 123, fig. 3): ". . . suddenly a light from heaven shined round about him. And falling on the

FIG. 2 Dirck Pietersz. Crabeth. *The Battle for the Ark of the Covenant*. Painted and leaded-glass panel. 1543. Paris, Musée des Arts Décoratifs

FIG. 3 Dirck Pietersz. Crabeth. *Samuel Anointing Saul*. Painted and leaded-glass panel. 1543. Paris, Musée des Arts Décoratifs

FIG. 4 Dirck Pietersz. Crabeth. *Paul before the Magistrates of Philippi*. Painted and leaded-glass panel. 1543. Paris, Musée des Arts Décoratifs

FIG. 5 Dirck Pietersz. Crabeth. *Paul amid the Areopagus*. Painted and leaded-glass panel. 1543. Paris, Musée des Arts Décoratifs

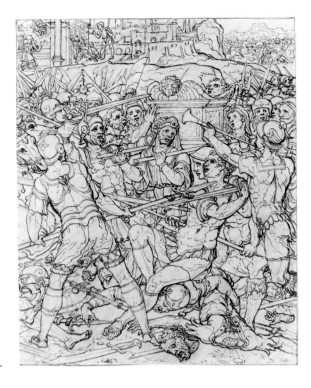

121

122

ground, he heard a voice" (Acts 9: 3–4).; 9. *The Preaching of Paul*: "And immediately he preached in the synagogues, that he is the Son of God" (Acts 9: 20).; 10. *The Blinding of Elymas*: ". . . the hand of the Lord is upon thee, and thou shalt be blind, not seeing the sun for a time" (Acts 13: 11).; 11. *Paul before the Magistrates of Philippi* (fig. 4): "And presenting them to the magistrates, they said: These men disturb our city" (Acts 16: 20).; and 12. *Paul amid the Areopagus* (fig. 5): ". . . Paul standing in the midst of the Areopagus" (Acts 17: 22).[6]

The misordering of the known panels and the loss of an uncertain number of others make the reconstruction of the series all but impossible (see cat. nos. 123 and 124). The use of parallel stories from the Old and New Testaments recalls medieval typological arrangements in which the old order prefigures the new. Of all the extant scenes in this series, however, only *God Calling Samuel* and *The Vision of Saint Paul*, in the traditional sense, relate typologically. This may indicate that many scenes are missing, but, more probably, a figurative apposition was intended in which the emphasis was placed not on the affirmation of prophecy but on Man, his calling by God, and the fulfillment of his mission on earth. This interpretation is consistent with the current tendency to place greater importance on individual responsibility in developing a relationship with God.[7]

There were at least three different hands—presumably from one workshop—involved in the execution of the narrative scenes.[8] *Samuel Is Brought to the High Priest Eli*, *The Banquet of Samuel and Saul*, and *Samuel Anointing Saul*—

notwithstanding the darker tonalities of the paint and the silver stain in the last—belong to one group; *The Philistines Taking the Ark* and *Paul before the Magistrates* to another; and the remaining three scenes with Paul represent yet another hand. The quality of the painting remains exceedingly high throughout; characteristic of the workshop are a skillful balance in the use of the stylus, the point of the brush, and the badger brush to achieve the subtle and finely gradated modeling, and the calculated distribution of silver stain as a counterpoint to the monochromatic planes, enhancing the sense of spatial depth.

1. For a study of this house, its history, and its restoration see Dröge, *Pieterskerkgracht 9*, 1982.

2. Although no document exists, there is little doubt that the windows originally were commissioned for this residence by Adriaen van Crimpen.

3. Leiden, Stedelijk Museum de Lakenhal, 31280-5 (1-3). See Wurfbain et al., *Catalogus*, 1983, pp.78–79, no.553.

4. See Bouchon, in Amsterdam, *Kunst voor de beeldenstorm* (exhib. cat.), 1986, pp. 284–85, nos. 160.1–8.

5. Ibid., p. 285.

6. Numbers 3, 7, 11, and 12 are in the Musée des Arts Décoratifs, Paris, 46517 A, 46517 B, 46518 A, and 46518 B, respectively; number 8 is known only from the Crabeth drawing in the Collection Frits Lugt, Paris, 8429; and numbers 2 and 4 are known only through Bos's 1846 drawing.

7. For a discussion of the influence on typological imagery of Humanist thought and new forms of religiosity, from about the 1530s, see Miedema, "De bijbelse ikonografie van twee monumenten," 1978, esp. pp. 71 and 87.

8. See Bouchon, in Amsterdam, *Kunst voor de beeldenstorm* (exhib. cat.), 1986, p. 285.

BIBLIOGRAPHY: (117–120) Pelinck, "Geschilderde vensters," 1940, pp. 193–200; Dröge, *Pieterskerkgracht 9*, 1982, pp. 13–14; Wurfbain et al., *Catalogus*, 1983, pp. 79–80, nos. 553, 712, 712 A and B; Amsterdam, *Kunst voor de beeldenstorm* (exhib. cat.), 1986, pp. 284–85, nos. 160.1–8.

### 121

### The Battle for the Ark of the Covenant

Gouda, about 1543

Pen and dark brown ink, with traces of black chalk, on paper, 10⅛ x 8 in. (25.7 x 20.3 cm)

Leiden, Prentenkabinet der Rijksuniversiteit, PK 3687

### 122

### The Banquet of Samuel and Saul

Gouda, about 1543

Pen and dark brown ink, with traces of black chalk, on paper, 10¼ x 8 in. (26 x 20.3 cm)

Leiden, Prentenkabinet der Rijksuniversiteit, PK 2159

### 123

### The Banquet of Samuel and Saul

North Lowlands, about 1543

Panel, 10¼ x 7⅞ in. (26 x 20 cm)

The Netherlands, Private collection

These two drawings, along with three others, appear to be original working designs by Dirck Crabeth for the central scenes of the windows installed in the *Pax Huic Domui* at Pieterskerkgracht 9 in Leiden (cat. nos. 117–120). Two of the three other drawings, representing *Samuel Is Brought to the High Priest Eli* (fig. 1) and *Samuel Offering a Sacrificial Lamb to Yahweh and the Israelites Defeating the Philistines* (fig. 2), recently were acquired by the Rijksmuseum.[1] The third sheet, representing *The Vision of Saint Paul* (fig. 3), is in Paris;[2] a panel based on this design is in the parish church of Saint Mary the Virgin in Addington, Buckinghamshire.[3] These drawings reveal Crabeth's gifted draftsmanship, already apparent in his early work. In *The Battle for the Ark of the Covenant* a dense throng of soldiers is in the middle of a fray; swords are brandished, a spear impales a throat, a trumpet is sounded, men fall on the dying and the dead, and the ground is littered with weaponry, a severed head, and a hand. The bristling halberds, spears, and pikes create a play of lines that draw attention to the ark of the covenant—the focus of the composition—traditionally surmounted by cherubim and borne on poles on the shoulders of the priests. In the left background, Samuel has a vision foretelling the ruination of Eli and his family, and Eli,

123

FIG. 1 Dirck Pietersz. Crabeth. *Samuel Is Brought to the High Priest Eli by His Parents.* Pen and black ink, over black chalk, on paper. 1543. Amsterdam, Rijksmuseum, Rijksprentenkabinet

FIG. 2 Dirck Pietersz. Crabeth. *Samuel Offering a Sacrificial Lamb to Yahweh and the Israelites Defeating the Philistines.* Pen and black ink, over black chalk, on paper. About 1543. Amsterdam, Rijksmuseum, Rijksprentenkabinet

FIG. 3 Dirck Pietersz. Crabeth. *The Vision of Saint Paul.* Pen and black ink on paper. About 1543. Paris, Collection Frits Lugt, Institut Néerlandais

hearing that his sons Hophni and Phinehas have been killed in battle, falls backward in shock and breaks his neck. In the right background the Israelites and Philistines are engaged in battle. The composition is dominated by a sense of *horror vacui*. Bodies merge with one another; full-muscled forms—Crabeth often depicts at least one figure from behind—are firmly outlined with bold pen strokes; the sheer drapery flutters, falling in small, agitated folds where it clings to the body, revealing the underlying anatomy; and facial features are given expression with terse wavy or hooked lines. The composition is at once narrative and decorative, dense but legible. The Romanist tendencies reflect the direct influence of Jan van Scorel and Jan Swart.

Swart's influence is evident in *The Banquet of Samuel and Saul*: Its composition has much in common with that of Swart's *Feast of Ahasuerus* (see cat. no. 93). Here, the short, nervous lines of the drapery folds are in profusion, and the dinner table, although densely populated with figures pressed close together, brings a welcome calm to the composition, in sharp contrast to the frenetic tone of the first sheet. The design for *The Vision of Saint Paul* (fig. 3) is the only one in the series to include a biblical inscription: on the rays from above are the words *Saul quid me p[er]sequeris* ("Saul, why persecutest thou me?") (Acts 9: 4), and below center, Saul (Paul)'s response, *dñe qd meVisfacere* ("Lord, what wilt thou have me to do?") (Acts 9: 6). Unusual in the composition of *Samuel Is Brought to the High Priest Eli by His Parents* (fig. 1) are the strong diagonals of the figural groupings, the use of architecture to frame these groups, and the apposition of voids and solids to define spatial relationships, all of which seem to reflect an awareness of Dirick Vellert's later roundel compositions (see cat. nos. 77–80).

In addition to the panels from the *Pax Huic Domui*, there are replicas of *The Banquet of Samuel and Saul* and of *The Anointing of Saul* (fig. 4).[4] Both are executed in shades of gray to black paint and hues of pale and deep yellow silver stain. The contours are indicated with strong trace lines, while the forms are modeled with stippled matte reinforced with heavier trace lines. The silver stain is used to enhance details such as pillows, elements of the costumes, and the foreground. Stylus work is employed throughout to indicate details of the hair and beards and to highlight drapery folds and parts of the costumes, while etching with the aid of a straightedge serves to highlight the outlines of the architecture. Both panels appear to have been painted by the same hand responsible for the Leiden versions (cat. nos. 119 and 117–120, fig. 3). Indeed, these panels came to the present owners by descent, as a gift from the widow of Johannes Kneppelhout, the owner of the *Pax Huic Domui* from 1858.[5] Although roundel series were generally made in multiples according to market demand, why two versions of the same composition would share the same provenance is unclear. The glass of the present *Banquet* panel is warped, causing a vertical bow. There is a vertical break just to the left of center that has been glued, and it is possible that

FIG. 4 After Dirck Pietersz. Crabeth. *The Anointing of Saul*. Painted glass panel. About 1543. The Netherlands, Private collection

FIG. 5 Dirck Pietersz. Crabeth. *The Israelites Slaying Sihon and the Amorites*. Pen and black ink, over black chalk, on paper. About 1543. Amsterdam, Rijksmuseum, Rijksprentenkabinet

FIG. 6 Jan Swart van Groningen. *The Israelites Slaying Sihon and the Amorites*. Woodcut. Before 1528. Amsterdam, Rijksmuseum, Rijksprentenkabinet

FIG. 7 After Dirck Pietersz. Crabeth. *The Destruction of the Rebels against Moses.* Pen and umber ink, over black chalk, on paper. About 1540–50. Paris, École Nationale Supérieure des Beaux-Arts

FIG. 8 After Dirck Pietersz. Crabeth. *The Destruction of the Rebels against Moses.* Painted glass panel. About 1545–55. Dundalk, Ireland, Church of Saint Nicholas

FIG. 9 After Dirck Pietersz. Crabeth. *Moses Closing the Red Sea on the Pharaoh's Army.* Painted glass panel. About 1545–55. Rotterdam, Museum Boymans-van Beuningen

the panel has been slightly recut along the lower edge.

The Samuel and Saul series was not Crabeth's only project for small-scale glass; an extensive cycle of the Story of Moses and Aaron, from the Book of Numbers, can be partially reconstructed from surviving designs and executed glass. In the Rijksprentenkabinet of the Rijksmuseum in Amsterdam is a design for a panel representing *The Israelites Slaying Sihon and the Amorites* (Numbers 21: 21–24) (fig. 5).[6] Details of the composition are identical to those of *The Battle for the Ark of the Covenant,* and both recall Jan Swart's woodcut composition of the former subject for the 1528 Vorsterman Bible (fig. 6). Three other drawings from the same Moses series— *The People of Israel in Elim* (Numbers 33: 9), *Joshua and Caleb Returning from Eschol* (Numbers 13: 24), and *The Blossoming Rod of Aaron* (Numbers 17: 8)—are also in the Rijksmuseum, Amsterdam.[7] Another drawing, apparently by the same hand as these Rijksmuseum drawings, and representing *The Destruction of the Rebels against Moses,* is in Paris (fig. 7);[8] the composition of this drawing, which includes the design for the upper lunette of the window, appears in a similar form in a woodcut illustration in the 1528 Vorsterman Bible and in a 1530 woodcut by Hans Sebald Beham.[9] The scene, which shows Korah, Dathan, and Abiram consumed by flames and swallowed up in the earth as the Israelites depart with Moses and Aaron (Numbers 16: 15–35), is unusual for its bifurcated composition. A panel based on this design is in the parish church of Saint Nicholas in Dundalk, Ireland (fig. 8).[10]

Another panel, by an altogether different hand, representing *Moses Closing the Red Sea on the Pharaoh's Army* (Exodus 14: 27–28), now in the Museum Boymans-van Beuningen, Rotterdam (fig. 9),[11] is probably from a different cycle of the Story of Moses, based on the Book of Exodus. Both panels are of lesser quality than those in the Samuel and Paul series.

1. Inv. nos. RPK-T-1984-84 and 85. The former was published and illustrated by van Gelder ("Nog een teekening voor klein glas," 1946, pp. 33–34) but its whereabouts were unknown; the latter heretofore was unrecorded. See "Keuze uit de aanwinsten," *Bulletin van het Rijksmuseum* 41, no. 1, 1993, pp. 32–33, figs. 2 and 3.

2. Collection Frits Lugt, Institut Néerlandais, 8429. See Boon, *Drawings of the Frits Lugt Collection,* 1992, pp. 105–6, no. 62.

3. See Cole, *Roundels in Britain,* 1993, p. 5, no. 35.

4. See Coebergh-Surie, in Amsterdam, *Kunst voor de beeldenstorm* (exhib. cat.), 1986, pp. 289–90, nos. 162 and 163.

5. Ibid., p. 289, no. 162.

6. Inv. no. RPK-T-13-9. See Boon, *Netherlandish Drawings,* 1978, pp. 58–59, no. 159.

7. Inv. nos. RPK-T-13-7, 8, and 10, respectively. See Boon, *Netherlandish Drawings,* 1978, p. 58, nos. 156–159.

8. École Nationale Supérieure des Beaux-Arts, M. 700. See Brugerolles, in Paris, *Renaissance et Maniérisme* (exhib. cat.), 1985, pp. 132–33, no. 65.

9. See Amsterdam, *Kunst voor de beeldenstorm* (exhib. cat.), 1986, pp. 290–92, no. 165, esp. p. 292, fig. 166a.

10. Ibid., pp. 292–93, no. 166.

11. Ibid., nos. 166 and 167.

BIBLIOGRAPHY: (121 and 122) van der Boom, *Monumentale glasschilderkunst,* 1940, pp. 280–82; Pelinck, "Geschilderde vensters," 1940, pp. 199–200; van Regteren Altena, "Klein glas van 1543 door Dirck Crabeth," 1940, pp. 200–206, figs. 4 and 2, respectively; Paris, *Old Master Drawings* (exhib. cat.), 1985, pp. 80–86, nos. 29 and 30; Amsterdam, *Kunst voor de beeldenstorm* (exhib. cat.), 1986, pp. 290–91, nos. 165 and 164, respectively. (123) van der Boom, *Monumentale glasschilderkunst,* 1940, pp. 280–83; van Regteren Altena, "Klein glas van 1543 door Dirck Crabeth," 1940, pp. 200–206, fig. 1; Rijksen, *Glasschilderingen van de St. Janskerk te Gouda,* 1947, p. 70; Pelinck, "Het huis Pieterskerkgracht 9 en zijn bewoners," 1957, p. 121; Amsterdam, *Kunst voor de beeldenstorm* (exhib. cat.), 1986, p. 290, no. 163.

## 124

**Interior View of the House at Pieterskerkgracht 9, Leiden**

Gerardus Johannes Bos

Leiden, 1846

Pen and ink, pencil, and watercolor, on paper, 7⅝ x 6⅛ in. (19.4 x 15.6 cm)

Leiden, Stedelijk Museum de Lakenhal, 712

## 125

**Window Frame, from the House at Pieterskerkgracht 9, Leiden**

Leiden, about 1543

Carved and fitted oak, 91¾ x 63⅜–64¼ in. (233 x 161–163.2 cm)

Leiden, Stedelijk Museum de Lakenhal, 2449

In addition to the drawings of the three two-over-two windows once in the *Pax Huic Domui* at Pieterskerkgracht 9 in Leiden (cat. nos. 117–120, fig. 1), Gerardus Bos also executed three watercolor views of the interior showing the original situation of these windows. The present sheet depicts an upstairs corridor in the *"achterhuis,"* with the panels installed in their mullioned window frames; the undecorated lower sections open onto the interior, and the upper sections are secured with caryatid stiles. A second view, this one through an open door looking back into the corridor from the other direction, shows that, in the connecting corridor, there was an additional single-register two-light window with partially draped female caryatid stiles, also facing into the inner courtyard (fig. 1), while a third watercolor depicts another window the same in format but with composite-beast stiles (fig. 2).[1] By 1846, both of these single-register windows were without stained glass.

Two carved window frames were removed from the house in 1897 and entered the collections of the Stedelijk Museum de Lakenhal the following year.[2] Both are very similar in design and format to the three depicted in Bos's 1846 drawing (cat. nos. 117–120, fig. 1), differing primarily in the form of the caryatids: The present window has female figures draped from the waist down and the other, grotesque composite beasts (fig. 3). This means that there must have been at least five such two-over-two windows, in addition to the two single-register double-light windows seen in the upper corridor (see figs. 1 and 2). The original position of the surviving windows is unknown, but they may have been located, like the other three, on the upper floor, facing into the inner courtyard.[3] Whether these windows were glazed with further scenes of Samuel and Paul set within architectural surrounds is, likewise, unknown, but, theoretically, twenty-four panels could have been accommodated. The fanciful stiles, vigorous if somewhat unrefined, are a striking foil to the precision and grace of the classical forms and strapwork surrounding the stained-glass panels.

124

125

FIG. 1 Gerardus Johannes Bos. *Interior View of Windows at Pieterskerkgracht 9, Leiden.* Watercolor. 1846. Leiden, Stedelijk Museum de Lakenhal

FIG. 2 Gerardus Johannes Bos. *Interior View of Windows at Pieterskerkgracht 9, Leiden.* Watercolor. 1846. Leiden, Stedelijk Museum de Lakenhal

FIG. 3 *Window Frame from the House at Pieterskerkgracht 9, Leiden.* By 1543. Leiden, Stedelijk Museum de Lakenhal

1. Inv. nos. 712 B and 712 A, respectively. See Wurfbain et al., *Catalogus*, 1983, pp. 79–80.

2. See Amsterdam, *Kunst voor de beeldenstorm* (exhib. cat.), 1986, p. 289, nos. 161.1–2.

3. See Pelinck, "Het huis Pieterskerkgracht 9 en zijn bewoners," 1957, pp. 120, 123.

BIBLIOGRAPHY: (124) Wurfbain et al., *Catalogus*, 1983, pp. 79–80, no. 712; Amsterdam, *Kunst voor de beeldenstorm* (exhib. cat.), 1986, p. 289, fig. 160 b. (125) Pelinck, "Het huis Pieterskerkgracht 9 en zijn bewoners," 1957, pp. 120–21, 127; Dröge, *Pieterskerkgracht 9*, 1982, pp. 13–15; Amsterdam, *Kunst voor de beeldenstorm* (exhib. cat.), 1986, pp. 288–89, nos. 161.1–2.

## 126

### The Triumph of Christ and Faith as the True Way

Frans Huys

Antwerp, about 1560

Engraving, 10⅝ x 14 in. (27 x 35.6 cm)

Amsterdam, Rijksmuseum, Rijksprentenkabinet, RP-P-1989-172

## 127

### Christ as the Redeemer of Mankind

Gouda, about 1560–65

Pen and brown ink, over black chalk, on paper, 12⅝ x 7½ in. (32.1 x 19.1 cm)

Amsterdam, Rijksmuseum, Rijksprentenkabinet, RP-T-1960-175

Inscribed in a later hand: (on the arm of the cross) *Exaltatus a terra traham vīā ad me ipsum*; (above the mouth of John the Baptist) *ecce ag.nos* [?] *dei qui tollit pecā mūdi*; (to the right of the mouth of Man) *trahe me*

## 128 *see plate 20*

### Christ as the Redeemer of Mankind

North Lowlands, about 1560–65

Panel, 24 x 7¾ in. (61 x 19.7 cm)

Amsterdam, Rijksmuseum, RBK-1984-45

The present engraving is the eleventh in a series of twelve, after the work of an unknown designer; the last bears the monogram of the engraver Frans Huys, who was active in Antwerp in the mid-sixteenth century. The set of prints, which comprises twenty-four numbered scenes paired on twelve sheets, is unmistakably Protestant in tone; the detailed allegorical imagery traces Man's search for salvation in the wake of the Fall, relating his struggle against sin, false practices, doubt, and faithlessness, and his ultimate redemption through faith and the grace of God.[1] On each sheet, two scenes are framed within a double arcade below which is a frieze with inscriptions providing elucidation in both Latin and a dialect apparently spoken in East Friesland, especially in Emden.[2] As Horst has clearly established, Dirck

126

Der aen dem Cruts verwonnen hätt
Sundt duvell hell vnd ewich dött
Vp den Iohannes weiset claer
Met sambt der gants Propheten schaer

Vnd wirt dan smenschen gloeff gemehertt
Von dagh tho dagh dair durch geheertt
Dat Christus is die doer vnd baen
Durch den men moet thom Vader gaen .

*Qui, neci fronte virs, & vicit Auerni
Regna, & stygi regna profunda soli.
Deniq, quem digito monstrat Baptista Ioannes.
Quemq, prophetarum cælica turba docet . 22 .*

*Tuæ fidei crescens hominis sub pectore lumen,
Te, quamis maius lucibiud, dic
Atq, viam, rutuli quæ ducat ad ætria cæli.
Sydereti natum principis esse docet . 22 .*

127

128

FIG. 1 Frans Huys. *The Creation of Eve and The Fall*. Engraving. About 1560. Amsterdam, Rijksmuseum, Rijksprentenkabinet

FIG. 2 Frans Huys. *Man Is Bound by Disobedience and Man Is Chastised by Sin*. Engraving. About 1560. Amsterdam, Rijksmuseum, Rijksprentenkabinet

Crabeth borrowed from these prints in designing a series of glass panels devoted to the same theme.[3] The first print in the series represents God creating Eve from Adam's rib, paired with the Fall and the personification of God's wrath seen holding a skull, to indicate the punishment for mortal sin (fig. 1). In the second print in the series, Man is bound to a tree by Disobedience in one scene, and, in the next, he is chastised by Sin (fig. 2). In the first panel of his series, Crabeth conflates the first three engraved scenes, loosely following their compositions (fig. 3). In ensuing scenes, Man encounters Moses and the Law, which underscores his sin, and is driven hopelessly to the mouth of hell, after which Man is then deluded into believing he can variously save himself through blind intellect, by penitential acts, or by good works. God's will to save all those who place faith above intellect is expressed by juxtaposing the Annunciation with Man rendered deaf by his intellect to Christ's words (fig. 4); the composition of this last scene is closely followed in Crabeth's design (fig. 5).[4] The subsequent episodes represent Man and Intellect carrying the image of Good Works, only to find that Good Works are of no avail when Man is pursued by the fear of Death; with the fear of Death come Doubt and Conscience, which turn Man toward the mercy of God. The mantle of Man's sinful ways is sloughed off and he is spiritually reborn, whereupon he violently attacks Good Works with a club (fig. 6). The present engraving, the next in the sequence, depicts, in one scene, Christ's victory over Sin and Death and, in the other, an angel demonstrating that only through Christ can Man reach God; the pres-

ent drawing combines elements of these two scenes. The two scenes in the final engraving show Man, accompanied by "old Adam" and supported by Faith, Hope, and Patience, being persecuted for his convictions; finally, with a preacher reading the Scriptures to him, Man peacefully succumbs to "Sweet Death."

As the rejection of penitential acts lay at the heart of virtually all the Protestant theologies, the scene of redeemed Man violently confronting Good Works, in particular, is unusually strident in its anti-Catholicism. Boon has demonstrated that the author of the engraved verses was familiar with the writings of the Anabaptist reformer David Joris (1505–1556), which frequently addressed the concept of spiritual rebirth, the road to which is filled with trials and tribulation.[5] That Man must suffer and turn away from worldly concerns was preached by, among others, Thomas Müntzer of Zwickau, who, contrary to Martin Luther, also believed that the Bible should not be taken literally, but given spiritual interpretation. Other Spiritualists, including Joris, espoused similar, if less radical, views. Joris held that the Crucifixion provided an exemplum through which the true believer could overcome all evil and death itself, and could spiritually rise again. In Crabeth's design, here, and in the glass panel based on it, spiritually reborn or baptized Man, standing naked between Saint John the Baptist and Faith—who holds a Eucharistic chalice—points to Christ, carrying the burdens of mankind up the ladder to his sacrificial death. A quatrain on the back of the Amsterdam sheet states the message that is explicitly illustrated in the second scene in the

present engraving: "*Doort Geloove liet hi dan gewis / Dat hoope in Christo alleene gelt / Die tot den Vader D'eenige poorter is Soe ons claerlich . . . schrift . . . melt*" ("By faith he learns for certain that Christ is the only gate leading to the Father").[6]

The pen work of the present drawing, which is executed with linear clarity, appears to develop and clarify a preliminary charcoal sketch; as there is virtually no indication of reworking with the pen, Crabeth apparently made all adjustments to the composition in charcoal, rubbing away discarded details. Typically, Crabeth filled the picture field with large, tightly massed figures that bleed off the edges, and provided only the slightest indication of landscape.

The glass panel, which appears to be trimmed at the top, displays a fairly narrow range of brownish to dark gray paint. A dark, orangy yellow silver stain enhances the costumes, the chalice, and Christ's halo, while a pale yellow is employed throughout the ground area. The silver stain is used to particular effect on Christ's halo, as it draws attention to his head, which, otherwise, would be less conspicuous in the design among the mass of figures climbing the ladder. Contours are strongly outlined in black trace lines, and forms are modeled with a fine-pointed brush over mattes, augmented by an overall working with the stylus. The brush and stylus are used equally to define volumes and contours, and for sculptural effect. The skill of the painter is best demonstrated in the fine stylus work and trace-line rendering of Faith's trailing drapery, which reveals the modeled muscular forms underneath.

FIG. 3 After Dirck Pietersz. Crabeth. *The Creation and The Fall*. Painted glass panel. About 1560. Amsterdam, Rijksmuseum

FIG. 4 Frans Huys. *The Annunciation and Man Is Rendered Deaf by Intellect to Christ*. Engraving. About 1560. Amsterdam, Rijksmuseum, Rijksprentenkabinet

FIG. 5 After Dirck Pietersz. Crabeth. *Man Is Rendered Deaf by Intellect to Christ*. Pen and dark brown ink, over black chalk, on paper. 1560. Paris, École Nationale Supérieure des Beaux-Arts

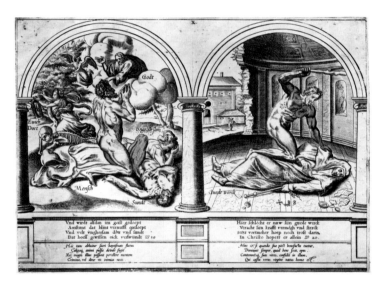

FIG. 6 Frans Huys. *Man's Sinful Ways Are Sloughed Off and Man Attacking Good Works*. Engraving. About 1560. Amsterdam, Rijksmuseum, Rijksprentenkabinet

1. For a thorough study of this series, and the relationship of the engravings to Dirck Crabeth, see Horst, "de Heilsweg van de Mens," 1990, pp. 3–24.

2. See Boon, *Drawings of the Frits Lugt Collection*, 1992, p. 109, n. 5.

3. See note 1.

4. Paris, École Nationale Supérieure des Beaux-Arts, M. 698. See Paris, *Renaissance et Maniérisme* (exhib. cat.), 1985, p. 130, no. 64.

5. See Boon, *Drawings of the Frits Lugt Collection*, 1992, pp. 107–8, 109, n. 5.

6. Ibid., p. 108.

BIBLIOGRAPHY: (126) Boon, *Netherlandish Drawings*, 1978, pp. 60–61, no. 163; Horst, "de Heilsweg van de Mens," 1990, pp. 3–24, esp. pp. 12–14, fig. 18; Boon, *Drawings of the Frits Lugt Collection* 2, 1992, p. 254, fig. 19. (127) Florence, *L'Époqué de Lucas de Leyde* (exhib. cat.), 1981, pp. 88, 89, n. 1; "Keuze uit de aanwinsten," *Bulletin van het Rijksmuseum* 33, no. 2, 1985, p. 128, fig. 8 a; Amsterdam, *Kunst voor de beeldenstorm* (exhib. cat.), 1986, p. 359, no. 240; Horst, "de Heilsweg van de Mens," 1990, pp. 13–15, fig. 20; Husband, *Silver-Stained Roundels*, 1991, p. 26, fig. 25; Boon, *Drawings of the Frits Lugt Collection*, 1992, pp. 107, 108–9, n. 3, and 2, p. 254, fig. 19. (128) Boon, *Netherlandish Drawings*, 1978, p. 60, under no. 163; "Keuze uit de aanwinsten," *Bulletin van het Rijksmuseum* 33, no. 2, 1985, p. 125, no. 8, p. 129, fig. 8; Amsterdam, *Kunst voor de beeldenstorm* (exhib. cat.), 1986, pp. 359–61, no. 241.

# Bibliography

"Accessions," 1958
  "Accessions of American and Canadian Museums, October–December, 1957," *The Art Quarterly* 21, 1958, p. 92.

"Accessions," 1960
  "New Accessions," *Museum News* (The Toledo Museum of Art), 3, 1960, p. 50.

Adolf, "The Ass and the Harp," 1950
  Helen Adolf, "The Ass and the Harp," *Speculum* 25, 1950, pp. 49–57.

Amsterdam, *Bijbelsche Kunst* (exhib. cat.), 1939
  Amsterdam, *Tentoonstelling Bijbelsche Kunst* (exhib. cat.), Rijksmuseum, 1939.

Amsterdam, *Middeleeuwse kunst* (exhib. cat.), 1958
  Amsterdam, *Middeleeuwse kunst der Noordelijke Nederlanden* (exhib. cat.), Rijksmuseum, 1958.

Amsterdam, *Vorstenportretten* (exhib. cat.), 1972
  Amsterdam, *Vorstenportretten uit de eerste helft van de 16de eeuw. Houtsneden als propaganda* (exhib. cat.), by D. de Hoop Scheffer and A. J. Klant-Vlielander Hein, Rijksmuseum, Rijksprentenkabinet, 1972.

Amsterdam, *Lucas van Leyden — grafiek* (exhib. cat.), 1978
  Amsterdam, *Lucas van Leyden — grafiek (1489 of 1494–1533)* (exhib. cat.), by Jan Piet Filedt Kok et al., Rijksmuseum, Rijksprentenkabinet, 1978.

Amsterdam, *Kunst voor de beeldenstorm* (exhib. cat.), 1986
  Amsterdam, Rijksmuseum, *Kunst voor de beeldenstorm. Noordnederlandse kunst 1525–1580 (De eeuw van de beeldenstorm)* (exhib. cat.), ed. by J. P. Filedt Kok et al., The Hague, 1986.

Andrews, *Fifty Master Drawings*, 1961
  Keith Andrews, *Fifty Master Drawings in the National Gallery of Scotland*, Edinburgh, 1961.

Andrews, *Catalogue of Netherlandish Drawings*, 1985
  Keith Andrews, *Catalogue of Netherlandish Drawings in the National Gallery of Scotland*, 2 vols., Edinburgh, 1985.

Antwerp, *Antwerp* (exhib. cat.), 1993
  Antwerp, Hessenhuis, *Antwerp, story of a metropolis. 16th–17th century* (exhib. cat.), ed. by Jan Van der Stock, Ghent, 1993.

Anzelewsky et al., *Zeichnungen im Berliner Kupferstichkabinett*, 1973
  Fedja Anzelewsky et al., *Vom späten Mittelalter bis zu Jacques Louis David. Neuerworbene und neubestimmte Zeichnungen im Berliner Kupferstichkabinett*, Berlin, Staatliche Museen Preußischer Kulturbesitz, Kupferstichkabinett, 1973.

Appuhn et al., *Riesenholzschnitte*, 1976
  Horst Appuhn and Christian von Heusinger, *Riesenholzschnitte und Papiertapeten der Renaissance*, Unterschneidheim, Germany, 1976.

Armstrong, *Moralizing Prints*, 1990
  Christine Megan Armstrong, *The Moralizing Prints of Cornelis Anthonisz*, Princeton, 1990.

Ludwig von Baldass, "Notizen über holländische Zeichner des XVI. Jahrhunderts. I. Pieter Cornelisz," *Mitteilungen der Gesellschaft für vervielfältigende Kunst. Beilage der "Graphischen Künste"* 38, 1915, pp. 25–29.

Baldass, "Jan Swart," 1918
  Ludwig von Baldass, "Notizen über holländische Zeichner des XVI. Jahrhunderts. III. Jan Swart van Groningen," *Mitteilungen der Gesellschaft für vervielfältigende Kunst. Beilage der "Graphischen Künste"* 41, 1918, pp. 11–21.

Baldass, "Dirk Vellert als Tafelmaler," 1922

Ludwig von Baldass, "Dirk Vellert als Tafelmaler," *Belvedere* 1, 1922, pp. 162–67.

Baltimore, *Time Sanctified* (exhib. cat.), 1988
  Baltimore, Walters Art Gallery, *Time Sanctified. The Book of Hours in Medieval Art and Life* (exhib. cat.), by Roger S. Wieck et al., New York, 1988.

Bangs, *Documentary Studies*, 1976
  Jeremy D. Bangs, *Documentary Studies in Leiden Art and Crafts, 1475–1575* [Leiden], 1976.

Jeremy D. Bangs, "Maerten van Heemskerck's *Bel and the Dragon* and Iconoclasm," *Renaissance Quarterly* 30, 1977, pp. 8–11.

Jeremy D. Bangs, *Cornelis Engebrechtsz.'s Leiden. Studies in Cultural History*, Assen, The Netherlands, 1979.

Bangs, "The Leiden monogramist," 1981
  Jeremy D. Bangs, "The Leiden monogramist PC and other artists' enigmatic fire buckets," *Source* 1, no. 1, 1981, pp. 12–15.

Jeremy M. Bangs, "Rijnsburg Abbey: Additional Documentation on Furniture, Artists, Musicians, and Buildings, 1500–1570," *Bulletin van de Koninklijke Nederlandse Oudheidkundige Bond* 74, 1975, pp. 182–90.

Engelbert Baumeister, "Zwei Glasfensterentwürfe des Jan Swart van Groningen," *Wallraf-Richartz-Jahrbuch*, n.s., 1, 1930, pp. 222–24.

T. D. S. Bayley and Francis W. Steer, "Glass at Stanley Hall, Pebmarsh," *Journal of the British Society of Master Glass-Painters* 12, no. 3, 1958, pp. 183–90.

Beeh-Lustenberger, *Glasmalerei in Darmstadt*, 1973
  Suzanne Beeh-Lustenberger, *Glasmalerei um 800–1900 im Hessischen Landesmuseum in Darmstadt* (Kataloge des Hessischen Landesmuseums, no. 2), 2 vols., Frankfurt am Main, 1973 (plate volume published 1967).

Beets, "Dirick Jacobsz. Vellert," 1908
N[icolaas]. Beets, "Dirick Jacobsz. Vellert, Schilder van Antwerpen. III. Vroege teekeningen," *Onze Kunst* 13, 1908, pp. 165–88.

Beets, "Pieter Cornelisz. Kunst," 1909
N[icolaas]. Beets, "Pieter Cornelisz. Kunst, glasschrijver en . . . . . schilder?" *Bulletin van den Nederlandschen Oudheidkundigen Bond*, 2nd ser., 2, 1909, pp. 10–16.

Beets, "Aanwinsten," 1911
N[icolaas]. Beets, "Aanwinsten Nederl. Museum voor geschiedenis en kunst," *Bulletin van den Nederlandschen Oudheidkundigen Bond*, 2nd ser., 4, 1911, pp. 243–47.

Beets, "Dirick Jacobsz. Vellert," 1912
N[icolaas]. Beets, "Dirick Jacobsz. Vellert, Schilder van Antwerpen. IV. Teekeningen na 1520," *Onze Kunst* 22, 1912, pp. 133–52.

Beets, "Catalogus van de tekeningen," 1913
N[icolaas]. Beets, "Catalogus van de tekeningen," in *Supplement van den catalogus der tentoonstelling van Noord-Nederlandsche schilder- en beeldhouwkunst vóór 1575*, Utrecht, 1913.

Beets, *Lucas de Leyde*, 1913
N[icolaas]. Beets, *Lucas de Leyde* (Collection des grands artistes des Pays-Bas), Brussels and Paris, 1913.

Beets, "Schilder- en beeldhouwkunst," 1914
N[icolaas]. Beets, "De Tentoonstelling van Noord-Nederlandsche Schilder- en beeldhouwkunst vóór 1575 (Utrecht, 3 September–3 October 1913)," *Onze Kunst* 25, 1914, pp. 85–103.

Beets, "Jan Swart," 1914
N[icolaas]. Beets, "Zestiende-eeuwsche Kunstenaars. I. Jan Swart," *Oud Holland* 32, 1914, pp. 1–28.

Beets, *De houtsneden*, 1915
N[icolaas]. Beets, *De houtsneden in Vosterman's bijbel van 1528. Afbeeldingen der prenten van Jan Swart, Lucas van Leyden, e. a., met een inleiding en een kritische lijst*, Amsterdam, 1915.

Beets, "Dirick Jacobsz. Vellert," 1922
N[icolaas]. Beets, "Dirick Jacobsz. Vellert, Schilder van Antwerpen. V. Gebrande glazen," *Onze Kunst* 40, 1922, pp. 85–114.

Beets, "Verres Peints," 1925
N[icolaas]. Beets, "Dirick Jacobsz. Vellert, Peintre d'Anvers. V. Verres Peints," *La Revue d'Art* 26, 1925, pp. 116–45.

N[icolaas]. Beets, "Zestiende-eeuwsche Kunstenaars. II. Barent van Orley," *Oud Holland* 48, 1931, pp. 145–71.

Beets, "Zestiende-eeuwsche Kunstenaars," 1935
N[icolaas]. Beets, "Zestiende-eeuwsche Kunstenaars. IV. Lucas Corneliszoon de Kock," *Oud Holland* 52, 1935, part 1: Een Familie- en Detective-verhaal, pp. 49–76; part 2: Teekeningen van Lucas Cornelisz en van Pieter Cornelisz, pp. 159–73, 217–28.

N[icolaas]. Beets, "Nog eens 'Jan Wellens de Cock' en de zonen van Cornelis Engebrechtsz: Pieter Cornelisz Kunst, Cornelis Cornelisz Kunst, Lucas Cornelisz de Kock," *Oud Holland* 67, 1952, pp. 1–30.

N[icolaas]. Beets, "Cornelis Engebrechtsz. en nog drie rondjes uit zijn school," *Oud Holland* 68, 1953, pp. 111–12.

Benesch, *Albertina Katalog*, 1928
Otto Benesch, *Die Zeichnungen der Niederländischen Schulen des XV. und XVI. Jahrhunderts* (Beschreibender Katalog der Handzeichnungen in der Graphischen Sammlung Albertina, vol. 2), Vienna, 1928.

Otto Benesch, *Meisterzeichnungen der Albertina. Europäische Schulen von der Gotik bis zum Klassizismus*, Salzburg, 1964.

G. Bergsträsser, *Niederländische Zeichnungen 16. Jahrhundert im Hessischen Landesmuseum Darmstadt*, Darmstadt, 1979.

Bernet Kempers, "De speler," 1973
A. J. Bernet Kempers, "De speler met de ronde bus," *Oud Holland* 87, 1973, pp. 240–42.

Berserik, "Leiden, ca. 1480–1545," 1982
C[aes]. J. Berserik, "Niet-monumentaal gebrandschilderd glas en ontwerpen uit Leiden, ca. 1480–1545, een catalogus," thesis, Leiden, Rijksuniversiteit, 1982.

Bertelli, "*Image of Pity*," 1967
Carlo Bertelli, "The *Image of Pity* in Santa Croce in Gerusalemme," in *Essays Presented to Rudolf Wittkower on His Sixty-Fifth Birthday* 2, ed. by Douglas Fraser, London, 1967, pp. 40–55.

Besançon, *Dessins*, 1951
Jacques Besançon, *Les Dessins flamands du XVe au XVIe siècle*, Paris, 1951.

Paul Biver and Edmond Socard, "Le vitrail civil au XIVe siècle," *Bulletin Monumental* 77, 1913, pp. 258–64.

Bock et al., *Zeichnungen*, 1930
Elfried Bock, Jakob Rosenberg, and Max J. Friedländer, *Die Zeichnungen alter Meister im Kupferstichkabinett. Die niederländischen Meister*, 2 vols., Staatliche Museen zu Berlin, 1930.

Bogtman, *Nederlandsche Glasschilders*, 1944
W. Bogtman, *Nederlandsche Glasschilders*, Amsterdam, 1944.

Bolte, "Bilderbogen," 1895
Johannes Bolte, "Bilderbogen des 16. Jahrhunderts," *Tijdschrift voor Nederlandse taal- en letterkunde* 14, 1895, pp. 119–53.

Bolte and Polívka, *Hausmärchen der Brüder Grimm* 3, 1918
Johannes Bolte and Georg Polívka, *Anmerkungen zu den Kinder- u. Hausmärchen der Brüder Grimm* 3, Leipzig, 1918.

van der Boom, *Monumentale glasschilderkunst*, 1940
A. van der Boom, *Monumentale glasschilderkunst in Nederland* 1, The Hague, 1940.

van der Boom, "Aerdt Ortkens," 1949
A. van der Boom, "Een Nederlands glasschilder in den vreemde, Aerdt Ortkens van Nijmegen," *Nederlandsch Kunsthistorisch Jaarboek*, 1948–49, pp. 75–103.

A. van der Boom, "Aertgen van Leyden en de glasruiten van het Leidse Anna-Hofje," *Oud Holland* 69, 1954, pp. 180–81.

A. van der Boom, *De Kunst der glazeniers in Europa 1100–1600*, Amsterdam, 1960.

Karel G. Boon, "Rondom Aertgen," in *Miscellanea. I. Q. van Regteren Altena*, 16/V/1969, Amsterdam, 1969, pp. 55–60.

Boon, *Netherlandish Drawings*, 1978
Karel G. Boon, *Netherlandish Drawings of the Fifteenth and Sixteenth Centuries* (Catalogue of the Dutch and Flemish Drawings in the Rijksmuseum, vol. 2), 2 vols., The Hague, 1978.

Boon, *Drawings of the Frits Lugt Collection*, 1992
Karel G. Boon, *The Netherlandish and German Drawings of the XVth and XVIth Centuries of the Frits Lugt Collection*, 3 vols., Paris, 1992.

Borromeo, *Musaeum*, 1625
Federico Borromeo, *Federici Cardinalis Borromaei Archiepisc Mediolani Musaeum*, Milan, 1625; reprinted, 1909.

Bourg-en-Bresse, *Van Orley* (exhib. cat.), 1981
Bourg-en-Bresse, *Van Orley et les artistes de la cour de Marguerite d'Autriche* (exhib. cat.), Musée de l'Ain, 1981.

de Brosses, *Lettres historiques* 1, 1739
Charles de Brosses, *Lettres historiques et critiques sur l'Italie* 1, Paris, 1739.

Bruges, *Pierre Pourbus* (exhib. cat.), 1984
Bruges, *Pierre Pourbus. Peintre brugeois 1524–1584* (exhib. cat.), by Paul Huvenne, Memlingmuseum, 1984.

Brussels, *Le siècle de Bruegel* (exhib. cat.), 1963
Brussels, *Le siècle de Bruegel. La peinture en Belgique au XVIe siècle* (exhib. cat.), Musées Royaux des Beaux-Arts de Belgique, 1963.

Brussels, *Albrecht Dürer in de Nederlanden. Zijn reis (1520–1521) en invloed* (exhib. cat.), Paleis voor Schone Kunsten, 1977.

Brussels, *Magie du Verre* (exhib. cat.), by Yvette Vanden Bemden et al., Galerie CGER, 1986.

J. Bruyn, "Twee St. Antonius-panelen en andere werken van Aertgen van Leyden," *Nederlands Kunsthistorisch Jaarboek* 11, 1960, pp. 37–119.

Bruyn, "Jan Gossaert Exhibition," 1965
J. Bruyn, "The Jan Gossaert Exhibition in Rotterdam and Bruges," *The Burlington Magazine* 107, 1965, pp. 462–67.

Bruyn, "Lucas van Leyden," 1969
J. Bruyn, "Lucas van Leyden en zijn Leidse tijdgenoten in hun relatie tot Zuid-Nederland," in *Miscellanea. I. Q. van Regteren Altena*, 16/V/1969, Amsterdam, 1969, pp. 44–47.

Bruyn, "Oude en nieuwe elementen," 1987
J. Bruyn, "Oude en nieuwe elementen in de 16de-eeuwse voorstellingswereld," *Bulletin van het Rijksmuseum* 35, 1987, pp. 138–63.

Bruyn, "Tekeningen uit de werkplaats van Pieter Coecke," 1988
J. Bruyn, "Tekeningen uit de werkplaats van Pieter Coecke van Aelst voor een serie glasruitjes met de 'Trionfi,'" *Nederlands Kunsthistorisch Jaarboek* 38, 1987 [1988], pp. 73–86.

Busch and Keller, *Meisterwerke der Kunsthalle Bremen*, 1959
Günter Busch and Horst Keller, *Meisterwerke der Kunsthalle Bremen*, Bremen, 1959.

Cambridge, *Medieval and Renaissance Stained Glass* (exhib. cat.), 1978
Cambridge, Massachusetts, Busch-Reisinger Museum, Harvard University, *Medieval and Renaissance Stained Glass from New England Collections* (exhib. cat.), ed. by Madeline H. Caviness, Medford, 1978.

Carroll, "Paintings of Jacob Cornelisz.," Ph.D. diss., 1987
Jane Louise Carroll, "The Paintings of Jacob Cornelisz. van Oostsanen (1472?–1533)," Ph.D. diss., Chapel Hill, University of North Carolina, 1987.

David Cast, "Marten van Heemskerck's *Momus criticizing the works of the gods*: a problem of Erasmian iconography," *Simiolus* 7, 1974, pp. 22–34.

*Catalogue of The Well-known Collection of Old Master Drawings . . . formed in the 18th century by*

*John Skippe* (sale cat.), London, Christie, Manson & Woods, November 20–21, 1958, no. 275.

Châtelet, "Sur un Jugement dernier," 1965
Albert Châtelet, "Sur un Jugement dernier de Dieric Bouts," *Nederlands Kunsthistorisch Jaarboek* 16, 1965, pp. 17–42.

Châtelet, *Primitifs hollandais*, 1980
Albert Châtelet, *Les Primitifs hollandais. La peinture dans les Pays-Bas du Nord au XVe siècle*, Paris, 1980.

William Cole, "The Flemish Roundel in England," *Journal of the British Society of Master Glass-Painters* 15, no. 2, 1973–74, pp. 16–27.

William Cole, "Early Continental Stained Glass," *Antique Collector* 49, no. 7, 1978, pp. 60–63.

William Cole, "Glass-paintings after Heemskerck in England," *The Antiquaries Journal* 60, 1980, pp. 247–67.

William Cole, "A Description of the Netherlandish Glass in the Church of St Peter, Nowton, Suffolk," in *Crown in Glory. A Celebration of Craftsmanship—Studies in Stained Glass*, ed. by Peter Moore, Norwich, n.d. [1982], pp. 40–47.

Cole, *Roundels in Britain*, 1993
William Cole, *A Catalogue of Netherlandish and North European Roundels in Britain* (Corpus Vitrearum Medii Aevi, Great Britain, Summary Catalogue, 1), Oxford, 1993.

*Collection formed by F. E. Sidney* (sale cat.), 1937
*The Collection of English and Continental Furniture, Porcelain and Objects of Art and Stained Glass formed by F. E. Sidney, Esq.* (sale cat.), London, Christie, Manson & Woods, December 9, 1937.

Cologne, *Herbst des Mittelalters* (exhib. cat.), 1970
Cologne, *Herbst des Mittelalters. Spätgotik in Köln und am Niederrhein* (exhib. cat.), Kunsthalle, 1970.

Cologne, *Die Messe Gregors des Grossen* (exhib. cat.), 1982
Cologne, *Die Messe Gregors des Grossen. Vision, Kunst, Realität* (exhib. cat.), by Uwe Westfehling, Schnütgen-Museum, 1982.

Colvin, "Handzeichnungen des Lukas van Leyden," 1893
Sidney Colvin, "Eine Sammlung von Handzeichnungen des Lukas van Leyden," *Jahrbuch der königlich preußischen Kunstsammlungen* 14, 1893, pp. 165–76, 231–32.

Dal, *The Ages of Man*, 1980
Erik Dal, *The Ages of Man and the Months of the Year. Poetry, Prose and Pictures Outlining the Douze mois figurés Motif Mainly Found in Shepherds' Calendars and in Livres d'Heures (14th to 17th Century)* (Det Kongelige Danske Videnskabernes Selskab, Historisk-filosofiske Skrifter 9:3), Copenhagen, 1980.

Darmstadt, *Das Bild in Glas. Von der europäischen Kabinettscheibe zum New Glass* (exhib. cat.), by Suzanne Beeh-Lustenberger, Hessisches Landesmuseum, 1979.

De Coo, "Twee Orley-retabels," 1979
Jozef De Coo, "Twee Orley-retabels," *Jaarboek van het Koninklijk Museum voor Schone Kunsten Antwerpen*, 1979, pp. 67–104.

Detroit, *Flanders* (exhib. cat.), 1960
Detroit, *Flanders in the Fifteenth Century: Art and Civilization* (exhib. cat.), The Detroit Institute of Arts, 1960.

De Vocht, *Jerome de Busleyden*, 1950
Henry De Vocht, ed., *Jerome de Busleyden, Founder of the Louvain Collegium Trilingue. His Life and Writings* (Humanistica Lovaniensia, 9), Turnhout, 1950.

Anne-Marie Didier-Lamboray, "Les Vitraux de l'Histoire de Joseph à l'église Saint-Antoine de Liège et leurs modèles," *Institut Royal du Patrimoine Artistique Bulletin* 8, 1965, pp. 202–22.

Anne-Marie Didier-Lamboray, "Deux Vitraux de l'Histoire de Daniel d'après Martin van Heemskerck à l'église Saint-Antoine de Liège," *Institut Royal du Patrimoine Artistique Bulletin* 11, 1969, pp. 134–41.

Anne-Marie Didier-Lamboray, "Trois Vitraux d'après Jean Wierix conservés à l'église Saint-Antoine de Liège," *Institut Royal du Patrimoine Artistique Bulletin* 18, 1980–81, pp. 143–54.

Anne-Marie Didier-Lamboray and Jacques Papeleux, "Note sur des Vitraux de l'Histoire de Joseph à l'église Saint-Antoine de Liège et une série de dessins de même composition," *Institut Royal du Patrimoine Artistique Bulletin* 8, 1965, pp. 199–201.

Dodgson, "Holzschnitten Jan Swarts," 1910
Campbell Dodgson, "Zu den Holzschnitten Jan Swarts," *Mitteilungen der Gesellschaft für vervielfältigende Kunst. Beilage der "Graphischen Künste"* 33, 1910, pp. 33–35.

Campbell Dodgson, "Two Drawings by Aert Claesz," *The Burlington Magazine* 38, 1921, pp. 25–26.

Campbell Dodgson, "Pieter Cornelisz Kunst (c. 1490–1542)," *Old Master Drawings*, no. 46, September 1937, pp. 24–25.

Drake, *English Glass-Painting*, 1912
Maurice Drake, *A History of English Glass-Painting, with Some Remarks upon the Swiss Glass Miniatures of the Sixteenth and Seventeenth Centuries*, London, 1912.

Dröge, *Pieterskerkgracht 9*, 1982
J. F. Dröge, *De bouw- en bewoningsgeschiedenis van Pieterskerkgracht 9*, Leiden, 1982.

Dubiez, *Cornelis Anthoniszoon*, 1969
F. J. Dubiez, *Cornelis Anthoniszoon van Amsterdam. Zijn Leven en Werken, ca. 1507–1553*, Amsterdam, 1969.

Franz Dülberg, "Die Nachkommen des Lucas van Leyden," *Oud Holland* 17, 1899, pp. 156–62.

Dülberg, "Die Persönlichkert des Lucas van Leyden," 1899
Franz Dülberg, "Die Persönlichkeit des Lucas van Leyden," *Oud Holland* 17, 1899, pp. 65–83.

Dülberg, *Frühhölländer 3*, n.d. [1907]
Franz Dülberg, *Frühhölländer 3, Frühhölländer in Italien*, Haarlem, n.d. [1907].

Dülberg, *Frühholländer 4*, n.d. [1908]
Franz Dülberg, *Frühholländer 4, Früholländer in Paris*, Haarlem, n.d. [1908].

Düsseldorf, *Niederländische Handzeichnungen 1500–1800 aus dem Kunstmuseum Düsseldorf* (exhib. cat.), Städtische Kunsthalle, 1968.

I[sabella]. H[enriette]. van Eeghen, *De gilden. Theorie en praktijk*, 2nd ed., Bussum, The Netherlands, 1974.

I[sabella]. H[enriette]. van Eeghen, "Jacob Cornelisz, Cornelis Anthonisz en hun familierelaties," *Nederlands Kunsthistorisch Jaarboek* 37, 1986, pp. 95–132.

"Een Kunstverzamelaar," 1882–83
"Een Kunstverzamelaar der 17e eeuw. Medegedeeld als voren," in *Archief voor Nederlandsche Kunstgeschiedenis. Verzameling van Meerendeels Onuitgegeven Berichten en Mededeelingen* 5, comp. by Fr. D. O. Obreen, Rotterdam, 1882–83, pp. 293–315.

Eisler, *Master of the Unicorn*, 1979
Colin Eisler, *The Master of the Unicorn. The Life and Work of Jean Duvet*, New York, 1979.

Prince d'Essling and Eugène Müntz, *Pétrarque, ses études d'art, son influence sur les artistes, ses portraits et ceux de Laure, l'illustration de ses écrits*, Paris, 1902.

*European Works of Art* (sale cat.), 1988
*European Works of Art, Arms and Armour, Furniture and Tapestries* (sale cat.), New York, Sotheby's, November 22–23, 1988.

Evers, "Valentijn van Orley en zijn atelier," thesis, 1986
Linda Evers, "Valentijn van Orley en zijn atelier," thesis, Leiden, Rijksuniversiteit, 1986.

Faggin, *La pittura*, 1968
Giorgio T. Faggin, *La pittura ad Anversa nel Cinquecento*, Florence, 1968.

von Falke, *Kunstsammlung von Pannwitz*, 1925
Otto von Falke, ed., *Die Kunstsammlung von Pannwitz 2, Skulpturen und Kunstgewerbe*, Munich, 1925.

Ferguson, *Signs and Symbols in Christian Art*, 1976
George Ferguson, *Signs and Symbols in Christian Art*, New York, 1976.

Filedt Kok, "Underdrawing and other technical aspects," 1978
Jan Piet Filedt Kok, "Underdrawing and other technical aspects in the paintings of Lucas van Leyden," *Nederlands Kunsthistorisch Jaarboek* 29, 1978 [1979], pp. 1–184.

Jan Piet Filedt Kok, "Een *Biblia pauperum* met houtsneden van Jacob Cornelisz. en Lucas van Leyden gereconstrueerd," *Bulletin van het Rijksmuseum* 36, 1988, pp. 83–116.

Josef Ludwig Fischer, *Handbuch der Glasmalerei für Forscher, Sammler und Kunstfreunde, wie für Künstler, Architekten und Glasmaler* (Hiersemanns Handbücher, vol. 8), Leipzig, 1914.

Florence, *L'Époque de Lucas de Leyde* (exhib. cat.), 1981
Florence, *L'Époque de Lucas de Leyde et Pierre Bruegel. Dessins des anciens Pays-Bas, Collection Frits Lugt, Institut Néerlandais, Paris* (exhib. cat.), by Karel G. Boon, Istituto Universitario Olandese di Storia dell'Arte, and Paris, Institut Néerlandais, 1981.

Folie, "Les Dessins de Jean Gossart," 1951
Jacqueline Folie, "Les Dessins de Jean Gossart dit Mabuse," *Gazette des Beaux-Arts*, 6th ser., 38, 1951, pp. 77–98.

Folmer-von Oven, "Meester," Ph.D. diss., 1974
T. Folmer-von Oven, "De Meester van de Dood van Absolom," Ph.D. diss., Leiden, Rijksuniversiteit, 1974.

David Freedberg, "The Problem of Images in Northern Europe and its Repercussions in the Netherlands," *Hafnia. Copenhagen Papers in the History of Art*, 1976, pp. 25–45.

David Freedberg, "Aertsen, Heemskerck en de crisis van de kunst in de Nederlanden," *Bulletin van het Rijksmuseum* 35, 1987, pp. 224–41.

Friedländer, "Aerdt Ortkens," 1917
Max J. Friedländer, "Der niederländische Glasmaler Aerdt Ortkens," *Amtliche Berichte aus den Königlichen Kunstsammlungen* 38, 1916–17, cols. 161–67.

Friedländer, "Brüsseler Tafelmalerei," 1923
Max J. Friedländer, "Die Brüsseler Tafelmalerei gegen den Ausgang des 15. Jahrhunderts," *Belgische Kunstdenkmäler* 1, 1923, pp. 309–20.

Max J. Friedländer, "Zu Jan Swart van Groningen," *Oud Holland* 63, 1948, pp. 3–9.

Friedländer, *Lucas van Leyden*, 1963
Max J. Friedländer, *Lucas van Leyden*, ed. by Friedrich Winkler, Berlin, 1963.

Friedländer, *Early Netherlandish Painting*, 1967–76
Max J. Friedländer, *Early Netherlandish Painting*, trans. by Heinz Norden, 14 vols., New York and Washington, D.C., 1967–76.

von Frimmel, "Davidbildern," 1921
Theodor von Frimmel, "Zu den Davidbildern des Lukas van Leyden. Ein neu aufgefundenes Gemälde," *Studien und Skizzen zur Gemäldekunde* 5, 1920–21, pp. 149–53.

Frodl-Kraft, *Die Glasmalerei*, 1970
Eva Frodl-Kraft, *Die Glasmalerei. Entwicklung, Technik, Eigenart*, Vienna and Munich, 1970.

Galbiati, *Itinerario*, 1951
Giovanni Galbiati, *Itinerario per il visitatore della Biblioteca Ambrosiana della Pinacoteca e dei monumenti annessi*, Milan, 1951.

Garff, *Tegninger af Maerten van Heemskerck*, 1971
Jan Garff, *Den kongelige Kobberstiksamling. Tegninger af Maerten van Heemskerck*, Copenhagen, Statens Museum for Kunst, 1971.

Geldenhauer, *Collectanea* 16
Gerhard Geldenhauer, *Collectanea* (Historisch Genootschap, 3rd ser., no. 16), ed. by J. Prinsen, Amsterdam, 1901.

van Gelder, "Jan Gossaert in Rome," 1942
J. G. van Gelder, "Jan Gossaert in Rome, 1508–1509," *Oud Holland* 59, 1942, pp. 1–11.

van Gelder, "Nog een teekening voor klein glas," 1946
J. G. van Gelder, "Nog een teekening voor klein glas (1543) van Dirck Crabeth," *Kunsthistorische mededeelingen van het Rijksbureau voor Kunsthistorische Documentatie* 1, 1946, pp. 33–34.

Luc-Francis Genicot, "Un châssis de fenêtre du XVIe siècle au musée de Louvain-la-Neuve," *Revue des Archéologues et Historiens d'Art de Louvain* 20, 1987, pp. 234–52.

Teréz Gerszi, comp., *Netherlandish Drawings in the Budapest Museum. Sixteenth-Century Drawings. An Illustrated Catalogue*, 2 vols., Amsterdam and New York, 1971.

Ghent, *Charles-Quint et son temps* (exhib. cat.), 1955
Ghent, *Charles-Quint et son temps* (exhib. cat.), Museum voor Schone Kunsten, 1955.

Gibson, "Pieter Cornelisz. Kunst," 1967
Walter S. Gibson, "Pieter Cornelisz. Kunst as a Panel Painter," *Simiolus* 1, 1966–67, pp. 37–45.

Walter S. Gibson, "Lucas van Leyden and His Two Teachers," *Simiolus* 4, 1970, pp. 90–99.

Gibson, "Two Painted Glass Panels," 1970
Walter S. Gibson, "Two Painted Glass Panels from the Circle of Lucas van Leyden," *The Bulletin of The Cleveland Museum of Art* 57, 1970, pp. 81–92.

Walter S. Gibson, "*Imitatio Christi*: the Passion scenes of Hieronymus Bosch," *Simiolus* 6, 1972–73, pp. 83–93.

Gibson, *Hieronymus Bosch*, 1973
Walter S. Gibson, *Hieronymus Bosch*, New York and Washington, D.C., 1973.

Gibson, *Paintings of Cornelis Engebrechtsz*, 1977
Walter S. Gibson, *The Paintings of Cornelis Engebrechtsz* (Outstanding Dissertations in the Fine Arts), New York and London, 1977.

Gibson, "Artists and *Rederijkers*," 1981
Walter S. Gibson, "Artists and *Rederijkers* in the Age of Bruegel," *The Art Bulletin* 63, 1981, pp. 426–46.

Walter S. Gibson, "Lucas van Leyden's late paintings: The Italian connection," *Nederlands Kunsthistorisch Jaarboek* 37, 1986, pp. 41–52.

Glück, "Name des Meisters D*V," 1901
Gustav Glück, "Beiträge zur Geschichte der Antwerpner Malerei im XVI. Jahrhundert. I. Der wahre Name des Meisters D*V," *Jahrbuch der kunsthistorischen Sammlungen des Allerhöchsten Kaiserhauses* 22, 1901, pp. 1–34.

Glück, *Malerei*, 1933
Gustav Glück, *Aus Drei Jahrhunderten europäischer Malerei*, Vienna, 1933.

Gramatica, *Memorie*, 1919
Luigi Gramatica, ed., *Le Memorie su Leonardo da Vinci di Don Ambrogio Mazenta* (Analecta Ambrosiana, vol. 1), Milan, 1919.

Rainald Grosshans, *Maerten van Heemskerck. Die Gemälde*, Berlin, 1980.

Grosvenor Thomas Stock Book
Norwich, private library of Dennis King, Roy Grosvenor Thomas Stock Books, unpublished

Guicciardini, *Descrittione*, 1567
Lodovico Guicciardini, *Descrittione di m. Lodovico Guicciardini, patritio fiorentino, di tutti i Paesi Bassi, altrimenti detti Germania Inferiore. Con piu carte di geographia del paese, & col ritratto naturale di piu terre principali*, Antwerp, 1567.

Haarlem, Frans Halsmuseum, *Leerrijke reeksen van Maerten van Heemskerck* (De eeuw van de beeldenstorm) (exhib. cat.), by Ilja M. Veldman, The Hague, 1986.

Barbara Haeger, "Philips Galle's engravings after Maarten van Heemskerck's *Parable of the Prodigal Son*," *Oud Holland* 102, 1988, pp. 127–40.

Hagemann, *Der göttliche Pfeilschütze*, 1982
Ernst Hagemann, *Der göttliche Pfeilschütze. Zür Genealogie eines Pestbildtypus*, St. Michael, Austria, 1982.

Craig Harbison, "Lucas van Leyden, the Magdalen and the Problem of Secularization in early Sixteenth Century Northern Art," *Oud Holland* 98, 1984, pp. 117–29.

Craig Harbison, "Visions and meditations in early Flemish painting," *Simiolus* 15, 1985, pp. 87–118.

Hayward, "Stained-Glass Windows," 1972
Jane Hayward, "Stained-Glass Windows. An Exhibition of Glass in the Metropolitan Museum's Collection," *The Metropolitan Museum of Art Bulletin* 30, 1971–72, pp. 110–52.

Hayward, "Glazed Cloisters," 1973
Jane Hayward, "Glazed Cloisters and their Development in the Houses of the Cistercian Order," *Gesta* 12, 1973, pp. 93–109.

Helbig, "Arnould de Nimègue," 1937
Jean Helbig, "Arnould de Nimègue et le problème de son identité," *L'Art et la Vie* 4, no. 9, Ghent, September 1937, pp. 279–91.

Jean Helbig, "Circulation de modèles d'ateliers au XIVe siècle," *Revue Belge d'Archéologie et d'Histoire de l'Art* 8, 1938, pp. 113–18.

Helbig, Jean, *Meesterwerken van de glasschilderkunst in de oude Nederlanden* (Maerlantbibliotheek, II), Antwerp and Utrecht, 1941.

Helbig, *Glasschilderkunst*, 1943 and 1951
Jean Helbig, *De glasschilderkunst in België. Repertorium en documenten*, 2 vols., Antwerp, 1943 and 1951.

Helbig, *Vitraux 2*, 1968
Jean Helbig, *Les Vitraux de la première moitié du XIVe siècle conservés en Belgique. Province d'Anvers et Flandres* (Corpus Vitrearum Medii Aevi [Addenda], Belgium, vol. 2), Brussels, 1968.

Helbig and Vanden Bemden, *Vitraux 3*, 1974
Jean Helbig and Yvette Vanden Bemden, *Les Vitraux de la première moitié du XVIe siècle conservés en Belgique. Brabant et Limbourg* (Corpus Vitrearum Medii Aevi [Addenda], Belgium, vol. 3), Ledeberg and Ghent, 1974.

Held, *Dürers Wirkung*, 1931
Julius Held, *Dürers Wirkung auf die niederländische Kunst seiner Zeit*, The Hague, 1931.

M. D. Henkel, "Pieter Cornelisz Kunst (c 1490–c 1540)," *Old Master Drawings*, no. 24, March 1932, pp. 66–67.

Henkel, "Nederlandsche houtsneden," 1936
M. D. Henkel, "Nederlandsche houtsneden 1500–1550," *Maandblad voor beeldende kunsten* 13, 1936, pp. 99–107, 139–48.

s'Hertogenbosch, *Maria van Hongarije* (exhib. cat.), 1993
s'Hertogenbosch, Noordbrabants Museum, and Utrecht, Rijksmuseum Het Catharijneconvent, *Maria van Hongarije 1505–1558. Koningin tussen keizers en kunstenaars* (exhib. cat.), by Bob van den Boogert and Jacqueline Kerkoff, Zwolle, 1993.

Sadja Herzog, "Jan Gossart Called Mabuse (ca. 1478–1532). A Study of His Chronology With a Catalogue of His Works," 2 vols., Ph.D. diss., Bryn Mawr College, 1968.

Sadja Herzog, "Tradition and Innovation in Gossart's Neptune and Amphitrite and Danae," *Bulletin Museum Boymans-van Beuningen* 19, 1968, pp. 25–41.

Hirschmann, *Hendrick Goltzius als Maler*, 1916
Otto Hirschmann, *Hendrick Goltzius als Maler 1600–1617* (Quellenstudien zur holländischen Kunstgeschichte, 9), The Hague, 1916.

Hollstein 1–, 1949–
F. W. H. Hollstein, *Dutch and Flemish Etchings, Engravings and Woodcuts ca. 1450–1700*, Amsterdam, 1949–

Hoogewerff, *Noord-Nederlandsche Schilderkunst*, 1936–47
G. J. Hoogewerff, *De Noord-Nederlandsche Schilderkunst*, 5 vols., The Hague, 1936–47.

Horst, "de Heilsweg van de Mens," 1990
Daniel R. Horst, "Een zestiende-eeuwse reformatorische prentenreeks van Frans Huys over de Heilsweg van de Mens," *Bulletin van het Rijksmuseum* 38, 1990, pp. 3–24.

Hovey, "Stained Glass Windows," 1953
Walter Read Hovey, "Stained Glass Windows: Gift of

Mrs. Alan M. Scaife," *Pitt* (The University of Pitts-burgh), no. 49, 1953, pp. 18–19.

Hudig, "Zestiende eeuwsche ruiten," 1922
Ferrand Hudig, "Zestiende eeuwsche ruiten," *Onze Kunst* 40, 1922, pp. 37–52.

Hudig, "Quelques Vitraux," 1923
Ferrand Hudig, "Quelques Vitraux du XVIe Siècle," *La Revue d'Art* 24, 1922–23, pp. 98–112.

Vida Joyce Hull, *Hans Memlinc's Paintings for the Hospital of Saint John in Bruges* (Outstanding Dissertations in the Fine Arts), New York and London, 1981.

Husband, *Notable Acquisitions 1983–1984*, 1984
Timothy B. Husband, "Silver-stained Roundel: The Adoration," in *Notable Acquisitions 1983–1984. The Metropolitan Museum of Art*, New York, 1984, p. 19.

Husband, "'Ick Sorgheloose,'" 1989
Timothy B. Husband, "'Ick Sorgheloose . . . ': A Silver-Stained Roundel in The Cloisters," *Metropolitan Museum Journal* 24, 1989, pp. 173–88.

Husband, *Silver-Stained Roundels*, 1991
Timothy B. Husband, *Stained Glass before 1700 in American Collections: Silver-Stained Roundels and Unipartite Panels* (Corpus Vitrearum Checklist 4) (Studies in the History of Art, Monograph Series 1, vol. 39), Washington, D.C., 1991.

Huvenne, "Pieter Pourbus," 1980
Paul Huvenne, "Pieter Pourbus als tekenaar. Een overzicht," *Oud Holland* 94, 1980, pp. 11–31.

Hymans, *Livre des peintres*, 1884
Henri Hymans, trans. and ed., *Le Livre des peintres de Carel van Mander. Vie des Peintres flamands, hollandais et allemands (1604)* 1 (Bibliothèque Internationale de l'Art), Paris, 1884.

*Ill. Bartsch*
*The Illustrated Bartsch*, New York, 1978–

Isler-de Jongh, "Rondels de la Collection Hosmer," 1989
Ariane Isler-de Jongh, "Retour aux traditions—signe de réussite sociale: les rondels de la Collection Hosmer (Université McGill, Montréal)," *Revue d'art canadienne/Canadian Art Review* (RACAR) 16, 1989, pp. 29–42, 81–98.

H. Janse, *Vensters*, 2nd rev. ed., Schiedam, The Netherlands, 1977.

Jones, *Ambrosiana*, 1993
Pamela M. Jones, *Federico Borromeo and the Ambrosiana. Art Patronage and Reform in Seventeenth-Century Milan*, Cambridge, England, 1993.

de Jong, "Sorgheloos," 1978
P. J. de Jong, "Sorgheloos, een zestiende eeuwse rijmprentenreeks; tekst en commentaar," *Spektator* 7, 1977–78, pp. 104–20.

Junquera de Vega, "'L'Histoire de Noé,'" 1973
Paulina Junquera de Vega, "Les séries de tapisseries de 'Grotesques' et 'l'Histoire de Noé' de la Couronne d'Espagne," *Bulletin des Musées Royaux d'Art et d'Histoire*, 6th ser., 45, 1973, pp. 143–71.

Rosy Kahn, *Die Graphik des Lucas van Leyden. Studien zur Entwicklungsgeschichte der holländischen*

*Kunst im XVI. Jahrhundert* (Zur Kunstgeschichte des Auslandes, part 118), Strasbourg, 1918.

Kerrich, *Catalogue of prints*, 1829
Thomas Kerrich, *A catalogue of the prints, which have been engraved after Martin Heemskerck; or rather, an essay towards such a catalogue*, London, 1829.

H. T. Kirby, "The Lesser Glass in St. Mary's Church, Warwick," *Apollo* 39, 1944, pp. 45–48.

H. T. Kirby, "Some Warwickshire Medallions of Sixteenth-Century Stained-Glass," *Journal of the British Society of Master Glass-Painters* 12, no. 2, 1957, pp. 127–30.

Kloek, *Beknopte catalogus*, 1975
Wouter Th. Kloek, *Beknopte catalogus van de Nederlandse tekeningen in het Prentenkabinet van de Uffizi te Florence*, Utrecht, 1975.

Kloek, "Drawings of Lucas van Leyden," 1978
Wouter Th. Kloek, "The drawings of Lucas van Leyden," *Nederlands Kunsthistorisch Jaarboek* 29, 1978 [1979], pp. 425–58.

Wouter Th. Kloek, "Jacob Cornelisz van Oostsanen, Drieluik met de aanbidding der koningen en de heiligen Hiëronymus en Catharina met stichters en op de keerzijden der luiken de heiligen Christoforus en Antonius Abt, 1517," *Bulletin van het Rijksmuseum* 37, 1989, pp. 169–70.

Kloek and Filedt Kok, "De Opstanding van Christus," 1983
Wouter Th. Kloek and Jan Piet Filedt Kok, "'De Opstanding van Christus', getekend door Lucas van Leyden," *Bulletin van het Rijksmuseum* 31, 1983, pp. 4–20.

Konowitz, "Drawings as intermediary stages," 1991
Ellen Konowitz, "Drawings as intermediary stages: some working methods of Dirk Vellert and Albrecht Dürer re-examined," *Simiolus* 20, 1990–91, pp. 143–52.

Konowitz, "Vellert," Ph.D. diss., 1992
Ellen Konowitz, "Dirk Jacobsz. Vellert: A Study of His Stained Glass Windows, Drawings, and Prints," Ph.D. diss., New York University, 1992.

Krönig, "Frühzeit Jan Gossarts," 1934
Wolfgang Krönig, "Zur Frühzeit Jan Gossarts," *Zeitschrift für Kunstgeschichte* 3, 1934, pp. 163–77.

Krönig, *Der italienische Einfluß*, 1936
Wolfgang Krönig, *Der italienische Einfluß in der flämischen Malerei im ersten Drittel des 16. Jahrhunderts. Beiträge zum Beginn der Renaissance in der Malerei der Niederlande*, Würzburg, 1936.

Lafond, "Arnoult de Nimègue," 1939
Jean Lafond, "Arnoult de Nimègue et le Vitrail de l'Arbre de Jessé à St. George's, Hanover Square, de Londres," in *Actes du Congrès d'Histoire de l'Art*, London, 1939, section IV A.

Jean Lafond, *Pratique de la peinture sur verre à l'usage des curieux, suivie d'un essai historique sur le jaune d'argent et d'une note sur les plus anciens verres gravés*, Rouen, 1943.

Lafond, "Le peintre-verrier Arnoult de Nimègue," 1952
Jean Lafond, "Le peintre-verrier Arnoult de Nimègue (Aert van Oort) et les débuts de la Renaissance à Rouen et à Anvers," in *Actes du XVIIme Congrès International d'Histoire de l'Art. Amsterdam, 23–31 juillet 1952*, The Hague, 1955, pp. 333–44.

Jean Lafond, "Un vitrail du Mesnil-Villeman (1313) et les origines du jaune d'argent," *Bulletin de la Société nationale des antiquaires de France*, 1954–55, pp. 93–95.

Jean Lafond, "Le vitrail civil français à l'église et au musée," *Médecine de France* no. 77, 1956, p. 29.

Jean Lafond, "The Traffic in Old Stained Glass from Abroad during the 18th and 19th Centuries in England," *Journal of the British Society of Master Glass-Painters* 14, no. 1, 1964, pp. 58–67.

Laren, *Oude tekeningen* (exhib. cat.), 1966
Laren, *Oude tekeningen. Een keuze uit de verzameling P. en N. de Boer* (exhib. cat.), Singer Museum, 1966.

Larsen, *Primitifs flamands*, 1960
Erik Larsen, *Les Primitifs flamands au Musée métropolitain de New York*, Utrecht and Antwerp, 1960.

László, *Flemish and French Tapestries in Hungary*, 1981
Emöke László, *Flemish and French Tapestries in Hungary*, Budapest, 1981.

Laurent, "Le Vitrail de Dirick Vellert," 1925
Marcel Laurent, "Bruxelles. Musée du Cinquantenaire.—Le Vitrail de Dirick Vellert," *La Revue d'Art* 25, 1925, pp. 81–84.

Lawrence Lee, George Seddon, and Francis Stephens, *Gebrandschilderd Glas, schilderen met licht*, Utrecht, 1977.

Leuven, *Ars sacra antiqua* (exhib. cat.), 1962
Leuven, *Ars sacra antiqua* (exhib. cat.), Stedelijk Museum, 1962.

Leuven, *Oude kunst uit Leuvens privébezit* (exhib. cat.), by R. de Strycker et al., Stedelijk Museum, 1964.

Lillich, "Monastic Stained Glass," 1984
Meredith Parsons Lillich, "Monastic Stained Glass: Patronage and Style," in *Monasticism and the Arts*, ed. by Timothy Gregory Verdon, Syracuse, 1984, pp. 207–54.

Meredith Parsons Lillich, "European Stained Glass around 1300: The Introduction of Silver Stain," in *Europäische Kunst um 1300* (Akten des XXV. Internationalen Kongresses für Kunstgeschichte, vol. 6, section 6), ed. by Elisabeth Liskar, Vienna, 1986, pp. 45–60.

Lugt, "Beiträge," 1931
Frits Lugt, "Beiträge zu dem Katalog der niederländischen Handzeichnungen in Berlin," *Jahrbuch der preußischen Kunstsammlungen* 52, 1931, pp. 36–80.

Lugt, *Dessins*, 1968
Frits Lugt, *Musée du Louvre. Inventaire Général des Dessins des écoles du nord, publié sous les auspices du Cabinet des dessins. Maîtres des Anciens Pays-Bas nés avant 1550*, Paris, 1968.

Paul Victor Maes, "Oud Leuvens Brandglas in Engeland," *Arca Lovaniensis artes atque historiae reserans documenta*, Jaarboek 1, 1972, pp. 189–203.

Maes, "Leuvense brandglasmedaillons," 1976
Paul Victor Maes, "De Leuvense brandglasmedaillons. Een historisch en typologisch onderzoek," *Arca Lovaniensis artes atque historiae reserans documenta*, Jaarboek 5, 1976, pp. 313–48.

Maes, *Leuvens Brandglas*, 1987
Paul Victor Maes, *Leuvens Brandglas. De produktie tijdens de 16de eeuw en de nabootsing van oude brandglasmedaillons in de 19de en 20ste eeuw. Met een inventaris van het 16de-eeuws brandglas bewaard in het Stedelijk Museum Vander Kelen-Mertens en in*

de collectie van het O.C.M.W. te Leuven, Arca Lovaniensis artes atque historiae reserans documenta, Jaarboek 13, 1987.

Mâle, *Twelfth Century*, 1978
Émile Mâle, *Religious Art in France, The Twelfth Century. A Study of the Origins of Medieval Iconography* (Bollingen Series, XC:1), Princeton, 1978.

Mâle, *Thirteenth Century*, 1984
Émile Mâle, *Religious Art in France, The Thirteenth Century. A Study of Medieval Iconography and Its Sources* (Bollingen Series, XC:2), Princeton, 19 4.

Émile Mâle, *Religious Art in France, The Late Middle Ages. A Study of Medieval Iconography and Its Sources* (Bollingen Series, XC:3), Princeton, 1986.

Karel van Mander, *Dutch and Flemish Painters. Translation from the Schilderboeck*, trans. by Constant van de Wall, New York, 1936.

Karel van Mander, *The Lives of the Illustrious Netherlandish and German Painters, from the first edition of the Schilder-boeck (1603–1604). Preceded by The Lineage, Circumstances and Place of Birth, Life and Works of Karel van Mander, Painter and Poet and likewise his Death and Burial, from the second edition of the Schilder-boeck (1616–1618)* 1, trans. and ed. by Hessel Miedema, Doornspijk, 1994.

Marlier, *Pierre Coeck*, 1966
Georges Marlier, *La Renaissance flamande. Pierre Coeck d'Alost*, Brussels, 1966.

James H. Marrow, *Passion Iconography in Northern European Art of the Late Middle Ages and Early Renaissance. A Study of the Transformation of Sacred Metaphor into Descriptive Narrative* (Ars Neerlandica, vol. 1), Kortrijk, 1979.

Marrow, "Symbol and meaning," 1986
James H. Marrow, "Symbol and meaning in northern European art of the late middle ages and the early Renaissance," *Simiolus* 16, 1986, pp. 150–69.

*Master Drawings 1500–1900* (exhib. cat.), 1992
*Master Drawings 1500–1900* (exhib. cat.), Thomas le Claire, Kunsthandel VIII, at W. M. Brady & Co., Inc., New York, 1992.

Mechelen, *Margareta van Oostenrijk* (exhib. cat.), 1958
Mechelen, *Margareta van Oostenrijk en haar hof* (exhib. cat.), 1958.

Meder, *Die Handzeichnung*, 1923
Joseph Meder, *Die Handzeichnung. Ihre Technik und Entwicklung*, Vienna, 1923.

Meder, "Het leven in twaalf maanden," 1990
Theo Meder, "Een sproke van Willem van Hildegaersberch. Het leven in twaalf maanden," *Literatuur* 7, 1990, pp. 22–28.

Miedema, "De bijbelse ikonografie van twee monumenten," 1978
Hessel Miedema, "De bijbelse ikonografie van twee monumenten: De 'kraak' te Oosterend (Fr.), en het grafmonument van Edo Wiemken te Jever," *Bulletin van de Koninklijke Nederlandse Oudheidkundige Bond* 77, 1978, pp. 61–88.

E[rnst]. W[ilhelm]. Moes, *Iconographia Batava. Beredeneerde lijst van geschilderde en gebeeldhouwde portretten van Noord-Nederlanders in vorige eeuwen*, 2 vols., Amsterdam, 1897–1905.

Moes, *Oude teekeningen*, 1904–6
E[rnst]. W[ilhelm]. Moes, *Oude teekeningen van de hollandsche en vlaamsche school in het Rijks-prentenkabinet te Amsterdam*, 2 vols., The Hague, 1904–6.

Mundy, "Gerard David's *Rest on the Flight into Egypt*," 1982
E. James Mundy, "Gerard David's *Rest on the Flight into Egypt*: further additions to grape symbolism," *Simiolus* 12, 1981–82, pp. 211–22.

Munich, *Niederländische Zeichnungen* (exhib. cat.), 1989
Munich, *Niederländische Zeichnungen des 16. Jahrhunderts in der Staatlichen Graphischen Sammlung München* (exhib. cat.), Staatliche Graphische Sammlung, 1989.

*National Art-Collections Fund*, 1952
*National Art-Collections Fund. Forty-Eighth Annual Report 1951*, London, 1952.

New Brunswick, *Dürer to Cézanne* (exhib. cat.), 1982
New Brunswick, New Jersey, *Dürer to Cézanne. Northern European Drawings from the Ashmolean Museum* (exhib. cat.), by Christopher Lloyd, The Jane Voorhees Zimmerli Art Museum, Rutgers University, and The Cleveland Museum of Art, 1982.

Newton, *Oxford, CVMA*, 1979
Peter A. Newton, *The County of Oxford. A Catalogue of Medieval Stained Glass* (Corpus Vitrearum Medii Aevi, Great Britain, vol. 1), London, 1979.

New York, *The Wild Man* (exhib. cat.), 1980
New York, *The Wild Man. Medieval Myth and Symbolism* (exhib. cat.), by Timothy B. Husband, The Metropolitan Museum of Art, 1980.

New York, *Form and Light* (exhib. cat.), 1985
New York, *Form and Light. 400 Years of European Glass* (exhib. cat.), by Timothy Husband and Marvin D. Schwartz, Michael Ward, Inc., 1985.

New York, *Pisanello to Cézanne* (exhib. cat.), 1990
New York, The Pierpont Morgan Library, Fort Worth, Kimbell Art Museum, and The Cleveland Museum of Art, *From Pisanello to Cézanne. Master Drawings from the Museum Boymans-van Beuningen, Rotterdam* (exhib. cat.), by Ger Luijten and A. W. F. M. Meij, Rotterdam, and Cambridge, England, 1990.

New York, *Petrus Christus* (exhib. cat.), 1994
New York, *Petrus Christus. Renaissance Master of Bruges* (exhib. cat.), by Maryan W. Ainsworth, The Metropolitan Museum of Art, 1994.

Nieuwdorp, *Musée Mayer van den Bergh*, 1992
Hans Nieuwdorp, *Musée Mayer van den Bergh Anvers* (Musea Nostra, 26), Brussels, 1992.

Nijhoff, *Nederlandsche houtsneden 1500–1550*, 1931–39
Wouter Nijhoff, ed., *Nederlandsche houtsneden 1500–1550. Reproducties van oude Noord- en Zuid-Nederlandsche houtsneden op losse bladen met en zonder tekst in de oorspronkelijke grootte*, 2 vols., The Hague, 1931–39.

*Old Master Drawings from Holkham* (sale cat.), 1991
*Old Master Drawings from Holkham* (sale cat.), London, Christie, Manson & Woods, July 2, 1991.

*Oppenheim Collection* (sale cat.), 1914
*Collection Baron Albert Oppenheim, Cöln* (sale cat.), Berlin, Rudolph Lepke's Kunst-Auctions-Haus, October 28–29, 1914.

von der Osten, "Studien zu Jan Gossaert," 1961
Gert von der Osten, "Studien zu Jan Gossaert," in *De Artibus Opuscula XL. Essays in Honor of Erwin Panofsky* 1, ed. by Millard Meiss, New York, 1961, pp. 454–75.

von der Osten, "Blick in die Geburtshöhle," 1967
Gert von der Osten, "Der Blick in die Geburtshöhle. Ein Nachtrag," *Kölner Domblatt* 26–27, 1967, pp. 111–14.

von der Osten and Vey, *Painting and Sculpture*, 1969
Gert von der Osten and Horst Vey, *Painting and Sculpture in Germany and the Netherlands 1500 to 1600* (The Pelican History of Art), Baltimore, 1969.

Erwin Panofsky, "Jean Hey's 'Ecce Homo.' Speculations about Its Author, Its Donor, and Its Iconography," *Musées Royaux des Beaux-Arts Bulletin* 5, 1956, pp. 95–138.

Erwin Panofsky, "Erasmus and the Visual Arts," *Journal of the Warburg and Courtauld Institutes* 32, 1969, pp. 200–227.

Paris, *Rubens, ses maîtres, ses élèves* (exhib. cat.), 1978
Paris, *Rubens, ses maîtres, ses élèves. Dessins du musée du Louvre* (exhib. cat.), Musée du Louvre, 1978.

Paris, *Old Master Drawings* (exhib. cat.), 1985
Paris, Institut Néerlandais, and other venues, *Old Master Drawings from the Print Room of the University, Leiden/Alte Zeichnungen aus dem Kupferstichkabinett der Universität zu Leiden* (exhib. cat.), ed. by Jaap Bolten, The Hague, 1985.

Paris, *Renaissance et Maniérisme* (exhib. cat.), 1985
Paris, *Renaissance et Maniérisme dans les Écoles du Nord. Dessins des collections de l'École des Beaux-Arts* (exhib. cat.), by Émmanuelle Brugerolles, École Nationale Supérieure des Beaux-Arts, and Hamburg, Kunsthalle, 1985.

Parker, *Drawings in the Ashmolean Museum*, 1938
K. T. Parker, *Catalogue of the Collection of Drawings in the Ashmolean Museum* 1, Oxford, 1938.

Peter W. Parshall, "Lucas van Leyden's narrative style," *Nederlands Kunsthistorisch Jaarboek* 29, 1978 [1979], pp. 185–237.

Parshall, "Kunst en reformatie," 1987
Peter W. Parshall, "Kunst en reformatie in Noordelijke Nederlanden—enkele gezichtspunten," *Bulletin van het Rijksmuseum* 35, 1987, pp. 164–75.

Pelinck, "Geschilderde vensters," 1940
E. Pelinck, "Geschilderde vensters uit 1543 in Leiden," *Oud Holland* 57, 1940, pp. 193–200.

E. Pelinck, "Pieter Couwenhorn, glasschrijver te Leiden," *Oud Holland* 68, 1953, pp. 51–56.

Pelinck, "Het huis Pieterskerkgracht 9 en zijn bewoners," 1957
E. Pelinck, "Pax Huic Domui, het huis Pieterskerkgracht 9 en zijn bewoners," *Leids Jaarboekje*, 1957, pp. 119–29.

Perdrizet, *La Vierge de Miséricorde*, 1908
Paul Perdrizet, *La Vierge de Miséricorde. Étude d'un thème iconographique*, Paris, 1908.

"Pierre de Dappere," 1866–70
"Pierre de Dappere: Peintre-Verrier, 1513–1546," *Le Beffroi* 3, 1866–70, pp. 288–91.

Pleij, "Sorgheloos," 1980
Herman Pleij, "Sorgheloos," in *Het zal koud zijn in 't water als 't vriest. Zestiende-eeuwse parodieën op gedruckte jaarvoorspellingen*, The Hague, 1980.

Pleij, *Blauwe Schuit*, 1983
Herman Pleij, *Het gilde van de Blauwe Schuit. Literatuur, volksfeest en burgermoraal in de late middeleeuwen*, 2nd ed., Amsterdam, 1983.

J. M. G. van der Poel, "Gebrandschilderd glas in Nederlandse boederijen," *Antiek* 1, no. 6, 1967, pp. 11–19.

Popham, "Engravings and Woodcuts of Vellert," 1925
A[rthur]. E[wart]. Popham, "The Engravings and Woodcuts of Dirick Vellert," *The Print Collector's Quarterly* 12, 1925, pp. 343–68.

Popham, "Teekeningen," 1925
A[rthur]. E[wart]. Popham, "Teekeningen van de Vlaamsche School onlangs aangeworven in het British Museum," *Onze Kunst* 41, 1925, pp. 205–11.

Popham, *Drawings of the Early Flemish School*, 1926
A[rthur]. E[wart]. Popham, *Drawings of the Early Flemish School*, London, 1926.

Popham, "Notes-I," 1928
A[rthur]. E[wart]. Popham, "Notes on Flemish Domestic Glass Painting-I," *Apollo* 7, 1928, pp. 175–79.

Popham, "Notes-II," 1929
A[rthur]. E[wart]. Popham, "Notes on Flemish Domestic Glass Painting-II," *Apollo* 9, 1929, pp. 152–57.

A[rthur]. E[wart]. Popham, "Antwerp School (about 1500–1510)," *Old Master Drawings*, no. 19, December 1930, pp. 54–55.

Popham, "Dutch Designer," 1931
A[rthur]. E[wart]. Popham, "A Dutch Designer for Glass," in *Mélanges Hulin de Loo*, Brussels and Paris, 1931, pp. 272–77.

Popham, "French Drawings," 1931
A[rthur]. E[wart]. Popham, "A Group of French Drawings of the Fifteenth Century," *Old Master Drawings*, no. 20, March 1931, pp. 65–67.

Popham, "Josefslegende," 1931
A[rthur]. E[wart]. Popham, "Die Josefslegende," *Berliner Museen. Berichte aus den preußischen Kunstsammlungen* 52, 1931, pp. 73–76.

Popham, *Drawings in the British Museum*, 1932
A[rthur]. E[wart]. Popham, *Catalogue of Drawings by Dutch and Flemish Artists Preserved in the Department of Prints and Drawings in the British Museum* 5, London, 1932.

A[rthur]. E[wart]. Popham, "Master of the Story of Tobit (working about 1480–90)," *Old Master Drawings*, no. 40, March 1936, pp. 65–66.

Popham, "Flemish Miniaturists," 1938
A[rthur]. E[wart]. Popham, "Paintings and Drawings by Flemish Miniaturists (First Part)," in *Annuaire des Musées Royaux des Beaux-Arts de Belgique*, Brussels, 1938, pp. 9–17.

Popham and Lloyd, *Drawings at Holkham Hall*, 1986
A[rthur]. E[wart]. Popham and Christopher Lloyd, *Old Master Drawings at Holkham Hall* (Chicago Visual Library Text-Fiche, no. 50), Chicago, 1986.

Pugin, *Old Dutch Windows*, 1899
Thornton F. Pugin, *Catalogue of Two Old Dutch Painted and Stained Windows in the Royal and Free Library of Canterbury*, Canterbury, 1899.

van Puyvelde, *Flemish Drawings*, 1942
Leo van Puyvelde, *The Flemish Drawings in the Collection of His Majesty The King at Windsor Castle*, London, 1942.

Bernard Rackham, "English Importations of Foreign Stained Glass in the Early Nineteenth Century," *Journal of the British Society of Master Glass-Painters* 2, no. 2, 1927, pp. 86–94.

Rackham, "Stained Glass in the Collection of Mr. F. E. Sidney," 1929
Bernard Rackham, "Stained Glass in the Collection of Mr. F. E. Sidney. II. Netherlandish and German Medallions," *Old Furniture* 8, 1929, pp. 13–18.

Rackham, *Guide to Stained Glass*, 1936
Bernard Rackham, *A Guide to the Collections of Stained Glass*, London, Victoria and Albert Museum, Department of Ceramics, 1936.

Regensburg, *Altdorfer* (exhib. cat.), 1988
Regensburg, *Albrecht Altdorfer. Zeichnungen, Deckfarbenmalerei, Druckgraphik* (exhib. cat.), by Hans Mielke, Museen der Stadt, and Berlin, Staatliche Museen Preußischer Kulturbesitz, Kupferstichkabinett, 1988.

J. Q. van Regteren Altena, "Aertgen van Leyden," *Oud Holland* 56, 1939, pp. 17–25, 74–87, 129–38, 222–35.

van Regteren Altena, "Klein glas van 1543 door Dirck Crabeth," 1940
J. Q. van Regteren Altena, "Klein glas van 1543 door Dirck Crabeth," *Oud Holland* 57, 1940, pp. 200–206.

van Regteren Altena, "Hugo Jacobsz," 1955
J. Q. van Regteren Altena, "Hugo Jacobsz," *Nederlands Kunsthistorisch Jaarboek* 6, 1955, pp. 101–17.

Renger, *Lockere Gesellschaft*, 1970
Konrad Renger, *Lockere Gesellschaft. Zur Ikonographie des Verlorenen Sohnes und von Wirtshausszenen in der niederländischen Malerei*, Berlin, 1970.

de Ridder, "Gerechtigheidstaferelen," 1980
Juliaan de Ridder, "Gerechtigheidstaferelen in de 15de en de 16de eeuw, geschilderd voor Schepenhuizen in Vlaanderen," *Gentse Bijdragen tot de Kunstgeschiedenis* 25, 1979–80, pp. 42–62.

Rijksen, *Glasschilderingen van de St. Janskerk te Gouda*, 1947
A. A. J. Rijksen, *Gespiegeld in kerkeglas. Hollands leed en vreugd in de glasschilderingen van de St. Janskerk te Gouda*, Lochem, The Netherlands, 1947.

Sixten Ringbom, *Icon to Narrative. The Rise of the Dramatic Close-Up in Fifteenth-Century Devotional Painting*, 2nd ed., Doornspijk, 1983.

*Rodrigues Collection* (sale cat.), 1921
*Catalogue d'une vente importante de Dessins Anciens. Collection R[odrigues]. . . , de Paris, principalement des écoles des Pays-Bas et de l'Allemagne* (sale cat.), Amsterdam, Frederik Muller & Cie., July 12–13, 1921.

Rombouts and van Lerius, *Antwerpsche Sint-Lucasgilde*, 1872
Ph. F. Rombouts and Th. F. X. van Lerius, *De liggeren en andere historische archieven der Antwerpsche Sint-Lucasgilde*, 2 vols., Amsterdam, 1872.

Rombouts and van Lerius, *Antwerpsche Sint-Lucasgilde*, 1961
Ph[ilippe]. F[élix]. Rombouts and Th[éodore]. F[rançois]. X[avier]. van Lerius, *De liggeren en andere historische archieven der Antwerpsche Sint-Lucasgilde*, 2 vols., reprint, Amsterdam, 1961.

Rome, *Old Master Drawings* (exhib. cat.), 1992
Rome, *Old Master Drawings from the Ashmolean Museum* (exhib. cat.), by Christopher White, Catherine Whistler, and Colin Harrison, Palazzo Ruspoli, and Oxford, Ashmolean Museum, 1992.

Rooses, "De Romanisten," 1902
Max Rooses, "De Teekeningen der Vlaamsche Meesters. De Romanisten," *Onze Kunst* 1, 1902, pp. 168–72.

Roosval, "Peintures des retables," 1934
Johnny Roosval, "Les Peintures des retables néerlandais en Suède," *Revue Belge d'Archéologie et d'Histoire de l'Art* 4, 1934, pp. 311–20.

de Roovere, *Gedichten*, 1955
Anthonis de Roovere, *De Gedichten*, ed. by J. J. Mak, Zwolle, 1955.

Rotterdam, *Noord-nederlandsche Primitieven* (exhib. cat.), 1936
Rotterdam, *Jeroen Bosch. Noord-nederlandsche Primitieven* (exhib. cat.), Museum Boymans, 1936.

Rotterdam, *Verzameling van Sir Bruce en Lady Ingram* (exhib. cat.), 1961
Rotterdam, *150 Tekeningen uit vier eeuwen uit de verzameling van Sir Bruce en Lady Ingram* (exhib. cat.), by Carlos van Hasselt, Museum Boymans-van Beuningen, and Amsterdam, Rijksmuseum, Rijksprentenkabinet, 1961.

Rotterdam, *Jan Gossaert genaamd Mabuse* (exhib. cat.), 1965
Rotterdam, *Jan Gossaert genaamd Mabuse* (exhib. cat.), by H. Pauwels, H. R. Hoetink, and S. Herzog, Museum Boymans-van Beuningen, and Bruges, Groeningemuseum, 1965.

Rowlands, *Master Drawings*, 1984
John Rowlands, ed., *Master Drawings and Watercolours in the British Museum*, London, 1984.

Rupprich, *Dürer Schriftlicher Nachlass* 1, 1956
Hans Rupprich, ed., *Dürer Schriftlicher Nachlass*, 3 vols., Berlin, 1956–69.

Zsuzsanna van Ruyven-Zeman, "Some Drawings Attributed to Wouter Crabeth, the Glass Painter from Gouda," *Master Drawings* 23–24, 1985–86, pp. 544–51.

Zsuzsanna van Ruyven-Zeman, "Het Laatste Avondmaal-glas in de Onze-Lieve-Vrouwekerk te Antwerpen. Een oude toeschrijving herzien," *Revue Belge d'Archéologie et d'Histoire de l'Art* 57, 1988, pp. 51–66.

van Ruyven-Zeman, "Lambert van Noort Inventor," Ph.D. diss., 1990
Zsuzsanna van Ruyven-Zeman, "Lambert van Noort Inventor," Ph.D. diss., 2 vols., Amsterdam, Vrije Universiteit, 1990.

*Sammlung des Freiherrn Adalbert von Lanna* (sale cat.), 1911
*Sammlung des Freiherrn Adalbert von Lanna, Prag* (sale cat.), Berlin, Rudolph Lepke's Kunst-Auctions-Haus, March 21–28, 1911, part 2, p. 97, no. 799, pl. 65.

Sander, "*Jacob and Rachel*," 1989
Jochen Sander, "*The Meeting of Jacob and Rachel*: Hugo van der Goes' Drawing at Christ Church, Oxford," *Master Drawings* 27, 1989, pp. 39–52.

Eleanor A. Saunders, "A commentary on iconoclasm in several print series by Maarten van Heemskerck," *Simiolus* 10, 1978–79, pp. 59–83.

Schade, "*Jacob and Rachel*," 1991
Werner Schade, "*The Meeting of Jacob and Rachel* by Hugo van der Goes: A Reappraisal," *Master Drawings* 29, 1991, pp. 187–93.

Schapelhouman, "Lucas van Leyden, De opstanding van Christus," 1989
Marijn Schapelhouman, "Lucas van Leyden, De opstanding van Christus, ca. 1529," *Bulletin van het Rijksmuseum* 37, 1989, pp. 171–73.

Schmitz, *Glasgemälde*, 1913
Hermann Schmitz, *Die Glasgemälde des Königlichen Kunstgewerbemuseums in Berlin, mit einer Einführung in die Geschichte der deutschen Glasmalerei*, 2 vols., Berlin, 1913.

Schmitz, *Rund- und Kabinettscheiben*, 1923
Hermann Schmitz, *Deutsche Glasmalereien der Gotik und Renaissance Rund- und Kabinettscheiben* (Sammelbände zur Geschichte der Kunst und Kunstgewerbes, vol. 4), Munich, 1923.

Schönbrunner and Meder, *Handzeichnungen*, 1896
J. Schönbrunner and J. Meder, eds., *Handzeichnungen alter Meister aus der Albertina und anderen Sammlungen* 3, Vienna, 1896.

Schwartz, "Iconography of the Rest on the Flight," Ph.D. diss., 1975
Sheila Schwartz, "The Iconography of the Rest on the Flight into Egypt," Ph.D. diss., New York University, 1975.

Heinrich Schwarz, "Jan Gossaert's *Adam and Eve* Drawings," *Gazette des Beaux-Arts*, 6th ser., 42, 1953, pp. 145–68.

Seligman, "Roundel attributed to Lucas van Leyden," 1923
Dorothy C. Seligman, "A Roundel of Painted Glass attributed to Lucas van Leyden," *The Connoisseur* 66, 1923, pp. 13–15.

Julien le Sénécal, "Les Occupations des mois dans l'Iconographie du Moyen Âge," *Bulletin de la Société des Antiquaires de Normandie* 35, 1921–23 [1924], pp. 108–218.

Shaw, *Drawings at Christ Church Oxford*, 1976
James Byam Shaw, *Drawings by Old Masters at Christ Church Oxford* 1, Oxford, 1976.

Larry Silver, "The *Sin of Moses*: Comments on the Early Reformation in a Late Painting by Lucas van Leyden," *The Art Bulletin* 55, 1973, pp. 401–9.

Silver, *Paintings of Quinten Massys*, 1984
Larry Silver, *The Paintings of Quinten Massys with Catalogue Raisonné*, Montclair, 1984.

Larry Silver, review of *Maerten van Heemskerck. Die Gemälde*, by Rainald Grosshans, *Zeitschrift für Kunstgeschichte* 47, 1984, pp. 269–80.

Larry Silver, "*Figure nude, historie e poesie*: Jan Gossaert and the Renaissance Nude in the Netherlands," *Nederlands Kunsthistorisch Jaarboek* 37, 1986, pp. 1–40.

Larry Silver, "The 'Gothic' Gossaert. Native and Traditional Elements in a Mabuse Madonna," *Pantheon* 45, 1987, pp. 58–69.

Larry Silver and Susan Smith, "Carnal knowledge: The late engravings of Lucas van Leyden," *Nederlands Kunsthistorisch Jaarboek* 29, 1978 [1979], pp. 239–98.

Smith, *Lucas Catalogue Raisonné*, 1992
Elise Lawton Smith, *The Paintings of Lucas van Leyden. A New Appraisal, with Catalogue Raisonné*, Columbia, Missouri, and London, 1992.

Smith, "Power of Women," Ph.D. diss., 1978
Susan Louise Smith, "'To Women's Wiles I Fell': The Power of Women *Topos* and the Development of Medieval Secular Art," Ph.D. diss., University of Pennsylvania, 1978.

Sonkes, *Dessins*, 1969
Micheline Sonkes, *Dessins du XVe Siècle: Groupe van der Weyden. Essai de catalogue des originaux du maître, des copies et des dessins anonymes inspirés par son style* (Les Primitifs flamands. III. Contributions à l'étude des primitifs flamands, 5), Brussels, 1969.

Stampfle, *Netherlandish Drawings*, 1991
Felice Stampfle, *Netherlandish Drawings of the Fifteenth and Sixteenth Centuries and Flemish Drawings of the Seventeenth and Eighteenth Centuries in The Pierpont Morgan Library*, New York and Princeton, 1991.

Edith A. Standen, "Drawings for the 'Months of Lucas' Tapestry Series," *Master Drawings* 9, 1971, pp. 3–14.

Steinbart, "Paramente," 1921
Kurt Steinbart, "Paramente nach verschollenen Malereien des Jakob Cornelisz von Amsterdam," *Kunstchronik und Kunstmarkt*, September 23, 1921, pp. 931–37.

Steinbart, *Tafelgemälde des Jakob Cornelisz*, 1922
Kurt Steinbart, *Die Tafelgemälde des Jakob Cornelisz von Amsterdam. Versuch einer kritischen Biographie und Beitrag zur holländischen Malerei im ersten Drittel des 16. Jahrhunderts* (Studien zur deutschen Kunstgeschichte, part 221), Strasbourg, 1922.

Steinbart, "Nachlese," 1929
Kurt Steinbart, "Nachlese im Werke des Jacob Cornelisz," *Marburger Jahrbuch für Kunstwissenschaft* 5, 1929, pp. 213–60.

Steinbart, *Holzschnittwerk*, 1937
Kurt Steinbart, *Das Holzschnittwerk des Jakob Cornelisz von Amsterdam*, Magdeburg, Germany, 1937.

Sterck, *Onder Amsterdamsche Humanisten*, 1934
J. F. M. Sterck, *Onder Amsterdamsche Humanisten. Hun opkomst em bloei in de 16e eeuwsche stad*, Hilversum and Amsterdam, 1934.

Stiassny, "Oberitalienischen Sammlungen," 1888
Robert Stiassny, "Altdeutsche und Altniederländer in oberitalienischen Sammlungen," *Repertorium für Kunstwissenschaft* 11, 1888, pp. 369–95.

Stockholm, *Dutch and Flemish Drawings in the Nationalmuseum and Other Swedish Collections* (Nationalmusei Utställningskatalog, no. 200), Nationalmuseum, 1953.

Swarzenski, *Stiftungkunsthaus Heylshof*, 1927
George Swarzenski, *Stiftungkunsthaus Heylshof. Die Kunstsammlung im Heylshof zu Worms*, Frankfurt am Main, 1927.

de Tervarent, *Attributs et Symboles*, 1958
Guy de Tervarent, *Attributs et Symboles dans l'Art profane 1450–1600. Dictionnaire d'un langage perdu* 1, Geneva, 1958.

Ulrich Thieme and Felix Becker, *Allgemeines Lexikon des bildenden Künstler von der Antike bis zur Gegenwart*, 37 vols., Leipzig, 1907–50.

Toledo, *Glass Collections*, 1969
Toledo, *Art in Glass. A Guide to the Glass Collections*, The Toledo Museum of Art, 1969.

Tümpel, *Rembrandt*, 1970
Christian Tümpel, *Rembrandt legt die Bibel aus. Zeichnungen und Radierungen aus dem Kupferstichkabinett der Staatlichen Museen Preußischer Kulturbesitz Berlin*, Berlin, 1970.

Tuttle, "Bosch's Image of Poverty," 1981
Virginia G. Tuttle, "Bosch's Image of Poverty," *The Art Bulletin* 63, 1981, pp. 88–95.

Vanden Bemden, "Histoire de Joseph," 1976
Yvette Vanden Bemden, "Peintures sur verre représentant l'Histoire de Joseph," *Bulletin des Musées Royaux d'Art et d'Histoire*, 6th ser., 48, 1976, pp. 85–100.

Vanden Bemden, "Rondels représentant les Triomphes de Pétrarque," 1977
Yvette Vanden Bemden, "Rondels représentant les Triomphes de Pétrarque," *Revue Belge d'Archéologie et d'Histoire de l'Art* 46, 1977 [1979], pp. 5–22.

Vanden Bendem, "Fichier du Rondel," 1979
Yvette Vanden Bemden, "Le Fichier International de Documentation du Rondel," *Revue des Archéologues et Historiens d'Art de Louvain* 12, 1979, pp. 149–68.

Yvette Vanden Bemden, "Les Rondels, cousins mal aimés des vitraux?" in *Vitrea. Revue du Centre International du Vitrail* 1, 1988, pp. 22–23.

Vandenbroeck, "Bubo significans," 1985
Paul Vandenbroeck, "Bubo significans. Die Eule als Sinnbild von Schlechtigkeit und Torheit, vor allem in der niederländischen und deutschen Bilddarstellung und bei Jheronimus Bosch. I." *Jaarboek van het Koninklijk Museum voor Schone Kunsten Antwerpen*, 1985, pp. 19–135.

Van Roy, "Kunstschatten," 1962
A. Van Roy, "Kunstschatten uit Oud-Affligen. De 'Meester van Affligen,'" *Brabantse Folklore*, no. 155, 1962, pp. 226–29.

Vasari, *Vite*, 1881
Giorgio Vasari, *Le Vite de' più eccellenti Pittori, Scultori, ed Architettori* 7, ed. by Gaetano Milanese, Florence, 1881.

Vasari Society, 1912–13
*The Vasari Society for the Reproduction of Drawings by Old Masters*, 1st ser., part 8, Oxford, 1912–13.

Veldman, "The idol on the ass," 1973
Ilja M. Veldman, "The idol on the ass; Fortune and the sleeper: Maarten van Heemskerck's use of emblem and proverb books in two prints," *Simiolus* 6, 1972–73, pp. 20–28.

Ilja M. Veldman, "Maarten van Heemskerck and Hadrianus Junius: the relationship between a painter and a humanist," *Simiolus* 7, 1974, pp. 35–54.

Ilja M. Veldman, "Maarten van Heemskerck and the Rhetoricians of Haarlem," *Hafnia. Copenhagen Papers in the History of Art*, 1976, pp. 96–112.

Veldman, *Heemskerck*, 1977
Ilja M. Veldman, *Maarten van Heemskerck and Dutch humanism in the sixteenth century*, trans. by Michael Hoyle, Maarssen, The Netherlands, 1977.

Ilja M. Veldman, "Seasons, planets and temperaments in the work of Maarten van Heemskerck. Cosmo-astrological allegory in sixteenth-century Netherlandish prints," *Simiolus* 11, 1980, pp. 149–76.

Ilja M. Veldman, "Leerzame dwaasheid. De invloed van het *Sotten schip* (1548) op zottenvoorstellingen van Maarten van Heemskerck en Willem Thibaut," *Nederlands Kunsthistorisch Jaarboek* 37, 1986, pp. 195–224.

Ilja M. Veldman, "Lessons for ladies: a selection of sixteenth and seventeenth-century Dutch prints," *Simiolus* 16, 1986, pp. 113–27.

Ilja M. Veldman, *De Wereld tussen Goed en Kwaad. Late prenten van Coornhert*, The Hague, 1990.

Veldman, New Hollstein, 1993
Ilja M. Veldman, comp., and Ger Luijten, ed., *The New Hollstein. Dutch & Flemish Etchings, Engravings and Woodcuts 1450–1700. Maarten van Heemskerck*, part 1, Roosendaal and Amsterdam, 1993.

Ilja M. Veldman, comp., and Ger Luijten, ed., *The New Hollstein. Dutch & Flemish Etchings, Engravings and Woodcuts 1450–1700. Maarten van Heemskerck*, part 2, Roosendaal and Amsterdam, 1994.

Veronée-Verhaegen in "La Chute des Damnés," 1972
Nicole Veronée-Verhaegen, "La Chute des Damnés de Thierry Bouts au Musée des Beaux-Arts de Lille. Note Iconographique," *Institut Royal du Patrimoine Artistique Bulletin* 13, 1971–72, pp. 20–28.

"Verschillende verzamelingen," 1969
"Verschillende verzamelingen," in *Verslagen der Rijksverzamelingen van geschiedenis en Kunst* 88 [1966], The Hague, 1969.

Ewald Vetter, *Der Verlorene Sohn* (Lukas-Bücherei zur christlichen Ikonographie, vol. 7), Düsseldorf, 1955.

Vienna, *Kunst der Graphik* (exhib. cat.), 1964
Vienna, *Kunst der Graphik. Das Zeitalter Albrecht Dürers* (exhib. cat.), Graphische Sammlung Albertina, 1964.

Vos, "Life of Lucas," 1978
Rik Vos, "The Life of Lucas van Leyden by Karel van Mander," *Nederlands Kunsthistorisch Jaarboek* 29, 1978 [1979], pp. 459–507.

Vos, *Lucas*, 1978
Rik Vos, *Lucas van Leyden*, Bentveld and Maarssen, The Netherlands, 1978.

Washington, *Lucas van Leyden* (exhib. cat.), 1983
Washington, D.C., *The Prints of Lucas van Leyden & His Contemporaries* (exhib. cat.), by Ellen S. Jacobowitz and Stephanie Loeb Stepanek, National Gallery of Art, and Boston, Museum of Fine Arts, 1983.

Washington, *Curtis O. Baer Collection* (exhib. cat.), 1985
Washington, D.C., *Master Drawings from Titian to Picasso. The Curtis O. Baer Collection* (exhib. cat.), by Eric M. Zafran, National Gallery of Art, Atlanta, High Museum of Art, and other venues, 1985.

Washington, *Age of Bruegel* (exhib. cat.), 1986
Washington, D.C., *The Age of Bruegel: Netherlandish Drawings in the Sixteenth Century* (exhib. cat.), by John Oliver Hand et al., National Gallery of Art, and New York, The Pierpont Morgan Library, 1986.

Washington, *Old Master Drawings* (exhib. cat.), 1990

Washington, D.C., *Old Master Drawings from the National Gallery of Scotland* (exhib. cat.), by Hugh Macandrew, National Gallery of Art, and Fort Worth, Kimbell Art Museum, 1990.

Wayment, "A Rediscovered Master—I," 1967
Hilary Wayment, "A Rediscovered Master: Adrian van den Houte (c. 1459–1521) and the Malines/Brussels School—I. A Solution to the 'Ortkens' Problem," *Oud Holland* 82, 1967, pp. 172–202.

Wayment, "A Rediscovered Master—II," 1968
Hilary Wayment, "A Rediscovered Master: Adrian van den Houte (c. 1459–1521) and the Malines/Brussels School—II. Adrian van den Houte as a Tapestry Designer," *Oud Holland* 83, 1968, pp. 71–94.

Wayment, "The Dido and Aeneas Tapestries," 1969
Hilary Wayment, "Bernard van Orley and Malines: The Dido and Aeneas Tapestries at Hampton Court," *The Antiquaries Journal* 49, 1969, pp. 367–76.

Wayment, "A Rediscovered Master—III," 1969
Hilary Wayment, "A Rediscovered Master: Adrian van den Houte of Malines (c. 1459–1521) and the Malines/Brussels School—III. Adrian's development and his relation with Bernard van Orley," *Oud Holland* 84, 1969, pp. 257–69.

Wayment, *Windows of King's College*, 1972
Hilary Wayment, *The Windows of King's College Chapel Cambridge. A Description and Commentary* (Corpus Vitrearum Medii Aevi, Great Britain, supplementary vol. 1), London, 1972.

Wayment, "'Vidimus,'" 1980
Hilary Wayment, "The Great Windows of King's College Chapel and the Meaning of the Word 'Vidimus,'" *Proceedings of the Cambridge Antiquarian Society* 69, 1979 [1980], pp. 53–69.

Wayment, "Six Netherlandish Roundels," 1983
Hilary Wayment, "Six Netherlandish Roundels from the collection of Dr. C. A. Ralegh Radford, F. S. A.," *The Antiquaries Journal* 63, 1983, pp. 387–88.

Hilary Wayment, "Three *Vidimuses* for the Windows in King's College Chapel, Cambridge," *Master Drawings* 22, 1984, pp. 43–46.

Wayment, *King's College*, 1988
Hilary Wayment, *King's College Chapel Cambridge. The Side-Chapel Glass*, Cambridge, England, 1988.

Hilary Wayment, "The Master of the Mass of Saint Gregory Roundel. A Dutch Glass-painter in Brabant during the 1520s," *Oud Holland* 103, 1989, pp. 61–96.

Wegner, *Niederländischen Handzeichnungen*, 1973
Wolfgang Wegner, *Die Niederländischen Handzeichnungen des 15.–18. Jahrhunderts* (Kataloge der Staatlichen Graphischen Sammlung München, vol. 1), 2 vols., Berlin, 1973.

Weigel, *Werke der Maler*, 1865
Rudolph Weigel, *Die Werke der Maler in ihren Handzeichnungen*, Leipzig, 1865.

Wescher, "Cornelis Teunissen," 1928
Paul Wescher, "Beiträge zu Cornelis Teunissen von Amsterdam. Zeichnungen und Holzschnitte," *Oud Holland* 45, 1928, pp. 33–39.

Paul Wescher, "Holländische Zeichner zur Zeit des Lucas van Leiden," *Oud Holland* 45, 1928, pp. 245–54.

Wescher, "Pieter Coecke van Aelst," 1938
Paul Wescher, "Pieter Coecke van Aelst (1502–1550)," *Old Master Drawings*, no. 48, March 1938, pp. 58–59.

Paul Wescher, "Aertgen van Leyden: Some Additions," *Wallraf-Richartz-Jahrbuch* 30, 1968, pp. 215–22.

Winkler, "Anfänge Jan Gossarts," 1921
Friedrich Winkler, "Die Anfänge Jan Gossarts," *Jahrbuch der preußischen Kunstsammlungen* 42, 1921, pp. 5–19.

Winkler, "Meister der Anna Selbdritt," 1922
Friedrich Winkler, "Der Meister der Anna Selbdritt im Louvre," *Kunstchronik und Kunstmarkt*, June 9–16, 1922, pp. 611–17.

Friedrich Winkler, "Pieter Cornelisz Kunst (c. 1490–1544)," *Old Master Drawings*, no. 14, September 1929, pp. 27–28.

Winkler, "Jacob Cornelisz," 1932
Friedrich Winkler, "Jacob Cornelisz van Oostsanen (c. 1470–1533)," *Old Master Drawings* 6, 1931–32, pp. 10–12.

Friedrich Winkler, "Eine flämische Folge von Rundscheiben der Sakramente," *Pantheon* 19, 1961, pp. 284–88.

Winkler, "Aus der ersten Schaffenszeit des Jan Gossaert," 1962
Friedrich Winkler, "Aus der ersten Schaffenszeit des Jan Gossaert," *Pantheon* 20, 1962, pp. 145–55.

Winkler, *Hugo van der Goes*, 1964
Friedrich Winkler, *Das Werk des Hugo van der Goes*, Berlin, 1964.

Winzinger, *Altdorfer—Graphik*, 1963
Franz Winzinger, *Albrecht Altdorfer—Graphik. Holzschnitte, Kupferstiche, Radierungen*, Munich, 1963.

Worcester, *Northern Renaissance Stained Glass* (exhib. cat.), 1987
Worcester, *Northern Renaissance Stained Glass. Continuity and Transformations* (exhib. cat.), by Virginia Chieffo Raguin et al., College of the Holy Cross, Iris and B. Gerald Cantor Art Gallery, 1987.

M. L. Wurfbain, "Zes gebrandschilderde ruitjes eerste kwart 16de eeuw," *Jaarverslag Vereniging Rembrant* 1970, pp. 14–16.

Wurfbain et al., *Catalogus*, 1983
M. L. Wurfbain, J. P. Sizoo, and D. Wintgens, *Catalogus van de schilderijen en tekeningen*, Stedelijk Museum de Lakenhal, Leiden, 1983.

Wurzbach, *Künstler-Lexicon*, 1910
Alfred von Wurzbach, *Niederländisches Künstler-Lexikon* 2, Vienna and Leipzig, 1910.

Zijp, "De iconografie van de reformatie," 1987
R. P. Zijp, "De iconografie van de reformatie in de Nederlanden, een begripsbepaling," *Bulletin van het Rijksmuseum* 35, 1987, pp. 176–92.

# Index

# Photograph Credits

*Photographs by Patricia Mazza of the Photograph Studio, The Metropolitan Museum of Art, New York, except for those reproduced through the courtesy of the following institutions, photographic services, and photographers:*

Alinari / Art Resource, New York: cat. nos. 8 and 9, fig. 1; cat. no. 10, fig. 8; cat. no. 26, fig. 5; cat. no. 27, fig. 1

Jorg P. Anders, Photoatelier, Berlin: figs. 18, 19, p. 26; fig. 22, p. 28; fig. 23, p. 29; cat. nos. 2, 8; cat. nos. 8 and 9, figs. 2, 5, 7; cat. no. 10, fig. 1; cat. nos. 15, 19, 38; cat. no. 38, fig. 2; cat. no. 48, fig. 2; cat. no. 59, fig. 6; cat. nos. 67 and 68, figs. 3, 4; cat. no. 69; cat. nos. 69 and 70, fig. 1; cat. no. 71; fig. 3, p. 167; cat. nos. 94 and 95, fig. 1; cat. no. 96, fig. 5; cat. no. 103, fig. 1; cat. no. 105, fig. 2

Ashmolean Museum, Oxford: cat. no. 10, fig. 6; cat. no. 11, and fig. 1; cat. no. 15, fig. 3; cat. no. 19, fig. 2; cat. no. 24; cat. no. 62, fig. 2; cat. no. 66; cat. no. 105, fig. 3

Bayerische Staatsgemäldesammlungen, Munich: cat. no. 10, fig. 2; cat. nos. 16 and 17, fig. 2; cat. no. 26, fig. 4

British Library, London: cat. no. 24, figs. 1, 3

British Museum, London: cat. nos. 4 and 5, fig. 1; cat. no. 7, fig. 2; cat. nos. 43, 49; cat. no. 51, fig. 1; cat. no. 57; cat. no. 59, fig. 5; fig. 1, p. 135; cat. nos. 67 and 68, fig. 2; cat. nos. 69 and 70, fig. 3; cat. no. 70; cat. nos. 74, 75, 77, 78; cat. nos. 77, 78, and 79, fig. 3; figs. 2, 3, 4, p. 159; fig. 1, p. 167; cat. no. 94; cat. no. 96, and figs. 2, 3; cat. no. 97, fig. 1; cat. no. 102, figs. 1, 2; cat. nos. 110 and 111, fig. 2

Centraal Museum, Utrecht: cat. no. 105, fig. 1; cat. no. 107, fig. 1

Christ Church College, Governing Body, Oxford: fig. 1, p. 52

The Cleveland Museum of Art: cat. no. 60

Dr. William Cole, Hindhead, Surrey: cat. no. 7, fig. 1; cat. nos. 8 and 9, fig. 6

Conway Library, Courtauld Institute of Art, London: cat. nos. 115, 116

Roland Dreßler, Weimar: cat. nos. 72 and 73, fig. 1

École Nationale Supérieure des Beaux-Arts, Service Photographique, Paris: Plate 14; cat. no. 58; cat. nos. 81 and 82, figs. 1, 3, 6; cat. no. 83; cat. nos. 100 and 101, fig. 3; cat. no. 111; cat. nos. 110 and 111, fig. 1; cat. nos. 121, 122, and 123, fig. 7; cat. nos. 126, 127, and 128, fig. 5

Linda Evers: fig. 7, p. 137

Fitzwilliam Museum, Cambridge: cat. nos. 81 and 82, fig. 4; cat. nos. 82, 100

Fondation Custodia (Coll. F. Lugt). Institut Néerlandais, Paris: fig. 20, p. 27; cat. no. 6, fig. 1; cat. no. 15, fig. 2; cat. nos. 32 and 33, fig. 3; cat. no. 48, fig. 1; fig. 2, p. 117; cat. nos. 58 and 59, fig. 2; cat. nos. 62, 63; cat. nos. 69 and 70, fig. 2; cat. nos. 83 and 84, fig. 1; cat. nos. 91 and 92, fig. 1; cat. no. 96, fig. 6; cat. no. 104, figs. 1, 2; cat. no. 112; cat. nos. 121, 122, and 123, fig. 3

Foto Studio Forini, Milan: Plate 13

Frequin-Photos, Voerburg (The Netherlands): cat. no. 59, fig. 4; fig. 1, p. 158

Giraudon, Paris / Art Resource: fig. 5, p. 18; cat. nos. 39 and 40, fig. 6; cat. no. 102, fig. 3

Tom Haartsen, Ouderkerk a/d Amstel: Plates 2, 12; fig. 9, p. 20; cat. nos. 4, 51; cat. nos. 121, 122, and 123, figs. 6, 9

Harvard University Art Museums, Cambridge: cat. nos. 63 and 64, figs. 1, 2, 3

Ruben de Heer, Utrecht: cat. no. 27, fig. 2

Hessisches Landesmuseum, Darmstadt: cat. no. 36; cat. no. 55, fig. 1; cat. no. 73

Timothy B. Husband, New York: cat. nos. 121, 122, and 123, figs. 4, 8

Institut Royal du Patrimoine Artistique (Copyright A.C.L.), Brussels: fig. 13, p. 23; cat. no. 1, fig. 1; cat. no. 10, figs. 3, 4; cat. nos. 16 and 17, fig. 1; cat. no. 28, figs. 1, 2; cat. nos. 46 and 47, figs. 1, 4, 5, 6; fig. 3, p. 136; fig. 5, p. 137; cat. no. 71, fig. 2; cat. nos. 77, 78, and 79, fig. 2; cat. no. 80, fig. 1; fig. 5, p. 159; cat. no. 98; cat. no. 107, fig. 2; cat. nos. 108 and 109, figs. 6, 8; cat. no. 113, fig. 3

Laurent Sully Jaulmes, Musée des Arts Décoratifs, Paris: Plate 21; cat. nos. 117, 118, 119, and 120, and figs. 2, 3, 4, 5

Koninklijke Bibliotheek, The Hague: fig. 1, p. 16; fig. 3, p. 17; cat. nos. 67 and 68, fig. 5

Kunsthalle, Bremen: fig. 10, p. 21; cat. nos. 67 and 68, fig. 6

Kunsthistorische Musea Fotodienst, Antwerp: Plate 6; cat. nos. 8 and 9, fig. 3; cat. no. 12, fig. 7

Kunsthistorisches Museum, Vienna: cat. no. 60, fig. 1

Kunstmuseum, Basel: cat. nos. 32 and 33, fig. 2; cat. no. 34, fig. 1; cat. nos. 35 and 36, fig. 2; cat. no. 37, fig. 1

Kunstsammlungen, Veste Coburg: cat. nos. 39 and 40, figs. 1, 2

Lightner Photography, Timonium, Maryland: cat. no. 27, fig. 5; cat. no. 34, fig. 2

Jannes Linders, Rotterdam: cat. no. 108

John Mills (Photography) Ltd., Liverpool: cat. no. 25, fig. 1

Musée Bonnat, Bayonne: cat. no. 10, fig. 5

Museum der bildenden Künste, Leipzig: fig. 8, p. 20

Museum of Fine Arts, Department of Photographic Services, Boston: cat. no. 1; cat. nos. 58 and 59, fig. 1; cat. no. 107